PAGANISM AND
CHRISTIANITY
100–425 C.E.

PAGANISM AND CHRISTIANITY

100–425 C.E.

A Sourcebook

Edited by
RAMSAY MACMULLEN
and
EUGENE N. LANE

FORTRESS PRESS   MINNEAPOLIS

PAGANISM AND CHRISTIANITY, 100–425 C.E.
A Sourcebook

Cover design by Ned Skubic
Interior design by Publishers' WorkGroup
Cover illustration: A portrait on gold glass dating from the fourth century C.E.

Library of Congress Cataloging-in-Publication Data

Paganism and Christianity, 100–425 C.E. : a sourcebook / edited by
  Ramsay MacMullen and Eugene N. Lane.
    p. cm.
  Includes bibliographical references and indexes.
  ISBN 0–8006–2647–8 (alk. paper)
    1. Christianity and other religions—Roman—Sources. 2. Church
history—Primitive and early church, ca. 30–600—Sources. 3. Rome-
–Religion—Relations—Christianity—Sources. I. MacMullen, Ramsay,
1928– . II. Lane, Eugene, 1936– . III. Title: Paganism and
Christianity.
BR128.R7P34   1992
270.1—dc20   92–3069
                                                CIP

The paper used in this publication meets the minimum requirements of American National Standard for Information Sciences—Permanence of Paper for Printed Library Materials, ANSI Z329.48–1984.

Manufactured in the U.S.A.   AF 1–2647

96   95   94   93   92   1   2   3   4   5   6   7   8   9   10

CONTENTS

PREFACE

The emergence of Christianity from the tangled mass of older religious beliefs, eventually to a position of unchallenged superiority, is surely the most important single phenomenon that can be discerned in the closing centuries of the ancient world. In its impact on the way life was to be lived thereafter in the West, it outmatches even the decline of Rome itself. For the study of the process there exist such books as those of von Harnack and others more recent; as primary sources there is the indispensable account of the early history of the church by Eusebius, amplified by Stevenson. On these and other works, see the bibliography, below. It must be said in criticism of these works, however, that they make little or no mention of the body in which Christianity grew—as if obstetrics were limited to passing references in a handbook on babies. How about the mother? Will she not help determine the manner in which the child enters the world and, to some extent, its shape and nature?

To illustrate: In most regions of St. Paul's or St. Augustine's world, attendance at holy places on religious anniversaries was a time for friends and family together to enjoy the meal that followed the sacrifice. That was how reverence was paid to the sanctuaries of saints in the fourth century—not because those attending were still "pagan" (they would have indignantly rejected any such label) but because the ceremony still lacked any distinctively Christian form. Or again: The impulse to join actively in reverence at shrines most often took the form of dancing, whether restrained or vigorous, we do not know; and congregations that we glimpse in various cities of the west and east alike expressed themselves in this fashion without the least sense of inappropriateness, because to them it seemed the natural way to show religious feeling. Their bishops disagreed, and such activity was gradually suppressed. Or finally: The wish to predict the near term, whether in choosing to favor the suit of Jack or Tom, or to begin a journey on the first or last day of the week, or to address the sickness of a child with this or some other treatment, was just as pressing for Christians as for non-Christians. But the former as such lacked a specifically Christian means; so, without any sense of wrong-doing, they resorted to amulets and spells and other forms of everyday divination. Perhaps the most familiar instance is St. Augustine's use both of divination from the words of children overheard and of the random choice of a line in some revered text (for non-Christians, the *Aeneid*; for him, the Bible). This was in 384 C.E. in the suburbs of Milan (*Confessions* 8.12.29).

Therefore, if one were to design a course of formal study about the historical process here in focus, by which Christianity attained its suprem-acy, one would need something quite different from Harnack and Eusebius. One would need a body of material describing what, in the realm of religion, was taken for granted in the period from 125 to 425 C.E. (We choose the earlier of these dates as the point at which the historian of antiquity must begin seriously to track and evaluate the church as an institution of importance, exerting some impact on the world that sur-rounded it; and by 425 Augustine approaches the end of his days.) The selections that follow are meant to supply just that need. They must do so, first, by revealing something of the nature of the pagan matrix. Then, we inquire about how the pious viewed Christians (and Jews, too, since the two were for long confused). How were they, in turn, viewed by their neighbors who were Christians? We next offer selections to show how the public authorities expressed their perceptions, through threats and vio-lence and offers of bribes and, after the authorities began to be Christian, how threats and violence and bribes were aimed in the other direction, aiding the operation of other inducements to conversion. In its inward-ness, religious conversion is nowhere nearly so often reported as one might expect, and our emphasis must fall, more than we would wish, on acts rather than on thoughts. However, we have included a good sampling of what does remain, notably, the sole surviving account of missionary activity in post-scriptural antiquity, Gregory's, hitherto available only in Greek.

The choice of selections to be included was difficult. Within non-Christian religion, some matters such as healing cults were of broader significance to people of the past than to students of today. They could not be wholly blocked out by matters less significant but more intriguing, for whatever reason, such as Mithraism and Gnosticism. The more accessi-ble and, to us, intelligible beliefs of the upper classes could not be allowed to monopolize attention; and the cohesiveness of the whole mix of beliefs could not be allowed to hide the endless diversity of regions and classes. We have tried to bear in mind both the ancient reality and the shape of the lens through which it is likely to be examined today.

Turning to the subject of Christianity, we thought it safe to leave aside, as familiar, matters of its early history and self-definition—likewise, therefore, Eusebius, whose work is readily available in convenient translations. We left out what even small institutional libraries can usually supply—the range of texts of the church fathers, of which several readily accessible series of translations exist. Nevertheless, we included most of one Apology, by Athenagoras, for convenience's sake, just as we earlier included Lucian's account of the cult-founder Alexander and an entire book of Apuleius's novel (both easily found in translation). Finally, the long selections given over to the persecutions in north Africa earned their inclusion through their being so nearly unknown, despite the extraordinary level of detail and the vividness which they bring to the narrative of the Great Persecution. No accessible English version exists, and a French version has appeared only in quite recent years.

As both of us have taught a course in which this collection in some form was staple fare (and one of us has taught it many times over some twenty-five years), we well understand how different might be the approaches to this same subject matter, changing over time as interests shift. We certainly do not expect to have served every legitimate need for documentary illustration. However, to repair some of the deficiencies in this collection, help may be found among titles which we have found useful, listed in the bibliography.

SELECT
BIBLIOGRAPHY

Non-Christian Religion

Ferguson, John. *The Religions of the Roman Empire*. London, 1970.

*MacMullen, Ramsay. *Paganism in the Roman Empire*. New Haven, Conn., 1981.

Vermaseren, M. J. *Mithras, the Secret God*. London, 1963.

Price, S.R.F. *Rituals and Power: The Roman Imperial Cult in Asia Minor*. Cambridge, 1984.

Christianity

Primary Sources

*Eusebius. *The History of the Church*, trans. G. A. Williamson, 2d ed. Penguin, 1989.

———. *The Martyrs of Palestine* (appended to The History of the Church, ed. and trans. by H. J. Lawlor and J.E.L. Oulton, vol. 1. London, 1954).

Stevenson, J. *A New Eusebius. Documents Illustrative of the History of the Church to A.D. 337*. London, 1963.

Musurillo, Herbert. *The Acts of the Christian Martyrs*. Oxford, 1972.

Secondary Sources

*Frend, W.H.C. *The Early Church*. Philadelphia: Fortress Press, 1962, 1985.

———. *The Rise of Christianity*. Philadelphia: Fortress Press, 1984.

———. *Martyrdom and Persecution in the Early Church*. Oxford, 1965.

*Harnack, A. von. *The Mission and Expansion of Christianity in the First Three Centuries*. New York 1961 = vol. 1 of the 1902 German original.

*MacMullen, Ramsay. *Christianizing the Roman Empire*. New Haven, Conn., 1984.

*Nock, A. D. *Conversion*. Oxford, 1930.

*In paperback.

ABBREVIATIONS

Abh. preuss Akad.	*Abhandlungen der preussischen/deutschen Akademie der Wissenschaften zu Berlin, Philologisch-Historische Klasse* (Berlin: Akademie-Verlag,1908–49)
AE	*Année Epigraphique* (Paris: Presses Universitaires de France, from 1888, up to 1961 published as part of the *Revue archéologique)*
BGU	*Berliner Griechische Urkunden (Ägyptische Urkunden aus den Kgl. Museen zu Berlin)* (Berlin: Akademie-Verlag, 1895–)
CCSL	*Corpus Christianorum, Series Latina* (Turnholti: Brepols, 1954–)
CIL	*Corpus Inscriptionum Latinarum* (Berlin: Akademie der Wissenschaften, 1863–)
CIMRM	Maarten J. Vermaseren, *Corpus Inscriptionum et Monumentorum Religionis Mithriacae* (The Hague: Nijhoff, 1956–60)
CMRDM	Eugene N. Lane, *Corpus Monumentorum Religionis Dei Menis* (Leiden: Brill, 1971–78)
CRAIBL	*Comptes Rendus de l'Académie des inscriptions et belles-lettres* (Paris: A. Durand, 1858–)
Euseb.	Eusebius
GRBS	*Greek, Roman, and Byzantine Studies* (Durham, N.C.: Duke University Press, 1958–)
Hist. eccl.	*Historia Ecclesiastica,* church histories by Eusebius, Rufinus, Socrates, Sozomen, and Theodoret.
HTR	*Harvard Theological Review* (various publishers, 1908–)
IA	Christian Habicht, *Die Inschriften des Asklepieions (Altertümer von Pergamon 8.3)* (Berlin: W. de Gruyter, 1969)

IG	*Inscriptiones Graecae* (Berlin: Georg Reimer, 1873–)
IGR	*Inscriptiones Graecae ad Res Romanas Pertinentes*, ed. René Cagnat (Paris: E. Leroux, 1906–27; reprint; Chicago: Ares, 1975)
ILS	Hermann Dessau, *Inscriptiones Latinae Selectae*, 3 vols. (Berlin: Weidmann, 1892–1916)
LCL	Loeb Classical Library (New York: Putnam; and London: Heinemann, 1912–)
MAMA	*Monumenta Asiae Minoris Antiqua*, 8 vols. (Manchester, Eng.: Manchester University Press, 1928–)
NHS	*Nag Hammadi Studies* (Leiden: Brill, 1971–)
OCD	*Oxford Classical Dictionary*, 2d ed. (Oxford: Clarendon Press, 1970)
PG	J.-P. Migne, *Patrologia graeca* (Paris: Garnier, 1857–91)
PGM	Karl Preisendanz (ed.), *Papyri Graecae Magicae*, 2d ed., 2 vols. (Stuttgart: Teubner, 1973)
PL	J.-P. Migne, *Patrologia latina* (Paris: Garnier, 1878–90)
P. Oxy.	B. P. Grenfell and A. S. Hunt, *The Oxyrhynchus Papyri* (London: Egypt Exploration Society, 1898–)
SEG	*Supplementum Epigraphicum Graecum* (Leiden: Sijthoff 1923–)
SIG	Wilhelm Dittenberger, *Sylloge Inscriptionum Graecarum*, 3d ed. (Leipzig: Hirzel, 1915–24)

1

MAGIC, DREAMS, ASTROLOGY, "SUPERSTITION"

In presenting a selection of illustrative texts on our topic, it is natural to begin with the beliefs and practices that accompanied a person through the day—every day, not only on special festivals or anniversaries—and that constituted the more peripheral, lightly held, and unofficial parts of religion: namely, magic and superstition. Established religion (covered in subsequent sections) was something else again—settled in shrines and tended by communities and their representatives. A most important characteristic, however, shared by both the official and the unofficial, was the considerable degree of homogeneity of belief that developed over time, at least among the urbanized population. The process has no clear beginning, but it was certainly accelerated by the gradual formation of a single political structure that united and imposed peace, the *pax Romana,* on the Mediterranean world. To the extent that a single civilization was thus achieved, it testified to the free, constant movement of people and ideas through the empire's cities, which consequently enriched the whole. By such movement, and within the bounds of broad common expectations about religion (illustrated in the middle sections of this collection), innovation could take place and historical change occur. To these latter phenomena, our concluding sections are devoted.

1.1 The Tale of Josephus's Conversion from Judaism to Christianity, from Epiphanius's *Panarion*

The following little drama illustrates the high degree of intermingling of beliefs to be found, it so happens, in the best lit of areas for the historian of ancient religion—the Holy Land. Among the actors are Christians, some of whose religion is non-Christian, Jews, some of whose religion is non-Jewish (being both pagan and Christian), still a third category of person belonging to the great majority of the population who are neither Christian nor Jew even at this time and in this

1

region—and finally, a substratum which all three groups and we our-selves might plainly call superstition. Yet it was omnipresent, and important.

The author of the account, Epiphanius, was born in Judea ca. 315 C.E., becoming head of the monastery there and, later, a bishop in Cyprus for thirty-three years (till his death in 403). He took a prominent part in religious controversies of his age, traveled a lot and wrote a lot. Best known is his *Panarion* (*Adversus haereses*), in which he reports on and argues against various Christian heresies. In the selection below he looks back some thirty years to a story told him by a friend, most of which can be dated to the latter years of Constantine. It shows the intermingling in the cities that was so noteworthy: non-Christian festi-vals are attended by people of every religious persuasion, quite openly, while on the other hand non-Christians are aware of Christianity espe-cially as a healing power, and may invoke it on that account.

The selection also contains material on magic, especially as it was practiced among the Jews. Also discussed are relationships and percep-tions among several religious groups, and conversion, wrought in an instant through physical demonstration that the Christian God's power can prevail over any other. In short, then, the passage introduces a large number of the topics and elements with which this anthology is concerned.

Source: Epiphanius, *Panarion* 30.4–12, *PG* 41, col. 409ff., original translation.

One of these [Jews who turned Christian] was Josephus, not the ancient author and historian but a man from Tiberias of the period when the late Constantine the Elder reigned. He obtained the rank of Count from the emperor and had authority to erect a church to Christ in Tiberias itself, as well as in Diocaesarea, Capernaum, and other cities. He suffered severely from the Jews until the emperor heard about him. For this Josephus was numbered among their highest officials—men who, after the Patriarch, are called "Apostles" and take their seats next to the Patriarch and are often present in his company constantly, day and night, since they are his councillors and refer to him any business regarding Law. At that time the Patriarch was called Hillel (for I believe Josephus said this was his name, unless from the passage of time I am mistaken). He was of the descent of Gamaliel who had been Patriarch among them. It can be supposed—and others have thought so—that this is the line of the first Gamaliel who lived in the Savior's time and by God's inspiration offered his counsel against any persecution of the apostles. When he lay dying, Hillel summoned the then bishop of the neighboring Tiberias and pro-cured from him the holy bath at the end of his life, alleging as the reason its medicinal powers. Sending for him through that Josephus just mentioned, on the grounds that he was a physician, and making everyone else leave, he addressed the bishop in these words: Give me the seal in Christ. The bishop called his assistants and ordered the water prepared as if to bring aid for an illness to the Patriarch who was at that point gravely ill. They did as he said, without understanding, and the Patriarch, pretending a wish for privacy, cleared them out and was deemed worthy of baptism and the holy mysteries.

5. Josephus conversed with me personally. I have heard all this from his own mouth and no one else's, in his old age (he was then around seventy or more). I stayed at his house in Scythopolis, for he had moved from Tiberias and had acquired some splendid buildings there in Scythopolis. It was in his house that the blessed Eusebius, bishop of Vercellae in Italy, exiled by Constantius [emperor 337–61] for his faithfulness to orthodoxy, was being entertained. I and the other brothers going there to visit him were ourselves put up by him. Encountering Josephus in his house and questioning him, and knowing that he had been one of the renowned among the Jews, and inquiring also about his situation and how he was converted to Christianity, we have heard the whole tale from him clearly, not from anyone else's say-so. We thought then that the man's doings were worth relating for the edification of the faithful, because of the translations into Hebrew in the Treasury, and we proposed to go through the whole case of Josephus very carefully. For he was not only a Christian and judged worthy to be of the faithful but also violently pilloried the Arians. For in that city, I mean Scythopolis, he was the only orthodox person, and all the others were Arians; and had he not been Count, and had the rank of Count not prevented the Arians' persecuting him, the man would not have been able to live in the city, particularly with an Arian bishop Patrophilus, who enjoyed great influence through his wealth and harshness and through his acquaintance and familiarity with Constantius the emperor. There was also another younger man in the city who had come over from Hebrew to orthodox belief, who did not dare openly but secretly visited us. Josephus told a likely and amusing story, and I believe that he was telling the truth. He said that, when his wife died, he feared lest the Arians seize him and make him a priest; for they often, flattering him to talk him around to their heresy, promised greater advancements and, if need be, to reward him with a bishopric. But he said he remarried out of fear of this, to escape election by them.

6. But I return to focusing my account on the situation of the Patriarch and of Josephus, too, so as to make all clear, down to the details, for anyone wishing to read them, through what that man related to me. And now, as he reported, the Patriarch being accorded baptism, "Peeking

through the crack between the doors," he said, "I understood everything the bishop was doing for the Patriarch, and I stored it away in my mind and treasured it up. The Patriarch, having a certain considerable weight of gold on hand, put out his hand and gave it to the bishop saying, 'Offer it up on my behalf; for it is written, All things are bound or loosened by God's priests, and the same shall be bound or loosened by heaven.'" When this was done, he said, and the doors were opened, the Patriarch was asked by those visiting how he felt from the help; and he replied that he was feeling fine. And he knew what he was saying. But afterwards, two or three days later, when the bishop had looked in on him often with the excuse of serving as his physician, the Patriarch died, happy in his release, entrusting his own son (still little) to Josephus and to a second most able person. These two now took care of everything because the [new] Patriarch was a child, indeed an infant, and he was raised by them. At this juncture, Josephus's spirit was often troubled by the mystic rites, and he considered what he should do in the matter of baptism. There was there a Treasury room [*gazophylakion*] that was sealed [the word "Treasure" is *gaza* in Hebrew], and many people had many different ideas about the Treasury because of that seal. Now Josephus ventured secretly to open it; but he didn't find any money, only papyrus rolls [of value] beyond money. Reading in them, as I have already said, he discovered the Gospel according to John translated from Greek into Hebrew, and the Acts of the Apostles. Indeed, reading Matthew's Hebrew genealogy, he was tortured in his mind and was troubled about belief in Christ, being pricked by two matters, the reading of the books and the initiation of the Patriarch. Nevertheless, as often happens, he hardened his heart.

7. While he was in the midst of these perplexities, the child left behind by Hillel to be brought up into the Patriarchate began to grow up. Among the Jews, no other person seizes official positions but, rather, a son succeeds his father. When, therefore, the youth reached maturity, he came under the corrupting influence of certain young men of dissolute ways and too much leisure (I think perhaps, this youth's name was Judas but, from the lapse of time, I don't well remember). Those age-mates of his won him over to many bad practices: the seduction of women, unholy lechery; and they tried to make him join in their unbridled conduct through working magical spells, carrying out some inducing rituals, and forcing women of free birth through incantations to engage against their will in his corruption. Josephus, however, and the elder with him, being obliged to follow the young man about, were distressed by all this and in their conversation offered frequent reproach or advice, while he for his part listened rather to the young men, concealed his wicked deeds, or denied them. Josephus and his associates did not venture to speak about him explicitly. They

could only incline him through praise and wisdom. They made a trip one
time to Gadara, to the hot springs. There is an annual festival there,
attended from all over by people wishing to bathe on certain fixed days
supposedly in order to be freed of illnesses. It is all a strategem of the
Devil. For where God's miracles took place, there the enemy managed to
spread his destructive snares. Couples of both sexes bathed there together,
and, by chance, one of them was a young woman of free birth and
beautiful perfection of form. The young man, walking about outdoors, was
smitten, through his now habitual licentiousness, and brushed his side
against hers. She crossed herself in Christ's name, for she was a Christian,
and there was no necessity for her to sin and bathe in mixed couples—but
such things happen to the naive and ignorant, thanks to the slackness of
their teachers who have failed to fortify them through instruction. But so
that God might show his wonders, the young man failed in his attempt, I
mean the Patriarch. He sent word to her and promised gifts, but she
treated his messengers abusively and was not worn down by the vain
conduct of the licentious fellow.

8. Next, his comrades, when they learned of the suffering he owed
to the woman, tried to devise some better wizardry for him, as Josephus
himself described to me in detail. They got the unhappy youth away after
sundown among the neighboring tombs. These caves are called Polyandria
in the local tongue. They are fashioned out of the living rock. The
charlatans [goetes] who were with him taking him there worked certain
spells for him and invocations and preparations replete with unholiness,
all on the name of the woman mentioned. But by God's wish this came to
the attention of that other elder who happened to be with Josephus, and
he, aware of what was going on, imparted it to Josephus. At first, bewail-
ing himself, he said, "Wretched men that we are, my brother," says he,
"and instruments of destruction! Whom are we watching over?" But as
Josephus asked how it happened, and before he had heard from him by
words, the elder took Josephus's hand and led him where the evil men
together with the youth made their gathering among the tombs for the
sake of sorcery. Standing outside the doors, they heard all that was going
on among them; when they came out, they [Josephus and those with him]
slipped away. It was not yet late evening—still close to sunset—and it was
still possible to see things dimly. After the impious fellows had left the
sepulchre, Josephus and those with him entered. They found still further
preparations for mischief scattered on the ground, on which they [the
miscreants] had poured urine and blood, mixing in dust, as he said, before
they went out. They understood the plan and for which woman it was that
these evil things had been done by them; and they were watching closely
whether they would prevail. When the charlatans didn't (for the woman

had help from the sign of Christ and her belief), they knew that the youth waited for three nights for the woman to come, and then fought with those who made the mischief, because he didn't succeed. For Josephus, this was the third element in his instruction: the power of sorcery had failed where Christ's name and the sign of the cross are. Nevertheless he was not persuaded to become a Christian.

9. Then the Lord appeared to him in a dream, saying, "I am Jesus whom your ancestors crucified; yet believe in me." However, he [Josephus], unpersuaded, fell gravely ill and was despaired of. The Lord appeared to him again, bidding him believe and be cured. Yet he recovered after the apparition and remained once again fixed in his stubbornness. Again, he succumbed to a second illness and was now again despaired of. His Jewish kin supposed that he was dying, and he heard them saying the secret rites that have always been customary among them; for one of the senior men among those learned in the Law came up close to his ear and announced, "Believe in Jesus who was crucified under Pontius Pilate the governor, the son of God, born afterwards of Mary, being the Christ of God and raised from the dead, and that he comes again to judge the living and the dead." Josephus himself told me these things distinctly in his narration, as an honest man ought to tell it; but I have heard something similar from someone else who remains a Jew out of fear of the Jews though he passes much time among Christians, honors Christians and loves them, and traveled with me in the desert of Bethel and Ephraim when I went up to the mountain from Jericho. I questioned him about Christ's coming, and he offered no argument. I showed astonishment and asked him to explain (he was learned in the Law and able to argue) just why he offered no argument, but was persuaded about Christ Jesus our Lord, hearing such great things, and the man revealed to me that, on the point of death, he heard from them in his own ear in a whispered voice "Jesus Christ the crucified son of God will judge you." But enough for my purposes about this—on this subject let it be recorded, from the true report.

10. Josephus was still ill, as I said earlier, when he heard from the elder, among other things, that "Jesus Christ will judge you." He nonetheless remained stubborn. The Lord, however, from his mercifulness spoke to him through an apparition in a dream, saying, "See, I heal you; but when you recover health, believe!" But, recovering again from his illness, he did not believe. The Lord appeared to him in his health once again through a dream, reproaching him for not believing. The Lord promised him, saying "For certainty of belief, if you want to perform a miracle through my name, call on me and I will do it." Now, there was a certain madman who went about naked in the city, I mean Tiberias.

Though often clothed, he ripped that clothing off again—as such men do. Josephus then, wanting a test of the apparition and still in doubt, was held back by shame. He took this [madman] indoors, closed the door, and, taking water in his hand and making a cross over it, sprinkled it on the madman, saying, "In the name of Jesus of Nazareth who was crucified, come out of him, demon, and may he have his health." The man let out a mighty cry and fell prone, foaming greatly at the mouth and writhing. He stayed there motionless for a long time. Josephus thought perhaps the man was dead. After a time, however, with his face scraped, he stood up and, seeing his own nakedness, covered himself by putting his hands over his private parts. He could no longer bear his own nakedness. He put on one of Josephus's cloaks and returned to his sense and to modesty. He gave great thanks to the man and to God in the knowledge that he had been saved through him. And in the city he advertised the man greatly, and the miracle [sign] became well known there among the Jews. A lot of excited talk developed in the city, people saying that Josephus had opened the Treasury, had there found writings with God's name on them and read them, and then was performing great miracles. And what was said by them was true, but not as they suspected. Josephus remained stubborn in his heart; but merciful God, who always provides good occasions of salvation to those that love him, offers them to those men whom he deems worthy of [eternal] life.

11. It happened to Josephus, after Judas the Patriarch reached manhood (as I indicated—that was perhaps his name) that, as reward, he bestowed on Josephus as an honor the profit of an Apostleship. He was sent with letters into Cilicia. Arriving, he collected in each city the tithe and the first fruits from the Jews in the province. At this time he stayed in the neighborhood of a church, I don't know in which city. He made friends with its bishop and in confidence asked for a Bible from him,* which he read. Then, as Apostle (for so the post is named among them), very knowledgeable and supposedly purifying everything to a condition of good legal order—as he had been appointed to do—he cleaned out many synagogue heads who had settled into evil ways, many priests and elders, and the deacons or assistants that they call Azanites. He removed them from office and aroused the resentment of many who tried as if to be revenged upon him—people who were most eager to meddle about the matter and to track down everything that he had been responsible for. While they were being such busybodies, of a sudden they turned against his very hearth and attacked him in the midst of his Bible reading. They seized the book and laid hands on the man, dragging him along the

---

*This passage is evidently corrupt, and the translation here restores the probable sense.—[EDS.]

ground and shouting; they directed no ordinary accusations against him, haled him before the synagogue, and whipped him. This was the first trial made of him according to the Law. But the city bishop presided and acquitted him. Another time, they caught him when he was on a certain journey, as he related to us, and threw him into the river Cydnus; and they assumed he had been pulled down by the force of the stream and destroyed beneath the water—at which they rejoiced. A little later, however, he was deemed worthy of baptism; for he was saved. He rose to the imperial service, became the emperor Constantine's friend, and revealed to him his whole story: that he had been in highest esteem among the Jews, honored among the first, and that many a divine apparition had come to him, and that the Lord had summoned him to a holy calling and to this safeguarding of the Lord's beliefs and revelations. And the good emperor, in truth Christ's servant, possessing a zeal for God with David, Ezekiel, and Josiah among rulers, rendered him the honor, as I said, of a court post in the realm. For he made him Count, adding that he should ask for whatever he wanted. But he [the Count] requested nothing further than this highest favor from the emperor, namely, to be entrusted through imperial command with the building of churches to Christ in the cities and villages of the Jews. There, no one had ever been capable of building churches, because neither Greek, Samaritan, nor Christian was to be found in their midst. This is particularly closely watched in Tiberias and in Diocaesarea (also called Sepphoris), Nazareth, and Capernaum, namely, that there should be no people of another race.

12. Josephus, taking his instructions, authority, and rank, went to Tiberias. He also took letters from the imperial officials for expenditures, while he himself had been honored by the emperor with his own stipends. He began to build then in Tiberias. The city contained a vast shrine—I think it may have been called Hadrianeum—but it had remained unfinished, and the citizens were trying to turn it into a public bath. When he found this situation, he took it for a signal for action; and as he found it already of squared, four-cubit stone carried up to a certain point, he began work on his church exactly at that point. There was need of lime and other materials. He gave orders that there were to be lots of kilns outside the city, about seven of them (locally they call them "furnaces"). The terrible Jews, with the hardihood always to try anything, turned to the wizards' tricks that are customary among them. By certain magic and mischief, these marvelous Jews endeavored to prevent the fire from catching [in the kilns]; yet in the end they did not prevail. The fire checked and wouldn't work; but it was acting against its own nature, so to speak. When some were ordered to feed the fuel into the fire (I refer to the brush) and then the kindling, they couldn't get it going as they fed it in. They pointed

this out to Josephus. It operated on his spirit like a goad; he turned to the Lord full of ardor, ran out of the city, and ordered water to be brought in a bronze jug (I mean a kampsake, or, as the natives term it, a *kakybion*). He took the jug in the presence of everyone (and a throng of Jews had gathered for the sight, eager to see the outcome and what Josephus would try to do). In a loud voice, while he laid the mark of the cross on the jug with his own finger, he called on the name of Jesus, and spoke as follows: "In the name of Jesus of Nazareth whom my fathers and the fathers of all those here present crucified, may there be force in this water to set aside all spells and wizards' tricks that these persons have wrought—force also to supply the impulse to the power of fire, for the completion of the Lord's house." Speaking thus, he took the water in his hand and poured it over each of the "furnaces." The spells were dissolved, the fire burst forth in everyone's sight. The throng there present shouted, "One is the God who helps the Christians." Then they departed. Those persons often did evil to the man, but he continued construction to the last jot in Tiberias's shrine, and completed a small church. Then he left and came to Scythopolis, where he remained. In Diocaesareá and other [cities] he completed buildings. Such were his accomplishments. . . .

1.2   Five Spells from the
Greek Magical Papyri

Magical spells survive on papyrus (in the form of single short texts or entire books of a hundred pages or more) from Egypt only, and mostly of the second to fourth century (including some Christian ones); but, since the spells are closely similar to other very brief ones of earlier centuries, scratched on lead tablets, potsherds, or the like, and talked about in literary works, from all over the empire, it is likely that the Egyptian evidence is quite generally representative. Some of it was in the hands of professionals; its more elaborate forms show the edges of conventional belief, where a person could find what was foreign enough to seem worth trying (notice the Babylonian and Jewish Powers invoked in capitals, below), but not so very strange as to provoke instant disbelief; and spell-sellers had convincing testimonials to advertise, specifying real historical figures like Hadrian, Pachrates, or Apollonius. They most often served human desires that seemed too trivial for the familiar gods: help in one's daily chores, help in a river crossing, help in a love affair, hetero- or homosexual (below); or they were appealed to for purposes too dubious, morally, to enjoy the favor of the gods.

Source: *The Greek Magical Papyri in Translation*, ed. Hans Dieter Betz, vol. 1 (Chicago: University of Chicago Press, 1986). Individual references are to *PGM*.

4.2441f. [early fourth century C.E.?] Spell of Attraction: (implements: those for a lunar burnt offering); it attracts those who are uncontrollable and require no magical material and who come in one day. It inflicts sickness excellently and destroys powerfully, sends dreams beautifully, accomplishes dream revelations marvelously and in its many demonstrations has been marveled at for having no failure in these matters.

Burnt offering: Pachrates, the prophet of Heliopolis, revealed it to the emperor Hadrian [117–38 C.E.], revealing the power of his own divine magic. For it attracted in one hour; it made someone sick in 2 hours; it destroyed in 7 hours, sent the emperor himself dreams as he thoroughly tested the whole truth of the magic within his power. And marveling at the prophet, he ordered double fees to be given to him.

Take a field mouse and deify it in spring water. And take two moon beetles and deify them in river water, and take a river crab and fat of a dappled goat that is virgin and dung of a dog-faced baboon, 2 eggs of an ibis, 2 drams of storax, 2 drams of myrrh, 2 drams of crocus, 4 drams of Italian galingale, 4 drams of uncut frankincense, a single onion. Put all these things into a mortar with the mouse and the remaining items and, after pounding thoroughly, place in a lead box and keep for use. And whenever you want to perform a rite, take a little, make a charcoal fire, go up on a lofty roof, and make this offering as you say this spell at moonrise and at once she comes.

Spell: "Let all the darkness of clouds be dispersed for me, and let the goddess AKTIOPHIS shine for me, and let her hear my holy voice. For I come, announcing the slander of NN, a defiled and unholy woman, for she has slanderously brought your holy mysteries to the knowledge of men, she, NN, is the one, [not] I, who says, 'I have seen the greatest goddess, after leaving the heavenly vault, on earth without sandals, sword in hand, and [speaking] a foul tongue.' It is she, NN, who said, 'I saw [the goddess] drinking blood.' She, NN, said it, not I, AKTIOPHIS ERESCHIGAL NEBOUTOSOUALETH PHORPHORBA SATRAPAMMON CHOIRIXIE, flesh eater. Go to her, NN, and take away her sleep and put a burning heat in her soul, punishment and frenzied passion in her thoughts, and banish her from every place and every house, and attract her here to me, NN."

And after these things, sacrifice. Then raise loud groans and go backward as you descend. And she will come at once. But pay attention to the one being attracted so that you may open the door for her; otherwise the spell will fail."

36.35–68. Charm to restrain anger and to secure favor, and an excellent charm for gaining victory in the courts (it works even against kings; no charm is greater): Take a silver lamella and inscribe with a bronze stylus the following seal of the figure and the names, and wear it under your garment, and you will have a victory.

The names to be written are these: "IAO SABAOTH ADONAI ELOAI ABRASAX ABLANATHANALBA AKRAMMACHAMARI PEPHTHA PHOZA PHEBENNOUNI, supreme angels, give to me, NN whom NN bore, victory, favor, reputation, advantage over all men and over all women, especially over NN, whom NN bore, forever and all time." Consecrate it. [Under this is a figure of a headless man with his face on his chest, but also a miniature head protruding from his right shoulder. With his right hand he is holding a fat snake, with his left an ankh. An elongated object inscribed ZAGYRE is at his feet. Seven magical symbols are on each side, and around the field are arranged the words IAO ARIAD OBADOZEIRA DABAEITHAOPRETHEIAIEA ARIOBADOZEIRAD ABAITHA EROUCH I LEIELICHYORE ARIOBATHA DARIZO DABOIRA.]

29.1–21 [with a drawing of the dwarf god Bes and a figure holding a sword in its right hand, a severed head in its left]

thattharathautholthara	thattharathautholthara
attharathautholthara	attharathautholthara
ttharathautholthara	ttharathautholthara
tharathautholthara	tharathautholthara
arathautholthara	arathautholthara
rathautholthara	rathautholthara
athautholthara	athautholthara
thautholthara	thautholthara
autholthara	autholthara
utholthara	utholthara
tholthara	tholthara
olthara	olthara
lthara	lthara
thara	thara
ara	ara
ra	ra
a	a

I adjure you by the twelve elements of heaven and the twenty-four elements of the world, that you attact Herakles, whom Taaipis bore, to me, to Allous, whom Alexandra bore, immediately, immediately, quickly, quickly.

11.A.1–40. Apollonius of Tyana's old serving woman: Take Typhon's skull and write the following characters on it with the blood of a black dog: (magical signs) SABERRA. Then, going to a suitable place, by a river, the sea, or at the fork of a road, in the middle of the night put the skull on the ground, place it [under] your left foot, and speak as follows.

The formula: "ERITHYIA MEROPE GERGIRO CHETHIRA ANAPER-OUCH . . . LYROPHIA GEGETHIRA LOLYN GOUGOGE AMBRACHA BI . . . AEBILE MARITHAIA MPROUCHE AABEL ETHIRAO AP . . . OCHO-RIELA MORETHIRA PHECHIRO OSRI POIRA AMERI . . . PHE. OUTHERA GARGERIO TITHEMYME MERAPSECHIR AORIL. Come, Appear, O goddess called Mistress of the House."

After you say this, you will behold sitting on an ass a woman of extraordinary loveliness, possessing a heavenly beauty, indescribably fair and youthful. As soon as you see her, make obeisance and say: "I thank [you] lady for appearing to me. Judge me worthy of you. May your Majesty be well disposed to me, and accomplish whatever task I impose on you."

The goddess will reply to you, "What do you have in mind?"

You say, "I have need [of you] for domestic service."

At that she will get off the ass, shed her beauty, and will be an old woman. And the old woman will say to you, "I will serve and attend you."

After she tells you this, the goddess will again put on her own beauty, which she had just taken off, and she will ask to be released.

But you say to the goddess, "No, Lady! I will use you until I get her."

As soon as the goddess hears this, she will go up to the old lady, and will take her molar tooth and a tooth from the ass and give both to you; and after that it will be impossible for the old woman to leave you, unless perhaps you want to release her. From that time forth you will receive a bounty of great benefits, for everything that your soul desires will be accomplished by her. She will guard all your possessions and in particular will find out for you whatever anyone is thinking about you.

Indeed she will tell you everything and will never desert you: such is her store of good will toward you. But if ever you wish, there is a way to release her (but never do this!). Take her tooth and the ass's tooth, make a bonfire and throw them into the fire, and with a shriek the old woman will flee without a trace. Do not be prone to release her, since it will be impossible for you to replace her.

But do release the goddess, when you are sure that the old woman will serve you, by speaking as follows: "MENERPHER PHIE PRACHERA LYLORI MELICHARE NECHIRA." When the old woman hears this, the goddess will mount the ass and depart.

The phylactery to be used throughout the rite: The skull of the ass. Fasten the ass's tooth with silver and the old lady's tooth with gold, and wear them always; for if you do this, it will be impossible for the old woman to leave you. The rite has been tested.

[The goddess referred to in this spell is Nephtys, wife of the donkey-headed Seth, or Typhon.]

A part of a page of a mid-fourth-century book of magical spells and instructions (the whole, over a thousand lines in eight double pages) from Egypt. The invocation indicates typical conceptions of divine powers.

Source: *PGM* 13.762ff.

Come to me, you from the four winds, ruler of all, who breathed spirit into men for life, whose is the hidden and unspeakable name— it cannot be uttered by human mouth—at whose name even the daimons, when hearing, are terrified, whose is the sun, ARNEBOUAT BOLLOCH BARBARICH B BAALSAMEN PTIDAIOY ARNEBOUAT, and [the] moon, ARSENPENPROOUTH BARBARAIONE OSRAR MEMPSECHEI— they are unwearied eyes, shining in the pupils of men's eyes—of whom heaven is head, ether body, earth feet, and the environment water, the Agathos Daimon. You are the ocean, begetter of good things and feeder of the civilized world. . . . Yours is the eternal processional way in which your seven-lettered name is established for the harmony of the seven sounds [of the planets which] utter their voices according to the twenty-eight forms of the moon, SAR APHARA APHARA I ABRAARM APAPHA PERTAOMECH AKMECH IAO E IAOOYE AIOY AEO AAOY IAO. Yours are the beneficent effluxes of the stars, daimons, and Fortunes and Fates, by whom is given wealth, good old age, good children, good luck, a good burial. And you, lord of life, King of the heavens and the earth and all things living in them, you whose justice is not turned aside, you whose glorious name the Muses sing, you whom the eight guards attend, E O CHO CHOUCH NOUN NAUNI AMOUN AMAUNI; you who have truth that never lies. Your name and your spirit rest upon the good. Come into my mind and my under-standing for all the time of my life and accomplish for me all the desires of my soul.

For you are I, and I, you. Whatever I say must happen, for I have your name as a unique phylactery in my heart, and no flesh, although moved, will overpower me; no spirit will stand against me—neither daimon nor visitation nor any other of the evil beings of Hades, because of your name, which I have in my soul and invoke. Also [be] with me always for good, a good [god dwelling] in a good [man], yourself immune to magic, giving me health no magic can harm, well-being, prosperity, glory, victory, power, sex appeal. Restrain the evil eyes of each and all of my legal opponents, whether men or women, but give me charm in everything I do. ANOCH AIEPHE SAKTIETE BIBIOU BIBI-OU SPHE SPHE NOUSI NOUSI SEEE SEEESIETHO SIETHO OUN CHOUN-TIAI SEMBI IMENOUAI BAINPHNOUN PHNOUTH TOUCHAR SOUCHAR SABACHAR ANA of [the] god IEOU ION EON THOPTHO OUTHRO ARAO KOL KOL KAATON KOLKANTHO BALALACH ABLALACH OTH-ERCHENTHE BOULOCH BOULOCH OSERCHNTHE MENTHEI, for I have received the power of Abraham, Isaac, and Jacob, and of the great god, daimon IAO ABLANATHANALBA SIABRATHILAO LAMPSTER IEI OO, god. Do [it], lord PERTAOMECH CHACHMECH IAO OYEE IEOU AEO EEOY IAO.

1.3 Two Hex Tablets from Britain

> These two lead hex tablets (curse tablets, *defixiones*) will serve to indicate the wide diffusion of magical practices of a more or less uniform character, no matter where encountered. They are inscribed on both sides, roughly $4^1/_2$ x $3^1/_2$ inches, from south central England, of the second (?) century. The local Celtic deity in his Italianized name, Silvanus (= Mars), came first to the mind of the inscriber, before being corrected into another name more familiarly associated with Egyptian magic, Mercury = Hermes = Thoth.

> *Source:* M.W.C. Hassall and R.S.O. Tomlin, *Britannia* 10 (1979): 342f.

Cenacus complains to the god Mercury about Vitalinus and Natalinus his son concerning the draught animal that was stolen. He begs the god Mercury that neither may have health before/unless they repay me promptly the animal they have stolen and repay to the god the devotion [i.e., submit to the god for the punishment] which he himself has demanded from them.

A memorandum to the god Mercury [erased: "Mars Silvanus"] from Saturnina a woman concerning the linen cloth she has lost. Let him who stole it not have rest before/unless/until he brings the aforesaid things to the temple, whether he is man or woman, slave or free. She gives a third part to the aforesaid god on condition that he exact those things which have been aforewritten. A third part from what has been lost is given to the god Silvanus on condition that he exact this, whether the thief is man or woman, slave or free.

1.4   Examples of Divination by Dreams, from Artemidorus's *Oneirocritica*

Oneiromancy, divination through dreams, took the night's visions as messages sent by some deity, just as they have been seen in the conversion of Josephus, above, or will be seen again in many texts, below. The art of their interpretation enjoyed a history reaching back many centuries before the Greco-Roman, and developed conventions that can be sensed through no more than an observant first reading of oneiromantic texts, for example, regarding the civic or socioeconomic status of the person involved. Among various known handbooks, one by Artemidorus of Daldis (*Oneirocritica*) of the mid-second century is typical. He considers larger religious questions as well as the meaning of the things one sees in one's sleep, in discussions that answer the query, What if one has dreamt that. . . ?

Source: Artemidorus, *Oneirocritica* 33, 34, 68, trans. Robert J. White (Park Ridge, N.J.: Noyes Press, 1975).

33. Sacrificing to the gods what is prescribed for each means good luck for everyone. For men sacrifice to the gods when they have received benefits or when they have escaped some evil. But to sacrifice to the gods offerings that are unholy or inappropriate foretells the wrath of the gods to whom the person has sacrificed. If a sick man dreams that other men are sacrificing, even if he sees them sacrificing to Asclepius, it is a bad sign, since the sacrificial victim is destroyed. It portends death.

To wreathe the gods with flowers and branches that are fitting and prescribed by law as sacred to these deities signifies good fortune for all men, but it will not come to pass without anxieties. This dream admonishes a slave to obey his master and to do things that are pleasing to him. To wipe off, to anoint, or to clean the statues of the gods, to sweep in front of statues and to sprinkle everything in the temple with water signifies that a man has committed a sin against those very gods. I know of a man who forswore himself after this dream by the very god whose statue he had dreamt he was cleaning. What the dream was telling him was this, that he must implore the god for forgiveness.

To destroy statues of the gods, to throw out of a house the statues that are inside, to raze a temple, or to commit any sacrilegious act in a temple is inauspicious for all men and portends great crises. For men who are in great distress also abandon their reverence towards gods.

If the gods depart of their own free will and their statues fall down, it portends death for the dreamer or for one of his family. If gods are sacrificing to other gods, it signifies that the house of the dreamer will be deserted. For the gods sacrifice to one another only when they feel there are no human beings present.

If the statues of the gods move, it signifies fears and disturbances for all but those who are imprisoned or who intend to take a trip. It signifies that the former will be released, so that they can move about easily. It moves the latter from their dwelling place and leads them out.

34. Some gods can be apprehended only by the intellect while others can be perceived by the senses. The majority of the gods can be grasped by the intellect, whereas only a few can be perceived by the senses. The following section will make this clearer.

We divide the gods into the Olympians, whom we call the aetherial gods, the celestial gods, the terrestrial gods, the sea and river gods, the chthonic gods <and those in their circle>. The aetherial gods are called, reasonably enough, Zeus, Hera, Aphrodite Urania, Artemis, Apollo, Aetherial Fire, and Athena. The celestial deities are Helius [the Sun], Selene [the Moon], the stars, the clouds, the winds, the mock suns that come under them, the meteors, the "shooting star" and Iris [the Rainbow]. All of these can be preceived by the senses.

Among the terrestrial gods, those that can be perceived by the senses are Hecate, Pan, Ephialtes, and Asclepius (who is also said to be intelligible at the same time). The intelligible gods are the Dioscuri, Heracles, Dionysus, Hermes, Nemesis, Aphrodite Pandemus, <Hephaestus>, Tyche [chance], Peitho [Persuasion], the Graces, the Hours, the Nymphs, and Hestia.

The sea gods who are intelligible are Poseidon, Amphitrite, Nereus, the Nereids, Leucothea, and Phorcys. Those that can be perceived by the senses are the Sea itself, the Waves, the Seashores, the Rivers, the Marshes, the Nymphs, and Achelous.

The chthonic gods are Pluto, Persephone, Demeter, Core, Iacchus, Serapis, Isis, Anubis, Harpocrates, chthonic Hecate, the Furies, the demons who attend them, Fear and Panic, who are called the sons of Ares by some men. One must count Ares himself as much among the terrestrial gods as among the chthonic. The gods in their circle are Ocean, Tethys, Cronus, the Titans, and Universal Nature.

68. If a man dreams that he is flying not very far above the earth and in an upright position, it means good luck for the dreamer. The greater the distance above the earth, the higher his position will be in regard to those who walk beneath him. For we always call those who are more prosperous the "higher ones." It is good if this does not happen to a man in his own country, since it signifies emigration because the person does not set his foot upon the ground. For the dream is saying to some extent that the dreamer's native land is inaccessible to him.

Flying with wings is auspicious for all men alike. The dream signifies freedom for slaves, since all birds that fly are without a master and have no one above them. It means that the poor will acquire a great deal of money. For just as money raises men up, wings raise birds up. It signifies offices for the rich and very influential. For just as the creatures of the air are above those that crawl upon the earth, rulers are above private citizens. But to dream that one is flying without wings and very far above the earth signifies danger and fear for the dreamer.

Flying around tiled roofs, houses, and blocks of houses signifies confusion of the soul and disturbances. For slaves, dreaming that one is flying up into the heavens always signifies that they will pass into more distinguished homes and frequently even that they will pass into the court of a king. I have often observed that free men, even against their will, have journeyed to Italy. For just as the sky is the home of the gods, Italy is the home of kings. But the dream indicates that those who wish to hide and conceal themselves will be discovered. For everything in the sky is clear and easily visible to everyone.

Flying with the birds signifies that one will dwell with men of foreign nationalities and with strangers. The dream is inauspicious for criminals, since it signifies punishment for wrongdoers and frequently crucifixion. Flying a course that is not very high above the earth nor, again, very low but at a height where one is able to distinguish clearly objects on the ground signifies a trip or a change of address. One can ascertain from the things that are seen on the earth the kind of events that the dreamer will encounter during his trip abroad. For example, if a man sees plains, grain-lands, cities, villages, fields, all kinds of human activity, beautiful rivers, marshes, a calm sea, harbors, or ships that are sailing with a fair wind, it foretells a good trip. On the other hand, valleys, ravines, wooded glens, rocks, wild animals, river torrents, mountains, and steep cliffs signify that only misfortunes will occur on the trip. But it is always good, after one has flown above, to fly back down and to awaken in this way. But it is best of all to fly at will [wishing to soar above] and to stop at will. For it foretells great ease and skill in one's business affairs.

It is not auspicious, however, if a man dreams that he is flying while he is being pursued by a wild animal, a man, or a demon. For it portends great fears and dangers. For in these dreams the person's fear was so great that he did not think that he would be sufficiently safe fleeing upon the earth, but he took to the skies. If a slave dreams that he is flying in the house of his master, it means good luck. For he will surpass many in the house. But if he is flying outside the house, he will leave the house as a dead man after days of health and happiness, if he has gone out through the courtyard. If he has gone through the gate-house, he will be sold. If he has gone through a window, he will leave the house by running away.

1.5   The Foundations of Astrology, from Manilius's *Astronomica*

Like oneiromancy, prediction through the configuration of the stars and planets at one's birth had a long history, beginning in Mesopotamia and developing, at the hands of the Greeks, depth upon depth of lore and complexity. Among many of its handbooks, mostly Greek, two survive in Latin: Marcus Manilius's and Firmicus Maternus's. The first of these, written over several years on both sides of 15 C.E. by an otherwise unknown author, is in verse and aims for high effect; but it also conveys the basic teachings of astrology and thus, like such other developed arts as prophecy, healing, or invocation of superhuman power, it fits itself to the big, broad prevailing ideas about religion. Here the argument for the reasonableness of reading fate in the stars is presented.

Source: Manilius, *Astronomica* 2.65ff., trans. G. P. Goold, LCL.

Mine own theme shall I sing, my words shall I owe to none amongst bards, and there shall emerge no stolen thing, but work of my own contriving; in a lone car I soar to the heavens, in a ship of my own I sweep the seas. For I shall sing of god, silent-minded monarch of nature, who, permeating sky and land and sea, controls with uniform compact the mighty structure; how the entire universe is alive in the mutual concord of its elements and is driven by the pulse of reason, since a single spirit dwells in all its parts and, speeding through all things, nourishes the world and shapes it like a living creature. Indeed, unless the whole frame stood fast, composed of kindred limbs and obedient to an overlord, unless providence directed the vast resources of the skies, the earth would not possess its stability, nor stars their orbits, and the heavens would wander aimlessly or stiffen with inertia; the constellations would not keep their appointed courses nor would alternately the night flee day and put in turn the day to flight, nor would the rains feed the earth, the winds the upper air, the sea the laden clouds, rivers the sea and the deep the springs; the sum of things would not remain forever equal through all its parts, so disposed by the fairness of its creator that neither should the waves of the sea fail nor the land sink beneath them, nor the revolving heavens become larger or smaller than the mean. Motion sustains and does not alter the edifice. In this due order over the whole universe do all things abide, following the guidance of a master. This god and all-controlling reason, then, derives earthly beings from the signs of heaven; though the stars are remote at a far distance, he compels the recognition of their influences, in that they give to the peoples of the world their lives and destinies and to each his own character. Nor is the proof hard to find: thus it is that the sky affects the fields, thus gives and takes away the various crops, puts the sea to movement, casting it on land and fetching it therefrom, and thus this restlessness possesses ocean, now caused by the shining of the moon, now provoked by her retreat to the other side of the sky, and now attendant upon the sun's yearly revolution; thus that, submerged beneath the waves and in prison-shell confined, animals adapt their forms to the motions of the moon and copy your waning, Delia [the Moon], and your growth; thus you too return your features to your brother's car [Apollo's, the sun's] and a second time from it re-seek them, and as much as he has grudged or lavished on you do you reflect, your star dependent on his. Thus lastly with the herds and dumb animals on earth: though they remain forever ignorant of themselves and of law, nevertheless when nature summons them to the parent heaven, they lift up their minds and watch the sky and stars; they cleanse their bodies on beholding the horns of the nascent moon, and note the storms about to come, the fine weather about to return. Who after this can doubt that a link exists between heaven and man, to whom, in its desire for earth to rise to the stars, gifts outstanding did nature give and the power of speech and breadth of understanding and a wing-swift mind, and into whom alone indeed has god come down and dwells, and seeks himself in man's seeking of him?

1.6   Parts of an Astrological Handbook: Firmicus Maternus's *Mathesis*

Among works on astrology, Firmicus Maternus's is the best preserved from antiquity—also representative. It dates to the 330s C.E. Herewith a couple of typical selections, in a work of hundreds of pages. Observant reading is enough to draw out some of the conventions shared with oneiromancy.

Source: Firmicus Maternus, *Mathesis* 3.7.1–6 and 7.12.1–3, trans. Jean R. Bram (Park Ridge, N.J.: Noyes Press, 1975).

Mercury

1. Mercury located exactly on the ascendant in signs in which he rejoices, in a daytime chart, makes philosophers, teachers of the art of letters, geometers: often he makes those who measure heavenly phenomena or study them so that they can contemplate the presence of the gods,

or men skilled in sacred writings. Often he makes orators and lawyers, especially if in this house he is in his own sign or in other voiced signs.

2. If either the Sun, Saturn, or Jupiter are in aspect to Mercury in this house, he will make great men crowned with wreaths for being famous in sacred matters. He also makes men to whom the most important business of emperors is entrusted. But if Mars is in opposition or square aspect or together with Mercury on the ascendant, the native [i.e., the person of such a horoscope] is attacked by a variety of continual evils. These evils cannot be identified or defined. If Mars is in the trine aspect to Mercury in this house, this involves the natives in reputable and prosperous professions.

3. Mercury on the ascendant in a nocturnal chart makes men of divine sensibilities, easily attaining their wishes. They are sober and respectable in character, in charge of such activities as farming, construction, tax collecting, money-changing, or lending at interest. In this house by night Mercury also makes them interpreters of emperors or powerful judges. But all of these are indicated according to the different qualities of the signs.

4. Mercury in the second house in a morning rising makes the natives of humble class, of criminal disposition, with no knowledge of letters, destitute of all means of livelihood. But if Mercury is an evening star and in a nocturnal chart, he will make money-lenders or managers of others' money. In a diurnal chart he makes students of language skilled in difficult writings, unwilling to compare their own nature with that of other men. For they are fond of all things which have not been handed down by tradition. They are wretched in life and always wear themselves out with various troubles.

5. If Jupiter is in any aspect or conjunction with Mercury in this house and the Moon in favorable aspect, the natives will be great and famous but always subordinate to others, never attaining the first place. Nevertheless they will be in charge of great undertakings and have at their disposal royal facilities, will be managers of royal treasures and journeys. But all this good fortune is finished in a short space of time.

6. Mercury in the third house will make priests, magicians, healers, astrologers, men who through their own efforts discover things not handed down by tradition. They are intelligent, fortunate, easily taking part in any kind of activities. If Jupiter is in trine or sextile aspect, or together with Mercury, this indicates high intelligence and great and divine counsel. Mars in any aspect to Mercury and Jupiter in this position will make agents of kings, famous leaders, powerful administrators, to whom royal income is entrusted. They will overcome all obstacles with their courage and good fortune.

Number of Marriages

1. In all charts, if Saturn is found with Venus in the same sign and if Saturn has more degrees, this means one wife; if Venus has more degrees, many wives. You will find this true also in the charts of women. Venus on the descendant indicates a wife seduced by others; or they will live together without marriage tablets. If Mars is in aspect, the natives will take wives known for adultery. But if Venus is in Taurus or Libra she will provide well-born wives; in other signs, low-class.

2. To find the house of the wife in a man's chart, count from Saturn to Venus if it is a diurnal chart; in a nocturnal chart, the reverse. You compute the house of brothers from Saturn to Jupiter and again from the ascendant. If the house of the wife falls together with that of brothers, computed as we said, sisters or relatives are allotted as wives. You will find a similar effect in a woman's chart.

3. Also Venus in conjunction with the ruler of the chart gives sisters or relatives as wives. But if the house of the wife, computed exactly, is found in maternal or paternal signs, observed exactly, the natives will take mothers, stepmothers, or nurses as wives. You will find a similar effect in the charts of women, especially if Mars, Venus, and Mercury are in aspect to these same houses.

1.7   Cicero on Augury, from the *De Divinatione*

> Different people, naturally, had different ideas about the world above man: the gods, fate, means of communication with them and their intelligibility. In illustration of the variety of views, consider this short passage from an essay by Cicero written in the 40s B.C.E. The author imagines his brother, in a dialogue, presenting the case for the accessibility of the divine intent to man's reading, in which, however, the poet Ennius of around 200 B.C.E. did not believe, while Cicero's contemporary Appius believed too much. (Note, incidentally, that the Italian region of the Marsi, referred to as famous for its magicians by Pliny in the next selection, already had its reputation in Ennius's time.)

> **Source:** Cicero, *On Divination* 2.132–33, trans. William A. Falconer, LCL.

I will assert, however, in conclusion, that I do not recognize fortune-tellers, or those who prophesy for money, or necromancers, or mediums, whom your friend Appius makes it a practice to consult.

> In fine, I say, I do not care a fig
> For Marsian augurs, village mountebanks,
> Astrologers who haunt the Circus grounds
> Or Isis-seers, or dream interpreters—

—for they are not diviners either by knowledge or skill—
> But superstitious bards, soothsaying quacks,
> Averse to work, or mad, or ruled by want,
> Directing others how to go, and yet
> What road to take they do not know themselves;
> From those to whom they promise wealth they beg
> A coin. From what they promised let them take
> Their coin as toll and pass the balance on.

Such are the words of Ennius who only a few lines further back expresses the view that there are gods and yet says the gods do not care what human beings do. But for my part, believing as I do that the gods do care for man, and that they advise and often forewarn him, I approve of divination which is not trivial and is free from falsehood and trickery.

1.8   Roman Superstitions, from Pliny's *Natural History*

Pliny the Elder, eventually dying in the scientific but too close observation of the eruption of Vesuvius (79 C.E.), was the author of a monumental Natural History encyclopedia, in the course of which he looks at the gray zone between religion and superstition. He concludes with a story of the scientific method, applied rather roughly. As in the preceding passage from Cicero, one can sense here some of the various degrees of literalness of belief, and of tolerance for simple, mechanical views about divine roles, that characterized religiosity then as now.

Source: Pliny, *Natural History* 28.4.228, 28.6.30, trans. W.H.S. Jones, LCL.

There is indeed nobody who does not fear to be spell-bound by imprecations. A similar feeling makes everybody break the shells of eggs or snails immediately after eating them, or else pierce them with the spoon that they have used. And so Theocritus among the Greeks, Catullus and quite recently Virgil among ourselves, have represented love charms in their poems. Many believe that by charms pottery can be crushed, and not a few even serpents; that these themselves can break the spell, this being the only kind of intelligence they possess; and by the charms of the Marsi they are gathered together even when asleep at night. On walls too are written prayers to avert fires. It is not easy to say whether our faith is more violently shaken by foreign, unpronounceable words, or by the unexpected Latin ones, which our mind forces us to consider absurd, being always on the look-out for something big, something adequate to move a god, or rather to impose its will on his divinity. Homer said that by a magic formula Ulysses stayed the haemorrhage from his wounded thigh; Theophrastus, that there is a formula to cure sciatica; Cato handed down one to set dislocated limbs, Marcus Varro one for gout. The dictator Caesar, after one serious accident to his carriage, is said always, as soon as he was seated, to have been in the habit of repeating three times a formula or prayer for a safe journey, a thing we know that most people do today.

I should like to reinforce this part of my argument by adding an appeal to the personal feeling of the individual. Why on the first day of the year do we wish one another cheerfully a happy and prosperous New Year? Why do we also, on days of general purification, choose persons with lucky names to lead the victims? Why do we meet the evil eye by a special attitude of prayer, some invoking the Greek Nemesis, for which purpose there is at Rome an image of the goddess on the Capitol, although she has no Latin name? Why on mentioning the dead do we protest that their memory is not being attacked by us? Why do we believe that in all matters the odd numbers are more powerful, as is implied by the attention paid to critical days in fevers? Why at the harvest of the fruits do we say: "These are old," and pray for the new ones to take their place? Why do we say "Good health" to those who sneeze? This custom according to report even Tiberius Caesar, admittedly the most gloomy of men, insisted on even in a carriage, and some think it more effective to add to the salutation the name of the sneezer. Moreover, according to an accepted belief absent people can divine by the ringing in their ears that they are the object of talk. Attalus assures us that if on seeing a scorpion one says "Two," it is checked and does not strike.

We certainly still have formulas to charm away hail, various diseases, and burns, some actually tested by experience, but I am very shy of quoting them, because of the widely different feelings they arouse. Wherefore everyone must form his own opinion about them as he pleases. . . .

Persons possessed of powers of witchcraft and of the evil eye, along with many peculiar characteristics of animals, I have spoken of when dealing with marvels of the nations; it is superfluous to go over the ground again. Of certain men the whole bodies are beneficent, for example the members of those families that frighten serpents. These by a mere touch or by wet suction relieve bitten victims. In this class are the Psylli, the Marsi, and the Ophiogenes, as they are called, in the island of Cyprus. An envoy from this family, by name Evagon, was at Rome thrown by the consuls as a test into a cask of serpents, which to the general amazement licked him all over.

1.9   A Ghost Story, from the Letters of Pliny the Younger

Stories of ghosts and witchcraft were as popular in the Roman Empire as they are now, and introduce one further element into the picture we have of the supernatural and superhuman as they were understood in that period. A number of accounts survive, in verse or, in the next two selections, folded into novels or letters. Interest in them naturally rose with their credibility. For those offered here by Pliny, nephew to the natural philosopher (above) and a sensible, honest man, we have his assurance that they may be believed.

Source: Pliny the Younger, *Letters* 7.27, trans. Betty Radice, LCL.

To Licinius Sura. Our leisure gives me the chance to learn and you to teach me; so I should very much like to know whether you think that ghosts exist, and have a form of their own and some sort of supernatural power, or whether they lack substance and reality and take shape only from our fears. I personally am encouraged to believe in their existence largely from what I have heard of the experience of Curtius Rufus. While he was still obscure and unknown he was attached to the suite of the new governor of Africa. One afternoon he was walking up and down in the colonnade of his house when there appeared to him the figure of a woman, of superhuman size and beauty. To allay his fears she told him that she was the spirit of Africa, come to foretell his future: he would return to Rome and hold office, and then return with supreme authority to the same province, where he would die. Everything came true. Moreover, the story goes on to say that as he left the boat on his arrival at Carthage the same figure met him on the shore. It is at least certain that when he fell ill he interpreted his future by the past and misfortune by his previous success, and gave up all hope of recovery although none of his people despaired of his life.

Now consider whether the following story, which I will tell just as it was told to me, is not quite as remarkable and even more terrifying. In Athens there was a large and spacious mansion with the bad reputation of being dangerous to its occupants. At dead of night the clanking of irons and, if you listened carefully, the rattle of chains could be heard, some way off at first, and then close at hand. Then there appeared the spectre of an old man, emaciated and filthy, with a long flowing beard and hair on end, wearing fetters on his legs and shaking the chains on his wrists. The wretched occupants would spend fearful nights awake in terror; lack of sleep led to illness and then death as their dread increased, for even during the day, when the apparition had vanished, the memory of it was in their mind's eye, so that their terror remained after the cause of it had gone. The house was therefore deserted, condemned to stand empty, and wholly abandoned to the spectre; but it was advertised as being to let or for sale in case someone was found who knew nothing of its evil reputation.

The philosopher Athenodorus came to Athens and read the notice. His suspicions were aroused when he heard the low price, and the whole story came out on inquiry; but he was none the less, in fact all the more, eager to rent the house. When darkness fell he gave orders that a couch was to be made up for him in the front part of the house, and asked for his notebooks, pen, and a lamp. He sent all of his servants to the inner rooms, and concentrated his thoughts, eyes and hand on his writing, so that his mind would be occupied and not conjure up the phantom he had heard about nor other imaginary fears. At first there was nothing but the general silence of night; then came the clanking of iron and dragging of chains. He did not look up nor stop writing, but steeled his mind to shut out the sounds. Then the noise grew louder, came nearer, was heard in the doorway, and then inside the room. He looked round, saw and recognized the ghost described to him. It stood and beckoned, as if summoning him. Athenodorus in his turn signed to it to wait a little, and again bent over his notes and pen, while it stood rattling its chains over his head as he wrote. He looked round again and saw it beckoning as before, so without further delay he picked up his lamp and followed. It moved slowly, as if weighed down with chains, and when it turned off into the courtyard of the house, it suddenly vanished, leaving him alone. He then picked some plants and leaves and marked the spot. The following day he approached the magistrates, and advised them to give orders for the place to be dug up. There they found bones, twisted round with chains, which were left bare and corroded by the fetters when time and the action of the soil had rotted away the body. The bones were collected and given a public burial, and after the shades had been duly laid to rest the house saw them no more.

For these details I rely on the evidence of others, but here is a story I can vouch for myself. One of my freedmen, a man of some education, was sleeping in the same bed as his younger brother when he dreamed that he saw someone sitting on the bed and putting scissors to his hair, even cutting some off the top of his head. When day dawned he found this place shorn and the hair lying on the floor. A short time elapsed and then another similar occurrence confirmed the earlier one. A slave boy was sleeping with several others in the young slaves' quarters. His story was that two men clad in white came in through the window and cut his hair as he lay in bed, and departed the way they had come. Daylight revealed that his head also had been shorn and the hair was scattered about. Nothing remarkable followed except perhaps the fact that I was not brought to trial, as I should have been if Domitian (under whom all this happened) had lived longer. For among the papers in his desk was found information laid against me by Carus; from which, in view of the custom for accused persons to let their hair grow long, one may interpret the cutting of my slaves' hair as a sign that the danger threatening me was averted.

So please apply your learned mind to this question; it deserves your long and careful consideration, and I too am surely not undeserving as a recipient of your informed opinion. You may argue both sides of the case as you always do, but lay your emphasis on one side or the other and do not leave me in suspense and uncertainty; my reason for asking your opinion was to put an end to my doubts.

1.10   A Story of Witches, from Apuleius's *Metamorphoses*

> Further on the subject of what some contemporaries would certainly have called superstition, consider the following tale. It is taken from the first book of Apuleius's *Metamorphoses,* a work of which we will make further extensive use later. The narrator, a certain Aristomenes, recounts an adventure which had befallen him while traveling with a certain Socrates. This man had with Aristomenes's help escaped from a witch, Meroe, who possessively loved him. Aristomenes and Socrates have stopped for the night at an inn, when suddenly their room is broken into with such violence that Aristomenes finds himself lying under his own overturned bed.

> **Source:** Apuleius, *Metamorphoses* (*The Golden Ass*) 1:12–13, 18–19, trans. Jack Lindsay (Bloomington: Indiana University Press, 1962).

12. And while I lay where I had been pitched, I peeked out under the rim of the enveloping bed to see what was the matter. I saw two women of advanced age—one bearing a flashing lantern, the other a sponge and naked sword. Thus charactered, they took their stand about Socrates, who had slept peaceably through the whole commotion. The woman with the sword spoke first.

"Look at him, sister Panthia, look at my beloved Endymion, my sweet Catamite, who day and night has abused my youthful body. Look at him who sets my love beneath him, who not only defames me scandalously, but also prepares for wriggling out of my clutch. And I shall be deserted by this Ulysses in his craftiness. I shall be a Calypso wailing in eternal desolation."

Then she lifted her right hand and pointed me out to her sister Panthia. "And look at that fine fellow, his counsellor Aristomenes, who suggested this defalcation and who now quakes himself to death, flung prostrate beneath his bedstead. He is spying on all our movements and thinks to get off with his insults unrevenged. But I will make him repent someday, soon—in fact, at once—for his late reckless speeches and his present peeping-eye."

13. When I heard this, cornered as I was, a cold sweat broke out all over me, and my bowels quavered and opened, till the very bed shook and rattled above my palpitating spine.

"But why not rip him," remarked Panthia, "to shreds as the Bacchanals do, or let us set up the mark of his manhood and knock it off?"

But Meroe (for this clearly was the heroine of Socrates' story), answered, "No, he must survive to dump the corpse of this wretch under a sprinkle of earth."

Then she laid Socrates' head over on one side, and drove the sword into the left part of his throat up to the hilt, and caught the spout of blood in a leathern bottle which she held ready, so carefully that not a single drop was left visible. And more, I saw Meroe—to omit no correct detail of the sacrificial rite, I suppose—thrust her hand down through the wound to the very entrails, and, after groping about, finally wrench out the heart of my unhappy comrade. And he, with his gullet slit by the impact of the blade, uttered a cry through the wound (or rather a broken gurgle) and bubbled out his ghost. Then Panthia stopped the big wound in his throat with a sponge, and cried, "Beware, O sponge born of the salt-sea, beware that you pass not through a running stream."

After this declaration they raised up the bed and straddled above my body, emptying their bladders till I was drenched to the skin with filth. [The witches then depart and the damage to the door miraculously repairs itself. The next morning Socrates awakes apparently none the worse for wear, and our friends resume their journey. After a while they grow hungry:]

18. "Your breakfast is all ready," I said, and divesting myself of the scrip that hung about my shoulder I handed him some bread and cheese. "Let us take a seat," I continued, "near that plane-tree."

19. We seated ourselves and both started on a snack. Socrates was gobbling greedily, but as I looked at him more attentively, I saw that he was turning faint, and as pale as boxwood. Indeed the hues of life were in such pell-mell flight that my terrified imagination conjured up those Furies of the night; and the first morsel of bread, tiny as it was, that I put into my

mouth, lodged in the middle of my throat, and I could neither gulp it down nor urge it up. Moreover, the number of the passers-by intensified my fear for when one of two companions dies suddenly, who believes that the other is not somehow responsible?

But when Socrates had gnawed sufficiently at the bread, he grew impatiently thirsty. For he had hastily swallowed a fair portion of a very good cheese; and not far from the roots of the plane-tree a smooth stream wound sluggishly along, rather like a placid lake, lustrously rivalling silver or glass.

"Come here," I cried. "Drink your fill of this spring-water like milk." He rose and searched about a while till he found a flat space on the river bank. Then sinking on his knees he inclined himself down to take a draught. But he had no sooner touched the dewy sparkle of the water with the tips of his lips, when the wound in his throat gaped open wide, and the sponge suddenly sprang out, a little gush of blood accompanying it. And his body, now devoid of life, would have collapsed into the stream had I not gripped him by the leg and dragged him with difficulty higher up the bank. There I lamented over my hapless comrade as well as time would allow, and then buried him in the sandy soil that bordered the river, to lie there for ever.

2

HEALING SHRINES
AND TEMPLE MANAGEMENT

The ways in which sanctuaries were kept active and in repair indicates something of their place in the surrounding community and their role in promoting the circulation of people interested in religion—therefore, the circulation of religious ideas as well. Major shrines through major festivals attracted huge crowds from hundreds of miles away, not only in Greece, where Olympia is the most famous example, but in quite minor cities like Oenoanda in southern (modern) Turkey. (The festival there, centered in the local Apollo-cult, happens to be known in greater detail than any other. See the founding text as translated by S. Mitchell, *Journal of Roman Studies* 80 [1990]: 183–87.) Through integration not only into people's personal lives, but into the local civic calendar, economy, and administration as well, sanctuaries were centers of much interest and importance; and their structures sometimes accommodated more or less secular purposes, as safe-deposit vaults, meeting places for municipal senate sessions, or lecture halls for teachers and professors.

2.1 Two Accounts of Healing Shrines, from Strabo's *Geography*

Of this last purpose, for the advancement of learning, various sanctuaries provide examples. To begin with, there is a site in western Asia Minor, about which we have a report from Strabo. It appears in his monumental survey of a *National Geographic* character (and titled *Geography*), published in the reign of Augustus. The connection between a home of a god that heals, and truly scientific medical study, is seen here in his pages, as it could have been seen at any time from the fifth century B.C.E. on, perhaps best at Cos (the island) and Pergamon (below).

Source: Strabo, *Geography* 12.8.20, trans. Horace L. Jones, LCL.

Between Laodiceia and Carura is a temple of Men Carou, as it is called, which is held in remarkable veneration. In my own time a great Herophileian school [i.e., in the tradition of H., who flourished ca. 300 B.C.E.] of medicine has been established by Zeuxis, and afterwards carried on by Alexander Philalethes, just as in the time of our fathers the Erasistrateian school was established by Hicesius, although at the present time the case is not at all the same as it used to be.

A traveler to Egypt in the reign of Augustus might have seen, almost in the suburbs of Alexandria, a famous shrine for healing dedicated to Sarapis.

Source: Strabo, *Geography* 17.1.17, trans. Horace L. Jones, LCL.

Canobus is a city situated at a distance of one hundred and twenty stadia from Alexandria, if one goes on foot, and was named after Canobus, the pilot of Menelaüs, who died there. It contains the temple of Sarapis, which is honoured with great reverence and effects such cures that even the most reputable men believe in it and sleep in it—themselves on their own behalf or others for them. Some writers go on to record the cures, and others the virtues of the oracles there. But to balance all this is the crowd of revellers who go down from Alexandria by the canal to the public festivals; for every day and every night is crowded with people on the boats who play the flute and dance without restraint and with extreme licentiousness, both men and women, and also with the people of Canobus itself, who have resorts situated close to the canal and adapted to relaxation and merry-making of this kind.

2.2   Diogenes's Cynical Attitudes toward Divine Aid, from Diogenes Laertius

Illustrative of the tradition of extreme skepticism in Greek thought, and from the lips of its foremost practitioner, Diogenes the founder of Cynicism, is this comment on miracles of healing. The speaker was a contemporary of Plato, here being quoted in a biography of the third century C.E.

Source: Diogenes Laertius, *Lives of the Philosophers* 6.59, trans. R. D. Hicks, LCL.

When someone expressed astonishment at the votive offerings in Samothrace [an island whose divinities were credited with saving sailors], his comment was, "There would have been far more, if those who were not saved had set up offerings." But others attribute this remark to Diagoras of Melos.

2.3   Cures, Sacrificial Regulations, and Honorific Inscriptions from the Temple of Asklepios at Pergamum

The Asclepius-sanctuary, Asklepieion, of Pergamon was of exceptional size, grandeur, and fame. Through excavation as well as ancient descriptions, it is also relatively well known today. Surviving inscriptions include some that tell of cures wrought by the god and commemorated by grateful patients, of which the following three are examples.

Source: IA, p. 117, no. 86; p. 141, no. 139, original translation.

Eveteria, her eyes cured, [pays this] vow to Asclepius the Savior.

Julius Meidias, who has been bled under the biceps, set this up, by divine command.

The following second-century Pergamene inscription indicates how medicine was applied through the advice of the god (white pepper and onions were used commonly for stomach disorders).

Source: Helmut Müller, *Chiron* 17 (1987): 194; original translation.

To Asklepios the loving god [*philanthropos*]. Publius Aelius Theon of Rhodes, son of Zenodotus and Zenodota, through 120 days without drinking, and eating at the dawn of each day 15 grains of white pepper and a half onion, was manifestly [*enargos*, "unbelievably"] saved from many great threats [to health] by the god's commands, and set up this [structure or statue of some sort] for the use of children, on behalf of his nephew Publius Aelius Callistratus, also called Plancianus, son of Antipater, according to his vow.

Visitors at many a sanctuary could consult its rules through a text, a so-called *lex sacra,* inscribed on some prominent wall. The surviving example from the Asklepieion in Pergamon now unfortunately lacks its opening sections and other bits far her on, and represents not even the original but a recopying, perhaps in the first century, of a third- or second-century B.C.E. original. It indicates how visitors could arrange to receive healing messages from the god in their sleep, by dreams which the priests might be asked to interpret.

Source: *IA*, pp. 168–69, no. 161, original translation.

And he should offer on the table of sacrifices the right leg and the entrails, and, taking up another wreath of olive, first offer up to Zeus Apotropaios ["who wards off"] a nine-braided striped cake, and to Zeus Meilichios ["the merciful"] a nine-braided striped cake, and to Artemis [. . .] and to Artemis Prothyraia ["the gate-keeper"] and to Earth, each a nine-braided cake. Having done this, let him preliminarily offer up a suckling pig on the altar to Asclepius, and lay on the table of sacrifices the right leg and entrails. Let him then contribute three obols to the treasury. In the evening, let him offer three nine-braided cakes, two of them on the outer hearth to Luck and Remembrance, the third in the sleeping-room to Themis. Let him be ritually clean in the aforementioned respects, and from sexual intercourse, and goat's meat and cheese and [. . . come in after abstaining] on the third day. Let him who sleeps there take the wreath off and lay it on the bed. If anyone wants to submit inquiries concerning one single matter several times, let him offer up preliminarily a pig. But if he wants to ask about another matter, let him preliminarily offer up another pig according to the regulations. For the smaller sleeping-room, the entrant shall be similarly clean ritually. Let him make offering to Zeus Apotropaios of a nine-braided striped cake, and to Zeus Meilichios, a nine-braided striped cake, and to Artemis Prothyraia and Artemis [. . .] and to Earth, to each a nine-braided cake. Let him contribute three obols to the treasury. All persons offering cult to the god, as they follow the priest and [. . .], shall take part in the offering procession with a cake soaked in honey, oil, and incense. In the evening, let all those who have made the preliminary sacrifice [. . .] to the sleeping-room, and all those who have taken part in the offering procession offer up three nine-braided striped cakes, one each to Themis, to Luck, and to Remembrance. They shall provide the god with good securities for the healing instructions [received by dreams during the nights in the sleeping-rooms]—whatever he may do to them—to render their accounts within a year [. . .] thank-victims for cure, not less than a year old. They shall contribute the thank-offerings for a cure to Asclepius' treasury, a sixth of a Phocaean stater to Apollo and a sixth of a Phocaean stater to Asclepius, when they are restored to health, and whatever else the god may require. Claudius Glycon the priest for ritual set this up.

The Pergamene sanctuary also contains many inscriptions, most of them honorific, of the type, So-and-So is here honored by (some public body—, a very brief list of his high positions and attainments); also, thanks rendered for the god's favor shown in matters having nothing to do with health.

Source: *IA*, p. 84, no. 38; p. 23, no. 2; p. 103, no. 63; p. 106, no. 64; p. 109, no. 72; p. 137, no. 129; original translations.

(in the reign of Hadrian?): The senate and people of the capital city of Asia, twice the Temple-Warden, first city, the city of Pergamon, paid honor to Flavia Melitene, wife of Flavius Metrodorus the councillor, and mother of Flavius Metrodorus the councillor, who constructed [i.e., Melitene did] the library in the precinct of the Savior Asclepius.

"When the Pergamenes inquired from Apollo of Didyma where, according to sacred law, the heroes Marcellus and Rufinus might be entombed, in consideration of the past virtuousness of their lives, the god replied . . . " [but the inscription is broken off, the reply is lost, and Marcellus is unidentifiable. Rufinus, however, was the consul of 142 C.E. and builder of the great round temple to Zeus Asclepius the Savior, with its sacred groves. Burial was ordinarily taboo within a city or holy precinct— hence the problem here.]

(first century C.E.?): To Zeus Asclepius the Savior. Aemilius Sabinus and Aemilius Herennianus, saved by him from the far ocean (Atlantic) and the barbarians there.

(much restored): To the gods in general, and especially to Asclepius the Savior, and to the emperor Trajan Hadrian Augustus, and to the motherland, Gn. Otacilius(?) Pollio, himself and of his own funds with (. . .)ope his wife dedicated the portico and its decoration, and the grand entrance.

To Asclepius, to Hygieia, Koronis, and Epione, Oneso gave, by divine command, holy gifts on behalf of Gemellos and Epaphroditos Epiphanes, the same Oneso who had previously dedicated five bronze and four silver animal figurines, a dipper . . . a gold ring, three garments, a linen cloth, a statuette, a splint . . . a polished oil-flask, a writing tablet, and all the other things . . . of her faith . . . [Many of the words can refer to more than one object.]

Thou knowest, Cypris [Aphrodite], the reason why I ordered this golden [statuette] made of thee, and who dedicated it, and for whose sake.

2.4   Inscriptions Detailing Private Benefactions, from Various Parts of the Empire

Cult financing, in some representative inscriptions, shows how universal was the spirit of civic generosity. It was peculiarly characteristic of the Greco-Roman world in its developed centuries, producing in English and other modern languages the novel term "evergetism." Evergetism, insistently pressed upon the wealthy of a community by their fellow citizens and stimulated by their own ambitions, paid for the greater part of all urban festival costs, secular amenities, and construction intended for general use. It was heavily drawn on for the construction and upkeep of most temples, too. In the period of the empire, the civic prestige of service to the imperial cult, especially for the freedman class, attracted more than its share of evergetism. That is reflected in the selections that follow.

Source: CIL 13.4208, from Wasserbillig, near Luxembourg, original translation. The inscription is broken on the right and conjecturally restored.

To the god Mercury and the goddess Rosmerta, Acceptus, imperial clerk and freedman of the empress, made the temple with statues and all decorations and the lodging house also for celebrating the cult ceremonies, on behalf of himself and his children, dedicated [Date], July, Lupo and Maximus being consuls [232 C.E.].

Source: ILS 4454, from Sidi Amor Djedidi, or Zama Minor, in Tunisia; time of Antoninus Pius, original translation.

Sacred to Pluto the Great King. C. Pescennius Saturus Cornelianus, son of Saturus, of the tribe of Palatina, permanent priest of [the deified] Hadrian, quaestor, judicial prefect [*iure dicundo*], *duovir quinquennalis* of the colony Zama, for the office of priest by an additional offer of 40,000 HS [HS means *sestertii*, three or four of which made a normal day's pay for a laborer], set up two statues and twice gave a banquet, and dedicated [this] through a decree of the senators.

Source: AE 1916, 36, from Cuicul, north Africa, original translation.

L. Cosinius Primus, son of Lucius, of the tribe Arnensis, aedile, quaestor, duovir quinquennalis, pontifex, permanent priest, built this open market (*macellum*) from the ground up with columns, statues, public scales, and central rotunda (*tholos*), as he had promised, from the 30,000 HS for the office of permanent priest, with additional sums. He dedicated it, with his brother C. Cosinius Maximus in charge.

> *Source: CIL* 8.23888, from Sidi bou Arara, north Africa, original translation.

To Modia Quintia daughter of Q. Modius Felix, permanent priestess who for the office of priestess, beyond the legal assessment with added money, decorated the portico with marble [panelling], a coffered ceiling, and columns. . . .

> *Source: Karthago* 14, p. 177; from Mustis, north Africa, time of Antoninus Pius, original translation.

Sacred to Pluto bringer of harvests, August, the genius of Mustis. For the well-being of the emperor T. Aelius Hadrian Antoninus Augustus Pius. Marcus Cornelius Laetus, son of Marcus, of the tribe Cornelia, permanent priest, duovir, official priest of Caelestis and Aesculapius, when he had set 10,000 HS for the office of permanent priest and 2,000 HS for the office of duovir, and paid 3,000 HS to the treasury, set up a bronze statue and with additional sums built a four-column portico in the temple of Caelestis. By decree of the senate. And he also dedicated it. Moreover, the portico of his ancestors in that same temple having collapsed through age, he added funds and restored it with four columns.

> *Source: CIL* 9.1618, Beneventum, Italy, 2d century, original translation.

M. Nasellius Sabinus of the Palatine tribe, son of Marcus, prefect of the First Dalmatian Cohort, and his father Nasellius Vitalis, Augustal priest and duovir for the census (quinquennalis), to all the inhabitants of the district (pagus) presented a splendid decorated portico and cross-roads constructed wholly from their money, and directed that a gift of 125 denarii annually be made in perpetuity on the eighth of June, the birthday of Sabinus, to the district members banqueting on this spot, on condition that on June fifth they purify the district ritually and on the following days dine as usual, and that on the eighth of June they banquet on the birthday of Sabinus. If this is not done, then this spot, as aforesaid, with the yearly 125 denarii shall belong to the college of physicians and to our freedmen, for them to banquet here on the birthday of Sabinus, the eighth of June.

Source: *CIL* 2.4514, Barcino, Spain, of the late second century, original translation.

L. Caecilius Optatus of the Papirian tribe, son of Lucius [there follows a list of titles] . . . who thus made his will in favor of the municipality of Barcino: "I give, bequeath, and wish to present 7,500 denarii, from the 6 percent interest on which I wish to be staged, on June tenth each year, a boxing match up to the cost of 250 denarii, and on the same day, at a cost of 200 denarii, I wish oil to be provided the populace in the public baths and dinners (*lecta*) laid on, provided that my freedmen and likewise the freedmen of my freedmen and freedwomen in turn who have attained the rank of imperial cult priest (*sevir*) should be excused from all burdens of that office. And if any of them should be summoned to such burdens, these 7,500 denarii I then order to be conveyed over to the municipality of Tarraco, under the same conditions of responsibility to Tarraco for staging a boxing match as aforesaid.

2.5   The Accounts of the Temple of Jupiter Capitolinus from Egyptian Arsinoë

A long papyrus contains the accounts of the temple of Jupiter Capitolinus at Arsinoë in Egypt, dated 215 C.E. This selection emphasizes details that show what a sanctuary looked like on a holy day, what a religious parade looked like, and so forth.

Source: A. S. Hunt and C. C. Edgar, *Select Papyri* in LCL.

Received likewise from the same [person], as the price of iron removed . . . from the machine constructed to facilitate the erection of the divine colossal statue of our lord the emperor Severus Antoninus, weighing 52 minae, at 5 drachmas the mina, altogether 260 drachmas. Total of the receipts, 1,605 drachmas. And there remained from the preceding month a balance of 24 drachmas. Total, including the balance, 1,629 drachmas. Of this have been spent: . . . For payment of dues of the 22nd year at the following villages: at Alexandri Nesus . . . drachmas of silver coin, at Ptolemais Drumi likewise . . . drachmas. 5th, at Tricomia, likewise . . . drachmas. 6th, for payment of crown-tax for the 22nd year, at the village of Kerkesephis . . . drachmas, for payment of dues at the village of Pyrrheia . . . drachmas, for payment of bath-tax at the village of Philagris . . . drachmas, for payment of crown-tax for the 22nd year at Pyrrheia other . . . drachmas, . . . for the service of our ancestral god . . . Souchos the twice great, for crowning all the medallions and statues and sacred images in the temple, . . . drachmas, for oil for lighting lamps in the shrine . . . drachmas, charge for one donkey carrying trees and palm branches 4 drachmas. 18th, being a sacred day to celebrate the erection of the statue of our lord the emperor Severus Antoninus, for crowning all the monuments in the temple as aforesaid 16 drachmas. 20th, on the occasion of the visit of the most illustrious prefect Septimius Heraclitus, for crowning all the monuments in the temple as aforesaid 24 drachmas, for oil for lighting lamps in the shrine 6 drachmas, for pinecones and spices and other things 12 drachmas, charge for two donkeys carrying trees and palm branches 8 drachmas, for polishing all the statues in the temple with oil 20 drachmas, wage of copper-smith for polishing the statues 4 drachmas, to porters who carried the image of the god in procession to meet the prefect 32 drachmas, to an orator who made a speech in the presence of the most illustrious prefect Septimius Heraclitus in acknowledgement of the Victory [statue] which he contributed to the possessions of the god and of other gifts 60 drachmas . . . [and so on, through the wages of regular temple personnel].

2.6   Taboos from Thuburbo Maius in Tunisia

From Thuburbo Maius, an inland site in modern Tunisia, comes an inscription on a stone shaped to be the left doorpost of an opening in a stone balustrade. Besides indicating how temple construction is handled, it also provides what amounts to a brief *lex sacra*. Its list of taboos could easily be duplicated among shrines of eastern areas, where Asclepius was at home. The inscription is undated but is probably from the first century.

Source: Alfred Merlin, *CRAIBL* 1916, 263–64.

By command of the Lord Aesculapius, Lucius Numisius Vitalis son of Lucius erects this podium [a balustraded enclosure] at his own expense. Anyone wishing to ascend into the podium should abstain for three days from women, pork, beans, barber, and city baths, and should not enter the balustrade wearing shoes.

2.7   An Inscription regarding the Management of the Artemis Temple in Ephesus

Evergetism and piety, routinely advertised through inscriptions, together sufficed to pay for most of the everyday cost of cults. They would be supplemented by rents from lands owned by temples as corporations, or from fees charged to worshipers, or gifts or grants from cities, or other rights to income. Administration lay in the hands of local authorities: of priests who bought in, or were elected, supported by slaves paid for out of temple funds to do the lowly jobs; or administration lay in the hands of the magistrates of cities in whose territories the temples lay, or of families in dynasties of priests, or of benefactors and landowners. Provincial governors also exercised a potential, or distant, or emergency oversight of temples.

In illustration of much of this system are such items as this first, an inscription somewhat damaged from a particularly famous shrine: the Artemis-temple of Ephesus, known above all through the nineteenth chapter of the Acts of the Apostles. In 45 C.E., it required in the opinion of the Roman governor much better management, and he accordingly specified overdue improvements.

Source: *SEG* 4.516, trans. Naphthali Lewis, in *Greek Historical Documents. The Roman Principate: 25 B.C.–287 A.D.* (Toronto: Hakkert, 1974), pp. 130–32.

Paullus Fabius Persicus, pontifex, priest of Augustus, Arval brother, quaestor of Imperator Tiberius Caesar Augustus, praetor . . . , consul . . . , proconsul of Asia, on the injunction of Imperator Tiberius Claudius Caesar Augustus Germanicus, has proclaimed this decree beneficial to the city of Ephesos and the whole province . . .

Being ever myself of the opinion that governors of provinces should administer the offices entrusted to them with all steadfastness and good faith so as to provide for the lasting and lifelong advantage of both the province as a whole and of each city—and this not in their own year [of office] alone—I the more gladly acknowledge that I am further impelled to this policy by the example of our most excellent and truly most just ruler, who, receiving all the human race into his personal care, has graciously bestowed also this among his grants first in importance and to all most dear, to restore to each his own.

Therefore I have taken a decision, painful but necessary for the most illustrious city of Ephesos . . . Many houses have [recently] been gutted by fire or collapsed into unsightly rubble, and the temple of Artemis herself—which is an ornament of the whole province because of the sublimity of the structure, the antiquity of the worship of the goddess, and the liberality of the revenues allocated by the Emperor to the goddess—is deprived of its private income. These used to suffice for its upkeep and the adornment of the votive offerings, but now they are diverted for the illegal desires of the officers of the municipality, according as they think will be advantageous to themselves. For, as often as cheerful news comes from Rome, they misappropriate this to their private gain and, using the maintenance of the divine temple as their excuse, they sell the priesthoods as if at public auction: they invite to the sale men of every sort, and then they do not select the most suitable, on whose head the crown would appropriately be set; no, they limit the revenues allocated to those being consecrated to [the minimum] they are willing to accept, so that they may put aside as much as possible for themselves. . . . the city to sustain the [temple] expenses, so that the most suitable person will be judged worthy of the [priestly] honor awarded by the people and an excessive burden will by this decree be [removed?]. Since I know that returning the money will be too much for the city or absolutely impossible if it is compelled to pay up now what was received from the buyers [of the priesthoods], I order—in keeping with the decree of Vedius Pollio, which was also confirmed by the deified Augustus—that the city pay to those priests not more than one percent of the price they paid [at the auction], and that the priests pay nothing to the city council or receive anything of the sort from it. Likewise, all free men performing services of public slaves and [thus] adding a superfluous burden to the municipality are to be discharged and public slaves are to be put in their places. Likewise, public slaves who, it is reported, buy infants for a trifling sum and dedicate them to [the service of] Artemis in order to have these slaves of theirs raised at the expense of the [temple] revenues, are themselves to bear the expense of raising their own slaves. Likewise, all victors in the games who, it is reported, are votaries of Artemis for the purpose of free maintenance, are not to be maintained by [the temple of] Artemis but are to receive only what was accorded by the decree of Vedius Pollio. Likewise, no one of the priests of Artemis or of the annual magistrates is to borrow money for the municipality except in amounts that can be repaid from the revenue of that year; if anyone pledges the revenue of the following year as security, the lender is [hereby] given the right of execution against him for the amount of the loan. Likewise, all moneys bequeathed to the city or any part thereof or any body therein are to be borrowed on the terms on which they were bequeathed and not transferred by the magistrates to other uses and expenses. Likewise, not more than 4,500 denarii are to be spent on the quadrennial games, as provided in the decree of Vedius Pollio. Furthermore, the choristers, on whom no small part of the city's revenues is spent, are to be discharged from that service and the ephebes [the class of male adolescent citizens], who are especially suitable for such duty by virtue of age and status and learning aptitude, are to fulfill this function without pay. However, that I not be understood as applying this decision to choristers everywhere, I except those who celebrate the deified Augustus in Pergamon in the precinct dedicated by [the province of] Asia; their first assembly gathered together not for wages but voluntarily and without pay, and therefore the deified Augustus preserved the privileges subsequently voted them and their successors but ordered that their cost be borne not by Pergamon alone but by the whole [province] of Asia, reckoning that such a contribution would be heavy for a single city. Indeed, it will behoove the city of Ephesos, now that it has been freed of this expense and the service has been transferred to the ephebes, to see to it that the ephebes carry out their function with due care and attention, as befits those celebrating the imperial house.

[In the next clause a similar privilege is extended for the cult of Livia. Then begins, apparently, a recital of honors decreed by the provincial assembly, at which point the extant inscription breaks off.]

2.8   Two Other Inscriptions from the Temple of Artemis in Ephesus

From this same famous shrine come other representative inscriptions.

Source: *SIG* 839, Ephesus, original translation.

The autokrator Caesar, son of the divine Trajan Parthicus Maximus, and grandson of the divine Nerva, Trajan Hadrian Augustus and Olympius, holding tribunician power for the thirteenth time, consul thrice, father of his fatherland, [is honored by] the senate and people of Ephesus as their founder and savior for his unsurpassable gifts to Artemis, presenting to the goddess the rights of inheritance and property without heirs and the use of her own laws; providing shipments of grain from Egypt, and building navigable harbors, deflecting the river Cayster, which was harming the harbors by means of . . . .

This text, ca. 160 C.E., shows how an important change in the religious calendar was brought about by a leading citizen, local magistrates ("generals"), the senate, and the provincial governor.

Source: *SIG* 867, Ephesus, original translation.

Gaius Popillius Carus Pedo, proconsul, declares: I have learned from the resolution sent me by the most splendid senate of the Ephesians that the proconsuls before me had considered the days of the festival of Artemis to be holy and so announced by edict. I have thus thought it needful, myself mindful of the holiness of the goddess and of the honor of the most splendid city of the Ephesians, to make clear by edict that these days will be holy and that the truces will be kept on them, with Titus Aelius Marcianus Priscus, son of Aelius Priscus, and president of the games, being head of the festival—a man most esteemed and deserving of all honor and hospitality.

It seems good to the senate and the people of the First and Greatest Metropolis of Asia, the city of the Ephesians, twice temple-warden of the emperors, and their loyal subject: Concerning the question brought forward by [. . .] Laberius Amoenius, loyal subject, secretary of the people, the loyal generals of the city put the following to a vote: Inasmuch as the goddess Artemis, defender of our city, is honored not only in her own land, which she has rendered more glorious than all other cities through her holiness, but [she is honored] also by Greeks and barbarians, so that holy places and precincts are everywhere established for her, and shrines and altars and seats are set up to her because of her manifest epiphanies— and this is the greatest sign of her cult, that we have called a month after her name, Artemision, and among Macedonians and other Greeks and in their cities Artemisios, during which festivals and holidays are held, notably in our city, the nourisher of its own goddess the Ephesian—and the Ephesian people, considering it fitting for the entire month bearing the divine name to be holy and to be dedicated to the goddess, has resolved through this decree to establish the worship of it; wherefore, Resolved, that the month Artemision is holy in all its days and during its days the monthly and the yearly festivals and the celebration of the Artemisia and the [other] holidays shall be held, since the whole month is consecrated to the goddess. In this way, as the goddess will be the more honored, our city will abide for all time more famous and blessed.

His native place [honors] T. Aelius Marcianus Priscus, son of Titus of the tribe of Claudia, the president of the games, head of the festival of the Great Artemisia, first to present the festival in toto, obtaining a truce for the whole month named after the goddess, establisher of the Artemisian contest, who augmented the prizes for the contestants and set up statues of the victors.

L. Faenius Faustus set up [the honorific inscription] for his relation.

3

CULT SCENES

In trying to see more clearly what religion meant to people and how they expressed the thoughts and feelings associated with worship, one can walk up to a shrine of any sort in one's mind's eye, survey its buildings—some of which have been described or at least mentioned in the preceding selections—and look about at the "publications" inscribed in cut and brightly painted letters on its walls. Some are offered here, and, next, texts to help one to visualize and hear the worshipers themselves—in crowds or singly.

3.1 A Description of a Rural Shrine, from Pliny's *Letters*

A little, remote shrine about 30 miles north of Rome, in the mountains, is described by the senator Pliny the Younger in the early 100s C.E.

Source: Pliny, *Letters* 8.5f., trans. Betty Radice, LCL.

The banks are thickly clothed with ash trees and poplars, whose green reflections can be counted in the clear stream as if they were planted there. The water is as cold and as sparkling as snow. Close by is a holy temple of great antiquity in which is a standing image of the [river] god Clitumnus himself clad in a magistrate's bordered robe; the written oracles lying there prove the presence and prophetic powers of his divinity. All round are a number of small shrines, each containing its god and having its own name and cult, and some of them also their own springs, for as well as the parent stream there are smaller ones which have separate sources but afterwards join the river. The bridge which spans it marks the sacred water off from the ordinary stream: above the bridge boats only are allowed, while below bathing is also permitted. The people of Hispellum, to whom the deified Emperor Augustus presented the site, maintain a bathing place at the town expense and also provide an inn; and there are several houses picturesquely situated along the river bank. Everything in fact will delight you, and you can also find something to read: you can study the numerous inscriptions in honour of the spring and the god which many hands have written on every pillar and wall. Most of them you will admire, but some will make you laugh—though I know you are really too charitable to laugh at any of them.

3.2 A Divine Epiphany, from Thessalonike

Accounts of miracles were commonly posted up in sacred precincts like the following, the Sarapis-shrine of Thessalonike in northern Greece, where a third century B.C.E. (?) original text has been re-inscribed in the first century C.E. It is in a central Greek dialect (Locrian).

Source: IG 10.2, no. 255, original translation.

On his mission . . . to enter his house, it seemed in his sleep that Sarapis standing near him ordered him to come to Opus [in central Greece], that he might announce to Eurynomus son of Timesitheus that he should receive him and his sister Isis; and he should present to him the letter now under his pillow. Waking up, he wondered at the dream and was at a loss to know what to do, because he was a political enemy of Eurynomus. But falling asleep again, and seeing the same thing again, and waking, he found the letter under his pillow exactly as had been signified to him. Going home, he delivered the letter to Eurynomus and announced to him what orders had been laid on him by the god. Eurynomus, taking the letter and hearing what Xenainetos said, was at a loss at the moment, just because, as was said before, the two were political rivals. But, opening the letter and seeing written in it what accorded with what Xenainetos had said, he received Sarapis and Isis.

3.3 The Rights of a Phoenician Shrine

Chartered rights of a very famous shrine of a Phoenician sky-god, "Zeus" of Baetocaece, were inscribed on a marble tablet on the spot: four items, the second and oldest no doubt re-inscribed from an original.

Source: IGR 3.1020; translation of the Greek letter of Antiochus is taken from C. Bradford Welles, *Royal Correspondence in the Hellenistic Period*, no. 70 (New Haven, 1934), with suggestions from René Mouterde, *Mélanges Université St. Joseph* (1934): 192; and Henri Seyrig, *Syria*

(1951): 197ff. The letter of Valerian and his co-emperors is in Latin, the rest of the document in Greek. The translation of the Latin is original.

The emperors [titles, etc.] Valerian, Gallienus, and Saloninus [253–60 c.e.] to Aurelius Marea and others: The ancient privileges bestowed by kings, confirmed through custom in aftertimes, the authority in the provinces will take care to preserve in safety for you, free from any adversary's violence.

A letter from King Antiochus [293–61 b.c.e.]:

King Antiochus to Euphemus, greeting. The enclosed memorandum has been issued. See then that its provisions are carried out as far as concerns you.

Report having been brought to me of the power of the god Zeus of Baetocaece, it has been decided to grant him for all time the place whence the power of the god issues, the village of Baetocaece—formerly the property of Demetrius the son of Demetrius and grandson of Mnaseas in Tourgona of the Apamean satrapy—with all its property and possessions according to the existing surveys and with the harvest of present year, so that the revenue from this may be spent by priests chosen by the god in the customary manner for the monthly sacrifices and the other things which increase the dignity of the temple, and also so that there may be held each month on the fifteenth and thirtieth days fairs free from taxation; [it has been decided further] that the temple should be inviolable and the village exempt from billeting, as no objection has been raised; that anyone who should violate any of the above provisions should be held guilty of impiety, and that copies [of this memorandum] should be inscribed on a stone stele and placed in the same temple.

It will be necessary then to write to the usual officials so that these provisions may be carried out.

A decree of the city [of Aradus] dispatched to the divine Augustus:

All merchandise shall be required to be brought up by the market supervisors [agoretai] here and in the rural districts for sale at each fair, so that there is always a supply for pilgrims that come up. Moreover the agoretes of the city shall contribute his cooperation without interfering or offering disturbance through claiming any requisition or taxation or exaction or demand made. Likewise slaves, livestock, and other animals are to be sold in the location without tax or exaction or demand made.

The ministrants of the holy Heavenly Zeus have posted up the divine rescript, venerated by all people, of the Augustuses' piety toward the deity and of their exempting of the place.

3.4 An Isis Festival in Central Greece, Described by Pausanius

An Isis-festival in a rather poor region of central Greece is described by that ancient Michelin, Pausanias, in the 160s C.E. He also reports on another, Asclepius, shrine nearby.

Source: Pausanias, *Description of Greece* 10.32.8f., trans. Peter Levi (Harmondsworth, Eng.: Penguin, 1971).

Nine miles off from Tithorea is a shrine of Asklepios called the First Founder. The Tithoreans honor him and so does everyone else in Phokis. Inside the ring-wall the ritual suppliants and any of the god's slaves have cottages: in the middle is the temple, and a bearded stone statue over twelve feet high, and on the right of this statue a couch; they sacrifice anything at all to him except goats.

Five miles or so from Asklepios is a precinct with a sanctuary consecrated to Isis, the holiest sanctuary ever built by Greece for the Egyptian goddess. The Tithoreans have a sacred tradition that no one should live here, and no one can go into the holy place except those chosen by Isis and summoned by visions in their sleep. The gods of the underworld do the same in the cities on the Maiander, sending visionary dreams when they wish a man to enter the holy places. At this Tithorean sanctuary, they celebrate a festival to Isis twice a year, one in spring, the other in autumn. Two days before each festival, those allowed to enter clean out the holy place in a way not to be spoken about, always bringing any remains they may find from consecrated victims thrown in at the last festival to the same place to be buried; I reckon the spot as about a quarter of a mile from the holy place. That is what they do in the sanctuary on that day; on the next the traders make their booths out of reeds or any other material handy. On the last of the three days they hold a fair, selling slaves and cattle of every kind, and even clothes and gold and silver; then from mid-day they turn their attention to sacrificing. The more prosperous people slaughter cattle and deer, the less well off even slaughter geese and guinea-hens; but the use of sheep, pigs, or goats would be against the sacred law. Those who burn the victims . . . send into the holy place . . . must wind the victims in long bands of silk or linen; this is the Egyptian way of preparing them. Everything sacrificed goes in procession; some of them walk with the victims into the holy place while the others incinerate the booths in front of it and rush away. They say an unsanctified man with no right to go down to the holy place once went inside out of curiosity and daring, as the fire was just beginning to burn. He saw the spirits of the dead thronging everywhere: he went home to Tithorea, told the story of what he had seen, and breathed his last. I have heard something similar from a Phoenician. The Egyptians celebrated a festival for Isis when they say she grieves for Osiris; at that time the Nile begins to rise, and many people say that it is the tears of Isis that swell the river and water the ploughed land. Well, my friend said that at that time the Roman who was governor of Egypt bribed a man and sent him into the holy place of Isis at Koptos. The man he sent in did return from the holy place, but I find that the same thing happened to him: he described what he had seen, and immediately died. Homer's verse seems to be true, that it carries no blessing if the gods are seen plainly by the human race.

3.5   St. Augustine's Strictures on the Worship of Tanit

St. Augustine recalls religious ceremonies of Carthage, in honor of the city's chief female deity, Caelestis (Tanit), ca. 370s? C.E.

Source: Augustine, *City of God* 2.26, trans. Marcus Dods (New York: Modern Library, 1950), p. 70.

Where and when those initiated in the mysteries of Caelestis received any good instructions, we know not. What we do know is, that before her shrine, in which her image is set, and amidst a vast crowd gathering from all quarters, and standing closely packed together, we were intensely interested spectators of the games which were going on, and saw, as we pleased to turn the eye, on this side a grand display of harlots, on the other the virgin goddess: we saw this virgin worshipped with prayer and with obscene rites. There we saw no shamefaced mimes, no actress overburdened with modesty: all that the obscene rites demanded was fully complied with. We were plainly shown what was pleasing to the virgin deity, and the matron who witnessed the spectacle returned home from the temple a wiser woman. Some, indeed, of the more prudent women turned their faces from the immodest movements of the players, and learned the art of wickedness by a furtive regard. For they were restrained, by the modest demeanour due to men, from looking boldly at the immodest gestures; but much more were they restrained from con-demning with chaste heart the sacred rites of her whom they adored. And yet this licentiousness—which, if practised in one's home, could only be done in secret—was practised as a public lesson in the temple; and if any modesty remained in men, it was occupied in marvelling that wickedness which men could unrestrainedly commit should be part of the religious teaching of the gods, and that to omit its exhibition should incur the anger of the gods. What spirit can that be, which by a hidden inspiration stirs men's corruption, and goads them to adultery, and feeds on the full-fledged iniquity, unless it be the same that finds pleasure in such religious ceremonies, sets in the temples images of devils, and loves to see in play the images of vices; that whispers in secret some righteous sayings to deceive the few who are good, and scatters in public invitations to profligacy, to gain possession of the millions who are wicked?

3.6   In Defense of Dancing, from Lucian

Beyond the organization of cult or physical facilities and representations of religious subjects in art, the behavior of worshipers is relatively easy to illustrate from surviving evidence. In most regions of the Mediterranean from which descriptions survive, it included religious dancing—for example, in the Lucianic essay on dancing (later second century C.E.).

Source: Lucian, *On the Dance* 15–17, trans. A. M. Harmon, LCL.

I forbear to say that not a single ancient mystery-cult can be found that is without dancing, since they were established, of course, by Orpheus and Musaeus, the best dancers of that time, who included it in their prescriptions as something exceptionally beautiful to be initiated with rhythm and dancing. To prove that this is so, although it behooves me to observe silence about the rites on account of the uninitiated, nevertheless there is one thing that everybody has heard; namely, that those who let out the mysteries in conversation are commonly said to "dance them out."

At Delos, indeed, even the sacrifices were not without dancing, but were performed with that and with music. Choirs of boys came together, and while they moved and sang to the accompaniment of flute and lyre, those who had been selected from among them as the best performed an interpretative dance. Indeed, the songs that were written for these choirs were called Hyporchemes [interpretative dances], and lyric poetry is full of them.

3.7   Four Descriptions of Religious Spectacles and Processions, from Various Sources

There was, side by side with dancing, the natural musical accompaniment to cult ceremonies, often indicated in surviving sources. This one dates to 238 C.E.

Source: Censorinus, *De die natali* 12.2, ed. Otto Jahn (Berlin, 1845; reprint, Hildesheim: Olms, 1968), original translation.

If it [music] were not welcome to the immortal gods, theater spectacles (ludi scenici) would not have been established to conciliate the gods, the flute-player would not be used in all sacrifices in sacred temples, nor would a triumphal parade be conducted with the flute- or horn-player in honor of Mars, nor would the lyre be assigned to Apollo, nor the flute and such-like to the Muses.

A papyrus from Egypt of the late third century shows municipal magistrates making arrangements for performances at an upcoming festival by hiring professionals.

Source: *P. Oxy.* 7.1025, trans. Arthur S. Hunt.

Aurelius Agathus, gymnasiarch and prytanis in office, Aurelius Hermanobammon, exegete, Aurelius Didymus, chief priest, and Aurelius Coprias, cosmete of the city of Euergetis, to Aurelius Euripas, actor, and Aurelius Sarapas, Homeric reciter, greetings! Come at once, in accordance with your custom of taking part in the holiday, in order to celebrate with us our traditional festival on the birthday of Cronus the most great god. The spectacles begin tomorrow the 10th and will be held for the regular number of days; and you will receive the usual payments and presents.

Signed by me. I, Hermanobammon, exegete, pray for your health.

I, Didymus, chief priest, pray for your health.

I, Coprias, pray for your health.

A religious procession with musical accompaniment is described in *The Martyrdom of St. Theodotus* 14. The location is central Turkey, Ancyra, at the height of the persecutions. The date is 303 C.E.

Source: P. Franchi de' Cavalieri, *I martirii di S. Teodoto e di S. Ariadne* (Rome: Libreria Vaticana, 1901), p. 70, original translation.

It was the custom among them yearly to bathe the images in the nearby lake, and on that day was the chance for them to be cleansed along with the idols. Now each of the idols used to be set on a wagon. He [the governor, Theotecnus, who is elsewhere called a serpent's offspring] ordered the [Christian] virgins, too, to be taken to the lake, them too, to be washed along with the images in the same fashion. They led them, then, through the middle of the city, naked, set upright on carts to shame them and make mock of them; and the images were brought along a little behind the virgins. The populace of the whole city went out with them to see the sight, for the sound of the pipes and cymbals attracted attention, as did the dancing of the women with the hair let loose like maenads, and there was a great pounding of their feet striking the ground, and they had a lot of musical instruments along.

A similar religious procession from city (Ephesus) to shrine is described in a Greek novel.

Source: Xenophon Ephesius, *Ephesian Tales* 1.2.2–3, original translation.

The local Artemis festival was in swing, from the city to the shrine— a mile's distance. All the unmarried local girls must join the procession, dressed up richly, along with the youths (ephebes), who were of the same age as Abrokomes. He was about sixteen, and was joined to the ephebes, and carried the first objects in the procession. There was a great throng of local folk and visitors to see the sight; for it was customary on that holiday to pick out fiancés for the girls, and girls for the youths. The parade went along in a line, then, with the sacred things and torches carried up front, and the baskets and incense; next, horses and hounds and hunting equipment, and military, but mostly for peacetime. Each of the girls was fixed up to please her young admirer. And the leader of the girls' group was Anthia, daughter of Megamedes and Euippe, local people. Now Anthia's beauty was much to be wondered at, and she much exceeded the other girls. People of Ephesus had often worshiped her for Artemis, seeing her in the shrine. Now, too, at the sight of her the crowds raised a shout, expressing various reactions, some astonished, proclaiming her the goddess, others, that she was another woman, made by the goddess; and everyone offered prayers and knelt to her, and considered her parents blessed. [There follows a passage in which the people of Ephesus catch sight of Abrokomes and consider him just as fine a specimen of the male sex as Anthia is of the female.] When the parade was over, they had reached the sanctuary, where the whole crowd would offer sacrifice; and the order of the procession dissolved . . .

4

HYMNS

Of hymns there is an assortment of some dozens surviving, of which Isis gets more than her share. They had their origins in the eastern, Greek-speaking world, and their use spread only slowly and incompletely into the western. They were sung, it appears, only by trained choirs of youngsters, not by the worshipers themselves. Texts of the longer hymns survive on papyrus, especially helpful in conveying to us how ordinary people conceived of the beings they worshiped.

4.1   A Papyrus Hymn in Honor of Isis

P. Oxy. 1380 (early second century) is a copy of a hymn of the first century or earlier (perhaps best, in the reign of Augustus), composed in the style of earlier Egyptian hymns to Isis; but it is not a translation. It contains many elements or features familiar in Greek hymns. The fragments cannot represent much more (possibly much less) than a half of the original whole. Apparently Isis-worship in all of Upper Egypt was described in the lost sections; what survives makes a circuit of sixty-odd Delta towns, in the opening lines, and then moves on to another fifty-five places overseas. Isis received cult over an enormous area, taking on in different cities a different character derived from the goddess's attested acts of grace to her local worshipers.

Source: *P. Oxy.* 11.1380, trans. Bernard P. Grenfell and Arthur S. Hunt.

. . . at Aphroditopolis One- . . . ; in the House of Hephaestus . . . , Chmeunis; who at . . .ophis art called Bubastis, . . . ; at Letopolis Magna one, . . . ; at Aphroditopolis in the Prosopite nome fleet-commanding, many-shaped, Aphrodite; at Delta giver of favours; at Calamisis gentle; at Carene Affectionate; at Niciu immortal giver; at Hierasus . . . athroichis; at Momemphis ruler; at Psochemis bringer to harbor; at Mylon ruler; at Ce . . . culemis . . . ; at Hermoplois of beautiful form, sacred; at Naucratis fatherless, joy, saviour, almighty, most great; at Nithene in the Gynaecopolite nome Aphrodite; at Pephremis Isis, ruler, Hestia, lady of every country; at Es . . . Hera, divine; at . . . ; at Buto skilled in calculation; at Thonis love . . . ; in the Sais Hera, ruler, prefect; at Iseum Isis; at Sebennytus inventiveness, mistress, Hera, holy; at Hermopolis Aphrodite, queen, holy; at Diospolis Parva ruler; at Bubastus of old; at Heliopolis Aphrodite; at Athribis Maia, supporter; at Hiera in the Phthemphuthite nome lotus-bearing; at Teouchis sacred, mistress; among the Bucoli Maia; at Xois of old, oracular; at Catabathmus providence; at Apis understanding; at Leuce Acte Aphrodite, Mouchis, Eseremphis; at Phagrorioplois . . . ; at Choatine victorious; at . . . skilled in writing . . . ; at Cynopolis in the Busirite nome Praxidice; at Busiris fortune, good; at Hermopolis in the Mendesian nome leader; at Pharbaethus of beautiful form; at Isidium in the Sethoite nome saviour of men; at Heracleopolis in the Sethroite nome mistress; at Phernouphis ruler of cities; at Leontopolis serpent, good; at Tanis of gracious form, Hera; at Schedia inventiveness; at Heracleum lady of the sea; at Canopus leader of the muses; at Menouthis truth; at Meniouis seated before Io in whose honour . . . is founded; at M . . .enestium most great vulture-shaped, Aphrodite; at Taposiris Thauestis, Hera, giver; in the Island swiftly-victorious; at Peucestis pilot; at Melais (?) many-formed; at Menouphis war-like; in the Metelite nome Core; at Charax Athena; at Plinthine Hestia; at Pelusium bringer to harbour; in the Casian district Tachnepsis; at the Outlet Isis, preserver; in Arabia great, goddess; in the Island giver of victory in the sacred games; in Lycia Leto; at Myra in Lycia sage, freedom; at Cnidus dispeller of attack, discoverer; at Chalcedon Themis; at Rome warlike; in the Cyclades islands of threefold nature, Artemis; at Patmos young . . . ; at Paphos hallowed, divine, gentle; in Chios marching; at Salamis observer; in Cyprus all-bounteous; in Chalcidice holy; in Pieria youthful; in Asia worshipped at the three ways; at Petra saviour; at Hypsele most great; at Rhinocolura all-seeing; at Dora friendship; at Stratonos Pyrgos Hellas, good; at Ascalon mightiest; at Sinope many-named; at Raphia mistress; at Tripolis supporter; at Gaza abundant; at Delphi best, fairest; at Bambyce Atargatis among the Thracians and in Delos many-names; among the Amazons warlike; among the Indians Maia; among the Thessalians moon; among the Persians Latina; among the Magi Core, Thapseusis; at Susa Nania; in Syrophoenicia goddess; in Samothrace bull-faced; at Pergamum mistress; at Pontus immaculate; in Italy love of the gods; in Samos sacred; at the Hellespont mystic; at Myndus divine; in Bithynia Helen; in Tenedos name of the sun; in Caria Hecate; in the Troad and at Dindyma . . . , Palentra (?), unapproachable, Isis; at Bertyus Maia; at Sidon Astarte; at Ptolemais understanding; at Susa in the district by the Red Sea Sarkounis; thou who also interpretest first of all in the fifteen commandments, ruler of the world; guardian and guide, lady of the mouths of the seas and rivers; skilled in writing and calculation, understanding; who also bringest back the Nile over every country; the beautiful animal of all the gods; the glad face in Lethe; the leader of the muses; the many-eyed; the comely goddess in Olympus; ornament of the female sex and affectionate; providing sweetness in assemblies; the lock of hair (?) in festivals; the prosperity of observers of lucky days; Harpocratis of the gods; all-ruling in the processions of the gods, enmity-hating; true jewel of the wind and diadem of life; by whose command images and animals of all the gods, having . . . of thy name, are worshipped; O lady Isis, greatest of gods, first of names, Io Sothis; thou rulest over the mid-air and the immeasurable; thou devisest the weaving of . . . ; it is also thy will that women in health come to anchor with men; all the elders at E . . . ctus sacrifice; all the maidens who . . . Heracleopolis turn (?) to thee and dedicated the country to thee; thou art seen by those who invoke thee faithfully; from whom . . . in virtue of the 365 combined days; gentle and placable is the favour of thy two ordinances; thou bringest the sun from rising unto setting, and all the gods are glad; at the risings of the starts the people of the country worship thee unceasingly and the other sacred animals in the sanctuary of Osiris, they become joyful when they name thee; the spirits become thy subjects; . . . (174–89) and thou bringest decay on what thou wilt and to the destroyed bringest increase, and thou purifiest all things; every day thou didst appoint for joy; thou . . . having discovered all the . . . of wine providest it first in the festivals of the gods . . . ; thou becamest the discoverer of all things wet and dry and cold [and hot] of which all things are composed; thou bringest back alone thy brother, piloting him safely and burying him fittingly; . . . (193–96) leader of diadems; lady of increase and decay and of . . . (202–17) thou didst establish shrines of Isis in all cities for all time; and didst deliver to all men observances and a perfect year; and to all men . . . in every place; thou didst show . . . in order that all men might know that thou . . . ; thou didst establish thy son Horus Apollo everywhere the youthful lord of the whole world and . . . for all time; thou didst make the power of women equal to that of men; and in the sanctuary thou didst . . . nations . . . (222–31) thou, lady of the land, bringest the flood of rivers . . . , and in Egypt the Nile, in Tripolis the Eleutherus, in India the Ganges; owing to whom the whole and the . . . exists through all rain, every spring, all dew and snow, and all . . . and land and sea; thou art also the mistress of all things for ever; . . . (235–52) thou madest the . . . of Dioscuri; . . . thou hast dominion over winds and thunders and lightnings and snows; thou, the lady of war and rule, easily destroyest tyrants by trusty counsels; thou madest great Osiris immortal, and deliveredst to every country . . . religious observances; likewise thou madest immortal Horus who showed himself a benefactor . . . and good; thou art the lady of light and flames; thou . . . a sanctuary at Memphis; Horus having judged beforehand that thou hadst appointed him successor [of his father] . . . enthroning him, . . . (267–70) thou didst establish him lord of the throne and oracular king over his father's house for all time; in thy honour out of three temples that at Busiris called . . .

4.2   Isis Speaks Her Own Praises:
An Epigraphic Hymn from Cyme

Another hymn to Isis was copied on to stone in the first or second century for the goddess's temple at Cyme, on the west coast of modern Turkey. Phrasing and other echoes of it turn up in a number of other Isis-hymns which survive in modern Libya and the Greek islands and mainland. They all go back to an original in Memphis, Egypt.

Source: *IG*, Supplement 12, ed. F. Hiller von Gaertringen (Berlin, 1939), pp. 98–99, original translation.

Demetrius son of Artemidorus, also known as Thraseas, of Magnesia on the River Maeander, (fulfilled his) vow to Isis. The following was copied from a stone tablet in the city of Memphis, which stood near the Temple of Hephastus:

It is I who am Isis, the mistress of every land, and who was taught by Hermes, and who, with Hermes, invented writing, both hieroglyphics and the cursive script so that not every text might be written in the same style of script.

It is I who gave and ordained laws for men, which no one is able to
     change.

It is I who am the eldest daughter of Kronos.

It is I who am wife and sister of King Osiris.

It is I who am discoverer of crops for men.

It is I who am mother of King Horus.

It is I who rise in the Dog Star.

It is I who am called "goddess" by women.

It is by me that the city of Bubastis was built.

It is I who divided earth from heaven.

It is I who showed the courses of the stars.

It is I who ordered the course of the sun and the moon.

It is I who discovered maritime trade.

It is I who made justice strong.

It is I who joined woman and man together.

It is I who appoint to women to bring their infants to birth in the ninth
     [Greek: "tenth"] month.

It is I who ordained that parents should be loved by children.

It is I who laid punishment upon those who have no natural affection
    toward their parents.
It is I who together with my brother Osiris brought an end to
    cannibalism.
It is I who revealed mysteries to men.
It is I who taught men to honor images of the gods.
It is I who established sacred precincts of the gods.
It is I who dissolved despotic governments.
It is I who ended murders.
It is I who compelled women to be loved by men.
It is I who made the right to be stronger than gold and silver.
It is I who ordained that truth should be thought to be good.
It is I who devised marriage contracts.
It is I who assigned to Greeks and barbarians their languages.
It is I who made a distinction in nature between the beautiful and the
    shameful.
It is I who ordained that nothing should be more feared than an oath. . . .
It is I who am in the rays of the sun.
It is I who attend the movement of the sun.
Whatever I think well of, that comes to pass.
Through me things are right.
It is I who set free those in bondage. . . .
It is I who raised up islands out of the depths into the light of day.
It is I who am mistress of rainstorms.
It is I who conquer Fate;
It is I whom fate obeys.
        HAIL O EGYPT THAT NOURISHED ME!

4.3   Karpokrates Speaks His Own Praises

The rather well-controlled stylistic conventions of Isiac hymns can be
seen by comparing the preceding two texts with the one that follows:

Source: Richard Harder, "Karpokrates von Chalcis und die memphi-
tische Isispropaganda" (*Abh. Preuss. Akad.* 1943, 14 [1944]): 8, original
translation.

    To Karpokrates, to Sarapis, to the ears of Isis, to Osiris who gives
heed, to Hestia who rears from childhood . . . I am Karpokrates, son of
Sarapis and Isis, of Demeter and Kore and Dionysus and Iacchus [compan-
ion?], brother of Sleep and Echo. Every good season am I, providing for
every time, discoverer of the beginning [and end?]. I am the founder. I was

the first to construct shrines and palaces for the gods; the modes of weighing and counting [. . .] I devised. I it was that made Isis's sistrum, and devised the hunting of every sort of beast [. . .] and I who established forever in cities their magistrates. I watched over the children as they were brought up. Hymns and [. . . .] choruses of men and women with the Muses I established. I discovered the mixing of wine and water. Flutes and pipes [. . .] I always attend among those in court, so no injustice may be done. I join in Bacchic revels of men and women, I caused [grain?] to grow [. . .]. I cleansed all the earth, I who live in mountains, seas, and rivers, I who speak from oracular thrones and stars [. . . I who am] horn-shaped, and [Apollonian] Highway-guard, [Dionysian] Bassareus, [Jovian] Heights-dweller, [Dionysian] Indian-slayer, brandisher of the thyrsus, Syrian hunter, dream-visitor, sleep-giver [. . .] I welcome, while dealing justice to unlawful loves. I hate the accursed. To physicians for recovery, every medicine [I give?].

Titanius of Epidaurus. Greetings, O Chalcis, who bore and raised me. Liguris.

4.4   A Hymn to Tyche

A hymn to Chance, Tyche, has a quite different feel and form from the Isiac. This is a third-century papyrus text whose author was not very literate.

Source: John U. Powell, *Collectanea Alexandrina* (Oxford: Oxford University Press, 1925), p. 196.

Wing-footed goddess of many hues and forms,
Dwelling with mortals, all-powerful Tyche,
How may your strength and nature be made known?
The far-shining and holy (. . .) in your sight
You have split down to the ground, while wrapped in dark
     clouds.
Things lowly and humble, on wings
You have often raised to great heights, O Spirit.
Shall we call you dark Clotho,
Or swift-decreeing Necessity,
Or Iris, swift messenger of the gods?—
For you hold the beginning and the end of all things!

4.5   Selections from the *Orphic Hymns*

So-called Orphic hymns survive in a collection of 87. They follow in a long tradition, earlier examples of which have not survived except in fragments. The surviving ones seem all to be by one poet writing in the second or third century in western Asia Minor, who may have been a member of some religious fraternity or cult-group. There are echoes of common philosophic views here: Platonic, Stoic, neo-Pythagorean.

Source: *Orphic Hymns*, trans. Apostolos A. Athanassakis (Missoula, Mont.: Scholars Press, 1977).

4. To Ouranos (with offering of incense): Ouranos, father of all, eternal cosmic element, primeval, beginning of all and end of all, lord of the universe, moving about the earth like a sphere, home of the blessed gods. Your motion is a roaring whirl, and you envelop all as their celestial and terrestial guard. In your breast lies nature's invincible drive; dark blue, indomitable, shimmering, variform, all-seeing father Kronos, blessed and most sublime divinity, hearken and bring a life of holiness to the newly initiated.

48. To Sabazios (with offering of styrax): Hear! O father Sabazios, son of Kronos, famed spirit (daimon), who sewed into his thigh Bacchic Dionysus, the loud-yelling Eraphiotes, that he might, initiated, reach most holy Tmolus side by side with fair-cheeked Hipta. But, Blessed One, ruler of Phrygia, most kingly of all, come kindly to help those who perform the mystic rites.

49. To Hipta (with offering of styrax): I call upon Hipta, who reared Bacchus, favoring maid, who performs the mystic rites and offers cult through the rites of pure Sabos, and through nocturnal dances of loud-yelling Iacchos: hear me as I pray, earthmother and queen!—whether you are dwelling on the pure mount Ida in Phrygia or whether Tmolus is your delight, where the Lydians dance. Come to the rites showing joy on your sacred countenance!

4.6   An Epidaurian Hymn

One of the earliest surviving hymns is a paean to Health, Hygieia, by Ariphron of Sicyon (fourth century B.C.E.), copied on stone (two copies are known) in the third or fourth century C.E. at Epidaurus, site of a famous sanctuary to Asclepius.

Source: Paul Maas, *Epidaurische Hymnen* (Halle, 1933), p. 148; Georg Kaibel, *Epigrammata Graeca* 1027 (1878; reprint, Hildesheim: Olms, 1965), no. 1027; cited by Athenaeus, *Deipnosophistae* 702, original translation.

Hygieia, most reverend of the gods among mankind,
Would that I may dwell with you for the rest of my life!
Be present and well-disposed to me, for if there is any delight in
   money or in offspring
Or in royal rule, equal to that of the gods among men, or in
   desires,
That we hunt with hidden traps of Aphrodite,
Or if any other delight has been revealed to man from the gods,
   or any relief from pains,
It is through you, blessed Hygieia, that they are all flourishing and
   are brilliant in the Graces' speech.
Apart from you no man counts as blessed.

4.7   A Hymn to the Earth

A hymn of uncertain date, here, which comprises a prayer to the Earth
for the gathering of medicinal herbs. The last part is nonmetrical.

Source: Franz Buecheler and Alexander Riese, *Anthologia Latina*
(1893–1926; reprint, Amsterdam: Hakkert, 1964), 1:26–27. The following
original translation adopts the textual emendations made by J. I.
McEnerney, *Rheinisches Museum* 126 (1983): 175ff.

Holy goddess Earth, parent of the things of nature,
who generate and regenerate all the stars,
who alone furnish yourself a protection to the nations,
goddess ruler of the sky and sea and all things,
through you nature grows quiet and takes its sleep,
and again you bring light back and put night to flight;
you cover the shades of the underworld and immense chaos,
you restrain the winds, the rains and the storms,
and when you like send down and stir up the seas
and put the sun to flight and stir up gales,
and likewise when you want you bring forth cheerful day.
You grant the food of life with everlasting trust
and when the soul departs we find refuge in you
and whatever you grant, they all return to you.
Properly you are called the great mother of the gods
because you have overcome in piety the powers of the gods
and you are truly the parent of the nations and the gods
without whom nothing dies nor can be born.
You, goddess, are great and are queen of the gods!

You, goddess, I adore and your power I invoke
and easily may you furnish me this thing I ask you for
and I will give thanks, goddess, with deserved trust.
Hear me, I beg, and favor my undertakings.
This which I ask of you, goddess, furnish me willingly.

Whatever herbs your majesty generates, you grant to all nations for the sake of health. Entrust this medicine of yours to me. Come to me with your virtues. Whatever I make of them, may it have a good outcome, and whatever people take them from me, may you make them well. Now, goddess, I request that your majesty furnish me what I beseechingly ask.

4.8   A Narrative Hymn to Dionysus

A cult-hymn (apparently—the work is in verse, but only preserved in part) exists from the third century, telling the tale of Lycurgus and Dionysus.

Source: *Select Papyri*, ed. and trans. Denys L. Page, LCL.

[. . . whence] the playful Satyrs were born. Neither flowed the spring beside the elm, nor were there ways of watering, nor paths nor fences nor trees, but all had vanished. Only the smooth plain appeared again.

Where a meadow was before, close came Lycurgus, heart-stricken with mighty fear and speechlessness. For irresistibly, beyond mortal defence, all their works were upset and turned about before their eyes. But when Lycurgus knew him for the glorious son of Zeus, pale terror fell upon his spirit; the ox-goad, wherewith he had been at labour smiting, fell from his hand before his feet. He had no will to utter or to ask a word. Now might that poor wretch have escaped his gloomy fate: but he besought not then the divinity to abate his wrath. In his heart he foresaw that doom was nigh to him, when he saw Dionysus come to assail him amid lightning-bolts that flashed manifold with repeated thunderclaps, while Zeus did great honour to his son's destructive deeds.

So Dionysus urged his ministers, and they together sped against Lycurgus and scourged him with rods of foliage. Unflinching he stood, like a rock that juts into the marble sea and groans when a wind arises and blows, and abides the smiting of the seas: even so abode Lycurgus stead-fast, and recked not of their smiting. But even more unceasing wrath went deep into the heart of Thyone's son: he was minded not at all to take his victim with a sudden death, but rather to break him under a lengthy doom, that still alive he might repay a grievous penalty. He sent madness upon him, and spread about phantom shapes of serpents, that he might spend the time fending them away, till baneful Rumour of his madness should arrive at Thebes on wings and summon Ardys and Astacius, his two sons, and Cytis who married him and was subdued to his embrace.

They, when led by Rumour's many tongues they came, found Lycurgus just now released from suffering, worn out by madness. They cast their arms around him as he lay in the dust—fools! They were destined to perish at their father's hand before their mother's eyes! For not long after, madness, at the command of Dionysus, aroused Lycurgus yet again with real frenzy. He thought that he was smiting serpents; but they were his children from whom he stole the spirit forth. And now would Cytis have fallen about them: but in compassion Dionysus snatched her forth and set her beyond the reach of doom, because she had warned her lord constantly in his storms of evil passion. Yet she could not persuade her master, too stubborn; he, when his sudden madness was undone, recognized the god through experience of suffering. Still Dionysus abated not his wrath: as Lycurgus stood unflinching, yet frenzied by distress, the god spread vines about him and fettered all his limbs. His neck and both ankles imprisoned, he suffered the most pitiable doom of all men on earth: and now in a land of Sinners his phantom endures that endless labour— drawing water into a broken pitcher: the stream is poured forth into Hades. Such is the penalty which the loud-thundering son of Cronus ordained for men that fight against gods; that retribution may pursue them both living and again in death. [There follow traces of four obscene lines, evidently referring to a present festival of Dionysus. Then three lines of prose—perhaps a sketch for future verses.]

4.9   Menander Rhetor on the Composition of Prose Hymns

Menander the Rhetor is credited with authorship of two quite technical treatises on public (or performance) speaking. Rhetors were hired to give public addresses as small bands are hired today, at civic festivals (like the 4th of July), at weddings, and so forth—sometimes (as here) in the form of prose hymns. The treatises date to the late 200s and are meant for self-instruction by professionals. They are unusual in containing general statements about the religiosity to be expected in one's audience.

Source: *Menander Rhetor,* trans. D. A. Russell and N. G. Wilson (Oxford: Oxford University Press, 1981), pp. 7–8, 13–14, 63–64, 209–10, 217, 219, 221, 223–24.

Hymns to the Gods. Following our original division, let us first consider hymns to the gods. These hymns are themselves either cletic or apopemptic or scientific or mythical or genealogical or fictitious or precatory or deprecatory, or else combinations . . . [discussed at length, with references to examples by famous poets like Sappho and Bacchylides] . . .

Scientific Hymns. . . . Such hymns are found, for example, when, in delivering a hymn to Apollo, we identify him with the sun, and discuss the nature of the sun, or when we identify Hera with air or Zeus with heat. Such hymns are "scientific." Parmenides and Empedocles make use of this form exactly, but Plato also uses it . . . Plato in the Critias calls the Timaeus a "hymn of the universe," and the more scientific poets, whom we have mentioned, have constructed whole treatises. In these hymns there is no need of prayer at all. Such hymns should be carefully preserved and not published to the multitude or the people, because they look too unconvincing and ridiculous to the masses.

How to Praise Cities. . . . Piety to the gods consists of two elements: being god-loved and god-loving. The former means being loved by the gods and receiving many blessings from them, the latter consists of loving the gods and having a relationship of friendship with them . . . In this section [of a eulogy of a city] we have to show that the greatest number or the best of the gods have honoured the city . . . Love of the gods, as I said, is to be assessed [in the behaviour of a given city] in private terms, by inquiring whether each citizen devotes himself to the service of the gods; in public terms, in many ways: by inquiring whether they have instituted rites of initiation or established many festivals or sacrifices which are either very numerous or most punctiliously performed, or have built very many temples to all the gods or many to each god, or perform duties of the priesthoods very scrupulously. These are points under which love of the gods shown by cities is assessed. Nowadays, it is difficult to find piety in individuals, though many cities lay claim to common piety and zeal for the gods.

An example of a hymn to a major deity. After these introductory thoughts, you should deliver a hymn to the god himself: "Sminthian Apollo, how should we address thee? As the sun that is the dispenser of light and source of the brilliance of heaven? Or as Mind, as the theologians say, penetrating through the aether to this world of ours? As the creator of the universe, or as the Second Power? Through you the moon has her light, the earth is content with its bounds, and the sea does not pass beyond its depths. They say that, when Chaos filled the world and all things were in confusion and moving with that disordered and disharmonious(?) motion, you shone forth from the vaults of heaven, and scattered Chaos, and destroyed the darkness, and set order on all things. But this I leave to the children of the wise to study in their philosophy. I will try, however to relate the birth, as I have heard it from those who tell the myth(?). Nor will this story be inappropriate for you, for it holds concealed in itself a truer knowledge." Then you deliver the second section of your hymn, viz., "birth," and begin thus: "When Zeus . . ." [gets with child the goddess daughter of the Titans], "when she was about to give birth, the goddess luckily reached Delos—or, as some say, Lycia. Now those who say Delos was blessed with the privilege of receiving her allege that . . . Homer however. . ." After this, you should give an encomium of the country: "And it was natural that the god should favour our land, for he saw how it excels in beauty." At this point, you may describe what the country is like, not in detail, but going through those features of the country which may stir the audience, mentioning the most remarkable things it possesses. After dealing with the country, you should add, as a consequence, "He therefore continued to honor and support our people in wars, in prophecies, destroying our enemies . . ."

Similarly, when you are about to embark on the second section, you should state the greatest special accomplishment of the god, namely that he is a prophet. Here you should briefly discuss the general thesis that prophecy is a good thing and has been the medium by which the greatest human successes have been achieved. Apollo in particular honored it . . .

When you have dealt with this quality of the god, you should proceed to the fourth, viz., that he is a healer. . . . You should therefore state that the god discovered this art of medicine for us; and at this point you should add a general thesis, viz., that he discovered medicine out of pity for us, when the race was being destroyed by disease and hardship. . . . This is why all the poets and prose writers commonly call him "the gentle one," "protector from pain," and "saviour." You should note here the birth of Asclepius. "Wishing to increase his art and pass it on to the human race, the god contrived the birth of Asclepius: how can one speak worthily of this?"

. . . Therefore we also, who have always experienced the god's providence and kindness, are not laggard in his worship. He continues to give us abundant harvests and to rescue us from dangers, and we propitiate him with hymns. We therefore institute this great sacred contest, and arrange festivals and sacrifices, returning thanks for the benefits we receive.

You should describe the festival—what it is like, how crowded with visitors, how some display their excellence in literature or physical prowess, and so on, while some are spectators or listeners. You should briefly elaborate the general thesis (like Isocrates in the Panegyricus).

As you complete the subject, you should make use of the invocatory titles of the god. Thus: "O Sminthian and Pythian, from you my speech began, to you it shall return. By what names shall I address you? Some call you Lycian, some Delian, some Ascraean, some Actian. The Spartans call you Amyclaean, the Athenians Patroos, the Milesians Branchiate. You control every city and land and nation. You control the whole inhabited earth, even as you dance on your course through the heaven with the choir of stars about you. The Persians call you Mithras, the Egyptians Horus. . . . Thus, whether these are the titles you take pleasure in or some better than these, grant that this city may ever flourish in prosperity, and that this festival may forever be organized in your honor. And grant grace to these words; for both words and city are your gift."

4.10   A Hymn to Zeus

Between hymns and theology, the latter worked out in formal philosophical treatises, the connection is illustrated by an anonymous essay *On the World* (*De mundo*) of the first century c.e., where the author quotes from an "Orphic" hymn.

Source: Martin P. Nilsson, *HTR* 56 (1963): 102–3, trans. E. S. Forster.

God being one yet has many names, being called after all the various conditions which he himself inaugurates. We call him Zen and Zeus, using the two names in the same sense, as though we should say, "him through whom we live." He is called the son of Kronos and of Time (chronos), for he endures from eternal age to age. He is the God of Lightning and Thunder, God of the Clear Sky and of Ether, God of the Thunderbolt and of Rain, so called after the rain and thunderbolts and other physical phenomena. Moreover, after the fruits he is called the Fruitful God, after cities the City-God; he is God of Birth, God of the House-court, God of Kindred and God of our Fathers, from his participation in such things. He is god of Comradeship and Friendship and Hospitality, God of Armies and of Trophies, God of Purification and Vengeance and of Supplication and of Propitiation, as the poets name him, and in very truth the Saviour and God of Freedom, and to complete the tale of his titles, God of Heaven and of the World Below, deriving his names from all natural phenomena and conditions, inasmuch as he is himself the cause of all things. Wherefore it is well said in the Orphic Hymns:

> Zeus of the flashing bolt was the last to be born and the latest.
> Zeus is the head and the middle, of Zeus were all things created
> Zeus is the stay of the earth and the stay of the star-spangled
>   heaven.
> Zeus is male and female of sex, the bride everlasting,
> Zeus is the breath of all and the rush of the unwearying fire,
> Zeus is the root of the sea, and the sun and moon in the
>   heavens,
> Zeus of the flashing bolt is the king and the ruler of all men,
> Hiding them all away, and again to the glad light of heaven
> Bringing them back at his will, performing terrible marvels.

5

CULT GROUPS

With the exception of the group encountered in the first of these selections, people in the habit of assembling around one god were most likely to belong to the urban lower class, and their focus is best imagined as a shrine in their own neighborhood. They thus replicated in a city setting the focus of religiosity that would likely be found, without artificial organization, in villages and rural settings. As a group, they might improve both their finances and their dignity by soliciting the patronage of some city leader. Membership involved social activities as well as—indeed, of much more interest than—cult activities, and certainly had no overtones of sect, in the sense of controlled belief and religious behavior.

5.1   A Letter from Sulla to the Dionysiac Artists of Asia

Lucius Cornelius Sulla, dictator over Rome and without question the most powerful man on earth at the moment, responded as such to a continual great press of requests and embassies. Among them, in 81 B.C.E., was one from the Dionysiac Artists of the province of Asia, asking exemption from reparations demanded of the province in the wake of the civil disturbances of the earlier 80s. The Artists dedicated to Dionysus were professional performers, musical and other, in a sort of international guild with chapters in various regions and cities (Rome, Ephesus, and elsewhere), who hired themselves out to festival-organizers at the Olympic and other Games. Here they commemorate on stone the grant of what they gained, since it was really important to them.

Source: Rivista di Filologia 66 (1938): 253–54, trans. Naphtali Lewis and Meyer Reinhold, in *Roman Civilization* (New York: Harper and Row, 1951), 1:342–43.

May Good Fortune Attend! Lucius Cornelius Sulla Felix son of Lucius, dictator, to the chief magistrates, council, and people of Cos, greeting. I have granted the citharist Alexander of Laodicea, a gentleman of character and our friend, envoy of the Joint Society of "The Theatrical Artists of Ionia and the Hellespont" and "The Theatrical Artists of Dionysus our Leader," permission to erect, in the most conspicuous place in your community, a stele on which will be inscribed the privileges granted by me to the artists; and the senate having, in response to his embassy to Rome, passed a decree of approval, I accordingly desire you to take the necessary steps to provide a most conspicuous place, in which the stele concerning the artists may be set up. I append below a copy of my letter [to the artists] and of the decree of the senate [. . .] and also the good will you bear us, I therefore desire you to know that, on the advice of my council, I have made known my decision that you shall retain whatever privileges, offices, and exemptions from compulsory public services our senate, consuls, and proconsuls have given or granted you as kindnesses in honor of Dionysus, the Muses, and your profession; and that, just as in the past, you shall be exempt from all public and military service, you shall not pay any tax or contribution, you shall not be troubled by anyone for provisions or billets, and you shall not be compelled to receive any lodger in your homes against your will. . . . [The rest is lost.]

5.2 An Honorific Decree of the Dionysiac Artists, from Nysa

The Dionysiac Artists were especially given to and subsidized by the cult of the deified emperors, as can be seen, for example, in an honorific decree here in Nysa (southern Turkey). The turgidity of the syntax and fulsomeness of the vocabulary make translation difficult, but the main idea is that the Ephesian chapter does not want to be left behind the central organization in Rome in fawning on a benefactor who, after all, was from a place near their own headquarters in Ephesus.

Source: M. Clerc, *Bulletin de correspondance hellénique* 9 (1885): 124–25, original translation.

On the motion of Publius Aelius Pompeianus [. . .]aionus of Side, of Tarsus, and of Rhodes, ever-triumphant poet, composer, and song-writer for the deified Hadrian, theologian for the temples in Pergamon, producer by appointment to the August imperial Pythian Games; and by vote of Publius Aelius [. . .] of Cyzicus, guitar-singer extraordinary, triumphing at the Capitolian and Olympic Games:

Inasmuch as Aelius Alcibiades is a man of outstanding cultivation and spirit, endowed with many noble virtues for a long time past, not only for a dozen years but, recently, benefiting all the musicians and aiding the Society to its honor and glory, and taking personal pride in his relations for our own and the general good in many matters; and inasmuch as he has, through his wonderful books, richly equipped the sacred shrine in Rome belonging to the Universal Artists, and has afforded to us a splendid present of stabling facilities, assigning us a source of continual ongoing income for our benefit in the future, when we distribute the returns on the annual birthday of the deified Hadrian and in return for all these things, the Artists in Rome have voted him various suitable other honors and have nominated him to a perpetual high priesthood, and have judged him worthy of being preferred in the ranks of the other high priests, being enrolled first in the tablets, for his having adorned the imperishable memory of Hadrian and furnished the Association more honorably through his gifts, so that it outfits magnificent parades and carries out lavish monthly holidays, by reason of all this, and with good fortune, be it decreed by the artists crowned in holy victory, the artists who follow Dionysus and the Emperor Caesar Titus Aelius Hadrianus Antoninus Pius, and by their co-workers for the quinquennial contest of the Great Ephesia, in the greatest city of Ephesus, first metropolis of Asia and temple-warden of the Augusti, for themselves [i.e., the Ephesian group] in addition to the honors decreed to the man, to take care to vote a just reward and to set up gilded statues and images in the holy temples of the Emperors in Asia and in Augustus-loving Nysa, the homeland of Alcibiades, and to inscribe a stele in the sanctuary of Apollo with the decree, as well as in his other public works and throughout all the cities, so that there may be a useful record of both things, Alcibiades's generosity and the gratitude of its recipients [etc., on further honors voted to Alcibiades].

5.3   The Bylaws of an Italian Organization Worshiping Diana and Antinous

Bylaws for a religious association, dedicated to the worship of Diana and Antinous, were inscribed on the walls of the meeting-place at Lanuvium, a town not far from Rome, to govern the doings of the membership. The chief purpose of the association was to insure a respectful burial for members, all very poor persons. Diana is the huntress-deity, whose temple had been partially reassigned to the worship of the Hero (i.e., divinized mortal) Antinous, whose cult the emperor Hadrian initiated. The temple no doubt was chosen as a handy place for association meetings, and the cult followed from that.

Source: *CIL* 14.2112 = *ILS* 7212, trans. with emendations by William C. McDermott and Wallace E. Caldwell, in *Readings in the History of the Ancient World* (New York: Rinehart and Co., 1958), pp. 461–64, no. 86d.

June 9 in the consulship Lucius Ceionius Commodus and Sextus Vettulenus Civica Pompeianus [136 c.e.]. Lucius Caesennius Rufus, patron of the municipality, ordered that a meeting be called by Lucius Pompeius, . . . director of the worshipers of Diana and Antinous in the municipality of Lanuvium in the temple of Antinous, and there promised that he . . . would give them out of his generosity interest on 15,000 HS [i.e., *sestertii*— three or four of these made a normal day's pay for a laborer], that is, 400 HS to be paid on August 13 on the birthday of Diana, (and) 400 HS on November 27 on the birthday of Antinous. Also he gave instruction that the constitution adopted by them should be inscribed in the interior part of the tetrastyle temple of Antinous in the words written below: On January 1 in the consulship of Marcus Antonius Hiberus and Publius Mummius Sisenna [133 c.e.] the burial association of Diana . . . and Antinous was founded. Lucius Caesennius Rufus, son of Lucius of the Quirina tribe, was dictator for the third time and also patron. Section from the decree of the senate of the Roman people: Let them join, meet, and have an association. Let those who wish to contribute monthly dues for the funeral expenses join this association. Let them not under the pretext of this association meet except once a month to contribute money with which at their decease they may be buried. May this be fortunate, happy, and beneficial for the Emperor Caesar Trajan Hadrian Augustus and the household of the Augustus, for us, for our relatives, and our association, and may we assemble faithfully and diligently that we may honorably follow the funeral processions of our deceased members! Therefore all of us ought to agree in properly contributing, so that we may be established for a long time. Anyone who wishes to join this association as a new member should first read the constitution and join in such a spirit that he does not later complain and leave a quarrel for his heir.

The constitution of the association. It was unanimously decided that whoever wishes to enter this association shall pay an initiation fee of 100 HS and an amphora of good wine, and monthly dues of one-third HS. Further it was decided that whenever anyone has not paid for six consecutive months, and the mortal lot shall befall him, arrangements for his funeral will not be made, even if he has made a will [with provision for overdue payments]. Further, it was decided that whenever anyone of our membership shall die [with dues] fully paid, 300 HS shall be appropriated from the treasury for his funeral. From this sum 50 HS shall be used as procession money and be divided at the funeral pyre. Moreover, the funeral procession shall go on foot. Further, it was decided that whenever anyone dies beyond the twentieth milestone from this municipality, and his death has been announced, three men should be chosen from our membership and should go to that place to take care of his funeral, and they should render an account to the membership without deceit or fraud. If anything fraudulent be found in their accounts, let their fine be fourfold. The burial expenses of the deceased will be paid to these men, and each will receive in addition 20 HS for travel expenses there and back. But if anyone dies beyond the twentieth milestone and the death should not be announced, then the man who buried him should bear witness to it with accounts sealed by the seals of seven Roman citizens. When the accounts have been approved, funeral expenses should be paid to him in accordance with the constitution of the association, after stipends and procession money have been deducted. When an adequate amount has been paid, let no one seek more. Let all trickery and fraud be far from our association, and let there be no petition [for donations] from this association to the patron, patroness, master, mistress, or creditor unless some [member] be named an heir in a will. If any member dies without a will, he will be buried in accordance with the decision of the director and the membership.

Furthermore, it was decided that whoever from this association dies in slavery and his body is wickedly withheld by his master or his mistress, and he has not made a will, there shall be a funeral for his likeness. Further, it was decided that whenever anyone for any cause commits suicide, arrangements for his funeral will not be made. Further, it was decided that when any slave in this association is freed, he should donate an amphora of good wine. Further, it was decided that whoever becomes chairman for giving a dinner when it is his own year in accordance with the order of the membership list, and he does not perform his duty, he shall pay into the treasury 30 HS and the next man in sequence shall give the dinner and act in his place. The order of the dinners. March 8, on the birthday of Caesennius . . . the father. November 27, on the birthday of Antinous. August 13, on the birthday of Diana and the association. August 20, on the birthday of Caesennius Silvanus, the brother . . . 5 [or 7], on the birthday of Cornelia Procula, the mother. January 14, on the birthday of Caesennius Rufus, patron of the municipality. Chairmen in charge of dinners are selected in accordance with the order of the membership list. Whatever the order, four men at a time shall furnish: an amphora of good wine each, loaves of bread at two asses each in accordance with the number in the association, four sardines [per member], the furnishings for the dining room, and hot water with service. Further, it was decided that whoever is elected director of this association shall be immune from dues during the time in which he is director, and double portions shall be given to him in all distributions. Further, it was decided that a portion and a half in each distribution be given to the secretary and the sergeant-at-arms who are also relieved of dues. Further, it was decided that whoever fulfills his directorship honestly should be given as a mark of honor a portion and a half of everything, that the rest too may hope for the same thing by acting justly. Further, it was decided that, if anyone wishes to lodge a complaint or make a motion, he should do that at a business meeting, so that we may feast on holidays undisturbed and cheerful. Further, it was decided that whoever causes a disturbance by moving from one place to another shall be fined 4 HS. If anyone speaks insultingly of another or is riotous, his fine shall be 12 HS. If anyone speaks insultingly or in a quarrelsome manner to the director at a dinner, his fine shall be 20 HS.

Further, it was decided that the director on the solemn days of his own term shall make offering with incense and wine and perform his other duties clad in white, and, on the birthdays of Diana and Antinous, place in the public bath oil for the association before they dine.

5.4 The Rules of the Athenian Association of Iobacchi

Cult associations sooner or later in their history were likely to develop formal rules for internal conduct—like the following example from the 170s C.E., governing the Iobacchi, worshipers of Dionysus, in Attica. From the connection with a great local celebrity and millionaire, Herodes, and the size of membership fees, it is clear that this group was more middle- than lower-class.

Source: *IG* 2.1368, trans. Marcus N. Tod, *Classical Quarterly* (1932): 86ff.

To good luck. In the archonship of Arrius Epaphroditus, on the eighth day of the month Elaphebolion, a meeting was convened for the first time by the priest who had been nominated by Aurelius Nicomachus, who had served as vice-priest for seventeen years and as priest for twenty-three years and had in his lifetime resigned his position, for the honour and glory of the Bacchic Society, in favour of the most excellent Claudius Herodes. [Nichomacus, then, having served the society as Vice-president and then President, for forty years, appoints as his successor in the presidency Herodes, whom we may probably identify with Herodes Atticus, the most distinguished Athenian citizen of that day. His first official act is to nominate the outgoing President as Vice-President. The inscription continues thus]: Nicomachus, nominated by Herodes as vice-priest, read aloud the statutes drawn up by the ex-priests Chrysippus and Dionysius, and after the priest and the arch-bacchus and the patron had expressed their approval there were shouts of "These are what we always observe," "Hurrah for the priest!" "Revive the statutes: you ought to," "Long life to the Bacchic Society, and good order!" "Engrave the statutes," "Put the question." The priest then said: "Since my colleagues and I and all of you agree we shall put the question as you demand." Then the chairman, Rufus son of Aphrodisius, put the question: "Whoever wishes the statutes which have been read to be ratified and engraved on a column will raise his hand." All hands were raised. There were shouts of, "Long life to the most excellent priest Herodes!" "Now you are in fortune: now we are the first of all Bacchic Societies," "Hurrah for the vice-priest!" "Let the column be made!" The vice-priest said: "The column shall rest upon the pillar, and the statutes shall be engraved; the officers will take care to prevent any infringement of them." [Then follows the text of the statutes thus ratified, in these terms]: No one may be an Iobacchus unless he first lodge with the priest the usual notice of candidature and be approved by a vote of the Iobacchi as being clearly a worthy and suitable member of the Bacchic Society. The entrance-fee shall be fifty denarii [200 sesterces, let us say, $1,000] and a libation for one who is not the son of a member, while the sons of members shall lodge a similar notice and pay, in addition to twenty-five denarii, half the usual subscription until the attainment of puberty. The Iobacchi shall meet on the ninth of each month and on the anniversary of its foundation and on the festivals of Bacchus and on any extraordinary feast of the god, and each member shall take part in word or act or honorable deed, paying the fixed monthly contribution for the wine. If he fail to pay, he shall be excluded from the gathering and this exclusion shall be enforced by those whose names are recorded in the decree, save in case of absence from home or mourning or illness or if he who is to be admitted to the gathering was under strong compulsion, of which the priests are to judge. And if the brother of an Iobacchus enter the Society after approval by vote, he shall pay fifty denarii; but if any acolyte living outside pay the sums due to the gods and to the Bacchic Society, he shall be an Iobacchus together with his father, sharing with his father in a single libation. When anyone has lodged his application and has been approved by vote, the priest shall hand him a letter stating that he is an Iobacchus, but not until he has first paid to the priest his entrance fee, and in the letter the priest shall cause to be entered the sums paid under one head or another. No one may either sing or create a disturbance or applaud at the gathering, but each shall say and act his allotted part with all good order and quietness under the priest or the arch-bacchus. No Iobacchus who has not paid his contributions for the monthly and anniversary meetings shall enter the gathering until the priests have decided either that he must pay or that he may be admitted. If anyone start a fight or be found acting disorderly or occupying the seat of any other member or using insulting or abusive language to anyone, the person so abused or insulted shall produce two of the Iobacchi to state upon oath that they heard him insulted or abused, and he who is guilty of the insult or abuse shall pay to the Society twenty-five light drachmas, or he who is responsible for the fight shall pay the same sum of twenty-five drachmas, on pain of exclusion from the meetings of the Iobacchi until they make payment. And if anyone comes to blows, he who has been struck shall lodge a written statement with the priest or the vice-priest, and he shall without fail convene a general meeting, and the Iobacchi shall decide the question by vote under the presidency of the priest, and the penalty shall be exclusion for a period to be determined and a fine not exceeding twenty-five silver denarii. And the same punishment shall be imposed on one who, having been struck, fails to seek redress with the priest or the arch-bacchus but has brought a charge before the public courts. And the same punishment shall be imposed upon the orderly officer (eukosmos) if he failed to eject those who were fighting. And if any one of the Iobacchi, knowing that a general meeting ought to be convened for this purpose, fail to attend, he shall pay to the Society fifty light drachmas, and if he fail to pay on demand, the treasurer shall have power to prevent him from entering the Bacchic Society until he pay. And if any of those who enter fail to pay the entrance-fee to the priest or to the vice-priest, he shall be excluded from the banquet until he does pay, and the money shall be exacted in whatsoever way the priest may order. And no one shall deliver a speech without the leave of the priest or of the vice-priest on pain of being liable to a fine of thirty light drachmas to the society. The priest shall perform the customary services at the meeting and the anniversary in proper style, and shall set before the meeting the drink-offering for the return of Bacchus (ta katagogia) and pronounce the sermon, which Nicomachus the ex-priest inaugurated as an act of public spirit. And the arch-bacchus shall offer the sacrifice to the god and shall set forth the drink-offering on each tenth day of the month Elaphebolion. And when portions are distributed, let them be taken by the priest, vice-priest, arch-bacchus, treasurer, bucolicus, Dionysus, Core, Palaemon, Aphrodite and Proteurythmus; and let these names be apportioned by lot among all the members. And if any of the Iobacchi receive any legacy or honour or appointment, he shall set before the Iobacchi a drink-offering corresponding to the appointment—marriage, birth, Choes, coming of age (ephebeia), citizen-status, the office of wandbearer, councillor, president of the games, Panhellen, elder, thesmothetes, or any magistracy whatsoever, the appointment as synthytes or as justice of the peace, the title of hieroneikes, or any other promotion attained by any Iobacchus. The orderly officer shall be chosen by lot or appointed by the priest, and he shall bear the thyrsus of the god to him who is disorderly or creates a disturbance. And anyone beside whom the thyrsus is laid shall, with the approval of the priest or of the arch-bacchus, leave the banqueting-hall: but if he disobey, the "horses" who shall be appointed by the priests shall take him up and put him outside the front door and he shall be liable to the punishment inflicted upon those who fight. The Iobacchi shall elect a treasurer by ballot for a term of two years, and he shall take over all the property of the Bacchic Society in accordance with an inventory, and shall likewise hand it over to his successor as treasurer. And he shall provide out of his own pocket the oil for the lights on each ninth day of the month and on the anniversary and at the assembly and on all the customary days of the god and those days when legacies or honours or appointments are celebrated. And he shall, if he wish, appoint a secretary at his own risk, and he shall be allowed the treasurer's drink-offering and shall be free from the payment of subscriptions for the two years. And if any Iobacchus die, a wreath shall be provided in his honor not exceeding five denarii in value, and a single jar of wine shall be set before those who have attended the funeral; but anyone who has not attended may not partake of the wine.

5.5   Two Documents of Mithraism

An important cult in rivalry with Christianity was that of Mithras. From the earlier cult of this god in Persia arose the modern belief that there was an unbroken connection between the Persian cult and that of Roman imperial times, through its introduction into the western Mediterranean by the Cilician pirates whom Pompey captured and resettled in 67 B.C.E. But in fact Mithraism is not known to have appeared in the empire until the end of the first century C.E. The cult then spread rapidly. It involved worship by small groups of almost entirely male votaries in artificial caves, as well as various stages of initiation, of which the highest was that of father (*pater*). There is also a lot of astrological lore, as yet imperfectly understood, involved in Mithras-cult. The cult does not lend itself to extensive treatment in a book such as this, since most of the documentation on it is iconographical, primarily the bull-killing (*tauroctony*) reliefs, which adorned each cult-center, in which Mithras is shown stabbing a bull from whose tail grain sprouts, while on either side of him are the two torch-bearing youths, Cautes with upward-pointing torch, and Cautopates, whose torch points down. One of the few authors to take extensive notice of Mithraic religion is the neo-platonist Porphyry (late third century c.e.) in his work on the Cave of the Nymphs in the Odyssey.

Source: Porphyry, *De antro Nympharum* 6, 24, in *Arethusa Monographs,* vol. 1 (Buffalo, N.Y.: State University of New York Press, 1969), anonymous translation.

The Persians call the place a cave where they introduce an initiate to the mysteries, revealing to him the path by which souls descend and go back again. For Eubulus tells us that Zoroaster was the first to dedicate a natural cave in honor of Mithras, the creator and father of all; it was located in the mountains near Persia, and had flowers and springs. This cave bore for him the image of the Cosmos which Mithras had created, and the things which the cave contained, by their proportionate arrangement, provided him with symbols of the elements and climates of the Cosmos. After Zoroaster, others adopted the custom of performing their rites of initiation in caves and grottoes which were either natural or artificial. . . . The equinoctial region they assigned to Mithras as an appropriate seat. And for this reason he bears the sword of Aries, the sign of Mars; he also rides on a bull, Taurus being assigned to Venus. As creator and lord of genesis, Mithras is placed in the region of the celestial equator, with the north to his right and the south to his left; to the south, because of its heat, they assigned Cautes, and to the north <Cautopates> because of the coldness of the north wind.

A Latin inscription tells of the dedication of a Mithraic cave at Rome, where a number of little, late-imperial cult-centers have been excavated.

Source: *CIMRM* no. 423, original translation.

This place is happy, holy, blessed, well-intentioned, which Mithras pointed out, and he gave the idea to Proficientius father of the rites that he should make him and dedicate to him a cave; and presiding over rapid work he acquitted himself of a pleasant service which he undertook under good auspices but with anxious mind, so that the initiates [*syndexi*, joiners of right hands] might happily celebrate their vows for all time. Proficientius, most worthy pater of Mithras, composed these little verses. [Cf. also the prayer found in a Mithraeum, in chapter 7. This was rare, in that it was dedicated by a woman.]

6

IMPERIAL CULT

Encountered by Roman high commanders in the Greek world as early as the 190s B.C.E., homage to them as to demigods was by then an accepted Greek institution. It recognized the superhuman in the achievements of great leaders and conquerors. Eventually such veneration came to a focus right in amongst the Romans of Rome, on the person of Julius Caesar, in the weeks and years following his death. It was accorded also to his adopted son the first emperor Augustus—with familiar rituals in eastern provinces, in unfamiliar and awkward fashion in the west. Gradually it won acceptance throughout the empire in all parts and classes, finding especial honor among the freedman class in Italy, but also among more distinguished competitors for priesthoods in the provinces.

6.1 Imperial Cult in Gytheon

Imperial cult, in Gytheon in the territory of Sparta, was initiated right after the death of the first emperor Augustus (14 C.E.), under his successor Tiberius. Among inscriptions from Gytheon connected with the cult are Tiberius's grant of authority, and the regulations. In this city as elsewhere, the cult is in large part modeled on other traditional religious ceremonies and in facilities borrowed from other deities.

Source: Ernst Kornemann, *Neue Dokumente zum lakonischen Kaiserkult* (Breslau: M. & H. Marcus, 1929), pp. 7–10, original translation.

Letter of Tiberius: Tiberius Caesar Augustus, son of the god Augustus, pontifex maximus, holding tribunician power for the sixteenth time, to the magistrates and city of Gytheon, greetings. The envoy Decimus Tyrannius Nicanor whom you sent to me and my mother delivered your letter to me, in which were enclosed regulations you established for due worship of my father and the honoring of myself. In reply, I express my approval of your actions, for I suppose it is appropriate both to all men in common

and to your city in particular to keep exceptional those honors suitable to
the gods for the magnitude of the benefactions of my father toward all the
world. I myself, however, am satisfied with the more modest and mortal.
My mother [Julia Augusta] will respond to you when she learns from you
what decision you have made about honors for her. [And the *lex sacra* is
preserved in part (minus a bit at the beginning and again at the end), as
posted in 33/34 C.E.]: He [the priest?] should place an image of the god
Augustus Caesar the father on the first [chair?], one of Julia Augusta on the
second from the right, and one of Tiberius Caesar Augustus on the third,
the city providing him with them. Let a table [for sacrifices] be set by him
in the middle of the theater and an incense burner be placed there, and let
the representatives and all magistrates offer sacrifice—but not until the
musical performances enter—on behalf of our rulers' salvation. Let him
conduct the festival on the first day in honor of the god Augustus the
Savior and Liberator, son of the god Caesar; the second, of the emperor
Tiberius Caesar Augustus, father of the fatherland; the third, of Julia
Augusta, Good Fortune of our province and city; the fourth, of [her
grandson] Germanicus Caesar, who shares a temple with Victory; the fifth,
of [her grandson] Drusus Caesar, who shares a temple with Aphrodite; the
sixth, of Titus Quinctius Flamininus [Roman conqueror of Macedonia in
197 B.C.E.]; and let him see to the good order of competitors. After the
competition, in the first Assembly, let him supply the city with the accounts
for all the costs of the musical performances and administration of the
sacred monies. If he is found to have diverted funds or proved to have
falsified accounts, he may no longer hold any office and his property shall
be confiscated; and, if his possessions are ever confiscated, that money
shall be set aside as sacred and used by the annual magistrates to provide
amenities. Any citizen of Gytheon who wishes may prosecute for such
sacred monies, without personal liability. After the celebration of the days
for the gods and rulers, the market supervisor shall introduce the musical
portions of the theatrical competition, for two days, one in memory of
Gaius Julius Eurycles, [ruler and] benefactor of the nation and of our city in
many matters; the other day, in honor of Gaius Julius Laco [son and
successor to Eurykles, ca. 14 C.E.], patron of the watchfulness and safety of
our nation and city. Let him put on the competitions beginning with the
day of the goddess, on those days in which he may be able to do so; but
when he leaves office, let him turn over to his successor supervisor, by
written public record, all the sacrificial victims for the competitions, and
the city shall get a receipt from the recipient. When the supervisor is
putting on the theatrical competitions, he should direct the parade to
proceed from the temple of Asclepius and Hygieia [Health] with the youths
(*ephebes*) and all the young men and other citizens participating in the

parade wearing wreaths of bay and clad in white. The priestesses, maidens, and wives shall move in procession with them in their sacred garments. When the procession reaches the imperial cult temple [*Kaisareion*], let the magistrates make sacrifice of a bull for the well-being of the rulers and gods, and the eternal continuation of their rule; and, when they have made sacrifice, let them require the Table Companies [*Pheiditia*] and the officials to offer incense in the public square. If they do not carry out the procession, or sacrifice, or if, having done so, they do not require the Table Companies and officials to offer incense in the public square, they shall be fined 2,000 drachmae [$40,000–50,000], payable to the gods. Any citizen of Gytheon who wishes may bring accusation against them. In the presidency of Chairon and his priesthood of the god Augustus [14–19 C.E.], the magistrates under Terentius Viada shall present three painted portraits of the god Augustus, Julia Augusta, and Tiberius Caesar Augustus, and the stage for the chorus in the theater and four actors' entrances and stools for the orchestra. They shall set up a stone column, engraving on it the cult regulations [*hieros nomos* = *lex sacra*], and deposit a copy of the cult regulations also in the municipal archives, so that the regulations, in a public place and in the open and visible to all, may make continually manifest to all men the gratitude of the Gythean people toward the rulers. But if they should fail to inscribe these regulations or to erect the column in front of the temple or to write up [a copy . . .] . . .

6.2   Imperial Cult in Brittany

A temple for emperor worship at Rennes (Brittany) has yielded a number of inscriptions (though its groundplan has not been recovered), of which some are indicated here. They serve to show how widespread emperor worship was, and how adaptable to various religious traditions (texts are collected in A. M. Rouanet-Liesenfelt, *La civilisation des Riedones* (Brest: 1980), pp. 20, 24).

Source: *CIL* 13.3148, original translation; cf. 3149–50, almost identical, but of other districts.

In honor of the imperial house of Mars Mullo of the Matans district, [NN] and [NN 2] his son, priests of Rome and Augustus, set up this statue and its decoration at their own expense.

This further text belonged to the same sanctuary. Note that the decree for the third honor shows someone whose Roman citizenship was won from a Flavian emperor, i.e., 69–96 C.E., and the temple predates this by some number of years. It was probably of the native round type, touching a long portico, and dedicated to one of the many Celtic deities that could be best approximated to Roman Mars.

Source: *AE* 1969/70, no. 405; original translation.

In honor of the imperial house and of the Matans district, L. Campanius Priscus and Virilis his son, priests of Rome and Augustus, set up this statue and its decoration to Mars Mullo at their own expense, the place being given by decree of the senate (or "by the decision of the decurions"). To T. Flavius Postuminus, priest of Rome and Augustus, the first man to be honored by the state of the Riedones with the lifetime priesthood of Mars Mullo; twice councilman; who held all public offices among his fellow-citizens—the state of the Riedones sets up statues with their decoration, at public expense, by the following decree:

In the consulship of L. Tutilius Lupercus Pontianus and G. Calpurnius Atilianus [135 c.e.], they decreed in unanimous and complete agreement that, for T. Flavius Postuminus, most honored citizen, on account of his good deeds and generosity toward his city and toward individuals, and his outstanding character—for which they had often expressed their gratitude—statues should be awarded and set up in the great hall of the temple of Mars Mullo, with this inscription, along with the bases for statues which he said he would erect to the deities in the districts.

6.3 The Apotheosis of Trajan

From Egypt, a proclamation survives in rough draft by a local administrator in the Thebais addressed to the villagers on the occasion of Trajan's death and the accession of Hadrian, 117 c.e. It was the government's responsibility to oversee a smooth transition to a new reign.

Source: Ernst Kornemann, *Klio* 7 (1907): 278–88; Bernard W. Henderson, *The Life and Principate of the Emperor Hadrian* (London: Methuen, 1923), p. 38.

In white-horsed chariot have I now mounted [the word used is the one usually reserved for the sun rising] with Trajan to the heavens, whence come I now again to you, O my people, I, not unknown to you, the god Phoebus Apollo, and proclaim unto you the new lord Hadrian. To him be all things happily subject, alike by reason of his virtue and for the blessed fortune of his divine father. Wherefore sacrificing let us light the hearths, refreshing our souls with laughter, intoxicating drinks from the fountain, and ointments of the gymnasium, the whole whereof is furnished to you by the governor's piety toward his master and by his own love for you besides.

6.4   Tertullian's Criticism of Imperial Cult

Religious celebrations of the reigning emperor's birth- or accession-day in the cities of the empire are described, with elaborate disgust, by the Apologist Tertullian in ca. 200 C.E.

Source: Tertullian, *Apology* 35.2–3, trans. T. R. Glover, LCL.

Splendid service, I assure you! to bring braziers and couches out into the open air, street by street to dine together, to make the city look like nothing but a tavern, to make mud with [all the spilt] wine, to rush about in droves for outrage, impudence and the incitements to lust. Is it thus that a people's joy is expressed, in public shame? Does such conduct befit the festal days of princes, when it ill befits other days? Men who maintain order out of regard for Caesar, are they to abandon it for Caesar's sake? Shall their good feeling for him be their licence to follow bad ways? Shall religion be reckoned as an occasion for indulgence? Oh it is we deserve to be condemned! For why do we perform our vows and celebrate our joys for the Caesars, chaste, sober and decent? Why on the glad day do we not hang our doors with laurels and intrude upon the daylight with lamps? It is the honest man's duty, when a great public occasion calls, to rig your house up like some new brothel!

7

RELIGIOUS ATTITUDES

7.1 Seneca On Religious Awe

More or less explicit expression of people's response to religious stimuli—symbols, settings, ceremonies—is not very often encountered in the literature of any of the religious traditions illustrated in this collection; but the following examples do reveal how wide a variety of types of person and degrees of receptivity characterized the affective side of religion. In the first, Seneca, Nero's prime minister emeritus, addresses a friend on man's natural religiosity. The letter is one of a collection on Stoicism.

Source: To Lucilius 41.5, trans. Robin Campbell, *Letters from a Stoic* (Harmondsworth, Eng.: Penguin, 1969), p. 87.

If you have ever come on a dense wood of ancient trees that have risen to an exceptional height, shutting out all sight of the sky with one thick screen of branches upon another, the loftiness of the forest, the seclusion of the spot, your sense of wonderment at finding so deep and unbroken a gloom out of doors, will persuade you of the presence of a deity. Any cave in which the rocks have been eroded deep into the mountain resting on it, its hollowing out into a cavern of impressive extent not produced by the labours of men but the result of processes of nature, will strike into your soul some inkling of the divine. We venerate the sources of important streams; places where a mighty river bursts suddenly from hiding are provided with altars; hot springs are objects of worship; the darkness or unfathomable depth of pools has made their waters sacred. And if you come across a man who is never alarmed by dangers, never affected by cravings, happy in adversity, calm in the midst of storm, viewing mankind from a higher level and the gods from their own, is it not likely that a feeling will find its way into you of veneration for him? Is it not likely that you will say to yourself, "Here is a thing which is too great, too sublime for anyone to regard it as being in the same sort of category as that puny body it inhabits." Into that body there has descended a divine power.

7.2   Cicero's Thanksgiving

In a simple and intimate style, the following account from 49 B.C.E. is found in Cicero's correspondence with his wife. It reveals from its very inception a gesture of thanksgiving for his health which she would now render in the appropriate shrines.

Source: Cicero, *Letters to His Friends* 14.7.1, original translation.

All the troubles and concerns by which I've kept you in wretchedness—and nothing could be more troubling to me—along with my little [daughter] Tullia who is dearer to me than life itself, I have set aside and am rid of. The cause of it all I discovered the day after I left you: pure bile, which I threw up in the course of the night. I felt such immediate relief, it seemed some god had provided the treatment. To this god then, as you always do, do you acquit yourself devoutly and piously: that is, to Apollo and Aesculapius.

7.3   Prayers for Mercy and Thanksgiving

From the Mithraeum in the barracks of the Praetorian Guard in Rome survives this unusually long (but still, by our standards, short) prayer, inscribed on a small slab.

Source: G. Mussies, *La Soteriologia dei culti orientali nell' Imperio Romano,* eds. Ugo Bianchi and Maarten J. Vermaseren (Leiden: Brill, 1982), pp. 156–57, original translation.

Eternal Lord [*dominus*], Cascelia Elegans asks you through your mercy, on her behalf and that of all who are hers, as you have shown mercy to these created beings[?], I ask you, Eternal One, by earth and sea divine, by whatever good thing you have created, by salt and sacred seed[?], be merciful to me and mine, I beg, by your piety, your living law, your creatures, Eternal One, [I beg?] you [to be] favoring, on behalf of my fellow slave and my daughter and my master Primus and Celia wife of my patron, Lord.

This is a poem of thanksgiving from a shrine to the local Gallic deity Mars Lenus, near Trier (Trèves) on the Moselle (first or second century C.E.).

Source: *CIL* 13.7661, in both Greek and Latin versions. This is an original translation of the Latin.

While I am unable to bear the dire pangs of body
And spirit, wandering forever near the edges of death,
I, Tychicus, by Mars' divine love am saved.
This little thanks-offering I dedicate in return for his great caring.

7.4 Aelius Aristides's Religious Experience

The professor and exhibitor of the art of rhetoric, Aelius Aristides, much traveled in the cities of Greece and Asia Minor, spent especially important years in Pergamum, there seeking help for his chronic ill health from the god Asclepius. Among the experiences of this most devotedly religious man was a dream sent to him by the god in his temple in 146, as Aristides recorded it in, and later retrieved it from, his spiritual diary. It gives us a rare sense of the quite common initiatory experiences associated with Hellenistic cults.

Source: Aelius Aristides, *Oration* 48.32 Keil, trans. Charles A. Behr, *Aelius Aristides and the Sacred Tales* (Amsterdam: Hakkert, 1968) p. 230, altered.

For there was a feeling as if taking hold of him [the god] and of clearly perceiving that he himself had come, of being midway between sleeping and waking, of wanting to look, of struggling against his departure too soon; of having applied one's ears and of hearing some things as in a dream, some waking; hair stood straight, tears flowed in joy; the burden of understanding seemed light. What man is able to put these things into words? Yet if he is one of those who have undergone initiation, he knows and is familiar with them.

7.5 Seneca on the Nature of Divinity

Against the more direct and simple feelings of everday piety, as expressed above, religion approached from a unified philosophical position was potentially hostile. Seneca's Stoic piety produces this redirecting passage on right worship.

Source: Seneca, *Moral Letters* 95.47–48, trans. Richard L. Gummere, LCL.

Precepts are commonly given as to how the gods should be worshipped. But let us forbid lamps to be lighted on the Sabbath, since the gods do not need light, neither do men take pleasure in soot. Let us forbid men from offering morning salutation and to throng the doors of temples; mortal ambitions are attracted by such ceremonies, but god is worshipped by those who truly know him. Let us forbid bringing towels and flesh-scrapers to Jupiter, and proffering mirrors to Juno; for god seeks no servants. Of course not; he himself does service to mankind, everywhere and to all he is at hand to help. Although a man hear what limit he should observe in sacrifice, and how far he should recoil from burdensome superstitions, he will never make sufficient progress until he has conceived a right idea of god, regarding him as one who possesses all things, and allots all things, and bestows them without price. And what reason have the gods for doing deeds of kindness? It is their nature. One who thinks that they are unwilling to do harm, is wrong; they *cannot* do harm. They cannot receive or inflict injury; for doing harm is in the same category as suffering harm. The universal nature, all-glorious and all-beautiful, has rendered incapable of inflicting ill those whom it has removed from the danger of ill.

7.6 Augustine Quotes Seneca on the Folly of Paganism

Apparently the same author in a lost essay *Against Superstition* (less likely, by his father, Seneca the Elder) is quoted by Augustine. Augustine is concerned to show that non-Christian religious beliefs and practices are not only folly and worse, but are shown to be so by non-Christians themselves.

Source: Augustine, *City of God* 6.10–11, trans. William M. Green, LCL.

"To beings who are sacred, immortal and inviolable they consecrate images of the cheapest inert material. They give them the shapes of men or beasts or fishes; some, in fact, make them double creatures of both sexes combined or unlike bodies, united. They are called divinities [*numina*], but if they were suddenly brought to life and encountered, they would be regarded as monsters. [. . .]At this point someone says, 'Am I to believe that heaven and earth are gods [*dei*]? That some gods are above the moon and others below? Am I to tolerate either Plato or the Peripatetic Strabo, one of whom says that god has no body, the other that he has no soul?' [. . .]What then, pray? Tatius made a goddess of Cloacina ["of drains"], Romulus made gods of Picus and Pallor, the basest affections of men. One of them is mental, the emotion of a frightened mind, the other is physical, not even a disease, but only a color. Will you prefer to believe that these are deities [*numina*], and admit them to heaven? [. . .]One man cuts off his virile parts and another slashes his arms. What can they fear from the wrath of the gods when they use such means to win their favor? Moreover, gods deserve no worship [*coli debent*] of any kind if they want this kind. So great is the frenzy of a disordered and unsettled mind that means are used to placate the gods that have never been employed even by the most horrible men whose cruelty is recorded in myth and legend. . . . Some [men] have been castrated to serve the lust of a king, but no one has unmanned himself with his own hands at his master's order. They slash themselves in temples and make supplication with their own bleeding wounds. If anyone has leisure to view what they do and what they suffer, he will find practices so indecent for honorable men, so unworthy of free men, so unlike those of sane men, that if their number were fewer no one would have any doubt that they were demented. As it is, the only support for a plea of sanity is found in the number of the mad throng." He goes on [says Augustine] to relate the deeds which are customary performances in the very Capitol and completely demolishes them with absolute fearlessness. "Who could believe that they were performed unless by mockers and madmen? In the Egyptian rites the loss of Osiris is first bewailed, then shortly his restoration is celebrated with joy. Though both his loss and restoration are fictitious, yet the grief and joy of men who have lost nothing and found nothing is expressed as if it were real." After scoffing at these rites, Seneca remarks: "There is, however, a period fixed for their madness. It is permissible to be mad once in the year. But go to the Capitol and you will be ashamed of the folly there disclosed, and of the duties which a deluded madness has assigned itself. One [temple-servant] informs Jupiter of the names of his worshipper, another announces the hours; one is his bather, another his anointer, that is, he gestures with empty hands to imitate the act of anointing. There are women who are hairdressers for Juno and Minerva; while standing far away from the temple as well as from the image, they move their fingers as if they were dressing the hair, and there are others who hold a mirror. There are men who summon the gods to give bond for them, and some who offer them lawyers' briefs and explain their case. An expert leading actor in the mimes, now a decrepit old man, used to act a mime each day in the Capitol—as if the gods would enjoy the performance of a player when men had ceased to do so. Every kind of artisan sits there to devote his time to the mortal gods. [. . .]Still these men, though they offer useless service to the god, offer no base or indecent service. But there are women who sit in the Capitol, who imagine that Jupiter is their lover. They have no fear even of Juno's look, though she is much given to wrath, if we are to believe the poets."[. . .]The role that Seneca prefers the wise man to adopt is to exclude them from his personal worship, but to go through the motions of feigned conformity. For he says: "The wise man will observe all these rites as being enjoined by the laws, not as being pleasing to the gods. [. . .]What of the fact that we even join the gods in marriage and dishonorable marriage at that, the marriage of brother and sister? We give Bellona in marriage to Mars, Venus to Vulcan, and Salacia to Neptune. But some we leave unwed, as if no match could be arranged, especially since some are widows, such as Populonia, Fulgora, and the goddess Rumina. I am not at all surprised that there has been no suitor for these. As for all this obscure throng of gods, assembled through long years by ancient superstition, we shall invoke them, but with the reservation in mind that their worship belongs rather to custom than truth." Seneca also censures the sacred institutions of the Jews, especially the Sabbath [. . .]they lose in idleness almost a seventh of their life . . . he says: Meanwhile the customs of the accursed race have gained such influence that they are now received throughout all the world. [. . .] "The Jews, however, are aware of the origin and meaning of their rites. The greater part of the people go through a ritual not knowing why they do so."

7.7   Christians Admire Pagan Piety, from the *Didascalia Apostolorum*

As offset to the preceding, where a non-Christian cult is attacked from within its own ranks, there is this opposite testimony from a Christian observer of perhaps the mid-third century, writing in Syria and holding up non-Christian religiosity as exemplary, for its seriousness and punctuality.

Source: *Didascalia Apostolorum* 13, trans. R. Hugh Connolly (Oxford: Clarendon Press, 1929).

The heathen, when they daily rise from their sleep, go in the morning to worship and minister to their idols; and before all their works and undertakings they go first and worship their idols. Neither at their festivals and their fairs are they wanting, but are constant in assembling— not only they who are of the district but even those who come from afar; and all likewise assemble and come to the spectacle of their theater.

7.8   Lucius Is Saved by Conversion to Isis Worship, from Apuleius's *Metamorphoses*

Religious conversion in its most intense and fully described scenes in pagan literature is seen in Book 11 of the *Metamorphoses* (or *Golden*

Ass) of Apuleius. The hero of a novel, written in mid-second century but drawing on some earlier Greek version, is Lucius, here transformed by some evil magic into a donkey, living out his wretched life in central Greece. Wise advice has directed him to seek an exit from his transformation by praying to Isis. Critics have often supposed that the picture of a sudden focusing of devotion upon the goddess, and the consequent steps taken into further learning about her nature, wishes, and rites, are actually reflections of Apuleius's own personal experience. For this there is no direct evidence; but the account has much about it that inspires a reader's confidence—for example, the style of the hymn toward the beginning of this selection, the "theology" of Isis compared with that in real hymns, the appearance of the goddess compared with surviving statuary, the nature of the celebrations on her holy day, frequent epiphanies, and the prominence of communication with her through dreams.

Source: Apuleius, *Metamorphoses*, book 11 (London, n.p., 1853), anonymous translation.

Awaking in sudden alarm about the first watch of the night, I beheld the full orb of the moon shining with remarkable brightness, and just then emerging from the waves of the sea. Availing myself, therefore, of the silence and solitude of the night, as I was also well aware that the great primal goddess possessed a transcendent majesty, and that human affairs are entirely governed by her providence; and that not only cattle and wild beasts, but likewise things inanimate, are invigorated by the divine influence of her light; that the bodies which likewise are on the earth, in the heavens, and in the sea, at one time increase with her increments, and at another lessen duly with her wanings; being well assured of this, I determined to implore the august image of the goddess then present, Fate, as I supposed, being now satiated with many and great calamities, and holding out to me at last some prospect of relief.

Shaking off all drowsiness, therefore, I rose with alacrity, and directly, with the intention of purifying myself, began bathing in the sea. Having dipped my head seven times in the sea, because, according to the divine Pythagoras, that number is especially adapted to religious purposes, I joyously and with alacrity supplicated with a tearful countenance the transcendently powerful goddess: "Queen of heaven, whether thou art the genial Ceres, the prime parent of fruits, who, joyous at the discovery of thy daughter, didst banish the savage nutriment of the ancient acorn, and pointing out a better food, dost now till the Eleusinian soil; or whether thou art the celestial Venus, who, in the first origin of things, didst associate the different sexes, through the creation of mutual love, and having propagated an eternal offspring in the human race, art now worshipped in the sea-girt shrine of Paphos; or whether thou art the sister of Phoebus, who, by relieving the pangs of women in travail with remedies, hast brought into the world multitudes so innumerable, art now venerated, in the far-famed shrines of Ephesus; or whether thou art Proserpine, terrific with midnight howlings, with triple features checking the attack of ghosts, closing the recesses of the earth, and who wandering over many a grove, art propitiated by many modes of worship; with that feminine brightness of thine, illuminating the walls of every city, and with thy vaporous beams nurturing the joyous seeds of plants, and for the revolutions of the sun ministering thy fitful gleams: by whatever name, by whatever ceremonies, and under whatever form it is lawful to invoke thee; do thou graciously succour me in this my extreme distress, support my fallen fortune, and grant me rest and peace, after the endurance of so many sad calamities. Let there be an end of my sufferings, let there be an end of my perils. Remove from me the dire form of the quadruped, restore me to the sight of my kindred, restore me to Lucius, my former self. But if any deity pursues me with inexorable cruelty, may it at least be allowed me to die, if it is not allowed me to live." Having after this manner poured forth my prayers and added bitter lamentations, sleep again overpowered my stricken feelings on the same bed. Scarcely had I closed my eyes, when behold! a divine form emerged from the middle of the sea, and disclosed features that even the gods might venerate. After this, by degrees, the vision, resplendent throughout the whole body, seemed gradually to take its stand before me, rising above the surfaces of the sea. I will even make an attempt to describe to you its wonderous appearance, if, indeed, the poverty of human language will afford me the power of appropriately setting it forth; or, if the Divinity herself will supply me with a sufficient stock of eloquent diction.

In the first place, then, her hair, long and hanging in tapered ringlets, fell luxuriantly on her divine neck; a crown of varied form encircled the summit of her head, with a diversity of flowers, in the middle of it; just over her forehead, there was a flat circlet, which resembled a mirror, or rather emitted a white refulgent light, thus indicating that she was the moon. Vipers rising from furrows of the earth supported this on the right hand and the left, whole ears of corn projected on either side. Her garment was of many colours, woven of fine flax; in one part it was resplendent with a clear white colour; in another it was yellow like the blooming crocus, and in another flaming with rosy redness. And then, what rivetted my gaze far more than all, was her mantle of the deepest black, that shone with a glossy lustre. It was wrapped around her, and passing from below her right side over the left shoulder, was fastened in a knot that resembled the boss of a shield, while a part of the robe fell down in many folds, and gracefully floated with its little knots of fringe that edged its extremities. Glittering stars were dispersed along the embroidered extremities of the robe, and over its whole surface; and in the middle of them a moon of two weeks old breathed forth its flaming fires. Besides this, a garland, wholly consisting of flowers and fruits of every kind, adhered naturally to the border of this beautiful mantle, in whatever direction it was wafted by the breeze.

The objects which she carried in her hands were of a different description. In her right hand she bore a brazen sistrum, through the narrow rim of which, winding just like a girdle for the body, passed a few little rods, producing a sharp shrill sound, while her arm imparted motion to the triple chords. An oblong vessel, made of gold, in the shape of a boat, hung down from her left hand, on the handle of which, in that part in which it met the eye, was an asp raising its head erect, and with its throat puffed out on either side. Shoes, too, woven from the palm, the emblem of victory, covered her ambrosial feet.

Such was the appearance of the mighty goddess, as, breathing forth the fragrant perfumes of Arabia the happy, she deigned with her divine voice thus to address me: "Behold me, Lucius; moved by thy prayers, I appear to thee; I, who am nature, the parent of all things, the mistress of all things, the primordial offspring of time, the supreme among divinities, the queen of departed spirits, the first of the celestials, and the uniform manifestation of the gods and goddesses; who govern by my nod the luminous heights of heaven, the salubrious breezes of the ocean, and the anguished silent realms of the shades below: whose one sole divinity the whole orb of the earth venerates under a manifold form, with different rites, and under a variety of appellations. Hence the Phrygians, that primäval race, call me Pessinuntica, the Mother of the Gods; the Aborigines of Attica, Cecropian Minerva; the Cyprians, in their sea-girt isle, Paphian Venus; the arrow-bearing Cretans, Diana Dictynna; the three-tongued Sicilians, Stygian Proserpine; and the Eleusinians, the ancient goddess Ceres. Some call me Juno, others Bellona, others Hecate, and others Rhamnusia. But those who are illumined by the earliest rays of that divinity, the Sun, when he rises, the Äthopians, the Arii, and the Egyptians, so skilled in ancient learning, worshipping me with ceremonies quite appropriate, call me by my true name, Queen Isis. Behold then, commiserating your calamities, I am come to thy assistance; favouring and propitious I am come. Away, then, with tears; leave your lamentations; cast off all sorrow. Soon, through my providence, shall the day of deliverance shine upon you. Listen, therefore, attentively to these instructions. Eternal religion has consecrated to me the day which will be born from this night; tomorrow my priests offer to me the first fruits of the opened navigation, and dedicate to me a new ship, for that the wintry tempests are now appeased, and the stormy waves of the ocean lulled, and the sea itself has become navigable. That sacred ceremonial you must await, with a mind neither full of anxiety, nor intent upon subjects that are profane. For the priest, at my command, will carry in the procession a crown of roses, attached to the sistrum on his right hand. Without delay, then, pushing the crowd aside, join my procession, and put your trust in my gracious disposition; then, having approached close, as though to kiss the hand of the priest, gently pluck the roses, and at once divest yourself of the hide of that abominable beast, which I have long looked upon with detestation. Nor hold in dread any thing pertaining to my concerns as difficult. For even at this very same instant of time in which I appear to you here present, I am giving orders also to my priest how to bring about the things that are to take place hereafter. By my command, the dense crowds of people shall give way before you. Neither, amid the joyous rites and festive scenes, will any one view with abhorrence the unsightliness of the figure which you bear, or malignantly accuse you, by putting a sinister interpretation on the sudden change of your form. Only remember, and always keep it fast in the very depths of your heart, that the remaining period of your life must be dedicated to me, even to the moment of your latest breath. Nor is it unjust that you should devote your whole life to that goddess, by whose assistance you will have been restored to human form. But under my protection you will live happy, you will live glorious: and when, having passed through the allotted period of your life, you shall descend to the realms beneath, there, also, in the subterranean hemisphere, you, dwelling in the Elysian fields, shall frequently adore me whom you now behold thus propitious to you, and shall there see me shining amidst the darkness of Acheron, and reigning in the Stygian realms. And further, if you shall be found to deserve the protection of my divinity by sedulous obedience, religious devotion, and inviolable chastity, you shall be sensible that it is possible for me, and me alone, to extend your life beyond the limits that have been appointed to it by your destiny."

The venerable oracle having thus concluded, the invincible divinity dissolved into herself. Instantly shaking off sleep, I arose, in a state of fear and joy, and bathed in perspiration. Astonished in the highest degree at so evident a manifestation of the powerful goddess, having sprinkled myself with the spray of the sea, and intent on her high commands, I tried to recall to mind the successive particulars of her injunctions. Soon after this, the golden sun arose, and put to flight the clouds of dark night: and now, behold, a crowd of people filled all the streets with a religious procession, conducted in a style of triumph. All things likewise, independently of my own delight, seemed to me to be affected by the greatest hilarity, insomuch that I thought even the cattle of all kinds, every house, and the day itself, wore an aspect of gladness and serenity; for a sunny and placid day had suddenly succeeded to the frost of the previous one; so that, allured by the warmth of the spring, the tuneful little birds sang sweetly, and with their merry warbling soothed Her who was the mother of the stars, the parent of the seasons, and the mistress of the whole universe. And then the trees, too, both those prolific and those which only yielded a shade, unbounded from their wintry sleep by the warm southern breezes, and embellished with young foliage, sent forth a sweet rustling sound from their branches. The waves of the sea, no longer heaving turbidly to the roaring blast of the tempest, gently washed the shore; the dark clouds were dispersed, and the heavens shone with the serene splendour of their native light.

And now, behold, the prelude to the grand procession came gradually into action. The persons who composed it were all finely caparisoned in various ways, each according to his own taste and inclination. This man, being girded with a belt, represented a soldier; another was equipped as a hunter, with a short scarf, a hunting-knife, and javelin. Another, wearing gilded sandals, a silken garment, and precious female ornaments, and with false hair on his head, personated a woman by his appearance and his gait. Another, with his boots, his shield, his helmet, and his sword, appeared as though he had come straight from the school of the gladiators. There was one who played the part of a magistrate, with the fasces and the purple robe; another that of a philosopher, with his cloak, his staff, his wooden-clogged shoes, and his goatish beard; two persons, with dissimilar reeds, represented, the one a fowler with bird-lime, and the other a fisherman with his hook. I also saw a tame she-bear, wearing the dress of a woman, and carried in a chair; an ape, too, with a plaited straw hat on its head, and clothed with a Phrygian garment of saffron colour, carrying in its hand a golden cup, and representing the shepherd Ganymede; likewise an ass, on which wings were glued, and which walked near a feeble old man; so that you would certainly have said that the one was Bellerophon, and the other Pegasus; but still you would have enjoyed your laugh at both.

Amid this merry masquerade of the swarming people, the procession proper of the guardian goddess now advanced. Females, splendidly arrayed in white garments, expressing their joy by various gestures, and adorned with vernal chaplets, scattered flowers on the ground from their bosoms, along the path of the sacred procession. Others, again, with mirrors placed on their backs, showed all who followed to the Goddess, with their faces towards her as if they were coming to meet her. Others, carrying ivory combs, imitated the combing and bedecking of her regal hair, with the motion of their arms, and the twisting of their fingers. There were others, too, who sprinkled the streets with drops of genial balsam, and other kinds of perfume. In addition to all this, there was a great multitude of men and women, who propitiated the goddess, offspring of the celestial stars, by bearing lamps, torches, wax-tapers, and others of artificial light. Next came musicians, playing sweetly on pipes and flutes. A graceful choir of chosen youths, in snow-white garments, followed them, repeating a beautiful song, which an excellent poet had composed under the favour of the Muses, the words of which explained the first origin of the votive procession. Pipers also, consecrated to the great Serapis, played an air appropriate to the worship of the god, on pipes with transverse mouth-pieces, and tubes held obliquely towards their right ears. There were, also, a number of persons, whose office it was to give notice that room should be left for the sacred procession to pass. Then came a multitude of those who had been initiated into the sacred rites of the goddess, consisting of men and women of all classes and ages, resplendent with the pure whiteness of their linen garments. The women had their anointed hair enveloped in a transparent covering; but the men had shaven and shining pates; earthly stars were these of extreme sanctity, who kept up a shrill and incessant tinkling on brazen, silver, and even gold sistra. But the chief ministers of the sacred rituals, clothed in garments of white linen, drawn close over the breast, and hanging down to their feet, carried the insignia of the mighty goddess, exposed to full view. The first held aloft a brilliant lamp, not by any means resembling those lamps of ours which illumine banquets at night; but it was of gold, of a boat-like form, and emitted a flame of considerable magnitude, from an aperture in the middle. The second was arrayed in a similar manner, but carried in both his hands models of altars, to which the auxiliary providence of the supreme goddess gave the appropriate name of "auxilia." The third bore a palm tree, the leaves of which were beautifully wrought in gold, as also the caduceus of Mercury. The fourth displayed the symbol of Equity, a left hand, fashioned with the palm extended; which seems more adapted to administering Equity than the right, from its natural inertness, and its being endowed with no craft and no subtlety. The same person also carried a golden vessel, which was rounded in the shape of a female breast, and from which he poured forth milk on the ground. The fifth bore a golden corn-fan, made with thickest branches of gold; while another carried an amphora.

In the next place, appeared the gods who deigned to walk with the feet of men. Here, dreadful to view, was the messenger of the gods above, and of those of the realms beneath, standing erect, with a face partly black, and partly of a golden hue, bearing in his left hand a caduceus, and shaking in his right a green branch of palm; close upon whose footsteps followed a cow, in an erect position; this cow being the prolific resemblance of the all-parent goddess, and seated on the shoulders of one of the blessed devotees of this divinity, who acted gesticulating as he walked. Another carried a chest, containing the secret utensils of this stupendous mystery. Another bore in his beatified bosom a venerable effigy of his supreme Divinity, bearing no resemblance to any bird or beast, wild or tame, or even to man; but worthy of all veneration for the exquisite art with which it was wrought, as also for its very originality, and an ineffable symbol of the sublime religion, the mysteries of which were ever to be kept in deep silence. It was of burnished gold, after the following manner: there was a small urn, hollowed out in a most artistic manner, with a bottom quite round, and which outside was covered with the wonderful hieroglyphics of the Egyptians. The spout of this urn was very long, not much elevated; a handle was attached to the other side, and projected from the urn with a wide sweep. On this lay an asp, uplifting its scaly, wrinkled, and swollen throat, and embraced it with its winding folds.

At last the moment was at hand, when I was to experience the blessing promised me by the most potent goddess; and the priest, attired just as she had described, approached with the means of my deliverance. In his right hand he carried the sistrum of the goddess, and a crown of roses; and by Hercules, a crown it was for me; since by the providence of the mighty goddess, after having endured so many hardships, and escaped so many dangers, I should now achieve a victory over my cruel enemy, Fortune. Still, however, though agitated by a sudden burst of joy, I did not rush forward at once, lest the tranquil order of the procession should be disturbed by the impetuosity of a quadruped; but passed through the crowd with a quiet and altogether human step, and a sidelong movement of my body, and as the people gave way, through the interference, no doubt, of the goddess, I gradually crept nearer and nearer. But the priest, as I could plainly perceive, recollecting the nocturnal oracle, and struck with wonder at the coincidence with the duty which he had been commanded to perform, instantly stood still, and extending his right hand of his own accord, presented the chaplet to my very mouth. Trembling, and with great beating of my heart, I seized the bright rosy chaplet, and greedily, most greedily devoured it.

Nor did the celestial promise deceive me; for immediately my unsightly and brutal figure left me. First of all, my rough hair fell off, and next my thick skin became thin; my big belly shrank in; my hoofs spread out into feet and toes; my hands were no longer feet, but ready for the duties of their elevated position. My long neck was shortened; my face and my head became round; my enormous ears were restored to their former small dimensions; my stony teeth returned to the diminutive size of those of men; and the tail, which before especially annoyed me, was nowhere to be seen. The people were astonished, and the religious adored the power of the supreme divinity, so manifested in the facility of my restoration, which resembled the visions of a dream. Extending their hands towards the heavens, they attested, with loud and unanimous voice, the favour of the goddess thus signally displayed.

As for me, I stood riveted to the spot in excessive astonishment, my mind being unable to contain a delight so sudden and so great, quite at a loss what first and in especial to say, how to make a commencement with a new voice, how most auspiciously to prepare my address, my tongue being now born again, and in what words sufficiently to express my thanks to a goddess so great. The priest, however, who through the divine admonition knew all my misfortunes from the beginning, though he himself also was in a state of utter astonishment at this remarkable miracle, at once signified his wish by nodding his head, and ordered that a linen garment should be given me, for the purpose of covering my nakedness. For, the very instant that the ass had laid aside his abominable covering, I carefully shaded myself with a natural screen, as much as it was possible for a naked person to do so, by closely compressing my thighs, and applying my hands. Upon this one of the throng of devotees promptly throwing me his upper tunic, covered me therewith; which being done, the priest with a benign countenance, and, by Hercules, astonished at my perfectly human appearance, thus addressed me:

"At last, Lucius, you have arrived at the haven of peace and the altar of mercy, after the many and various hardships you have undergone, and all the buffetings of stormy Fortune. Neither the nobility of your descent, nor your dignified position, nor even the learning in which you excel, have benefited you in the slightest degree; but falling into the slavery of pleasure, in the wantonness of buxom youth, you have reaped the inauspicious reward of your ill-fated curiosity. Nevertheless, blind Fortune, while harassing you with the worst of dangers, has conducted you, in her short-sighted malice, to this state of religious beatitude. Let her go now, and rage with all her fury, and let her seek some other object for her cruelty; for direful calamity has no power over those whose lives the majesty of our goddess has claimed for her own service. What advantage has unscrupulous Fortune derived from robbers, from the wild beasts, from the servitude, from the long toils on rugged roads, and from the fear of death to which you were daily exposed? You are now received under the guardianship of Fortune, but of a Fortune who can see, and who even illuminates the other deities with the splendour of her light. Assume henceforth a more joyous countenance, such as befits that white garment which you wear. Follow the train of the goddess your deliverer with triumphant steps. Let the irreligious see, let them see and acknowledge their error. Behold now, Lucius, rejoicing in the providence of great Isis, and freed from his former miseries, triumphs over his destiny. Nevertheless, that you may be more secure and better protected, enroll your name in this holy militia, which you will hereafter rejoice to belong to; dedicate yourself to the service of our religion, and voluntarily bend your neck to the yoke of this ministry; for when you have once begun to serve the goddess, you will then in a still higher degree enjoy the fruit of your liberty.

The worthy priest having uttered these words, while his breath heaved with inspiration, concluded his address, and I mingling with the throng of devotees, accompanied the procession; an object of curiosity to the whole city. All pointed at me with their fingers and heads, and said, "This day has the august power of the almighty goddess restored that person to human form. Happy, by Hercules! and thrice blessed he, to have merited, by the innocence and probity of his past life, such special patronage of heaven; in that, being after a manner born again, he is immediately affianced to the service of the sacred ministry."

While these remarks were being made, and amid the tumult of their noisy congratulation, moving slowly on, we now approached the sea-shore, and came to that very place where, on the preceding day, I while yet an ass had laid me down. The images of the gods being there arranged in proper order, the chief priest dedicated and consecrated to the goddess a very skilfully built ship, pictured all over with the curious hieroglyphics of the Egyptians, after having most carefully purified it with a lighted torch, an egg, and sulphur, while at the same time his chaste lips poured forth solemn prayers. The shining white sail of this auspicious bark bore an inscription in large characters, which was a repetition of a vow that had been made on shore for the prosperity of the convoy at this season of the commencement of navigation. Now the mast was raised, which was a rounded pine tree, tall and well polished, and conspicuous for the beauteous appearance of its head. The prow also was turned in imitation of a goose's neck, and covered with gold leaf, the bark shone resplendently, while the whole of the highly polished keel consisted of shining citron wood. All the people, religious and profane, vied with each other in heaping together corn-fans laden with aromatics and other sacrificial offerings, and poured upon the waves a libation of milk mixed with other ingredients; until the ship, freighted with abundant gifts and auspicious prayers, and let slip from the ropes that held the anchor, put to sea with a serene breeze, which seemed to have sprung up for her sake alone. And after she had proceeded so far on her course that she could no longer be distinguished by us, the bearers of the sacred things again took what each had brought, and began joyfully to return to the temple, in an orderly manner, and in the same form of procession in which they had come.

Now as soon as we arrived at the temple, the chief priest and those who carried the sacred images, and those who had already been initiated into the venerable mysteries, being admitted into the sanctuary of the goddess, deposited in the accustomed form the breathing effigies. Then, one of these, whom all of them called the scribe, standing before the doors, whilst the company of the Pastophori, which is the name of the brotherhood of this sacred college, convoked together as to a council, uttered from a high pulpit auspicious wishes, from a book in which it was written:

"To the great Prince, to the Senate, to the Equestrian order, in naval matters and in ships, all those who are subject to our dominion;" and then he pronounced in the Greek language, and according to the Greek custom, the *laois aphesis* [the people may depart], to which the people responded with a clamor which testified their general satisfaction. Then everyone went home, full of joy, carrying branches of olive, sweet herbs, and garlands of flowers, and after kissing the feet of a silver image of the goddess, which stood on the step of the temple. But my feelings would not allow me to move so much as a nail's breadth from that place; but with my eyes intently fastened on the image of the goddess, I recalled to memory my past misfortunes.

Fleeting Fame, however, had not in the meantime let her wings remain idle, but had immediately circulated in all directions in my native country the adorable bounty of the provident goddess, and my own memorable adventures. Accordingly, my domestics and servants, and those who were nearest to me by blood, laying aside the sorrow with which they had been afflicted at the false intelligence of my death, and elated with sudden joy, hastened forthwith to see me, who had been divinely saved and brought back, as it were, from the shades below, and they presented me with gifts of various kinds. I, too, was delighted to see them, and returned them many thanks for their handsome presents, and the more especially, as my domestics had providently taken care to bring me what would be abundantly sufficient in the way of clothes and money. Having, therefore, spoken to each of them in such manner as I was in duty bound to do, and related to them my former sorrows and my present joyous prospects, I again returned to what was to me the greatest subject of delight, the contemplation of the goddess, and procured for myself a temporary habitation within the enclosure of the temple, constantly taking part in the private services of the goddess, and being inseparable from the brotherhood of the priests, and a constant adorer of the great divinity. Nor did I pass a single night or ever close my eyes without some vision from this divinity, in which she commanded me to be now initiated in her sacred mysteries, to which I had long since been destined. As for me, though prompted by eager inclination, I was still restrained by religious fear. For after diligent inquiry, I had found that the requirements of a religious life were full of difficulties; that the chastity required was a very difficult thing to observe, and that it needed extreme circumspection to preserve such a habit of life from casual defilements. Frequently pondering over these things, I somehow or other delayed being initiated, although hastening to that conclusion. One night I had a dream, in which I thought that the chief priest made his appearance, and presented to me his lap full of various things, and on my asking what they were, he answered me, that the things had been sent to me from Thessaly; for that a servant of mine, whose name was Candidus, had arrived from that province. When I awoke, I revolved in my mind over and over again what the vision portended, especially as I was certain that I never had any servant who was called by that name. Still, however, I believed that some profitable result was undoubtedly signified by the priest offering me the things. Thus, in a state of anxious and bewildered eagerness, I awaited the opening of the temple in the morning. The white curtains having been drawn aside, we prayed to the venerable presence of the goddess; and the priest going round the altars, performed the sacred ceremonial with solemn supplication, and poured forth libations from a chalice of water drawn from a fountain in the precinct of the sanctuary. The sacred rites, therefore, being now duly performed, the devotees, saluting the breaking dawn, in a loud voice announced the first hour of the day.

And now, behold! some servants arrived from my country whom I had left there at the time when Fotis, by her unfortunate mistake, had fitted me for a halter; so recognizing them as my own servants, and finding that they brought back that horse of mine, after it had been sold from place to place, and which I identified by a mark on its back; I was then especially struck with admiration at the fitness of my dream, because not only had it come true with respect to the gain it had promised, but it had also predicted to me the recovery of my horse, which was of a white color, under the designation of my servant Candidus.

I continued to apply myself wholly to attendance on the worship of the goddess, perceiving that the hopes which I had conceived of future good were now confirmed by present benefits. And besides, my desire of receiving initiation in the sacred duties, increased daily more and more. Accordingly, I frequently went to the chief priest, and most earnestly entreated him to initiate me into the mysteries of the holy night; but he, who was a man of a grave disposition, and remarkable for his strict observance of that abstemious religion, checked my urgent importunity in a mild and gentle manner, and in the way in which parents are in the habit of moderating the inconsiderate requests of their children, while at the same time he soothed me with hopes for the better. For he said, that the day on which each aspirant might be initiated was indicated by tokens from the goddess, and that by her providence the priest was selected who was to perform the sacred rites; and that in like manner by her mandate the expense necessary for the ceremonial was ordained. All these circumstances, he was of opinion, ought to be awaited with obsequious patience, since we ought, on every consideration, to avoid precipitation and contumacy, and neither be dilatory when called, nor precipitate when not called. Nor, indeed, was there a single one of their number who was so lost to a sense of propriety, or rather so bent on his own destruction, as to dare rashly and sacrilegiously to undertake the ministry of the goddess, and so bring upon himself a deadly mischance, unless she especially ordered him to do so; for the gates of the realms beneath, and the guardianship of life, are placed in the hands of the goddess, and the initiation into her mysteries is celebrated as bearing a close resemblance to a voluntary death, with a precarious chance of recovery. Wherefore the divine will of the goddess has been accustomed to choose for this purpose men who, having arrived at a great age, are standing at the very utmost limit of life, to whom, however, the mighty secrets of her religion may be safely entrusted, and whom, through her providence, being after a manner born again, she restores to the career of a new existence. Therefore it was requisite that I should await the celestial mandate, although by the clear and manifest favour of the great deity I had already been marked and destined for her blessed ministry; and I ought thenceforth to abstain from profane and forbidden food, in common with the other devotees, in order that I might with the most scrupulous strictness proceed on my course to the secret mysteries of the most pure religion.

Thus did the priest express himself, nor was my compliance interrupted by feelings of impatience; but I attentively performed the daily duties of the sacred ministry, intent upon maintaining a calm demeanour and laudable silence. Nor did the salutary benevolence of the powerful goddess disappoint me, or torment me with a long delay; but she clearly admonished me by no obscure mandates in the darksome night, that the day was now arrived that had always been the object of my desire, and in which she would put me in possession of my extreme wishes. She also stated what sum of money would be requisite for the expenses of the ceremonial, and at the same time appointed for me, as the dispenser of the rites, the same Mithras, her own high priest, who, she said, was united to me by a certain conjunction of the stars.

Refreshed in mind by these and other benevolent precepts of the supreme goddess, and shaking off slumber, though it was not yet clear day, I hastened at once to the dwelling of the priest, and saluted him just as he was coming out of his bedchamber. I had now determined to request more earnestly than ever initiation into the sacred rites, as being a thing that was due to me. He, however, the instant that he saw me, was the first to speak: "O my Lucius, how happy and blessed are you, whom the august divinity has thus greatly honored by her propitious will! And why," said he, "do you now stand idle, or make any delay? The day you so earnestly prayed for has now arrived, in which you will be initiated into the most holy mysteries by these hands of mine, in obedience to the divine mandates of the many-titled goddess."

And the old man, taking me by the right hand, led me immediately to the doors of the vast temple; and having performed the office of opening them in the accustomed solemn way, and celebrated the morning sacrifice, he drew forth from the secret recesses of the shrine certain books, written in unknown characters, partly representing in compendious form the words expressive of their meaning by figures of animals of every kind, and partly fortified against the inquisitive perusal of the profane, by characters wreathed like knots, and twisting round in shape of a wheel, and with extremities twining one with another, like the tendrils of vine. From these books he informed me what was necessary to be provided by me for the purpose of initiation.

Immediately, therefore, I diligently set about purchasing and pro-curing requisites, and even on a more liberal scale than I was ordered to do, partly at my own expense, and partly through my friends. And when, now the time, as the priest said, required it, he led me to the nearest bath, accompanied by a crowd of devotees; and after I had taken the customary bath, he himself washed and sprinkled me with the purest water, having first implored the pardon of the gods. Then, again, he brought me back to the temple, and there placed me at the very feet of the goddess, two-thirds of the day having now elapsed; and giving certain secret instructions, which are too holy to be uttered, he distinctly ordered, before all who were present, that I should abstain from luxurious food for the ten suc-ceeding days, and that I should eat the flesh of no animal, and should abstain from wine.

These ten days having been duly passed by me in reverential abstinence, the day now arrived for pledging myself to the sacred ministry, and the sun descending, was ushering in the evening. Then, behold, there was a concourse of the people flocking from every side, every one honoring me with various gifts, according to the ancient custom of these sacred rites. After this, the priest, all the profane being removed to a distance, taking hold of me by the hand, brought me into the inner recesses of the sanctuary itself, clothed in a new linen garment. Perhaps, curious reader, you may be eager to know what was then said and done? I would tell you, were it lawful for me to tell you; you should know it, if it were lawful for you to hear. But both the ears that heard these things, and the tongue that told them, would reap the evil results of their rashness. Still, however, kept in suspense as you probably are with religious longing, I will not torment you with long-protracted anxiety. Hear, therefore, but believe what is the truth. I approached the confines of death, and having trod on the threshold of Proserpine, I returned therefrom, being borne through all the elements. At midnight I saw the sun shining with its brilliant light; and I approached the presence of the gods beneath, and the gods of heaven, and stood near, and worshipped them. Behold, I have related to you things of which, though heard of by you, you must necessarily remain ignorant. I will therefore only relate that which may be enunciated to the understanding of the uninitiated without a crime.

The morning came, and, the solemnities being performed, I came forth consecrated by being dressed in twelve stoles, an habiliment no doubt of most religious character, but of which I am not forbidden by any obligation to speak, because it was seen by many who were present on the occasion. For, by order of the priest, I ascended a wooden pulpit, which was in the very middle of the sacred dwelling, and placed before the image of the goddess, full in view,. in a garment which was of linen, but elegantly coloured. A precious scarf also descended from my shoulders behind my back down to my ankles, and to whatever part of me you directed your view, you would have seen something to arrest your attention in the animals which were painted round my vestment in various colours. Here were Indian serpents, there Hyperborean griffins, which the other hemisphere generates in the form of a bird wearing wings. The persons devoted to the service of the divinity call this the Olympic stole. Then, in my right hand I carried a burning torch; while a graceful chaplet encircled my head, the shining leaves of the palm tree projecting from it like rays of light. Thus arrayed like the sun, and placed so as to resemble a statue, on a sudden, the curtains being drawn aside, I was exposed to the gaze of the multitude. After this, I celebrated the most joyful day of my initiation, as my natal day, and there was a joyous banquet and mirthful conversation. The third day was also celebrated with the like rites and ceremonies, and was accompanied by a religious breakfast, and the due termination of the ceremonial. After this, having stayed for some days in that place, I enjoyed the inexplicable pleasure of viewing the holy image, being indebted to it for a benefit which can never be sufficiently rewarded. At length, however, through the admonition of the goddess, having suppliantly given her thanks, not such as she deserved, but still to the best of my ability, I prepared myself, though very slowly, to return home. With difficulty did I rend asunder the ties of my most ardent affection. At last I prostrated myself in the presence of the goddess, and having for a long time watered her feet with my tears, interrupting my words by frequent sobs, and, as it were, half swallowing my voice, I thus addressed her:

"Thou, O holy and perpetual preserver of the human race, always munificent in cherishing mortals, dost bestow the sweet affection of a mother on the misfortunes of the wretched. Nor is there any day or night, nor so much as the minutest particle of time, which passes unattended by thy bounties. Thou dost protect men both by sea and land, and, dispersing the storms of life, dost extend the health-giving right hand, by which thou dost unravel the inextricably entangled threads of the Fates, and dost assuage the tempests of fortune, and restrain the malignant influences of the stars. The gods of heaven adore thee, those in the shades below do homage unto thee; thou dost roll the sphere of the universe around the steady poles, thou dost illumine the sun, thou dost govern the universe, thou didst tread the realms of Tartarus. The stars move responsive to thy command, the gods rejoice in thy divinity, the seasons return by thy appointment, and the elements are thy servants. At thy nod the breezes blow, the clouds are nurtured, the seeds germinate, and the blossoms increase. The birds as they hover through the air, the wild beasts as they roam in the mountains, the serpents that hide in the earth, and the monsters that swim in the sea, are terrified at the majesty of thy presence. But I, so weak in capacity for celebrating thy praises, and possessing such slender means for offering sacrifices, have far from eloquence sufficient to express all that I conceive of thy majesty; not a thousand mouths, and tongues as many, not an eternal flow of unwearied speech, would be equal to the task. I will, therefore, use my utmost endeavours to do what, poor as I am, still one truly-religious may do—I will figure to myself thy divine countenance, and will ever preserve this most holy divinity locked up in the deepest recesses of my breast."

After this manner, having offered up my prayer to the supreme goddess, I embraced the priest Mithras, who was now my parent, and hanging on his neck, and giving him many kisses, I begged him to forgive me, that I could not remunerate him in a manner adequate to such mighty benefits. At length, after having been long engaged in giving him thanks, I departed, and prepared to journey directly to my paternal abode, in order to revisit it after an absence so prolonged. A few days after, having hastily tied up my packages, through the admonition of the powerful goddess, embarking on board a ship I set sail for Rome. Being sure of a favourable wind during my voyage, I very speedily entered into port, and travelling by chariot with the greatest rapidity, arrived at the holy city [Rome], on the day before the Ides of December in the evening. Thenceforward no study was there of such primary importance with me, as that of daily supplicating the supreme divinity of Queen Isis; who is here propitiated with the greatest veneration under the name of Campensis, which appellation she derives from the situation of her temple. In fine, I became a constant worshipper, a foreigner indeed as to her temple, but indigenous as to her religion.

Behold the mighty sun, having passed through the sign-bearing circle of the zodiac, had completed the year, when the vigilant care of the benificent goddess again interrupted my sleep, and again reminded me of initiation and sacred rites. On this I wondered what object she had in view, and what future event she announced. For how could I do otherwise? as I considered myself to have been most fully initiated already. While, therefore, I revolved my religious doubts in my own mind, and availed myself of the counsels of the priest, I ascertained a thing that was novel and quite wonderful to me; that I was only initiated into the mysteries of the goddess, but that I had not yet been admitted to the knowledge of the rites of the great god, and supreme parent of the gods, the invincible Osiris. For though the essence of their divine nature and religion is connected, or rather, is transcendently united, nevertheless, there is a very considerable difference in the initiations into their mysteries. Hence, it was for me to know that I was called upon by the great god to become one of his servants. Nor did the matter long remain ambiguous. For on the following night, I saw in a dream one of the devotees, who, clothed in linen garments, and bearing in his hand thyrsi and ivy, and certain other things which I am not permitted to mention, placed them before my household gods, and then seating himself in my chair, announced to me that I must prepare a plentiful religious banquet. He also walked gently with a hesitating step, the ankle of his left foot being slightly bent in order no doubt that he might afford some sign, by which I might recognize him. All the mists of ambiguity were therefore removed, after such a manifest declaration of the will of the gods.

Accordingly, the instant I had performed the morning salutations to the goddess, I made a most careful examination of each, to see whether there was any one of the priests resembling him whom I had seen in the dream. Nor was he wanting. For I immediately beheld one of the Pastophori, exactly corresponding with the nocturnal vision, not only with regard to the mark of his foot, but also in his stature and general appearance; whose name I afterwards learnt to be Asinius ["Donkish"] Marcellus, an appellation not without some degree of reference to my transformation. Without delay, therefore, I addressed this priest, who was himself very far from ignorant of what I intended to say, because he had already been admonished by a similar mandate, that he should initiate me into the mysteries of Osiris. For on the preceeding night, while he was placing chaplets on the statue of the great god, he imagined that he had also heard from that mouth of his by which he pronounces the destinies of all things, that he should send him a native of Madaura, to whom, though he was very poor, he must immediately impart the sacred mysteries. That, through his providence, glory would accrue to that person from his religious exercises, and great profit for himself.

After this manner, being affianced to the sacred mysteries, I was retarded, contrary to my inclination, by reason of the slenderness of my means. For the expense to which I had been put in my journey had frittered away the small substance of my property; and the sums I was obliged to expend in the city, exceeded those which I had been disbursed in the provinces. Rigid poverty, consequently, greatly interfering with my wishes, I was much afflicted, being placed, as the old proverb says, between the altar and the stone. Nor yet was I less urged from time to time by the present mandates of the god. At last, after being repeatedly reminded, and finally commanded, not without considerable perturbation, taking off my back my garment, small as it was, I scraped together a sufficient sum. And this very thing I had been expressly commanded to do. For the god said to me, "Would you hesitate in the least to part with your garments, if you were attempting to procure any thing which might administer to your pleasures? and are you now, when you are going to enter upon so great a ceremonial, doubtful whether you shall commit yourself to a poverty of which you will never have to repent?"

All things, therefore, being abundantly prepared, again being satisfied for ten days with other than animal food, and besides this, being also admitted to the nocturnal orgies of Serapis, a god of the first rank, I now applied myself to the service of the god, full of that confidence which my knowledge of a kindred ritual produced. This event afforded me the greatest consolation for my sojourn in a foreign country, and at the same time supplied me more plentifully with the means of subsistence. For, under favour of the deity of Good Event, I supported myself on a little gain which I made in the forum by pleading causes in the Latin tongue.

A short time after, I was again addressed by the unexpected and perfectly miraculous mandates of the gods, and was compelled to undergo a third initiation. This caused me no slight anxiety, and much was I perplexed to know what could be the meaning of this new and unusual expression of the will of the gods; and what could still remain to be added by way of supplement to an initiation that had been already twice repeated. Surely, thought I, both the priests have advised me either wrongly or less fully than they ought to have done. And, by Hercules, I now began even to entertain a bad opinion of their fidelity. While, however, I was thus fluctuating amid a stormy tide of thought, and agitated to the verge of insanity, the benevolent figure of the divinity instructed me by a nocturnal vision. "There is no reason," said he, "that you should be terrified by the repeated series of religious rites, as if any thing had been previously omitted; but you ought rather exceedingly to rejoice on account of these reiterated marks of favour on the part of the divinities, and to exult that you will thrice obtain that which is scarcely even once granted to others. And you may confidently believe from that number that you will always be blessed. Besides, you will find that this ceremonial is most necessary for you, if you will only now consider with yourself, that the stole of the goddess with which you were invested in the province, still remains deposited in the same spot, and that you cannot so much as supplicate at Rome on solemn days in a garment of this kind, or be ennobled by that auspicious apparel, when you are commanded to assume it. In order, then, that you may enjoy health, happiness, and prosperity, once again with joyous feelings be initiated in the sacred mysteries, the mighty gods being your advisers."

Thus far did the persuasive majesty of the hallowed vision announce to me what was requisite to be done. Nor did I, after this, neglect the matter, or defer it; but immediately relating what I had seen to my priest, I forthwith submitted to the yoke of abstinence beyond those ten days prescribed by a perpetual law, I bought what was requisite for my initiation, spending more largely from pious zeal than with reference to the measure of the things provided. Nor, by Hercules, did I at all repent of my trouble and expense. And why should I? for by the bounteous providence of the gods, I was sufficiently enriched by my forensic emoluments. At length, after a very few days had elapsed, the god Osiris, who is the chief of the great gods, the highest among the greatest, the greatest among the highest, and the ruler of the greatest, not now veiling himself under some figure other than his own, but deigning to address me in his own person, and in his own divine words, seemed in my sleep to declare, that I should forthwith become renowned through my pleading causes in the forum, and that I should not fear the slanders of the malevolent, to which the learning I had acquired by laborious study had rendered me liable. Besides this, in order that I might minister to his sacred rites, mingling with the throng of devotees, he chose me to be a member of the college of his Pastophori, and still more, to be one of the quinquennial Decurions.

Finally, therefore, my hair being closely shaved off, I joyfully fulfilled the duties of that most ancient college, which had been established in the days of Sulla, not shading or covering my baldness, but freely exposing it to the public gaze, whithersoever I went. . . . [and Lucius lives happily ever afterward].

7.9 Pagan Asceticism, a Papyrus Account

A far less enthusiastic piety than that of Apuleius's Lucius—a far more philosophic-ascetic piety—speaks in this private letter of the third or early fourth century.

Source: P. Oxy. 42.3069, trans. P. J. Parsons.

Aquila to Sarapion, greetings. I was overjoyed to receive your letter. Our friend Callinicus was testifying to the utmost about the way of life you follow even under such conditions—especially in your not abandoning your austerities. Yes, we may deservedly congratulate ourselves, not because we do these things, but because we are not diverted from them by ourselves. Courage! Carry through what remains like a man! Let not wealth distract you, nor beauty, nor anything else of the same kind: for there is no good in them, if virtue does not join her presence, no, they are vanishing and worthless. Under divine protection, I expect you in Antinoopolis. Send Soteris the puppy, since she now spends her time by herself in the country. Good health to you and yours! Good health!

(Back) To Sarapion the philosopher from his friend Aquila.

7.10 The Guilt-Ridden Side of Pagan Belief: Some Inscriptions from Lydia

At times, however, pagan expectations could be quite oppressive. This is particularly true in the Lydian-Mysian borderland of Asia Minor. Here human ills might be attributed to divine punishment for misdeeds, even at times ones which the individual involved was unaware of committing. More often divine punishment for insults offered in a god's very presence was invoked to enforce the adjudication of disputes by oath before the gods. Belief was reinforced through the erection of confessional steles by the persons affected by divine punishment, or their heirs.

First, the story of the wicked and perjured mother-in-law. After a dating formula placing the inscription in 156–57 C.E., the narrative commences.

Source: CMRDM 1.44, original translation.

Great are Artemis Anaeitis and Men Tiamou! When Jucundus got into a manic state and it was being bruited about by all that poison was being given him by Tatias his mother-in-law, Tatias set up a scepter and placed oaths in the temple that she would get her satisfaction about her being talked about in such a blameworthy way. But the gods put her in a punishment, which she did not escape. Likewise her son Socrates, as he was going through the entrance that leads to the grove, holding a grape-cutting sickle in his hand—it fell on his foot, and thus he was dispatched in same-day punishment. Great then are the gods in Axitta! And they instructed the scepter and oaths which had been made in the temple to be dissolved, and Jucundus's and Moschius's children, Tatias's grandchildren, Sokrateia and Moschas and Jucundus and Menekrates did dissolve them, in all ways propitiating the gods, and from now on we bless them, writing the gods' powers on a stele.

Or consider the following involved story of multiple disregard of the gods' power and the ensuing punishment. Note that the stolen stone seems to have been used in a magical rite (love-magic?) and that Apphia's loss of virginity is attributed to the divinity, who, as god of the moon, acts only after a full month has passed.

Source: Georg Petzl and Hasan Malay, *GRBS* 28 (1987): 459–72; original translation after A. Chaniotes, *Epigraphica Anatolica* 15 (1990): 127–28.

Syntyche, [wife] of Theogenes, [made this dedication] to Men Artemidorou Axiot(t)enos. After her husband Theogenes had found a hyacinth stone, then [later] while it was lying in her house the stone was stolen, and when she was searching for it and being interrogated she prayed to Men Axiottenos to help her to satisfaction in regard to it; and it was found burned and disfigured, wrapped in a linen shirt, put by the thief in the place where it was lying when [still] undamaged. And so the god, having appeared [i.e., shown his power] on the thirty-first day, ravished Glycon's daughter Apphia, who was [still] a virgin, who had committed the theft and done this. And because she [i.e. Syntyche] slighted (?) the god's power, since she had been asked by the virgin's mother to keep silent, the god also became angry at this, [namely] because Syntyche did not make known and exalt the god. Therefore by means of [punishing] her thirteen-year-old son Heracleides he made her set up the [report of the] punishment at his place, because she acted in men's interest rather than in that of the god. It is Syntyche, daughter of Apollonius and Meltine, who has brought to public knowledge the punishment.

Lastly, an inscription which shows that in paganism also, not just in the Judeo-Christian tradition, gods could be seen as so remote that they needed angels (messengers) to communicate their will to man. The stele which bears the inscription has a particularly interesting relief: In an upper field stands the moon-god Men (or Meis), with a piece of clothing beside him, while in a smaller field below and to his left stands the culprit, his hands raised in adoration.

Source: *CMRDM*, 1.69, original translation.

Great is Meis Axiottenos who rules Tarsi! When a scepter was set up [to involve the god] if anybody steals anything from the bath-house, there being stolen a himation, the god punished the thief and caused him after some time to bring the himation to the god, and he confessed. The god then ordered by an angel the himation to be sold [for the benefit of the temple?] and [the thief] to write his powers on a stele. [Followed by a date corresponding to 164–65 C.E.]

8

MARCUS AURELIUS

8.1 Selections from Marcus Aurelius's *Meditations*

One of the most remarkable figures of the Roman Empire is the philosopher-emperor Marcus Aurelius (ruled 161–80 C.E.). His *Meditations* ("The Things Addressed to Himself," to give a literal translation of the Greek title) provide a unique look inside the mind of a conscientious, dutiful, and melancholy Stoic of the very highest level of society. Past generations, especially in Victorian England, turned to this figure with special affection, seeing in him a sort of reconciliation of the two streams of their education, classical and Christian; and translations of his work in many modern languages, literally dozens of them in English, almost as many in German, are legion. For Marcus Aurelius's view of Christianity, see 14.3, although it may not be genuine.

Source: Marcus Aurelius, *Meditations* 2.1, trans. A.S.L. Farquarson (Oxford: Clarendon Press, 1944).

Say to yourself in the early morning: I shall meet to-day inquisitive, ungrateful, violent, treacherous, envious, uncharitable men. All these things have come upon them through ignorance of real good and ill. But I, because I have seen that the nature of the good is the right, and of ill the wrong, and that the nature of man himself who does wrong is akin to my own (not of the same blood and seed, but partaking with me in mind, that is in a portion of divinity), I can neither be harmed by any of them, for no man will involve me in wrong, nor can I be angry with my kinsman or hate him; for we have come into the world to work together, like feet, like hands, like eyelids, like the rows of upper and lower teeth. To work against one another therefore is to oppose Nature, and to be vexed with another or to turn away from him is to tend to antagonism.

2. This whatever it is that I am, is flesh and vital spirit and the governing self. Disdain the flesh: blood and bones and network, a twisted

skein of nerves, veins, arteries. Consider also what the vital spirit is: a current of air, not even continuously the same, but every hour being expelled and sucked in again. There is then a third part, the governing self. Put away your books, be distracted no longer, they are not your portion. Rather, as if on the point of death, reflect like this: "You are an old man, suffer this governing part of you no longer to be in bondage, no longer be a puppet pulled by selfish impulse, no longer be indignant with what is allotted in the present or to suspect what is allotted in the future."

3. The work of the gods is full of Providence: the work of Fortune is not divorced from nature or the spinning and winding of the threads ordained by Providence. All flows from that other world; and there is, besides, necessity and the wellbeing of the whole universe, whereof you are a part. Now to every part of Nature, that is good which the nature of the Whole brings, and which preserves that nature; and the whole world is preserved as much by the changes of the compound bodies as by the changes of the elements which compose those bodies. Let this be sufficient for you, these be continually your doctrines. Put away your thirst for books, so that you may not die murmuring, but truly reconciled and grateful from your heart to the gods.

4. Remember how long you have been putting off these things, and how many times the gods have given you days of grace, and yet you do not use them. Now it is high time to perceive the kind of Universe of which you are a part and the nature of the governor of the Universe from whom you subsist as an effluence, and that the term of your time is circumscribed, and that unless you use it to attain calm of mind, time will be gone and you will be gone and that the opportunity to use it will not be yours again.

5. Each hour be minded, valiantly as becomes a Roman and a man, to do what is to your hand, with precise . . . and unaffected dignity, natural love, freedom, and justice; and to give yourself repose from every other imagination. And so you will, if only you do each act as though it were your last, freed from every random aim, from wilful turning away from the directing Reason, from pretence, self-love, and displeasure with what is allotted to you. You see how few things a man need master in order to live a smooth and godfearing life; for the gods themselves will require nothing more of him who keeps these precepts.

6. You are doing yourself violence, violence, my soul; and you will have no second occasion to do yourself honour. Brief is the life of each of us, and this of yours is nearly ended, and yet you do not reverence yourself, but commit your well-being to the charge of other men's souls.

7. Do things from outside break in to distract you? Give yourself a time of quiet to learn some new good thing, and do not wander out of

your course. But, when you have done that, be on your guard against a second kind of wandering. For those who are sick to death in life, with no mark on which they direct every impulse or in general every imagination, are triflers, not in words only but also in their deeds.

8. Men are not easily seen to be brought into evil case by failure to consider what passes in another's soul; but they who do not read aright the motions of their own soul are bound to be in evil case.

9. Always remember the following: what the nature of the whole is; what my own nature; the relation of this nature to that; what kind of part it is of what kind of Whole; and that no man can hinder your saying and doing at all times what is in accordance with that Nature whereof you are a part.

9

THEOLOGY

9.1   Plutarch's Rationalizing Strictures
on Egyptian Religion

As can be easily sensed in a great many passages already encountered,
people of a speculative turn of mind and more than average interest in
religion in the ancient world are easily found expressing that interest in
disciplined thought about the nature of supernatural power, its lodging
in one or in many beings, and its structure of greater or lesser complexity or abstraction. Such thought constitutes so large a subject that it
is difficult to present in brief without unacceptable distortion; but the
selections that follow attempt an outline of the most common features
of such thinking, without locating it too much among philosophers in
any formal sense.

In that intent of keeping within the mainstream of thought, we begin
with certain rationalizing remarks on both Greek and Egyptian religious
rites offered by a general man of letters and cultivated citizen of both
the Greek and Roman worlds, Plutarch (ca. 46–120 c.e.). He is writing
in general terms about Isiacism.

Source: Plutarch, *Isis and Osiris* 378E–379E trans. Frank Cole Babbitt,
LCL.

At Athens the women fast at the Thesmophoria sitting upon the
ground; and the Boeotians move the halls of the Goddess of Sorrow and
name that festival the Festival of Sorrow, since Demeter is in sorrow
because of her Daughter's descent to Pluto's realm. This month, in
the season of the Pleiades, is the month of seeding, which the Egyptians
call Athyr, the Athenians Pyanepsion, and the Boeotians Damatrius.
Theopompus records that the people who live toward the west believe
that the winter is Cronus, the summer Aphrodite, and the spring Persephone, and that they call them by these names and believe that from
Cronus and Aphrodite all things have their origin. The Phrygians, believing

109

that the god is asleep in the winter and awake in the summer, sing lullabies for him in the winter and in the summer chants to arouse him, after the manner of bacchic worshippers. The Paphlagonians assert that in the winter he is bound fast and imprisoned, but that in the spring he bestirs himself and sets himself free again.

The season of the year also gives us a suspicion that this gloominess is brought about because of the disappearance from our sight of the crops and fruits that people in the days of old did not regard as gods, but as necessary and important contributions of the gods toward the avoidance of a savage and bestial life. At a time of year when they saw some of the fruits vanishing and disappearing completely from the trees, while they themselves were sowing others in a mean and poverty-stricken fashion still, scraping away the earth with their hands and again replacing it, committing the seeds to the ground with uncertain expectation of their ever appearing again or coming to fruition, they did many things like persons at a funeral in mourning for their dead. Then again, even as we speak of the man who buys the books of Plato as "buying Plato," and of the man who represents the poems of Menander as "acting Menander," even so those men of old did not refrain from calling by the names of the gods the gifts and creations of the gods, honoring and venerating them because of the need which they had for them. The men of later times accepted this blindly, and in their ignorance referred to the gods the behaviour of the crops and the presence and disappearance of necessities, not only calling them the births and deaths of the gods, but even believing that they are so; and thus they filled their minds with absurd, unwarranted, and confused opinions although they had before their eyes the absurdity of such illogical reasoning. Rightly did Xenophanes of Colophon insist that the Egyptians, if they believed these to be gods, should not lament them; but if they lamented them, they should not believe them to be gods. Is it anything but ridiculous amid their lamentations to pray that the powers may cause their crops to sprout again and bring them to perfection in order that they again be consumed and lamented? This is not quite the case; but they do lament for their crops and they do pray to gods, who are the authors and givers, that they produce and cause to grow afresh other new crops to take the place of those that are undergoing destruction. Hence it is an excellent saying current among philosophers that they that have not learned to interpret rightly the sense of words are wont to bungle their actions. For example, there are some among the Greeks who have not learned nor habituated themselves to speak of the bronze, the painted, and the stone effigies as statues of the gods and dedications in their honour, but they call them gods; and then they have the effrontery to say that Lachares stripped Athena, that Dionysius sheared Apollo of the golden locks, and that Jupiter Capitolinus was burned and destroyed in the Civil War, and thus they unwittingly take over and accept the vicious opinions that are the concomitants of these names.

This has been in no small degree the experience of the Egyptians in regard to those animals that are held in honor. In these matters the Greeks are correct in saying and believing that the dove is the sacred bird of Aphrodite, that the serpent is sacred to Athena, the raven to Apollo, and the dog to Artemis—as Euripides says, "Dog you shall be, pet of bright Hecate." But the great majority of the Egyptians, in doing service to the animals themselves and in treating them as gods, have not only filled their sacred offices with ridicule and derision, but this is the least of the evils connected with their silly practices. There is engendered a dangerous belief, which plunges the weak and innocent into sheer superstition.

9.2 Eusebius Quotes Pagan Authors' Own Strictures on Paganism

Pagan criticism—"higher criticism," "more enlightened"—of pagan beliefs was offered from the sixth century B.C.E. on, at all times. Bishop Eusebius in the 330s C.E. in his *Praeparatio evangelica* drew heavily on certain works in this tradition, by the Epicurean Diogenianus (second century C.E.), the Cynic Oinomaus (a treatise of the 130s, *Frauds Detected*), and the Neoplatonist Porphyry (234–301/5 C.E. in an essay *Philosophy from Oracles*). His object, like that of St. Augustine in the selection above (7.6), is to expose the folly of non-Christian belief through the words of its own adherents.

Source: Eusebius, *Preparation for the Gospel*, 3.14.123c, trans. Edwin H. Gifford (Oxford: Clarendon Press, 1903).

Hear at least how Apollo himself teaches men a hymn which he put forth concerning himself, acknowledging that he was born of Leto in the island of Delos, and Asclepius again in Tricca, as also Hermes acknowledging that he was the child of Maia: for these things also are written by Porphyry in a book which he entitled *Of the Philosophy Derived from Oracles,* wherein he made mention of the oracles which run as follows:

Thou, joy of mortals, forth didst spring
From thy pure mother's sacred pangs.

To this he subjoins—

But when the pangs of holy birth
Through all her frame fair Leto seized,
And in her womb twin children stirr'd,
Still stood the earth, the air stood still,

> The isle grew fix'd, the wave was hush'd;
> Forth into life Lycoreus sprang,
> God of the bow, the prophet-king
> On the divining tripod thron'd.

Asclepius again thus speaks himself:

> From sacred Tricca, lo! I come, the god
> Of mortal mother erst to Phoebus born,
> Of wisdom and the healing art a king,
> Asclepius nam'd. But say, what would'st thou ask?

And Hermes says:

> Lo! whom thou callest, Zeus's and Maia's son,
> Hermes, descending from the starry throne,
> Hither I come.

Eusebius later turns (130df.) to the three traditional forms or genres in which pagans lay out their thoughts on god(s).

As to the first form then of their theology, being historical and mythical, let any of the poets arrange it as he will, and so let any of the philosophers deal with the second form, reported to us through the allegorical interpretation of the legends in a more physical sense: but since the third form, as being both ancient and politic, has been legally ordained by their rulers to be honored and observed, this, say they, let neither poet nor philosopher disturb; but let every one, both in rural districts and in cities, continue to walk by the customs which have prevailed from old time, and obey the laws of his forefathers.

In answer then to this, it is time to render the reason alleged on our [Christian] side, and to submit a defence of our Savior's evangelic system, as protesting against what has been described, and laying down laws opposed to the laws of all the nations.

Well then! it is manifest even to themselves that their lifeless images are no gods; and that their mythical theology offers no explanation that is respectable and becoming to deity, has been shown in the first book [of Eusebius's work], as likewise in the second and third it has been shown that neither does their more physical and philosophical interpretation of the legends contain an unforced explanation.

Come then, let us examine the third point—how we are to regard the powers that lurk in the carved images, whether as civilized and good and truly divine in character, or the very opposite of all these.

Others, peradventure, in entering upon the discussion of these questions, might have laid it down that the whole system is a delusion, and mere conjurors' tricks and frauds, stating their opinion generally and concisely, that we ought not to attribute even to an evil demon, much less to a god, the stories commonly told of them. For the poems and the compositions of the oracles, he would say, are fictions of men not without natural ability but extremely well furnished for deception, and are composed in an equivocal and ambiguous sense, and adapted, not without ingenuity, to either of these cases expected from the event: and the marvels which deceive the multitude by certain prodigies are dependent on natural causes. For there are many kinds of roots, and herbs, and plants, and fruits, and stones, and other powers both solid and liquid of every kind of matter in the natural world; some of them fit to drive off and expel certain diseases; others of a nature to attract and superinduce them; some again with power to secrete and disperse, or to harden and bind, and others to relax and liquidate and attenuate; some again to save and others to kill, or to give a thorough turn, and change the present condition, altering it now this way and now that; and some to work this effect for a longer and some for a shorter time; and again, some to be efficacious on many and others only on a few; and some to lead and others to follow; and some to combine in different ways, and to grow and decay together. Yet further, that some are conducive to health, not unconnected with medical science, and others morbific and deleterious; and lastly that some things occur by physical necessities, and wax and wane together with the moon, and that there are countless antipathies of animals and roots and plants, and many kinds of narcotic and soporific vapours and others that produce delusion: that the places also, and regions in which the effects are accomplished, give no little help; also that they have tools and instruments provided from afar in a way well fitted to their art, and that they associate with themselves in their jugglery many confederates from without, who make many inquiries about those who arrive, and the wants of each, and what he is come to request; also that they conceal within their temples many secret shrines and recesses inaccessible to the multitude; and that the darkness also helps their purpose not a little; and not least the anticipatory assumption itself, and the superstition of those who approach them as gods, and the opinion which has prevailed among them from the time of their forefathers.

To this must be added also the silliness of mind of the multitude, and their feeble and uncritical reasoning, and on the other hand the cleverness and craftiness of those who are constantly practising this mischievous art, and the deceitful and knavish disposition of the impostors, at one time promising what will please each person, and soothing the present trouble by hopes of advantage, and at other times guessing at what is to come, and prophesying obscurely, and darkening the sense of their oracles by equivocations and indistinctness of expression, in order that no one may understand what is foretold, but that they may escape detection by the uncertainty of their statement . . . But though there are thousands who have wrought the overthrow of the oracles by many arguments, for me I think it is sufficient at present, for a testimony of what I have stated, to make a single quotation from one of them in answer to the arguments devised by Chrysippus concerning fate from the predictions of the oracles. This author then writes against him to prove that he wrongly derives indications of fate from the oracles, and that the oracles of the Greeks give false answers in most cases, and that rarely from a coincidence some events agree with them, and that their prediction of the future is useless and mischievous. Hear, however, what he says, word for word [here quoting Diogenianus:] "But Chrysippus, in the book before mentioned, brings also another proof of the following kind. He says that the predictions of the prophets could not be true unless all things were fast bound by fate: which is itself a most silly argument. For he argues as if it were evident or would be more readily admitted by anyone, that all the predictions of the so-called prophets came to pass, than that all things take place according to fate, as if the former would not itself be an equally false statement, since plain experience shows the contrary; I mean that not all things foretold, or rather not the greatest part of them, come to pass." As to Oedipus, for instance, and Alexander son of Priam, even Chrysippus himself says that though their parents had recourse to many contrivances to kill them, in order that they might guard against the mischief predicted from them, they were unable to do so. "Thus there was no benefit," he says, "even to them from the prediction of the evils, because they were effects proceeding from fate. Let this then be enough, and more than enough, to have been said in regard to not merely the uncertainty but also the uselessness of the prophetic art."

Thus far the philosopher. Do thou however consider with thyself, how those who were Greeks, and had from an early age acquired the customary education of the Greeks, and knew more accurately than any man the customs of their ancestors concerning the gods, all Aristotelians, and Cynics, and Epicureans, and all who held like opinions with them, poured ridicule upon the oracles which were renowned among the Greeks themselves. And yet, if the stories current concerning the miraculous power of the oracles were true, it was natural that these men also should have been struck with wonder, being Greeks, and having an accurate understanding of the customs of their ancestors, and regarding nothing worthy to be known as of secondary importance. To collect, however, these and all similar evidences, in order to overthrow the argument on behalf of the oracles, there would be abundant means: but it is not in this way that I wish to pursue the present discussion, but in the same way as we started at first, by granting that those who stand forth in their defence speak truth; in order that from their own avowals, when they affirm that oracles are true, and that the alleged responses are divinely inspired Pythian oracles, we may learn the exact explanation of the things alleged.

Eusebius next turns to Porphyry (144d).

The aforesaid author, then, in his work which he entitled *Of the Philosophy to be Derived from Oracles,* gives responses of Apollo enjoining the performance of animal sacrifices, and the offering of animals not to demons only, nor only to the terrestrial powers, but also to the etherial and heavenly powers. But in another work the same author, confessing that all, to whom the Greeks used to offer sacrifices by blood and slaughter of senseless animals, are demons and not gods, says that it is not right nor pious to offer animal sacrifices to gods. Hear, therefore, his first utterances, in which, collecting the facts concerning The Philosophy to be derived from Oracles, he shows how Apollo teaches that the gods ought to be worshipped. This he sets forth in writing as follows: "Next in order after what has been said concerning piety we shall record the responses given by them concerning their worship, part of which by anticipation we have set forth in the statements concerning piety. Now this is the response of Apollo, containing at the same time an orderly classification of the gods.

'Friend, who hast entered on this heaven-taught path,
Heed well thy work; nor to the blessed gods
Forget to slay thine offerings in due form,
Whether to gods of earth, or gods of heaven,
Kings of the sky and liquid paths of air
And sea, and all who dwell beneath the earth;
For in their nature's fullness all is bound.
How to devote things living in due form
My verse shall tell, thou in thy tablets write.
For gods of earth and gods of heaven each three:
For heavenly gods pure white; for gods of earth
Cattle of kindred hue divide in three
And on the altar lay thy sacrifice.
For gods infernal bury deep, and cast
The blood into a trench. For gentle Nymphs

Honey and gifts of Dionysus pour.
For such as flit forever o'er the earth
Fill all the blazing altar's trench with blood,
And cast the feathered fowl into the fire.
Then honey mix'd with meal, and frankincense,
And grains of barley sprinkled over all.
But when thou comest to the sandy shore,
Pour green sea-water on the victim's head,
And cast the body whole into the deep.
Then, all things rightly done, return at last
To the great company of heavenly gods.
For all the powers that in pure ether dwell,
And in the stars, let blood in fullest stream
Flow from the throat o'er all the sacrifice:
Make of the limbs a banquet for the gods,
And give them to the fire; feast on the rest,
Filling with savors sweet the liquid air.
Breathe forth, when all is done, thy solemn vows.'"

Then with a few words later he explains this response, interpreting it as follows: "Now this is the method of the sacrifices, which are rendered according to the aforesaid classification of the gods. For whereas there are gods beneath the earth, and on the earth, and those beneath the earth are called also infernal gods, and those on the earth terrestrial, for all these in common he enjoins the sacrifice of black four-footed victims." But with regard to the manner of the sacrifice he makes a difference: for to terrestrial gods he commands the victims to be slain upon altars, but to the infernal gods over trenches, and moreover after the offering to bury the bodies therein. "For that the four-footed beasts are common to these deities, the god himself added when questioned:

'For gods of earth and Erebus alone
Four-footed must their common victims be;
For gods of earth soft limbs of newborn lambs.'

But to the gods of the air he bids men sacrifice birds as whole burnt-offerings, and let the blood run around upon the altars: birds also to the gods of the sea, of a black colour, but to cast them alive into the waves. For he says: 'Birds for the gods, but for the sea-gods black.'

"He names birds for all the gods save the Chthonians, but black for the sea-gods only, and therefore white for the others. 'But to the gods of the heaven and the ether he bids thee consecrate the limbs of the victims, which are to be white, and eat the other parts: for of these only must thou eat, and not of the others. But those whom in his classification he called gods of heaven, these he here calls gods of the stars.'" Will it then be necessary to explain the symbolic meanings of the sacrifices, manifest as they are to the intelligent? For there are four-footed land animals for the gods of the earth, because like rejoices in like. And the sheep is of the earth and therefore dear to Demeter, and in heaven the Ram, with the help of the sun, brings forth out of the earth its display of fruits. They must be black, for such color is the earth, being naturally dark: and three, for three is the symbol of the corporeal and earthly. "To the gods of earth then one must offer high upon altars, for these pass to and fro upon the earth; but to the gods beneath the earth, in a trench and in a grave, where they abide. To the other gods we must offer birds, because all things are in swift motion . . ." And after other matters he says [153a]: "But when a young man has learned that gods delight in costliness, and, as is said, in feasts upon kine and other animals, when would he ever choose to be thrifty and temperate? And if he believes that these offerings are pleasing to the gods, how can he avoid thinking that he has license to do wrong, being sure to buy off his sin by his sacrifices? But if he be persuaded that the gods have no need of these sacrifices, but look to the moral disposition of those who approach them, receiving as the greatest offering the right judgement concerning themselves and their affairs, how can he fail to be prudent, and just, and holy? "The best sacrifice to the gods is a pure mind and a soul free from passions; but also congenial to them is the offering of other sacrifices in moderation, not carelessly, however, but with all earnestness. For their honors must be like those paid in the case of good men, such as chief seats in public assemblies, rising up at their approach, and honorable places at table, and not like grants of tribute."

Eusebius turns next to Oinomaus (208c).

Take up again therefore the ancient records from the beginning, and observe what kind of answer the Pythian god [Apollo through the Delphic oracle] gives to the Athenian when afflicted with the pestilence on account of the death of Androgeus. The Athenians were all suffering from a pestilence for one man's death, and thought to receive the help of the gods. What advice then does this saviour and god give them? To cultivate justice and benevolence and all other virtue in the future, someone will perhaps suppose; or to repent of the offence, and to perform some holy and religious rites, as the gods would thereby be propitiated. Nay, nothing of the kind. For what indeed did their admirable gods, or rather their utterly wicked daemons, care for these things? So again they say what is natural and familiar to themselves, things merciless and cruel and inhuman, plague upon plague, and many deaths for one. In fact Apollo bids them every year send of their own children seven grown youths, and as many maidens, fourteen innocent and unconcerned persons for one, and that not once only but every year, to be sacrificed in Crete in the presence of Minos: so that even to the time of Socrates, more than five hundred years afterwards, this dreadful and most inhuman tribute was still kept in memory among Athenians. And this it was that caused the delay in the death of Socrates.

This answer of the oracle is at once stated and very justly condemned in a vigorous argument by a recent author, who has composed a seperate work on *The Detection of Impostors*: to whose own words, and not mine, now listen, as he aims his stroke at the author of the response in the manner following: "What then? When the Athenians had caused the death of Androgeus, and suffered a pestilence for it, would they not have said that they repented? Or if they did not say so, would it not have been proper for thee to say 'Repent,' rather than to say this?

'Of plague and famine there shall be an end,
If your own flesh and blood, female and male,
By lot assigned to Minos, ye send forth
Upon the mighty sea, for recompense
Of evil deeds: so shall the god forgive.'

I pass over the fact that you gods are indignant at the death of Androgeus at Athens, but sleep on while so many die in all places and at all times."

10

A NEW CULT

The appearance of cults far from their original home, in some new city, is a prominent feature of life in the Mediterranean world of the first four centuries C.E. That world was one of vital, constant interchange in religious ideas as in other aspects of culture. But of brand new religions, there are only very limited numbers: chief among them, Christianity, of course; perhaps next in historical importance, Manichaeism, destined for a life of a thousand years and diffusion into the remote corners of the east; Mithraism in the third place (as that form of worship emerged around 100 C.E., whether or not it had any real links at all to the Middle Eastern religion of the same name but at least two centuries earlier); after these examples, a poor fourth, the cult of Antinous, which was however, no more widespread and not so long-lasting as that of Glycon and that serpent-deity's high priest, Alexander. We are lucky enough to have a quite detailed account of this last, indicating in concrete form just what would be seen as credible, attractive, and powerful in impact, in the realm of religious ideas. For this reason, quite aside from its entertaining character, the following account is of great usefulness.

10.1 Lucian's Tale of Alexander the False Prophet

It is the work of the journalist and essayist, Lucian of Samosata. He wrote in the second half of the second century, generally in comical style, sometimes on local curiosities, travels, or personalities discovered in the eastern Roman provinces. He took special interest in religion— from the doubter's point of view—and had rich material to deal with in the Prophet of Abonouteichos (Abonutichus). Lucian's account is borne out by a certain amount of evidence from inscriptions, art, and coins of the eastern provinces.

Source: Henry W. Fowler and Francis G. Fowler, *The Works of Lucian of Samosata* (Oxford: Clarendon Press, 1905), 3:212–38.

You, my dear Celsus, possibly suppose yourself to be laying upon me quite a trifling task: Write me down in a book and send me the life and adventures, the tricks and frauds, of the impostor Alexander of Abonutichus. In fact, however, it would take as long to do this in full detail as to reduce to writing the achievements of Alexander of Macedon; the one is among villains, the other is among heroes. Nevertheless, if you will promise to read with indulgence, and fill up the gaps in my tale from your imagination, I will essay the task. I may not cleanse that Augean stable completely, but I will do my best, and fetch you out a few loads as samples of the unspeakable filth that three thousand oxen could produce in many years.

I confess to being a little ashamed both on your account and my own. There are you asking that the memory of an arch-scoundrel should be perpetuated in writing; here am I going seriously into an investigation of this sort—the doings of a person whose deserts entitled him not to be read about by the cultivated, but to be torn to pieces in the amphitheatre by apes or foxes, with a vast audience looking on. Well, well, if any one does cast reflections of that sort upon us, we shall at least have a precedent to plead. Arrian himself, disciple of Epictetus, distinguished Roman, and product of lifelong culture as he was, has just our experience, and shall make our defence. He condescended, that is, to put on record the life of the robber Tilliborus. The robber we propose to immortalize was of a far more pestilent kind, following his profession not in the forests and mountains, but in cities; he was not content to overrun a Mysia or an Ida; his booty came not from a few scantily populated districts of Asia; one may say that the scene of his depredations was the whole Roman Empire.

I will begin with a picture of the man himself, as lifelike (though I am not great at description) as I can make it with nothing better than words. In person—not to forget that part of him—he was a fine, handsome man with a real touch of divinity about him, white-skinned, moderately bearded; he wore besides his own hair artificial additions which matched it so cunningly that they were not generally detected. His eyes were piercing, and suggested inspiration, his voice at once sweet and sonorous. In fact there was no fault to be found with him in these respects. So much for externals. As for his mind and spirit—well, if all the kind gods who avert disaster will grant a prayer, it shall be that they bring me not within reach of such a one as he; sooner I will face my bitterest enemies, my country's foes. In understanding, resource, acuteness, he was far above other men; curiosity, receptiveness, memory, scientific ability—all these were his in overflowing measure. But he used them for the worst purposes. Endowed with all these instruments of good, he very soon reached a proud pre-eminence among all who have been famous for evil; the Cercopes,

Eurybatus, Phrynondas, Aristodemus, Sostratus—all thrown into the shade. In a letter to his father-in-law Rutilianus, which puts his own pretensions in a truly modest light, he compares himself to Pythagoras. Well, I should not like to offend the wise, the divine Pythagoras; but if he had been Alexander's contemporary, I am quite sure he would have been a mere child to him. Now, by all that is admirable, do not take that for an insult to Pythagoras, nor suppose I would draw a parallel between their achievements. What I mean is: if any one would make a collection of the vilest and most damaging slanders ever vented against Pythagoras—things whose truth I would not accept for a moment—the sum of them would not come within measurable distance of Alexander's cleverness. You are to set your imagination to work and conceive a temperament curiously compounded of falsehood, trickery, perjury, cunning; it is versatile, audacious, adventurous, yet dogged in execution; it is plausible enough to inspire confidence; it can assume the mask of virtue, and seem to eschew what it most desires. I suppose no one ever left him after a first interview without the impression that this was the best and kindest of men, ay, and the simplest and most unsophisticated. Add to all this a certain greatness in his objects; he never made a small plan; his ideas were always large.

While in the bloom of his youthful beauty, which we may assume to have been great both from its later remains and from the report of those who saw it, he traded quite shamelessly upon it. Among his other patrons was one of the charlatans who deal in magic and mystic incantations; they will smooth your course of love, confound your enemies, find your treasure, or secure you an inheritance. This person was struck with the lad's natural qualifications for apprenticeship to his trade, and finding him as much attracted by rascality as attractive in appearance, gave him a regular training as accomplice, satellite, and attendant. His own ostensible profession was medicine, and his knowledge included, like that of Thoon the Egyptian's wife, "Many a virtuous herb, and many a bane"—to all which inheritance our friend succeeded. This teacher and lover of his was a native of Tyana, an associate of the great Apollonius, and acquainted with all his heroics. And now you know the atmosphere in which Alexander lived.

By the time his beard had come, the Tyanean was dead, and he found himself in straits; for the personal attractions which might once have been a resource were diminished. He now formed great designs, which he imparted to a Byzantine chronicler of the strolling competitive order, a man of still worse character than himself, called, I believe, Cocconas. The pair went about living on occult pretensions, shearing "fat-heads" as they describe ordinary people in the native Magian lingo. Among these they got hold of a rich Macedonian woman; her youth was past, but not her desire for admiration; they got sufficient supplies out of her, and accompanied her from Bithynia to Macedonia. She came from Pella, which had been a flourishing place under the Macedonian kingdom, but was now a poor and much reduced population. There is here a breed of large serpents, so tame and gentle that women make pets of them, children take them to bed, they will let you tread on them, have no objection to being squeezed, and will draw milk from the breast like infants. To these facts is probably to be referred the common story about Olympias when she was with child of Alexander; it was doubtless one of these that was her bed-fellow. Well, the two saw these creatures, and bought the finest they could get for a few pence.

And from this point, as Thucydides might say, the war takes its beginning. These ambitious scoundrels were quite devoid of scruples, and they had now joined forces; it could not escape their penetration that human life is under the absolute dominion of two mighty principles, fear and hope, and that any one who can make these serve his ends may be sure of a rapid fortune. They realized that, whether a man is most swayed by the one or by the other, what he must depend upon and desire is a knowledge of futurity. So were to be explained the ancient wealth and fame of Delphi, Delos, Clarus, Branchidae; it was at the bidding of the two tyrants aforesaid that men thronged the temples, longed for foreknowledge, and to attain it sacrificed their hecatombs or dedicated their golden ingots. All this they turned over and debated, and it issued in the resolve to establish an oracle. If it were successful, they looked for immediate wealth and prosperity; the result surpassed their most sanguine expectations. The next things to be settled were, first the theatre of operations, and secondly the plan of campaign. Cocconas favoured Chalcedon, as a mercantile centre convenient both for Thrace and Bithynia, and accessible enough for the province of Asia, Galatia, and tribes still further east. Alexander, on the other hand, preferred his native place, urging very truly that an enterprise like theirs required congenial soil to give it a start, in the shape of "fat-heads" and simpletons; that was a fair description, he said, of the Paphla-gonians beyond Abonutichus; they were mostly superstitious and well-to-do; one had only to go there with some one to play the flute, the tambourine, or the cymbals, set the proverbial mantic sieve a-spinning, and there they would all be gaping as if he were a god from heaven.

This difference of opinion did not last long, and Alexander pre-vailed. Discovering, however, that a use might after all be made of Chalcedon, they went there first, and in the temple of Apollo, the oldest in the place, they buried some brazen tablets, on which was the statement that very shortly Asclepius, with his father Apollo, would pay a visit to Pontus, and take up his abode at Abonutichus. The discovery of the tablets took place as arranged, and the news flew through Bithynia and Pontus, first of all, naturally, to Abonutichus. The people of that place at once resolved to raise a temple, and lost no time in digging the foundations. Cocconas was now left at Chalcedon, engaged in composing certain ambiguous crabbed oracles. He shortly afterwards died, I believe, of a viper's bite.

Alexander meanwhile went on in advance; he had now grown his hair and wore it in long curls; his doublet was white and purple striped, his cloak pure white; he carried a scimitar in imitation of Perseus, from whom he now claimed descent through his mother. The wretched Paphlagonians, who knew perfectly well that his parentage was obscure and mean on both sides, nevertheless gave credence to the oracle, which ran:

> Lo, sprung from Perseus, and to Phoebus dear,
> High Alexander, Podalirius' son!

Podalirius, it seems, was of so highly amorous a complexion that the distance between Tricca and Paphlagonia was no bar to his union with Alexander's mother. A Sibylline prophecy had also been found:

> Hard by Sinope on the Euxine shore
> Th' Italic age a fortress prophet sees.
> To the first monad let thrice ten be added,
> Five monads yet, and then a triple score:
> Such the quaternion of th' alexic name.

This heroic entry into his long-left home placed Alexander conspicuously before the public; he affected madness, and frequently foamed at the mouth—a manifestation easily produced by chewing the herb soap-wort, used by dyers; but it brought him reverence and awe.

The two had long ago manufactured and fitted up a serpent's head of linen; they had given it more or less human expression, and painted it very like the real article; by a contrivance of horsehair, the mouth could be opened and shut, and a forked black serpent tongue protruded, working on the same system. The serpent from Pella was also kept ready in the house, to be produced at the right moment and take its part in the drama—the leading part, indeed. In the fullness of time, his plan took shape. He went one night to the temple foundations, still in process of digging, and with standing water in them which had collected from the rainfall or otherwise; here he deposited a goose egg, into which, after blowing it, he had inserted some new-born reptile. He made a resting-place deep down in the mud for this, and departed. Early next morning he rushed into the market-place, naked except for a gold-spangled loin-cloth; with nothing but this and his scimitar, and shaking his long loose hair, like the fanatics who collect money in the name of Cybele, he climbed onto a lofty altar and delivered a harangue, felicitating the city upon the advent of the god now to bless them with his presence. In a few minutes nearly the whole population was on the spot, women, old men, and children included; all was awe, prayer, and adoration. He uttered some unintelligible sounds, which might have been Hebrew or Phoenician, but completed his victory over his audience, who could make nothing of what he said, beyond the constant repetition of the names Apollo and Asclepius.

He then set off at a run for the future temple. Arrived at the excavation and the already completed sacred fount, he got down into the water, chanted in a loud voice hymns to Asclepius and Apollo, and invited the god to come, a welcome guest, to the city. He next demanded a bowl, and when this was handed to him, had no difficulty in putting it down at the right place and scooping up, besides water and mud, the egg in which the god had been enclosed; the edges of the aperture had been joined with wax and white lead. He took the egg in his hand and announced that here he held Asclepius. The people, who had been sufficiently astonished by the discovery of the egg in the water, were now all eyes for what was to come. He broke it, and received in his hollowed hand the hardly developed reptile; the crowd could see it stirring and winding about his fingers; they raised a shout, hailed the god, blessed the city, and every mouth was full of prayers—for treasure and wealth and health and all other good things that he might give.

Our hero now departed homewards, still running, with the new-born Asclepius in his hands—the twice-born, too, whereas ordinary men can be borne but once, and born moreover not of Coronis, nor even of her namesake the crow, but of a goose! After him streamed the whole people, in all the madness of fanatic hopes. He now kept the house for some days, in hopes that the Paphlagonians would soon be drawn in crowds by the news. He was not disappointed; the city was filled to overflowing with persons who had neither brains nor individuality, who bore no resemblance to men that live by bread, and had only their outward shape to distinguish them from sheep. In a small room he took his seat, very imposingly attired, upon a couch. He took into his bosom our Asclepius of Pella (a very fine and large one, as I observed), wound its body round his neck, and let its tail hang down; there was enough of this not only to fill his lap, but to trail on the ground also; the patient creature's head he kept hidden in his armpit, showing the linen head on one side of his beard exactly as if it belonged to the visible body.

Picture to yourself a little chamber into which no very brilliant light was admitted, with a crowd of people from all quarters, excited, carefully

worked up, all aflutter with expectation. As they came in, they might
naturally find a miracle in the development of that little crawling thing of a
few days ago into this great, tame, human-looking serpent. Then they had
to get on at once towards the exit, being pressed forward by the new
arrivals before they could get a good look. An exit had been specially
made just opposite the entrance, for all the world like the Macedonian
device at Babylon when Alexander was ill; he was in extremis, you
remember, and the crowd round the palace were eager to take their last
look and give their last greeting. Our scoundrel's exhibition, though, is
said to have been given not once, but many times, especially for the
benefit of any wealthy new-comers.

And at this point, my dear Celsus, we may, if we will be candid,
make some allowance for these Paphlagonians and Pontics; the poor
uneducated "fat-heads" might well be taken in when they handled the
serpent—a privilege conceded to all who choose—and saw in that dim
light its head with the mouth that opened and shut. It was an occasion for
a Democritus, nay, for an Epicurus or a Metrodorus, perhaps, a man
whose intelligence was steeled against such assaults by scepticism and
insight, one who, if he could not detect the precise imposture, would at
any rate have been perfectly certain that, though this escaped him, the
whole thing was a lie and an impossibility. By degrees Bithynia, Galatia,
Thrace, came flocking in, every one who had been present doubtless
reporting that he had beheld the birth of the god, and had touched him
after his marvellous development in size and in expression. Next came
pictures and models, bronze or silver images, and the god acquired a
name. By divine command, metrically expressed, he was to be known as
Glycon. For Alexander had delivered the line:

Glycon my name, man's light, son's son to Zeus.

And now at last the object to which all this had led up, the giving
of oracular answers to all applicants, could be attained. The cue was taken
from Amphilochus in Cilicia. After the death and disappearance at Thebes
of his father Amphiaraus, Amphilochus, driven from his home, made his
way to Cilicia, and there did not at all badly by prophesying to the
Cilicians at the rate of threepence an oracle. After this precedent, Alexander proclaimed that on a stated day the god would give anwers to all
comers. Each person was to write down his wish and the object of his
curiosity, fasten the packet with thread, and seal it with wax, clay, or other
such substance. He would receive these, and enter the holy place (by this
time the temple was complete, and the scene all ready), whither the givers
should be summoned in order by a herald and an acolyte; he would learn

the god's mind upon each, and return the packets with their seals intact and the answers attached, the God being ready to give a definite answer to any question that might be put.

The trick here was one which would be seen through easily enough by a person of your intelligence (or, if I may say so without violating modesty, of my own), but which to the ordinary imbecile would have the persuasiveness of what is marvellous and incredible. He contrived various methods of undoing the seals, read the questions, answered them as seemed good, and then folded, sealed, and returned them, to the great astonishment of the recipients. And then it was, "How could he possibly know what I gave him carefully secured under a seal that defies imitation, unless he were a true god, with a god's omniscience?" Perhaps you will ask what these contrivances were; well, then—the information may be useful another time. One of them was this. He would heat a needle, melt with it the under part of the wax, lift the seal off, and after reading warm the wax once more with the needle—both that below the thread and that which formed the actual seal—and re-unite the two without difficulty. Another method employed the substance called collyrium; this is a preparation of Bruttian pitch, bitumen, pounded glass, wax, and mastich. He kneaded the whole into collyrium, heated it, placed it on the seal, previously moistened with his tongue, and so took a mould. This soon hardened; he simply opened, read, replaced the wax, and reproduced an excellent imitation of the original seal as from an engraved stone. One more I will give you. Adding some gypsum to the glue used in bookbinding he produced a sort of wax, which was applied still wet to the seal, and on being taken off solidified at once and provided a matrix harder than horn, or even iron. There are plenty of other devices for the purpose, to rehearse which would seem like airing one's knowledge. Moreover, in your excellent pamphlets against magians (most useful and instructive reading they are) you have yourself collected enough of them—many more than those I have mentioned.

So oracles and divine utterances were the order of the day, and much shrewdness he displayed, eking out mechanical ingenuity with obscurity, his answers to some being crabbed and ambiguous, and to others absolutely unintelligible. He did however distribute warning and encouragement according to his lights, and recommend treatments and diets; for he had, as I originally stated, a wide and serviceable acquaintance with drugs; he was particularly given to prescribing "cytmides," which were a salve prepared from goat's fat, the name being of his own invention. For the realization of ambitions, advancement, or successions, he took care never to assign early dates; the formula was, "All this shall come to pass when it is my will, and when my prophet Alexander shall make prayer and entreaty on your behalf."

There was a fixed charge of a drachma two obols [= 1¼ denarii] per oracle. And, my friend, do not suppose that this would not come to much; he made something like 70 or 80,000 [denarii, say, one and a half million dollars] per year; people were insatiable—would take from ten to fifteen oracles at a time. What he got he did not keep to himself, nor put it by for the future; what with accomplices, attendants, inquiry agents, oracle writers and keepers, amanuenses, seal-forgers, and interpreters, he had now a host of claimants to satisfy.

He had been sending emissaries abroad to make the shrine known in foreign lands; his prophecies, discovery of runaways, conviction of thieves and robbers, revelations of hidden treasure, cures of the sick, restoration of the dead to life—all these were to be advertised. This brought them running and crowding from all points of the compass; victims bled, gifts were presented, and the prophet and disciple came off better than the god; for had not the oracle spoken?—

> Give what ye give to my attendant priest;
> My care is not for gifts, but for my priest.

A time came when a number of sensible people began to shake off their intoxication and combine against him, chief among them the numerous Epicureans; in the cities, the imposture with all its theatrical accessories began to be seen through. It was now that he resorted to a measure of intimidation; he proclaimed that Pontus was overrun with atheists and Christians, who presumed to spread the most scandalous reports concerning him; he exhorted Pontus, as it valued the God's favour, to stone these men. Touching Epicurus, he gave the following response. An inquirer had asked how Epicurus fared in Hades, and was told:

> Of slime is his bed,
> And his fetters of lead.

The prosperity of the oracle is perhaps not so wonderful, when one learns what sensible, intelligent questions were in fashion with its votaries. Well, it was war to the knife between him and Epicurus, and no wonder. What fitter enemy for a charlatan who patronized miracles and hated truth, than the thinker who had grasped the nature of things and was in solitary possession of that truth? As for the Platonists, Stoics, Pythagoreans, they were his good friends; he had no quarrel with them. But the unmitigated Epicurus, as he used to call him, could not but be hateful to him, treating all such pretensions as absurd and puerile. Alexander consequently loathed

Amastris beyond all the cities of Pontus, knowing what a number of Lepidus's friends and others like-minded it contained. He would not give oracles to Amastrians; when he once did, to a senator's brother, he made himself ridiculous, neither hitting upon a presentable oracle for himself, nor finding a deputy equal to the occasion. The man had complained of colic, and what he meant to prescribe was pig's foot dressed with mallow. The shape it took was:

> In basin hallowed
> Be pigments mallowed.

I have mentioned that the serpent was often exhibited by request; he was not completely visible, but the tail and body were exposed, while the head was concealed under the prophet's dress. By way of impressing the people still more, he announced that he would induce the god to speak, and give his responses without an intermediary. His ample device to this end was a tube of cranes' windpipes, which he passed, with due regard to its matching, through the artificial head, and, having an assistant speaking into the end outside, whose voice issued through the linen Asclepius, thus answered questions. These oracles were called autophones, and were not vouchsafed casually to anyone, but reserved for officials, the rich, and the lavish.

It was an autophone which was given to Severian regarding the invasion of Armenia. He encouraged him with these lines:

> Armenia, Parthia, cowed by thy fierce spear,
> To Rome, and Tiber's shining waves, thou com'st,
> Thy brow with leaves and radiant gold encircled.

Then when the foolish Gaul took his advice and invaded, to the total destruction of himself and his army by Othryades, the adviser expunged that oracle from his archives and substituted the following:

> Vex not th' Armenian land; it shall not thrive;
> One in soft raiment clad shall from his bow
> Launch death, and cut thee off from life and light.

For it was one of his happy thoughts to issue prophecies after the event as antidotes to those premature utterances which had not gone right. Frequently he promised recovery to a sick man before his death, and after it was at no loss for second thoughts:

> No longer seek to arrest thy fell disease;
> Thy fate is manifest, inevitable.

Knowing the fame of Clarus, Didymus, and Mallus for soothsaying much like his own, he struck up an alliance with them, sending on many of his clients to those places. So

> Hie thee to Clarus now, and hear my sire.

And again,

> Draw near to Branchidae and counsel take.

Or

> Seek Mallus; be Amphilochus thy counsellor.

So things went within the borders of Ionia, Cilicia, Paphlagonia, and Galatia. When the fame of the oracle travelled to Italy and entered Rome, the only question was, who should be first; those who did not come in person sent messages, the powerful and respected being keenest of all. First and foremost among these was Rutilianus; he was in most respects an excellent person, and had filled many high offices in Rome; but he suffered from religious mania, holding the most extraordinary beliefs on that matter; show him a bit of stone smeared with unguents or crowned with flowers, and he would incontinently fall down and worship, and linger about it praying and asking for blessings. The report about our oracle nearly induced him to throw up the appointment he then held, and fly to Abonutichus; he actually did send messenger upon messenger. His envoys were ignorant servants, easily taken in. They came back having really seen certain things, relating others which they probably thought they had seen and heard, and yet others which they deliberately invented to curry favor with their master. So they inflamed the poor old man and drove him into confirmed madness.

He had a wide circle of influential friends, to whom he communicated the news brought by his successive messengers, not without additional touches of his own. All Rome was full of his tales; there was quite a commotion, the gentlemen of the Court being much fluttered, and at once taking measures to learn something of their own fate. The prophet gave all who came a hearty welcome, gained their goodwill by hospitality and costly gifts, and sent them off ready not merely to report his answers, but to sing the praises of the god and invent miraculous tales of the shrine and its guardian.

This triple rogue now hit upon an idea which would have been too clever for the ordinary robber. Opening and reading the packets which reached him, whenever he came upon an equivocal, compromising question, he omitted to return the packet; the sender was to be under his thumb, bound to his service by the terrifying recollection of the question he had written down. You know the sort of things that wealthy and powerful personages would be likely to ask. This blackmail brought him in a good income.

I should like to quote you one or two of the answers given to Rutilianus. He had a son by a former wife, just old enough for advanced teaching. The father asked who should be his tutor, and was told,

> Pythagoras, and the mighty battle-bard.

When the child died a few days after, the prophet was abashed, and quite unable to account for this summary confutation. However, dear good Rutilianus very soon restored the oracle's credit by discovering that this was the very thing the god had foreshown; he had not directed him to choose a living teacher; Pythagoras and Homer were long dead, and doubtless the boy was now enjoying their instructions in Hades. Small blame to Alexander if he had a taste for dealings with such specimens of humanity as this. Another of Rutilianus's questions was,

> Whose soul he had succeeded to?

and the answer:

> First thou wast Peleus' son, and next Menander;
> Then thine own self; next, a sunbeam shalt be;
> And nine score annual rounds thy life shall measure.

At seventy, he died of melancholy, not waiting for the God to pay in full. That was an autophone too. Another time Rutilianus consulted the oracle on the choice of a wife. The answer was express:

> Wed Alexander's daughter and Selene's.

He had long ago spread the report that the daughter he had had was by Selene: she had once seen him asleep, and fallen in love, as is her way with handsome sleepers. The sensible Rutilianus lost no time, but sent for the maiden at once, celebrated the nuptials, a sexagenarian bridegroom, and lived with her, propitiating his divine mother-in-law with whole hecatombs, and reckoning himself now one of the heavenly company.

His finger once in the Italian pie, Alexander devoted himself to getting further. Sacred envoys were sent all over the Roman Empire, warning the various cities to be on their guard against pestilence and conflagrations, with the prophet's offers of security against them. One oracle in particular, an autophone again, he distributed broadcast at a time of pestilence. It was a single line:

Phoebus long-tressed the plague-cloud shall dispel.

This was everywhere to be seen written up on doors as a prophylactic. Its effect was generally disappointing; for it somehow happened that the protected houses were just the ones to be desolated. Not that I would suggest for a moment that the line was their destruction; but, accidentally no doubt, it did so fall out. Possibly common people put too much confidence in the verse, and lived carelessly without troubling to help the oracle against its foe; were there not the words fighting their battle, and long-tressed Phoebus discharging his arrows at the pestilence?

In Rome itself he established an intelligence bureau well manned with his accomplices. They sent him people's characters, forecasts of their questions, and hints of their ambitions, so that he had his answers ready before the messengers reached him. It was with his eye on this Italian propaganda, too, that he took a further step. This was the institution of mysteries, with hierophants and torch-bearers complete. The ceremonies occupied three successive days. On the first, proclamation was made on the Athenian model to this effect: "If there be any atheist or Christian or Epicurean here spying upon our rites, let him depart in haste; and let all such as have faith in the god be initiated and all blessing attend them." He led the litany with, "Christians, avaunt!" and the crowd responded, "Epicureans, avaunt!" Then was presented the child-bed of Leto and the birth of Apollo, the bridal of Coronis, Asclepius born. The second day, the epiphany and nativity of the god Glycon. On the third came the wedding of Podalirius and Alexander's mother; this was called Torch-day, and torches were used. The finale was the loves of Selene and Alexander, and the birth of Rutilianus's wife. The torch-bearer and hierophant was Endymion-Alexander. He was discovered lying asleep; to him from heaven, represented by the ceiling, enter as Selene one Rutilia, a great beauty, and wife of one of the imperial procurators. She and Alexander were lovers off the stage too, and the wretched husband had to look on at their public kissing and embracing; if there had not been a good supply of torches, things might possibly have gone even further. Shortly after, he reappeared amidst a profound hush, attired as hierophant; in a loud voice he called, "Hail, Glycon!" whereto the Eumolpidae and Ceryces of Paphlagonia, with their clod-hopping shoes and their garlic breath, made sonorous response, "Hail, Alexander!"

The torch ceremony with its ritual skippings often enabled him to bestow a glimpse of his thigh, which was thus discovered to be of gold; it was presumably enveloped in cloth of gold, which glittered in the lamp-light. This gave rise to a debate between two wiseacres, whether the golden thigh meant that he had inherited Pythagoras's soul, or merely that

their two souls were alike; the question was referred to Alexander himself
and King Glycon relieved their perplexity with an oracle:

> Waxes and wanes Pythagoras' soul: the seer's
> Is from the mind of Zeus an emanation.
> His father sent him, virtuous men to aid,
> And with his bolt one day shall call him home.

I will now give you a conversation between Glycon and one
Sacerdos of Tius; the intelligence of the latter you may gauge from his
questions. I read it inscribed in golden letters in Sacerdos's house at Tius.
"Tell me, lord Glycon," said he, "who are you?" "The new Asclepius."
"Another, different from the former one? Is that the meaning?" "That it is
not lawful for you to learn." "And how many years will you sojourn and
prophesy among us?" "A thousand and three." "And after that, whither will
you go?" "To Bactria; for the barbarians too must be blessed with my
presence." "The other oracles, at Didymus and Clarus and Delphi, have
they still the spirit of your grandsire Apollo, or are the answers that now
come from them forgeries?" "That, too, desire not to know; it is not
lawful." "What shall I be after this life?" "A camel; then a horse; then a
wiseman, no less a prophet than Alexander." Such was the conversation.
There was added to it an oracle in verse, inspired by the fact that Sacerdos
was an associate of Lepidus:

> Shun Lepidus; an evil fate awaits him.

As I have said, Alexander was much afraid of Epicurus, and the
solvent action of his logic on imposture. On one occasion, indeed, an
Epicurean got himself into great trouble daring to expose him before a
great gathering. He came up and addressed him in a loud voice. "Alexander, it was you who induced So-and-so the Paphlagonian to bring his
slaves before the governor of Galatia, charged with the murder of his son
who was being educated in Alexandria. Well, the young man is alive, and
has come back, to find that the slaves had been cast to the beasts by your
machinations." What had happened was this. The lad had sailed up the
Nile, gone on to the Red Sea port, found a vessel starting for India, and
had been persuaded to make the voyage. He being long overdue, the
unfortunate slaves supposed that he had either perished in the Nile or
fallen a victim to some pirates who infested it at that time; so they came
home to report his disappearance. Then followed the oracle, the sentence,
and finally the young man's return with the story of his absence. All this
the Epicurean recounted. Alexander was much annoyed by the exposure,
and could not stomach so well deserved an affront; he directed the
company to stone the man, on pain of being involved in his impiety and

called Epicureans. However, when they set to work, a distinguished Pontic called Demostratus, who was staying there, rescued him by interposing his own body; the man had the narrowest possible escape from being stoned to death—as he richly deserved to be; what business had he to be the only sane man in a crowd of madmen, and needlessly make himself the butt of Paphlagonian infatuation?

This was a special case; but it was the practice for the names of applicants to be read out the day before answers were given; the herald asked whether each was to receive his oracle; and sometime the reply came from within, To perdition! One so repulsed could get shelter, fire or water, from no man; he must be driven from land to land as a blasphemer, an atheist, and—lowest depth of all—an Epicurean. In this connection Alexander once made himself supremely ridiculous. Coming across Epicurus's Accepted Maxims, the most admirable of his books, as you know, with its terse presentment of his wise conclusions, he brought it into the middle of the market-place, there burned it on a fig-wood fire for the sins of its author, and cast its ashes into the sea. He issued an oracle on the occasion:

The dotard's maxims to the flames be given.

The fellow had no conception of the blessings conferred by that book upon its readers, of the peace, tranquillity, and independence of mind it produces, of the protection it gives against terrors, phantoms, and marvels, vain hopes and inordinate desires, of the judgement and candour that it fosters, or of its true purging of the spirit, not with torches or squills and such rubbish, but with right reason, truth, and frankness.

Perhaps the greatest example of our rogue's audacity is what I now come to. Having easy access to palace and court by Rutilianus's influence, he sent an oracle just at the crisis of the German war, when M. Aurelius was on the point of engaging the Marcomanni and Quadi [167 c.e.]. The oracle required that two lions should be flung alive into the Danube, with quantities of sacred herbs and magnificent sacrifices. I had better give the words:

To rolling Ister, swoln with Heaven's rain,
Of Cybelean thralls, those mountain beasts,
Fling ye a pair; therewith all flowers and herbs
Of savor sweet that Indian air doth breed.
Hence victory, and fame, and lovely peace.

These directions were precisely followed; the lions swam across to the enemy's bank, where they were clubbed to death by the barbarians, who took them for dogs or a new kind of wolves; and our forces immediately met after with a severe defeat, losing some twenty thousand men in one engagement. This was followed by the Aquileian incident, in the course of which that city was nearly lost. In view of these results, Alexander warmed up that stale Delphian defence of the Croesus oracle: the god had foretold a victory, forsooth, but had not stated whether Romans or barbarians should have it.

The constant increase in the number of visitors, the inadequacy of accommodation in the city, and the difficulty of finding provisions for consultants, led to his introducing what he called night oracles. He received the packets, slept upon them, in his own phrase, and gave answers which the god was supposed to send him in dreams. These were generally not lucid, but ambiguous and confused, especially when he came to packets sealed with exceptional care. He did not risk tampering with these, but wrote down any words that came into his head, the results obtained corresponding well enough to his conception of the oracular. There were regular interpreters in attendance, who made considerable sums out of the recipients by expounding and unriddling these oracles. This office contributed to his revenue, the interpreters paying him a talent [6000 denarii] each.

Sometimes he stirred the wonder of the silly by answers to persons who had neither brought nor sent questions, and in fact did not exist. Here is a specimen:

> Who is't, thou askst, that with Calligenia
> All secretly defiles thy nuptial bed?
> The slave Protogenes, whom most thou trustest.
> Him thou enjoyedst: he thy wife enjoys—

> The fit return for that thine outrage done.
> And know that baleful drugs for thee are brew
> Lest thou see or hear their evil deeds.
> Close by the wall, at thy bed's head, make search.
> The maid Calypso to their plot is privy.

The names and circumstantial details might stagger a Democritus, till a moment's thought showed him the despicable trick.

He often gave answers in Syriac or Celtic to barbarians who questioned him in their own tongue, though he had difficulty in finding compatriots of theirs in the city. In these cases there was a long interval between application and response, during which the packet might be securely opened at leisure, and somebody found capable of translating the question. The following is an answer given to the Scythian:

> Morphi ebargulis for night
> Chnenchicrank shall leave the light.

Another oracle to someone who neither came nor existed was in prose. "Return the way thou camest," it ran; "for he that sent thee hath this day been slain by his neighbour Diocles, with aid of the robbers Magnus, Celer, and Bubalus, who are taken in chains."

I must give you one or two of the answers that fell to my share. I asked whether Alexander was bald, and having sealed it publicly with great care, got a night oracle in reply:

Sabardalachu malach Attis was not he.

Another time I did up the same question—What was Homer's birth-place?—in two packets given under different names. My servant misled him by saying, when asked what he came for, a cure for lung trouble; so the answer to the one packet was:

Cytmide and foam of steed the liniment give.

As for the other packet, he got the information that the sender was inquiring whether the land or the sea route to Italy was preferable. So he answered, without much reference to Homer:

Fare not by sea; land-travel meets thy need.

I laid a good many traps of this kind for him; here is another. I asked only one question, but wrote outside the packet in the usual form, So-and-so's eight Queries, giving a fictitious name and sending eight drachmas. Satisfied with the payment of the money and the inscription on the packet, he gave me eight answers to my one question. This was, When will Alexander's imposture be detected? The answers concerned nothing in heaven or earth, but were all silly and meaningless together. He afterwards found out about this, and also that I had tried to dissuade Rutilianus both from the marriage and from putting any confidence in the oracle; so he naturally conceived a violent dislike for me. When Rutilianus once put a question to him about me, the answer was:

Night-haunts and foul debauch are all his joy.

It is true his dislike was justified. On a certain occasion I was passing through Abonutichus, with a spearman and a pikeman whom my friend the governor of Cappadocia had lent me as an escort on my way to the sea. Ascertaining that I was the Lucian he knew of, he sent me a very polite and hospitable invitation. I found him with a numerous company; by good luck I had brought my escort. He gave me his hand to kiss according to his usual custom. I took hold of it as if to kiss, but instead bestowed upon it a sound bite which must have come near disabling it. The company, who were already offended at my calling him Alexander instead of Prophet, were inclined to throttle and beat me for sacrilege. But he endured the pain like a man, checked their violence, and assured them that he would easily tame me, and illustrate Glycon's greatness in converting his bitterest foes to friends. He then dismissed them all, and argued the matter with me: he was perfectly aware of my advice to Rutilianus; why had I treated him so, when I might have been preferred by him to great influence in the quarter? By this time I had realized my dangerous position, and was only too glad to welcome these advances; I presently went my way in all friendship with him. The rapid change wrought in me greatly impressed the observers.

When I intended to sail, he sent me many parting gifts, and offered to find us (Xenophon and me, that is; I had sent my father and family on to Amastris) a ship and crew—which offer I accepted in all confidence. When the passage was half over, I observed the master in tears arguing with his men, which made me very uneasy. It turned out that Alexander's orders were to seize and fling us overboard; in that case his war with me would have been lightly won. But the crew were prevailed upon by the master's tears to do us no harm. "I am sixty years old, as you can see," he said to me; "I have lived an honest blameless life so far, and I should not like at my time of life, with a wife and children too, to stain my hands with blood." And with that preface he informed us what we were there for, and what Alexander had told him to do. He landed us at Aegiali, of Homeric fame, and thence sailed home. Some Bosphoran envoys happened to be passing, on their way to Bithynia with the annual tribute from their king Eupator. They listened kindly to my account of our dangerous situation, I was taken on board, and reached Amastris safely after my narrow escape.

From that time it was war between Alexander and me, and I left no stone unturned to get my revenge. Even before his plot I had hated him, revolted by his abominable practices, and I now busied myself with the attempt to expose him; I found plenty of allies, especially in the circle of Timocrates the Heracleot philosopher. But Avitus, the then governor of Bithynia and Pontus, restrained me, I may almost say with prayers and entreaties. He could not possibly spoil his relations with Rutilianus, he said, by punishing the man, even if he could get clear evidence against him. Thus arrested in my course, I did not persist in what must have been, considering the disposition of the judge, a fruitless prosecution.

Among instances of Alexander's presumption, high place must be given to his petition to the emperor: the name of Abonutichus was to be changed to Ionopolis; and a new coin was to be struck, with a representation on the obverse of Glycon, and on the reverse, Alexander bearing garlands proper to his paternal grandfather Asclepius, and the famous scimitar of his maternal ancestor Perseus. He had stated in an oracle that he was destined to live to a hundred and fifty, and then die by a thunderbolt; he had in fact, before he reached seventy, an end very sad for a son of Podalirius, his leg mortifying from foot to groin and being eaten of worms; it then proved that he was bald, as he was forced by pain to let the doctors make cooling applications to his head, which they could not do without removing his wig. So ended Alexander's heroics; such was the catastrophe of his tragedy; one would like to find a special providence in it, though doubtless chance must have the credit. The funeral celebration was to be worthy of his life, taking the form of a contest—for possession of the oracle. The most prominent of the impostors, his accomplices, referred it to Rutilianus's arbitration which of them should be selected to succeed to the prophetic office and wear the hierophantic oracular garland. Among these was numbered the grey-haired physician Paetus, dishonoring equally his grey hairs and his profession. But Steward-of-the-Games Rutilianus sent them about their business ungarlanded, and continued the defunct in possession of his holy office.

My object, dear friend, in making this small selection from a great mass of material has been twofold. First, I was willing to oblige a friend and comrade who is for me the pattern of wisdom, sincerity, good humour, justice, tranquillity, and geniality. But secondly I was still more concerned (a preference which you will be very far from resenting) to strike a blow for Epicurus, that great man whose holiness and divinity of nature were not shams, who alone had imparted true insight into the good, and who brought deliverance to all that consorted with him. Yet I think casual readers too may find my essay not unserviceable, since it is not only destructive, but, for men of sense, constructive also.

11

HOLY MEN AND
WOMEN

11.1 Philostratus on Apollonius of Tyana

A number of non-Christian men, and at least one woman (Sosipatra, described by Eunapius among the "sophists" of the fourth century), circulated in the empire and gained the reputation of being capable of working miracles, through partaking of a divine nature or of some god's special favor. The character and appearance expected of such persons has been seen in the priests who advised Lucius (in Apuleius's novel) and in Alexander as he appeared first to the "fat-heads" of Cappadocia. Among such real figures, the best known was the holy man from Tyana (southwestern Turkey), Apollonius. He was in fact the subject of more than one biography, intended to arouse belief and admiration—quite unlike Lucian's account of Alexander. (Be it noted, however, that Lucian claims Apollonius as Alexander's spiritual grand-father.) A little after 217 C.E., Philostratus wrote one of these accounts, a mixture of fact and fiction and sermonizing, in which the hero is often presented as a religious teacher and, through his special wisdom, a miracle-worker. The dramatic date is ca. 59 C.E.

Source: Philostratus, *Vita Apollonii* 4.17–18, trans. F. C. Conybeare, LCL.

So much for the conversation on board; but having sailed into the Piraeus at the season of the mysteries, when the Athenians keep the most crowded of Hellenic festivals, he went post haste up from the ship into the city; but as he went forward, he fell in with quite a number of students of philosophy on their way down to Phalerum. Some of them were stripped and enjoying the heat, for in autumn the sun is hot upon the Athenians; and others were studying books, and some were rehearsing their speeches, and others were disputing. But not one passed him by, for they all guessed that it was Apollonius, and they turned and thronged around him and welcomed him warmly; and ten youths in a body met him, and holding up their hands towards the Acropolis they cried: "By Athene yonder, we were on the point of going down to the Piraeus there to take a ship to Ionia in order to visit you." And he welcomed them and said how much he congratulated them on their study of philosophy.

It was then the day of the Epidaurian festival at which it is still customary for the Athenians to hold the initiation at a second sacrifice after both proclamation and victims have been offered; and this custom was instituted in honour of Asclepius, because they still initiated him when on one occasion he arrived from Epidaurus too late for the mysteries. Now most people neglected the initiation and hung around Apollonius, and thought more of doing that than being perfected in their religion before they went home; but Apollonius said that he would join them later on, and urged them to attend at once to the rites of religion, for that he himself would be initiated. But the hierophant was not disposed to admit him to the rites, for he said that he would never initiate a wizard and charlatan, nor open the Eleusinian rite to a man who dabbled in impure rites. Thereupon Apollonius, fully equal to the occasion, said: "You have not yet mentioned the chief of my offence, which is that knowing, as I do, more about the initiatory rite than you do yourself, I have nevertheless come for initiation to you, as if you were wiser than I am." The bystanders applauded these words, and deemed that he had answered with vigour and like himself; and thereupon the hierophant, since he saw that his exclusion of Apollonius was not by any means popular with the crowd, changed his tone and said: "Be thou initiated, for thou seemest to be some wise man that has come here." But Apollonius replied: "I will be initiated at another time, and it is so and so," mentioning a name, "who will initiate me." Herein he showed his gift of prevision, for he glanced at the hierophant who succeeded the one he addressed, and presided over the temple for years later.

At ibid. 8.7.7f., Apollonius toward the end of his life must defend himself against charges of being an agitator and wizard, before the emperor.

[My accuser] declares that men regard me as a god, and that those who have been thunderstruck and rendered stark-mad by myself proclaim this tenet in public. And yet before accusing me there are things which they should have informed us of, to wit, by what discourses, or by what miracles of word or deed I induced men to pray to me; for I never talked among Hellenes of the goal and origin of my soul's past and future transformations, although I knew full well what they were; nor did I ever disseminate such opinions about myself; nor came forth with presages and oracular strains, which are the harvest of candidates for divine honours. Nor do I know a single city in which a decree was passed that the citizens should assemble and sacrifice in honor of Apollonius. And yet I have been much esteemed in the several cities which asked for my aid, whatever the objects were for which they asked it, and they were such as these: that their sick might be healed of their diseases, that both their initiations and their sacrifices might be rendered more holy, that insolence and pride might be extirpated, and the laws strengthened. And whereas the only reward which I obtained in all this was that men were made much better than they were before, they were all so many boons bestowed upon yourself by me. For as cow-herds, if they get the cows into good order earn the gratitude of their owners, and as shepherds fatten the sheep for the owner's profit, and as bee-keepers remove diseases from the hive, so that the owner may not lose his swarm, so also I myself, I think, by correcting the defects of their politics, improved the cities for your benefit. Consequently if they did regard me as a god, the deception brought profit to yourself; for I am sure they were the more ready to listen to me, because they feared to do that which a god disapproved of. But in fact they entertained no such illusion, though they were aware that there is between man and god a certain kinship which enables him alone of the animal creation to recognize the gods, and to speculate both about his own nature and the manners in which it participates in the divine substance. Accordingly man declares that his very form resembles god, as it is interpreted by sculptors and painters; and he is persuaded that his virtues come to him from god, and that those who are endowed with such virtues are near to god and divine. . . . [Now he refers to his averting a plague from the city of Ephesus:] . . . Let me now, my prince, take the accusation which concerns Ephesus, since the salvation of that city was gained; and let the Egyptian be my judge, according as it best suits his accusation. For this is the sort of thing the accusation is. Let us suppose that among the Scythians or Celts, who live along the rivers Ister and Rhine, a city has been founded every whit as important as Ephesus in Ionia. Here you have a sally-port of barbarians, who refuse to be subject to yourself; let us then suppose that it was about to be destroyed by a pestilence, and that Apollonius found a remedy and averted it. I imagine that a wise man would be able to defend himself even against such a charge as that, unless indeed the sovereign desires to get rid of his adversaries, not by use of arms, but by plague; for I pray, my prince, that no city may ever be wholly wiped out, either to please yourself or to please me, nor may I ever behold in temples a disease to which those who lie sick should succumb in them. But granted that we are not interested in the affairs of barbarians, and need not restore them to health, since they are our bitter enemies, and not at peace with our race; yet who should desire to deprive Ephesus of her salvation, a city which took the basis of its race from the purest Attic source, and which grew in size beyond all other cities of Ionia and Lydia, and stretched herself out to the sea outgrowing the land on which she is built, and is filled with studious people, both philosophers and rhetoricians, thanks to whom the city owes her strength, not to her cavalry, but to the tens of thousands of her inhabitants in whom she encourages wisdom? And do you think that there is any wise man who would decline to do his best in behalf of such a city, when he reflects that Democritus once liberated the people of Abdera from pestilence, and when he bears in mind the story of Sophocles of Athens, who is said to have charmed the winds when they were blowing unseasonably, and who has heard how Empedocles stayed a cloud in its course when it would have burst over the heads of the people of Acragas?

The accuser here interrupts me—you hear him yourself do so, my prince, and he remarks that I am not accused of having brought about the salvation of the Ephesians, but for having foretold that the plague would fall upon them; for this, he says, transcends the power of wisdom and is miraculous, so that I could never have reached such a pitch of truth if I were not a wizard and an unspeakable wretch. What then will Socrates say of the lore which he declared he learned from his demonic genius? Or what would Thales and Anaxagoras, both Ionians, say, of whom one foretold a plenteous crop of olives, and the other not a few meteorological disturbances? That they foretold these things by dint of being wizards? Why, is it not a fact that they were brought before the law-courts upon other charges, but that no one ever heard among their accusations that of their being wizards, because they had the gift of foreknowledge? For that would have been thought ridiculous, and it would not have been a plausible charge to bring against men of wisdom even in Thessaly, where the women had a bad reputation for drawing the moon down to earth.

How then did I get my sense of the coming disaster at Ephesus? You have listened to the statement made even by my accuser, that instead of living like other people, I keep to a light diet of my own, and prefer it to the luxury of others, and I began by saying so myself. This diet, my king, guards my senses in a kind of indescribable ether or clear air, and forbids them to contract any foul or turbid matter, and allows me to discern, as in the sheen of a looking-glass, everything that is happening or is to be. For the sage will not wait for the earth to send up its exhalations, or for the atmosphere to be corrupted, in case the evil is shed from above; but he will notice these things when they are impending, not so soon indeed as the gods, but sooner than the many. For the gods perceive what lies in the future, and men what is going on before them, and wise men what is approaching. But I would have you, my prince, ask of me in private about the causes of pestilence; for they are secrets of a wisdom which should not be divulged to the many. Was it then my mode of living alone which develops such a subtlety and keenness of perception as can apprehend the most important and wonderful phenomena? You can ascertain the point in question, not only from other considerations, but in particular from what took place in Ephesus in connection with that plague. For the genius of the pestilence—and it took the form of a poor old man— I both detected, and having detected took it captive: and I did not so much stay the disease as pluck it out. And who the god was to whom I had offered my prayers is shown in the statue which I set up in Ephesus to commemorate the event; and it is a temple of the Hercules who averts disease, for I chose him to help me, because he is the wise and courageous god, who once purged of the plague the city of Elis, by washing away with the river-tide the foul exhalations which the land sent up under the tyranny of Augeas.

Who then do you think, my prince, being ambitious to be considered a wizard, would dedicate his personal achievement to a god? And whom would he get to admire his art, if he gave the credit of the miracle to god? And who would offer his prayers to Hercules, if he were a wizard? For in fact these wretches attribute such feats to the trenches they dig and to the gods of the under-earth, among whom we must not class Heracles, for he is a pure deity and kindly to men. I offered my prayer to him once on a time also in the Peloponnese, for there was an apparition of a lamia [an evil spirit in the shape of a woman] there too; and it infested the neighbourhood of Corinth and devoured good-looking young men. And Hercules lent me his aid in my contest with her, without asking of me any wonderful gifts—nothing more than honey-cake and frankincense, and the chance to do a salutary turn to mankind.

11.2 Porphyry on Plotinus

Plotinus (born ca. 205, probably in Egypt, where he studied) settled in Rome in 244 and there became established as a lecturer in philosophy, till his death in 270. He is described today (E. R. Dodds, *OCD*) as "the most powerful philosophic mind between Aristotle and Aquinas or Descartes." His student from 263 to 268 was Porphyry, who later (at the end of his own life, ca. 302) wrote a Life of Plotinus. Here are some passages presenting Plotinus as a mystic as well as a thinker.

Source: Porphyry, *Life of Plotinus*, 7ff., 10f., 16, and 22f., trans. Kenneth Sylvan Guthrie, in *Plotinos: Complete Works* 1:14–34 (London: G. Bell, 1918).

7. Zethus was one of the disciples of Plotinos. He was a native of Arabia, and had married the daughter of Theodosius, friend of Ammonius. He was a physician, and much loved by Plotinos, who sought to lead him to withdraw from public affairs, for which he had considerable aptitude; and with which he occupied himself with zeal. Plotinos lived in very close relations with him; he even retired to the country estate of Zethus, distant six miles from Minturnae [in southern Italy].

Castricius, surnamed Firmus, had once owned this estate. Nobody, in our times, loved virtue more than Firmus. He held Plotinos in the deepest veneration. He rendered Amelius the same services that might have been rendered by a good servant, he displayed for me the attentions natural towards a brother. Nevertheless this man, who was so attached to Plotinos, remained engaged in public affairs.

Several senators, also, came to listen to Plotinos. Marcellus, Orontius, Sabinillus and Rogatianus applied themselves, under Plotinos, to the study of philosophy. The latter, who also was a member of the senate, had so detached himself from the affairs of life, that he had abandoned all his possessions, dismissed all his attendants, and renounced all his dignities. On being appointed praetor, at the moment of being inaugurated, while the lictors were already waiting for him, he refused to sally forth, and carry out any of the functions of this dignity. He even failed to dwell in his own house (to avoid needless pomp); he visited his friends, boarding and sleeping there; he took food only every other day; and by this dieting, after having been afflicted with gout to the point of having to be carried around in a litter, he recovered his strength, and stretched out his hands as easily as any artisan, though formerly his hands had been incapacitated. Plotinos was very partial to him; he used to praise him publicly, and pointed him out as a model to all who desired to become philosophers.

Another disciple of Plotinos was Serapion of Alexandria. At first he had been a rhetorician, and only later applied himself to philosophy. Nevertheless he never was able to cure himself of fondness for riches, or usury. Me also, Porphyry, a native of Tyre, Plotinos admitted to the circle of his intimate friends, and he charged me to give the final revision to his works. . . .

8. Once Plotinos had written something, he could neither retouch nor even re-read what he had done, because his weak eyesight made any reading very painful. His penmanship was poor. He did not separate words, and his spelling was defective; he was chiefly occupied with ideas. Until his death he continuously persisted in this habit, which was for us all a subject of surprise. When he had finished composing something in his head, and when he then wrote what he had meditated on, it seemed as if he copied a book. Neither in conversation nor discussion did he allow

himself to be distracted from the purpose of his thoughts, so that he was able at the same time to attend to the needs of conversation, while pursuing the meditation of the subject which busied him. When the person who had been talking with him went away, he did not re-read what he had written before the interview, which, as has been mentioned above, was to save his eyesight; he could, later on, take up the thread of his composition as if the conversation had been no obstacle to his attention. He therefore was able simultaneously to live with others and with himself. He never seemed to need recuperation from his interior attention, which hardly ceased during his slumbers, which however were troubled both by the insufficiency of food, for sometimes he did not even eat bread, and by this continuous concentration of his mind. . . .

10. Among those who pretended to be philosophers, there was a certain man named Olympius. He lived in Alexandria, and for some time had been a disciple of Ammonius. As he desired to succeed better than Plotinos, he treated Plotinos with scorn, and developed sufficient personal animosity against Plotinos to try to bewitch him by magical operations. However, Olympius noticed that his enterprise was really turning against himself, and he acknowledged to his friends that the soul of Plotinos must be very powerful, since it was able to throw back upon his enemies the evil practices directed against him. The first time that Olympius attempted to harm him, Plotinos having noticed it said, "At this very moment the body of Olympius is undergoing convulsions, and is contracting like a purse." As Olympius several times felt himself undergoing the very ills he was trying to get Plotinos to undergo, he finally ceased his practices.

Plotinos showed a natural superiority to other men. An Egyptian priest, visiting Rome, was introduced to him by a mutual friend. Having decided to show examples of his mystic attainments, he begged Plotinos to come and witness the apparition of a familiar spirit who obeyed him on being evoked. The evocation was to occur in a chapel of Isis, as the Egyptian claimed that he had not been able to discover any other place pure enough in Rome. He therefore evoked Plotinos's guardian spirit. But instead of the spirit appeared a divinity of an order superior to that of guardians, which event led the Egyptian to say to Plotinos, "You are indeed fortunate, O Plotinos, that your guardian spirit is a divinity, instead of a being of a lower order." The divinity that appeared could not be questioned or seen for as long a period as they would have liked, as a friend who was watching over the sacrificed birds choked them, either out of jealousy, or fear.

As Plotinos's guardian spirit was a divinity, Plotinos kept the eyes of his own spirit directed on that divine guardian. That was the motive of his writing his book that bears the title *Of the Guardian Allotted to Us*. In it he tries to explain the differences between the various spirits that watch over mankind. Amelius, who was very scrupulous in his sacrifices, and who carefully celebrated the Festivals of the New Moon [as Numenius used to do?] (on the Calends of each month), one day besought Plotinos to come and take part in a function of that kind. Plotinos, however, answered him, "It is the business of those divinities to come and visit me, and not mine to attend on them." We could not understand why he should make an utterance that revealed so much pride, but we dared not question the matter.

11. So perfectly did he understand the character of men, and their methods of thought, that he could discover stolen objects, and foresaw what those who resided with him should some day become. A magnificent necklace had been stolen from Chione, an estimable widow who resided with him and the children [as matron?]. All the slaves were summoned, and Plotinos examined them all. Then, pointing out one of them, he said, "This is the culprit." He was put to the torture. For a long while, he denied the deed; but later acknowledged it, and returned the necklace. Plotinos used to predict what each of the young people who were in touch with him was to become. He insisted that Polemo would be disposed to amorous relations, and would not live long; which also occurred. As to me, he noticed that I was meditating suicide. He came and sought me, in his house, where I was staying. He told me that this project indicated an unsound mind, and that it was the result of a melancholy disposition. He advised me to travel. I obeyed him. I went to Sicily, to study under Probus, a celebrated philosopher, who dwelt in Lilybaeum. I was thus cured of the desire to die; but I was deprived of the happiness of residing with Plotinos until his death. . . .

16. At that time were many Christians, among whom were prominent sectarians who had given up the ancient philosophy [of Plato and Pythagoras], such as Adelphius and Aquilinus. They esteemed and possessed the greater part of the works of Alexander of Libya, of Philocomus, of Demostrates and of Lydus. They advertised the Revelations of Zoroaster, of Zostrian, of Nicotheus, Allogenes, of Mesus, and of several others. These sectarians deceived a great number of people, and even deceived themselves, insisting that Plato had not exhausted the depths of intelligible "being" or essence. That is why Plotinos refuted them at length in his lectures, and wrote the book that we have named "Against the Gnostics." The rest [of their books] he left me to investigate. Amelius wrote as much as forty books to refute the work of Zostrian; and as to me, I demonstrated by numerous proofs that this alleged Zoroastrian book was apocryphal, and had only recently been written by those of that ilk who wished to make people believe that their doctrines had been taught by Zoroaster. . . .

22. But when I have a long oracle of Apollo to quote, why should I delay over a letter of Longinus's, or in the words of the proverb, "Why should I dally near the oak-trees, or the rock?" If the testimony of the wise is to be adduced, who is wiser than Apollo, a deity who said himself, "I know the number of grains of sand, and the extent of the ocean; I understand the dust, and I hear him who does not speak!" This was the divinity who had said that Socrates was the wisest of men; and on being consulted by Amelius to discover what had become of the soul of Plotinos, said:

> "Let me sing an immortal hymn to my dear friend!
> Drawing my golden bow, I will elicit melodious sounds from my lyre.
> I also invoke the symphonic voice of the choir of Muses,
> Whose harmonious power raises exultant paeans,
> As they once sang in chorus in praise of Achilles,
> A Homeric song in divine inspiration.
> Sacred choir of Muses, let us together celebrate this man,
> For long-haired Apollo is among you!
> "O Deity, who formerly wert a man, but now approachest
> The divine host of guardian spirits, delivered from the narrowing bonds of necessity. . . .
> Persistently following the straightening path of the purified soul,
> Where the splendor of the divinity surrounds you, the home of justice,
> Far from contamination, in the holy sanctuary of initiation,
> When in the past you struggled to escape the bitter waves,
> When blood-stained life eddied around you with repulsive currents,
> In the midst of waters dazed by frightening tumult,
> Even then the divinities often showed you your end;
> And often, when your spirit was about to stray from the right path,
> The immortals beckoned you back to the real end; the eternal path,
> Enlightening your eyes with radiant beams in the midst of gloomy darkness. . . .

23. This oracle [pieced out of numerous quotations] says [in some now lost lines, perhaps] that Plotinos was kindly, affable, indulgent, gentle, such as, indeed, we knew him in personal intercourse. It also mentions that this philosopher slept little, that his soul was pure, ever aspiring to the divinity that he loved whole-heartedly, and that he did his utmost to

liberate himself [from terrestrial domination] "to escape the bitter waves of this cruel life."

That is how this divine man, who by his thoughts often aspired to the first [principle], to the divinity superior [to intelligence], climbing the degrees indicated by Plato [in his Banquet], beheld the vision of the formless divinity, which is not merely an idea, being founded in intelligence and the whole intelligible world. I, myself, had the blessed privilege of approaching this divinity, uniting myself to him, when I was about sixty-eight years of age.

That is how "the goal [that Plotinos sought to achieve] seemed to him located near him." Indeed, his goal, his purpose, his end was to approach the supreme divinity, and to unite himself with the divinity. While I dwelt with him, he had four times the bliss of reaching that goal, not merely potentially, but by a real and unspeakable experience. The oracle adds that the divinities frequently restored Plotinos to the right path when he strayed from it, "enlightening his eyes by radiant splendour." That is why it may truthfully be said that Plotinos composed his works while in contemplation of the divinities, and enjoying that vision. "Thanks to this sight that your 'vigilant' eyes had of both interior and exterior things, you have," in the words of the oracle, "gazed at many beauties that would hardly be granted to many of those who study philosophy." Indeed, the contemplation of men may be superior to human contemplation; but, compared to divine knowledge, if it be of any value whatever, it, nevertheless, could not penetrate the depths reached by the glances of the divinities.

Till here the oracle had limited itself to indicating what Plotinos had accomplished while enclosed in the vesture of the body. It then proceeds to say that he arrived at the assembly of the divinities where dwell friendship, delightful desire, joy, and love communing with the divinity, where the sons of god, Minos, Rhadamanthus, and Aeacus are established as the judges of souls. Plotinos joined them, not to be judged, but to enjoy their intimacy, as did the higher divinities. There indeed dwell Plato, Pythagoras, and the other sages who formed the choir of immortal love. Reunited with their families, the blessed angels spend their life "in continued festivals and joys," enjoying the perpetual beatitude granted them by divine goodness.

12

MISSIONIZING
(NON-CHRISTIAN)

12.1 Aelius Aristides on Philosophical Quacks

The purposeful spreading of information about some set of religious beliefs, in order to win adherents, is not often attested in non-Christian contexts. One description of a type of person engaged in such activities, given here in all its oratorical fullness, is only a digression from an oration on a different subject entirely, and in it the orator never makes clear just whom he has in mind—not, as some scholars in the past have thought, Christians, but, rather, people or groups defined by adherence to a simple or low-brow philosophical persuasion, and engaged in soap-box advertising of it. There are more frequent mentions of itinerant speakers lumped together as "Cynics" who circulated in the cities in the same manner, often attacked as agitators and vulgarizers; but their teachings, more moral than religious, do not survive.

Source: Aelius Aristides, *To Plato, on the Four,* Oration 46, ed. Wilhelm Dindorf (Leipzig, 1829; reprint, Hildesheim: Olms, 1964), 2:399–406, original translation.

But to know their untrustworthiness and greed, there is no need to entrust anything to them, for they take whatever they can; for they apply the term "sharing" to defrauding, "philosophizing" to envy, and "despising wealth" to plain lack (400:). Although they profess philanthropy, they have never done anyone a service, but insult those they deal with. And they will not look at people they meet up with, but go off to foreign parts seeking rich folk, like the Phrygians for the gathering of olives, and scent them immediately as they approach and take them and lead them away, and promise to bestow virtue on them. And others who do address them, they would not even address them back politely, but the bakers and millers of the rich and those in other sorts of posts, they welcome them from afar before they can even properly be seen, as if for this purpose they had risen from bed. They hang about in antechambers, consort with door-keepers more than with their masters, correcting their fawning by their impudence, having this one sign (401:), that they do not seek the company of people so as to oblige them, namely, that they wear everyone out by their disgusting importunity. From the moment one catches sight of them, they will sooner ask for something belonging to someone else than others can ask for something of their own. For those are the people who think impudence is liberty, but arousing hatred is frank speech, and to take is to offer a kindness. They are wise enough not to ask for money, but understand how to get their money's worth, and if by chance someone sends them something too little, they take their stand on their principles, but if it's a fine purse, then (402:) "Perseus has conquered the Gorgon." And their excuse is wisdom itself: their children and wives. O you most unfortunate member of the household! So it's on their account that you engage in trade? Why not allow your wife to take the wherewithal for an easier life? But to me they seem to have defined generosity in a new way, not for them to give much, but for them to take a lot; and they show it not by giving great gifts but by consenting to receive them. And, I hear, some make this a rule, to accept what's given, but as they take, to offer insult— though it would be wrong to place them either among flatterers or honest folk. For they deceive like flatterers while being abusive like great men, thus being guilty of two evils the most extreme and most opposed to each other, servility and presumption, in these manners very much resembling the impious of Palestine. Now for them the sign of impiety (403:) is this, that they do not recognize the Powers that Be, and in a way they have removed themselves from Greeks, indeed from all their superiors, in all respects making less noise than their own shadows, yet when there is need of abuse, you could not equal them with the bronze Dodonan, no, by Zeus, nor with the gnats that buzz in darkness. For in cooperating in any matter of need, they are of all men the most useless, but sheer wonders at breaking into a house, or making a disturbance (404:), or setting the inhabitants against each other, or claiming management over any affair. They have never once said, or invented, or done anything profitable, or added to a festival, or honored the gods, or advised a city, or comforted the sorrowing, or settled strife, or improved the youth (or anyone else), or observed propriety in their speeches; but, cowering down in their holes, there they invent their marvels, "covering over their speech with shadow," as Sophocles puts it, harvesting the asphodel, plaiting rope from sand, unbending who knows what loom; for however they progress in wisdom, to the same degree they lose ground through their grand conceit in speaking ill of eloquence, exceeding even slaves who often curse their masters under their breath—especially slaves who most need a whipping. So some Satyr on the stage curses Heracles, and then bows down when he appears. It seems to me very natural that they should speak ill of everyone, for they certainly have an abundance of material (406:) and even if they are not mentioning any specific person, they speak evilly what they do speak—so they can be generous with what they have. And they have the impudence to refer to the best of Greeks, as if by right. But if anyone separated out the lies and ill manners, that would mean the depriving them of their chief refuge in life. Then, too, they award themselves that most noble of titles, Philosophy, the way people usurp a theater seat, and it is necessary for others straightway to acquiesce.

12.2   A Pagan Missionary in Gaul, from an Inscription

A missionary for unidentified ethical beliefs (religious or philosophical, and pagan) is recorded in a versified epitaph from Lyon, from the second half of the second century.

Source: Jean-François Reynaud, et al., *Journal des savants* (1975): 58–59, original translation.

If you would like to know what man lies here, there is no secret: the inscription here tells you all his doings. By name Euteknios, and Ioulianos his fore-name, from Laodicea the admired ornament of Syria. He was of distinguished descent on the father's side, no less his mother's distinction—a good man and a just, beloved by all in return. When he spoke among the Gallic folk, persuasion flowed from his tongue. He circulated among various tribes and was acquainted with many peoples. He practised virtue of soul among them. He was continually entrusting himself to the waves and seas, bearing to the Gauls and western lands all the gifts that god commanded to be born of the abundant eastern earth; and on this account he loved him, mortal though he was. He bent the three Gallic tribes to the [. . .]

12.3   Philo Judaeus on Converts to Judaism

Jewish proselytizing and acceptance of converts, attested indirectly in many ways, are discussed by Philo in a work of the earlier first century, recommending proper attitudes for a Jew toward outsiders.

Source: Philo, *On the Virtues* 108, trans F. H. Colson, LCL.

If any of them [the Gentiles] should wish to pass over into the Jewish community, they must not be spurned with an unconditional refusal as children of enemies, but be so far favored that the third generation is invited to the congregation and made partakers in the divine revelations, to which also the native born, whose lineage is beyond reproach, are rightfully admitted.

A second passage from the same author, going into further detail.

Source: Philo, *The Special Laws* 1.52–53, trans. F. H. Colson, LCL.

While giving equal rank to all in-comers with all the privileges which he gives to the native-born, he exhorts the old nobility to honor them not only with marks of respect but with special friendship and with more than ordinary good will. And surely there is good reason for this: they have left, he says, their country, their kinsfolk and their friends for the sake of virtue and religion. Let them not be denied another citizenship or other ties of family and friendship, and let them find places of shelter standing ready for refugees to the camp of piety. For the most effectual love-charm, the chain which binds indissolubly the goodwill which makes us one, is to honor the one God. Yet he counsels them that they must not, presuming on the equal privilege and equal rank which He grants them because they have denounced the vain imaginings of their fathers and ancestors, deal in idle talk or revile with an unbridled tongue the gods whom others acknowledge, lest they on their part be moved to utter profane words against Him Who truly IS. For they know not the difference, and since their falsehood has been taught to them as truth from childhood and has grown up with them, they will go astray.

13

PERCEPTIONS OF JUDAISM

13.1 Josephus on Friction between Jews and Pagans

In trying to understand the historical aspect, which is the dynamic and changing aspect, of religious life in the empire, it is obviously important to assess the acceptability of beliefs as they were perceived by non-believers. None was likely to attract converts if it was seen to be too bizarre, too much at odds with one's traditional values, espoused chiefly by one's enemies, or inaccessible by reason of its expense or complexity.

Judaism certainly was a dynamic faith in the period illustrated by this collection of documents: it won over people both close to its center and in remote corners of the empire. But this was against the grain, so to speak: against widespread antipathy. In the background lay centuries of ill-feeling between Greeks and Jews of the eastern provinces, above all in the cities. As to the Romans, their first serious involvement in this hostility resulted from their competing among themselves for Jewish support during the civil wars of Caesar's day and then of Augustus's (more correctly, Octavian's). On that basis, the Jews could successfully appeal to the Romans for intervention in return for an offer of friendship. But a tolerated, or rather a specially favored, status assured by Roman law for the Jews only overlay a bad press among the Romans along lines long traditional among eastern Gentiles. Such negative reporting is evident in the passages that follow, drawing first on the most famous historian of the Jews, Flavius Josephus of the later first century.

Source: Josephus, *Antiquities of the Jews* 16.2.3–4, 16.6.1–2, trans. William Whiston (London, 1737).

When Agrippa [Augustus' principal supporter and delegate] . . . was in Ionia [that is, the coastal region that includes Ephesus and Smyrna], a great crowd of Jews who lived in the cities came to him [to complain] that they were not allowed their own laws but were forced to litigate, through the misconduct of their judges, on their holy days, . . . and were forced into the army and into other public positions that required them to spend their sacred money. . . . Our adversaries unjustly deprive us of our privileges, violently seize the money which is offered to God and called sacred, and do this openly in a sacrilegious way; they lay taxes on us and bring us into court on holy days, and collect similar debts in the same fashion, not because contracts demand it or for any special profit but simply to insult our religion, of which they are as conscious as we are. . . . Now the cities ill-treated the Jews in Asia and all those too of the same people who lived in Libya around Cyrene. . . . The Greeks treated them outrageously, to the point of making off with their sacred money and affronting them on other given occasions. [To their ambassadors, Caesar = Augustus affirmed the right of] the Jews . . . to make use of their own customs according to the laws of their forefathers. . . . Their sacred money should not be touched, but be sent to Jerusalem, they should not be made to appear before the judge on the Sabbath nor on the day of their preparation for it after sunset, and if anyone is caught stealing their holy books or their sacred money, whether it be out of the synagogue or public school, he shall be judged guilty of sacrilege.

13.2   A Letter of Claudius Regarding Jews and Pagans in Alexandria

> Evidence for the feelings that underlay gentile (pagan) appraisal of Jews and Judaism is mostly pre-125 C.E. and hostile. Anti-Semitism among the Jews' neighbors in cities of the eastern provinces appears both in acts of malicious mischief and in characterizations of Jewish beliefs. The hot-point of contact was for centuries Alexandria, containing a very large Jewish minority in its huge population. The emperor Claudius in 41 C.E. answered a letter from the authorities of that city on several important aspects of its internal affairs and problems, here prefaced by a public notice from the governor regarding the new imperial cult.

> **Source:** Pap. Lon. 1912, trans. A. S. Hunt and E. C. Edgar, *Select Papyri*, LCL.

Proclamation by Lucius Aemilius Rectus. Seeing that all the populace, owing to its numbers, was unable to be present at the reading of the most sacred and most beneficent letter to the city, I have deemed it necessary to display the letter publicly in order that reading it one by one you may admire the majesty of our god Caesar and feel gratitude for his goodwill towards the city. Year 2 of Tiberius Claudius Caesar Augustus

Germanicus Imperator, the 14th of Neus Sebastus. Tiberius Claudius Caesar Augustus Germanicus Imperator, Pontifex Maximus, holder of the Tribunician Power, consul designate, to the city of Alexandria, greeting. Tiberius Claudius Barbillus, Apollonius son of Artemidorus, Chaeremon son of Leonidas, Marcus Julius Asclepiades, Gaius Julius Dionysius, Tiberius Claudius Phanias, Pasion son of Potamon, Dionysus son of Sabbion, Tiberius Claudius Archibius, Apollonius son of Ariston, Gaius Julius Apollonius, Hermaiscus son of Apollonius, your ambassadors, having delivered to me the decree, discoursed at length concerning the city, directing my attention to your goodwill towards us, which from long ago, you may be sure, had been stored up to your advantage in my memory; for you are by nature reverent towards the Augusti, as I know from many proofs, and in particular have taken a warm interest in my house, warmly reciprocated, of which fact (to mention the last instance, passing over the others) the supreme witness is my brother Germanicus addressing you in words more clearly stamped as his own. Wherefore I gladly accepted the honours given to me by you, though I have no weakness for such things. And first I permit you to keep my birthday as a *dies Augustus* as you have yourselves proposed, and I agree to the erection in several places of the statues of myself and my family; for I see that you were anxious to establish on every side memorials of your reverence for my house. Of the two golden statues the one made to represent the Pax Augusta Claudiana, as my most honoured Barbillus suggested and entreated when I wished to refuse for fear of being thought too offensive, shall be erected at Rome, and the other according to your request shall be carried in procession on name-days in your city; and it shall be accompanied by a throne, adorned with whatever trappings you choose. It would perhaps be foolish, while accepting such great honors, to refuse the institution of a Claudian tribe and the establishment of groves after the manner of Egypt; wherefore I grant you these requests as well, and if you wish you may also erect the equestrian statues given by Vitrasius Pollio my procurator. As for the erection of those four-horse chariots which you wish to set up to me at the entrances into the country, I consent to let one be placed at Taposiris, the Libyan town of that name, another at Pharos in Alexandria, and a third at Pelusium in Egypt. But I deprecate the appointment of a high-priest to me and the building of temples, for I do not wish to be offensive to my contemporaries, and my opinion is that temples and such forms of honor have by all ages been granted as a prerogative to the gods alone.

> Claudius then goes on to discuss questions of municipal citizenship, choice of priests in imperial cult, and rotation of magistrates, ending

with a long lesson on mutual toleration which he delivers to both Jews and Gentiles.

Concerning the requests which you have been anxious to obtain from me, I decide as follows. All those who have become ephebes up to the time of my principate I confirm and maintain in possession of the Alexandrian citizenship with all the privileges and indulgences enjoyed by the city, excepting such as by beguiling you have contrived to become ephebes though born of servile mothers; and it is equally my will that all the other favors shall be confirmed which were granted to you by former princes and kings and praefects, as the deified Augustus also confirmed them. It is my will that the *neocori* of the temple of the deified Augustus in Alexandria shall be chosen by lot in the same way as those of the said deified Augustus in Canopus are chosen by lot. With regard to the civic magistracies being made triennial your proposal seems to me to be very good; for through fear of being called to account for any abuse of power your magistrates will behave with greater circumspection during their term of office. Concerning the senate, what your custom may have been under the ancient kings I have no means of saying, but that you had no senate under the former Augusti you are well aware. As this is the first broaching of a novel project, whose utility to the city and to my government is not evident, I have written to Aemilius Rectus to hold an inquiry and inform me whether in the first place it is right that a senate should be constituted and, if it should be right to create one, in what manner this is to be done.

As for the question which party was responsible for the riots and feud (or rather, if the truth must be told, the war) with the Jews, although in confrontation with their opponents your ambassadors, and particularly Dionysus son of Theon, contended with great zeal, nevertheless I was unwilling to make a strict inquiry, though guarding within me a store of immutable indignation against whichever party renews the conflict; and I tell you once for all that unless you put a stop to this ruinous and obstinate enmity against each other, I shall be driven to show what a benevolent prince can be when turned to righteous indignation. Wherefore once again I conjure you that on the one hand the Alexandrians show themselves forbearing and kindly towards the Jews, who for many years have dwelt in the same city, and dishonor none of the rites observed by them in the worship of their god, but allow them to observe their customs as in the time of the deified Augustus, which customs I also, after hearing both sides, have sanctioned; and on the other hand I explicitly order the Jews not to agitate for more privileges than they formerly possessed, and not in the future to send out a separate embassy as if they lived in a separate city, a thing unprecedented, and not to force their way into gymnasiarchic or cosmetic games, while enjoying their own privileges and sharing great abundance of advantages in a city not their own, and not bring in or admit Jews who come down the river from Syria or Egypt, a proceeding which will compel me to conceive serious suspicions; otherwise I will by all means take vengeance on them as fomenters of what is a general plague infecting the whole world. If desisting from these courses you consent to live with mutual forbearance and kindliness, I on my side will exercise a solicitude of very long standing for the city, as one which is bound to us by traditional friendship. I bear witness to my friend Barbillus of the solicitude which he has always shown for you in my presence and of the extreme zeal with which he has now advocated your cause, and likewise to my friend Tiberius Claudius Archibius. Farewell.

13.3 Josephus on the Outbreak of the Jewish War

Josephus was not only a great historian of his people but a prominent patriot and leader in the great rebellion (until he changed sides). Here he recounts how that rebellion was aroused, in the spring of 66 C.E., by typical provocations.

Source: Josephus, *Jewish War* 2.284f., trans. H. St. J. Thackeray, LCL.

The ostensible pretext for war was out of proportion to the magnitude of the disasters to which it led. The Jews in Caesarea had a synagogue adjoining a plot of ground owned by a Greek of that city; this site they had frequently endeavoured to purchase, offering a price far exceeding its true value. The proprietor, disdaining their solicitations, by way of insult further proceeded to build upon the site and erect workshops, leaving the Jews only a narrow and extremely awkward passage. Thereupon, some of the hot-headed youths proceeded to set upon the builders and attempted to interrupt operations. Florus [the governor] having put a stop to their violence, the Jewish notables, with John the tax-collector, having no other expedient, offered Florus eight talents of silver [48,000 denarii = $1 million] to procure the cessation of the work. Florus, with his eye only on the money, promised them every assistance, but, having secured his pay, at once quitted Caesarea for Sebaste, leaving a free field to sedition, as though he had sold the Jews a licence to fight the matter out.

On the following day, which was the sabbath, when the Jews assembled at the synagogue, they found that one of the Caesarean mischief-makers had placed beside the entrance a pot, turned bottom upwards, upon which he was sacrificing birds. This spectacle of what they considered an outrage upon their laws and a desecration of the spot enraged the Jews beyond endurance. The steady-going and peaceable members of the congregation were in favor of immediate recourse to the authorities; but the factious folk and the passionate youth were burning for a fight. The Caesarean party, on their side, stood prepared for action, for they had, by a concerted plan, set the man on to the mock sacrifice; and so they soon came to blows. Jucundus, the cavalry commander commissioned to intervene, came up, removed the pot and endeavoured to quell the riot, but was unable to cope with the violence of the Caesareans. The Jews, thereupon, snatched up their copy of the Law and withdrew to Narbata, a Jewish district sixty furlongs distant from Caesarea. Their leading men, twelve in number, with John at their head, waited upon Florus at Sebaste, bitterly complained of these proceedings and besought his assistance, delicately reminding him of the matter of the eight talents. Florus actually had them arrested and put in irons on the charge of having carried off the copy of the Law from Caesarea.

This news aroused indignation at Jerusalem. . . .

13.4   Josephus Defends Judaism against Slander

Josephus's short work *Against Apion* is the last piece of Jewish apologetic. It was also known to Porphyry under the title *Against the Greeks*, for Apion is only one of its targets; but Apion had indeed been a prominent Alexandrine anti-Semitic political leader and propagandist. Here are two excerpts.

Source: Josephus, *Against Apion* 2.7, 11–13, trans. William Whiston, (London, 1737).

7. However, I cannot but admire those other authors who furnished this man with such his materials; I mean Posidonius and Apollonius [the son of] Molo, who while they accuse us for not worshipping the same gods whom others worship, they think themselves not guilty of impiety when they tell lies of us, and frame absurd and reproachful stories about our temple: whereas it is a most shameful thing for freemen to forge lies on any occasion, and much more so to forge them about our temple, which was so famous over all the world, and was preserved so sacred by us; for Apion hath the impudence to pretend "That the Jews placed an ass's head in their holy place," and he affirms, "That this was discovered when Antiochus Epiphanes spoiled our temple, and found that ass's head there made of gold, and worth a great deal of money." To this my first

answer shall be this, That had there been any such thing among us, an Egyptian ought by no means to have thrown it in our teeth, since an ass is not a more contemptible animal than . . . and goats, and other such creatures, which among them are gods. But besides this answer, I say further, how comes it about that Apion does not understand this to be no other than a palpable lie, and to be confuted by the thing itself as utterly incredible? For we Jews are always governed by the same laws, in which we constantly persevere: and although many misfortunes have befallen our city, as the like have befallen others, and although Theos [Epiphanes, the second-century Syrian monarch] and Pompey the Great, and Licinius Crassus, and last of all Titus Caesar, have conquered us in war, and gotten possession of our temple, yet have they none of them found any such thing there, nor indeed any thing but what was agreeable to the strictest piety; although what they found we are not at liberty to reveal to other nations. But for Antiochus [Epiphanes], he had no just cause for that ravage in our temple that he made; he only came to it when he wanted money, without declaring himself our enemy, and attacked us while we were his associates and his friends; nor did he find any thing there that was ridiculous. This is attested by many worthy writers: Polybius of Megalopolis, Strabo of Cappadocia, Nicolaus of Damascus, Timagenes, Castor the chronologer, and Apollodorus, who all say that it was out of Antiochus' want of money, that he broke his league with the Jews, and despoiled their temple when it was full of gold and silver. Apion ought to have had a regard to these facts, unless he had himself either an ass's heart or a dog's impudence; of such a dog I mean as they worship: for he had no other external reason for the lies he tells of us. As for us Jews, we ascribe no honor or power to asses, as do the Egyptians to crocodiles and asps, when they esteem such as are seized upon by the former, or bitten by the latter, to be happy persons, and persons worthy of God. Asses are the same with us which they are with other wise men, viz. creatures that bear the burdens that we lay upon them; but if they come to our threshing-floors, and eat our corn, or do not perform what we impose upon them, we beat them with a great many stripes, because it is their business to minister to us in our husbandry affairs. But this Apion of ours was either perfectly unskilful in the composition of such fallacious discourses, or however, when he began [somewhat better,] he was not able to persevere in what he had undertaken, since he hath no manner of success in those reproaches he casts upon us.

11. Apion also tells a false story, when he mentions an oath of ours, as if we "swore by God, the maker of the heaven, and earth, and sea, to bear no good-will to any foreigner, and particularly to none of the Greeks."

Now this liar ought to have said directly, That "we would bear no good-will to any foreigner, and particularly to none of the Egyptians." For then his story about the oath would have squared with the rest of his original forgeries, in case our forefathers had been driven away by their kinsmen, the Egyptians, not on account of any wickedness they had been guilty of, but on account of the calamities they were under; for as to the Grecians, we are rather remote from them in place, than different from them in our institutions, insomuch that we have no enmity with them, or any jealousy of them. On the contrary, it hath so happened, that many of them have come over to our laws, and some of them have continued in their observation, although others of them had not courage enough to persevere, and so departed from them again; or did any body ever hear this oath sworn by us; Apion, it seems, was the only person that heard it, for he indeed was the first composer of it.

12. However, Apion deserves to be admired for his great prudence, as to what I am going to say, which is this, that "There is a plain mark among us, that we neither have just laws, nor worship God as we ought to do, because we are not governors, but are rather in subjection to Gentiles, sometimes to one nation, and sometimes to another; and that our city hath been liable to several calamities, while their city (Alexandria) hath been of old time an imperial city, and not used to be in subjection to the Romans." But now this man had better leave off his bragging, for everybody but himself would think, that Apion said what he hath said against himself; for there are very few nations that have the good fortune to continue many generations in the principality, but still the mutations in human affairs have put them into subjection by others; and most nations have been often subdued, and brought into subjection by others. Now for the Egyptians, perhaps they are the only nation that have had this extraordinary privilege, to have never served any of those monarchs who subdued Asia and Europe, and this on account, as they pretend, that the gods fled into their country, and saved themselves by being changed into the shapes of wild beasts! Whereas these Egyptians are the very people who appear to have never, in all the past ages, had one day of freedom—no, not so much as from their own lords. For I will not reproach them with relating the manner how the Persians used them, and this not once only, but many times, when they laid their cities waste, demolished their temples and cut the throats of those animals whom they esteemed to be gods; for it is not reasonable to imitate the clownish ignorance of Apion, who hath no regard to the misfortunes of the Athenians, or of the Lacedemonians, the latter of whom were styled by all men the most courageous, and the former the most religious of the Grecians. I say nothing of such kings

as have been famous for piety, particularly of one of them whose name was Croesus, nor what calamities he met in his life: I say nothing of the citadel of Athens, of the temple at Ephesus, of that at Delphi, nor of ten thousand others which have been burnt down, while nobody cast reproaches on those that were the sufferers, but on those that were the actors therein. But now we have met with Apion, an accuser of our nation, though one that still forgets the miseries of his own people the Egyptians; but it is that Sesostris, who was once so celebrated a king of Egypt, that hath blinded him: now we will not brag of our kings David and Solomon, though they conquered many nations: accordingly, we will let them alone. However, Apion is ignorant of what every body knows, that the Egyptians were servants to the Persians, and afterwards to the Macedonians, when they were lords of Asia, and were no better than slaves, while we have enjoyed liberty formerly; nay, more than that, have had the dominion of the cities that lie around us, and this nearly for a hundred and twenty years together, until Pompeius Magnus. And when all the kings every where were conquered by the Romans, our ancestors were the only people who continued to be esteemed their confederates and friends, on account of their fidelity to them.

13.5 Tacitus's Idea of the Jews

Tacitus, distinguished senator and still more distinguished historian, in the first decade of the second century introduces the Jews into his *Histories* (5.3ff.) with a sketch of their supposed origins. He knows of several theories or stories, and one most common.

Source: Tacitus, *Histories*, trans. A. J. Church and W. J. Brodribb (1888; reprint, New York: Modern Library, 1942).

Most writers, however, agree in stating that once a disease, which horribly disfigured the body, broke out over Egypt; that king Bocchoris, seeking remedy, consulted the oracle of Hammon, and was bidden to cleanse his realm, and to convey into some foreign land this race detested by the gods. The people, who had been collected after diligent search, finding themselves left in a desert, sat for the most part in a stupor of grief, till one of the exiles, Moses by name, warned them not to look for any relief from god or man, forsaken as they were of both, but to trust to themselves, taking for their heaven-sent leader that man who should first help them to be quit of their present misery. They agreed, and in utter ignorance began to advance at random. Nothing, however, distressed them so much as the scarcity of water, and they had sunk ready to perish in all directions over the plain, when a herd of wild asses was seen to retire from their pasture to a rock shaded by trees. Moses followed them, and, guided by the appearance of a grassy spot, discovered an abundant spring of water. This furnished relief. After a continuous journey for six days, on the seventh they possessed themselves of a country, from which they expelled the inhabitants, and in which they founded a city and temple.

Moses, wishing to secure for the future his authority over the nation, gave them a novel form of worship, opposed to all that is practised by other men. Things sacred with us, with them have no sanctity, while they allow what with us is forbidden. In their holy place they have consecrated an image of the animal by whose guidance they found deliverance from their long and thirsty wanderings. They slay the ram, seemingly in derision of Hammon, and they sacrifice the ox, because the Egyptians worship it as Apis. They abstain from swine's flesh, in consideration of what they suffered when they were infected by the leprosy to which this animal is liable. By their frequent fasts they still bear witness to the long hunger of former days, and the Jewish bread, made without leaven, is retained as a memorial of their hurried seizure of corn. We are told that the rest of the seventh day was adopted, because this day brought with it a termination of their toils; after a while the charm of indolence beguiled them into giving up the seventh year also to inaction. But others say that it is an observance in honor of Saturn, either from the primitive elements of their faith having been transmitted from the Idäi, who are said to have shared the flight of that god, and to have founded the race, or from the circumstance that of the seven stars which rule the destinies of men Saturn moves in the highest orbit and with the mightiest power, and that many of the heavenly bodies complete their revolutions and courses in multiples of seven.

This worship, however introduced, is upheld by its antiquity; all their other customs owe their strength to their very badness. The most degraded out of other races, scorning their national beliefs, brought to them their contributions and presents. This augmented the wealth of the Jews, as did the fact, that among themselves they are inflexibly honest and ever ready to shew compassion, though they regard the rest of mankind with all the hatred of enemies. They sit apart at meals, they sleep apart, and though, as a nation, they are singularly prone to lust, they abstain from intercourse with foreign women; among themselves nothing is unlawful. Circumcision was adopted by them as a mark of difference from other men. Those who come over to their religion adopt the practice, and have this lesson first instilled into them, to despise all gods, to disown their country, and set at nought parents, children, and brethren. Still they provide for the increase in their numbers. It is a crime among them to kill any newly-born infant. They hold that the souls of all who perish in battle or by the hands of the executioner are immortal. Hence a passion for propagating their race and a contempt for death. They are wont to bury rather than to burn their dead, following in this the Egyptian custom; they bestow the same care on the dead, and they hold the same belief about the lower world. Quite different is their faith about things divine. The Egyptians worship many animals and images of monstrous form; the Jews have purely mental conceptions of deity, as one in essence. They call those profane who make representations of god in human shape out of perishable materials. They believe that being to be supreme and eternal, neither capable of representation, nor of decay. They therefore do not allow any images to stand in their cities, much less in their temples. This flattery is not paid to their kings, nor this honor to our emperors. From the fact, however, that their priests used to chant to the music of flutes and cymbals, and to wear garlands of ivy, and that a golden vine was found in the temple, some have thought that they worshipped Father Liber, the conqueror of the East, though their institutions do not by any means harmonize with the theory; for Liber established a festive and cheerful worship, while the Jewish religion is tasteless and mean.

13.6   Jews Are Ridiculed in the Theater, from Rabbi Abbahu

> Rabbi Abbahu in the 290s describes the casual conversations and contrived comedy in the theaters that attack Jews.

> **Source:** Rabbi Abbahu, *Lamentations, Prologue* 14, trans. L. I. Levine, in *Christianity, Judaism, and Other Greco-Roman Cults: Studies for Morton Smith at Sixty*, ed. Jacob Neusner (Leiden: Brill, 1975), 4:60.

(Gentiles) sit in theaters and circuses. "And I am the song of the drunkards." After they have sat eating and drinking and become intoxicated, they sit and talk of me, scoffing at me saying, "We have no need to cut carobs [food for the poor] as Jews do!" They ask one another, "How long do you wish to live?" To which they reply, "As long as the shirt of a Jew which is worn on the Sabbath!" They then bring a camel into their theaters, put their shirts on it, and ask one another, "Why is it in mourning?" They reply, "The Jews observe the law of the Sabbatical year and they have no vegetables; so they eat this camel's thorns, and that is why it is mourning!" Next they bring a mime with a shaven head into the theater, and ask one another, "Why is his head shaven?" They reply, "The Jews observe the Sabbath and whatever they earn during the week they eat on the Sabbath. Since they have no wood to cook with, they break their bedsteads and use them as fuel; consequently they sleep on the ground and get covered with dust, and anoint themselves with oil, which is very expensive for that reason!" (After a while they can no longer afford the oil and have to shave their heads.)

14

PERCEPTIONS OF CHRISTIANITY

14.1 Pliny's Correspondence with Trajan about Christians in Pontus

Mention or comment about Christians by pagans before 300 C.E. is rare. The first of any length and importance outside of the New Testament is found in the official correspondence of Pliny the Younger, special High Commissioner to the provinces Bithynia and Pontus (modern northern Turkey). In the course of reporting regularly to the emperor Trajan, he raises the following problem, in ca. 111, from his headquarters in Pontus (Amastris).

Source: Pliny, *Letters* 10.98–99, trans. J. B. Firth (London: W. Scott, 1900), amended.

(Pliny to Trajan:) It is my custom, Sire, to refer to you in all cases where I do not feel sure, for who can better direct my doubts or inform my ignorance? I have never been present at any legal examination of the Christians, and I do not know, therefore, what are the usual penalties passed upon them, or the limits of those penalties, or how searching an inquiry should be made. I have hesitated a great deal in considering whether any distinctions should be drawn according to the ages of the accused; whether the weak should be punished as severely as the more robust; whether if they renounce their faith they should be pardoned, or whether the man who has once been a Christian should gain nothing by recanting; whether the name itself, even though otherwise innocent of crime, should be punished, or only the crimes that gather round it.

In the meantime, this is the plan which I have adopted in the case of those Christians who have been brought before me. I ask them whether they are Christians; if they say yes, then I repeat the question a second and a third time, warning them of the penalties it entails, and if they still persist, I order them to be taken away to prison. For I do not doubt, whatever the character of the crime may be which they confess, their pertinacity and inflexible obstinacy certainly ought to be punished. There were others who showed similar mad folly whom I reserved to be sent to Rome, as they were Roman citizens. Subsequently, as is usually the way, the very fact of my taking up this question led to a great increase of accusations, and a variety of cases were brought before me. A pamphlet was issued anonymously, containing the names of a number of people. Those who denied that they were or had been Christians and called upon the gods in the usual formula, reciting the words after me, those who offered incense and wine before your image, which I had given orders to be brought forward for this purpose, together with the statues of the deities—all such I considered should be discharged, especially as they cursed the name of Christ, which, it is said, those who are really Christians cannot be induced to do. Others, whose names were given me by an informer, first said that they were Christians and afterwards denied it, declaring that they had been but were so no longer, some of them having recanted many years before, and more than one so long as twenty years back. They all worshipped your image and the statues of the deities, and cursed the name of Christ. But they declared that the sum of their guilt or their error only amounted to this, that on a stated day they had been accustomed to meet before daybreak and to recite a hymn among themselves to Christ, as though he were a god, and that so far from binding themselves by oath to commit any crime, their oath was to abstain from theft, robbery, adultery, and from breach of faith, and not to deny trust money placed in their keeping when called upon to deliver it.

When this ceremony was completed, it had been their custom to depart and meet again to take food, but it was of no special character and quite harmless, and they had ceased this practice after the edict in which, in accordance with your orders, I had forbidden all secret societies. I thought it the more necessary, therefore, to find out what truth there was in these statements by submitting two women, who were called deaconesses, to the torture, but I found nothing but a debased superstition carried to great lengths. So I postponed my examination, and immediately consulted you. The matter seems to me to be worthy of your consideration, especially as there are so many people involved in the danger. Many persons of all ages, and of both sexes alike, are being brought into peril of their lives by their accusers, and the process will go on. For the contagion of this superstition has spread not only through the free cities, but into the villages and the rural districts, and yet it seems to me that it can be checked and set right. It is beyond doubt that the temples, which have been almost deserted, are beginning again to be thronged with worshippers, that the sacred rites which for a long time have been allowed to lapse are now being renewed, and that the food for the sacrificial victims is once more finding a sale, whereas, up to recently, a buyer was hardly to be found. From this it is easy to infer that vast numbers of people might be reclaimed, if only they were given an opportunity of repentance.

(Trajan to Pliny): You have adopted the proper course, my dear Pliny, in examining into the cases of those who have been denounced to you as Christians, for no hard and fast rule can be laid down to meet a question of such wide extent. The Christians are not to be hunted out; if they are brought before you and the offence is proved, they are to be punished, but with this reservation—that if any one denies that he is a Christian and makes it clear that he is not, by offering prayers to our deities, then he is to be pardoned because of his recantation, however suspicious his past conduct may have been. But pamphlets published anonymously must not carry any weight whatever, no matter what the charge may be, for they are not only a precedent of the very worst type, but they are not in consonance with the spirit of our age.

14.2   Lucian's Account of Peregrinus Proteus, and His Flirtation with Christianity

> The essayist Lucian, previously encountered in other selections, not long after 165 C.E. describes, for comic effect, the career of Peregrinus Proteus. Although he presents his subject as a sort of itinerant religious con man, Proteus was actually worshiped after his death as a "hero" in the Greek sense (i.e., divinized)—perhaps by no means a fake.

> **Source:** Lucian, *Vita Peregrini,* trans. Brooke Foss Westcott, in *The Two Empires, the Church and the World* (London: Macmillan, 1909), pp. 88–89.

He made himself master of the marvellous wisdom of the Christians by intercourse with their priests and scribes. . . . He soon showed them that they were all children, being himself prophet, master of the revels (*thiasarches*), chief of their assembly, everything in his single person. Some of their books he interpreted and explained, many he actually composed, and they held him to be a god, and followed him as a lawgiver, and adopted him as their patron; [I don't indeed vouch for this, but] at any rate they still worship that great one, the man who was crucified in Palestine, because he introduced this new religion into life [so that the statement is at least quite credible]. After a time Proteus was apprehended on this charge [of Christianity] and thrown into prison—a circumstance which gained him no small reputation to help him in later life and gratify his passion for imposture and glory. The Christians were distressed at his imprisonment, and set every power in motion in their endeavours to rescue him. When this proved impossible, they showed him every other attention, not as a matter of form, but in earnest. As soon as it was dawn you might see old women lingering about the prison, widows and orphans; and those in authority among them went so far as to sleep with him in the prison, bribing the keepers. Afterwards luxurious meals were carried in, and their holy discourses were repeated, and our excellent friend Peregrinus—for he was still known by this name—was called by them a new Socrates. Nor was this all; men came even from the cities in Asia charged by the Christians with a general mission to help and defend and console him. And it is marvellous what speed they show whenever any public misfortune of this kind happens; for, in a word, they spare nothing. So Peregrinus, as you may suppose, received considerable sums from them on the ground of his imprisonment, and found in this no small source of income.

For the poor wretches have convinced themselves that they will be absolutely immortal and live for ever, and in consideration of this they despise death and commonly offer themselves of their own accord [for martyrdom]; and besides this, their first lawgiver persuaded them that they are all brethren, when once they have transgressed and denied the gods of Greece, and pay worship to their crucified sophist, and live according to his laws. They despise, therefore, all possessions equally, and hold them as common, having received such principle without any exact faith. If, then, any cunning charlatan comes forward to join them, who knows how to use his opportunity, he shortly gains great wealth and makes himself merry at their simplicity. However, Peregrinus was discharged by the governor of Syria for the time being, who was a man fond of philosophy, for he perceived his desperate character, and knew that he would welcome death for the prospect of glory, and so dismissed him as being unworthy even of punishment.

14.3 Marcus Aurelius Mentions Christians

Writing about the same time (ca. 170), the emperor Marcus Aurelius, in his spiritual/philosophical diary or jottings, alludes to Christians—perhaps. The passage, by various good arguments, has been suspected of interpolation (insertion of the words "like the Christians").

Source: Marcus Aurelius, *Meditations* 11.3, trans. A.S.L. Farquharson (Oxford: Clarendon Press, 1944).

How admirable is the soul which is ready and resolved, if it must this moment be released from the body, to be either extinguished or scattered or to persist. This resolve, too, must arise from a specific decision, not out of sheer opposition like the Christians, but after reflection and with dignity, and so as to convince others, without histrionic display.

14.4   Galen Mentions Christians

Galen, the Greek immigrant to Rome and family physician to Marcus Aurelius and his son, the emperor Commodus, several times alludes to the Christians—very briefly, however, and just in passing. (These passages, like the above, have been challenged as not Galen's own words; but the challenge is not quite so serious.)

Source: Richard Walzer, *Galen on Jews and Christians* (London: Oxford University Press, 1949), passim, corrected thanks to D. Gutas, Yale.

One might more easily teach novelties to the followers of Moses and Christ than to the physicians and philosophers who cling fast to their schools.

. . . in order that one should not at the very beginning, as if one had come into the school of Moses and Christ, hear talk of undemonstrated laws, and that where it is least appropriate.

. . . If I had in mind people who taught their pupils in the same way as the followers of Moses and Christ teach theirs—for they order them to accept everything on faith—I should not have given you a definition.

. . . Most people are unable to follow any demonstrative argument consecutively; hence they need parables, and benefit from them—and he [Galen—adds the editor who preserved this extract from a lost work] understands by parables tales of rewards and punishments in a future life—just as now we see the people called Christians drawing their faith from parables (and miracles) and yet sometimes acting in the same way as those who philosophize. For their contempt of death (and of its sequel) is patent to us every day, and likewise their restraint in cohabitation. For they include not only men but also women who refrain from cohabitating all through their lives; and they also number individuals who have reached such a point in their control regarding their daily conduct and in their intense desire for rectitude that they have in fact become not inferior to those who are true philosophers.

14.5   A Theatrical Spoof Becomes a Conversion, from the *Acts of St. Genesius*

The *Acts of Saint Genesius* records a moment in Rome in the late third century when Genesius, the city's imperial theater director, decided on a bit of topical commentary.

Source: T. Ruinart, *Acta Primorum Martyrum Sincera et Selecta* (Amsterdam, 1713), pp. 270–71, original translation.

One day when he [Genesius] wanted to put on before the emperor Diocletian a play on the mysteries of the Christian liturgy, inasmuch as he [Diocletian] was a most savage tyrant, to whom the Christians were hateful, and when, with the emperor and the whole populace looking on on this account, appearing in the middle of the theater as a sick man he asked that he be baptized, he produced a skit with the following words: "Alas for me, I'm feeling heavy. I'd like to be made lighter." They [the other actors] answered, "How can we make you lighter if you're heavy? Do you think we're carpenters and can send you to the planing-mill?" These words raised a laugh among the people. Genesius continued, "Madmen, I want to die a Christian." "How come?" they asked. And Genesius answered them, "So in that very day I may be found like a refugee within God." When a presbyter and an exorcist were sent for, suddenly, with God looking over him, he believed. For when they sat near his bed, they said to him, "Why did you send to us, son?" Genesius responded now not merely pretending and fictitiously, but from a pure heart, "Because I want to receive Christ's grace, in which, reborn, I may be liberated from the destruction of my iniquities." When they had completed the mysteries of the sacraments and he was clad in white garments, and, seized by the soldiers as if part of the play, he was exhibited before the emperor, to be driven off from the name of Christ, standing in a high place, he delivered an oration as follows: . . . [Whereupon Genesius recants his former derision of the Christians, lets the emperor know that his conversion is genuine, and as a result is martyred by being beaten, dragged by a horse, burned with torches, and finally beheaded.]

14.6   Traveling Christian Missionaries, from the *Epistolae ad Virgines*

It is natural to assume that, for generations or even centuries after the missionary efforts of St. Paul, his companions, and immediate successors, Christianity continued to be spread in much the same, familiar manner. But the assumption is apparently mistaken. After the first century, known to us through the New Testament, the picture of the traveling Christian missionary fades almost entirely from the scene. It is a very rare glimpse that shows such activity among obviously tiny hamlets scattered fairly close together in some eastern setting (Syria is most likely), at a date somewhere in the (mid-?) 200s C.E. The description emerges out of the anonymous little *Epistles to the Non-marrying*, beginning with instructions on how the preachers may avoid scandal in their visits.

Source: *Epistolae ad Virgines* 2.3ff., trans. Benjamin P. Pratten, *Ante-Nicene Christian Library*, vol. 14 (Edinburgh: T. & T. Clark, 1869).

And the brother will say to the married persons who are in that place: We holy men do not eat or drink with women, nor are we waited on by women or by maidens, nor do the women wash our feet for us, nor do women anoint us, nor do women prepare our bed for us, nor do we sleep where women sleep, so that we may be without reproach in everything, lest any one should be offended or stumble at us. And, whilst we observe all these things, "we are without offence to everyman." As persons, therefore, "we know the fear of the Lord, we persuade men, and to God we are made manifest."

But if we chance to come into a place where there are no [Christian] men, but all the believers are women and maidens, and they press us to pass the night there in that place, we call them altogether to some suitable place, and ask them how they do; and according to that which we learn from them, and what we see to be their state of mind, we address them in a suitable manner, as men fearing God. And when they have all assembled and come [together], and we see that they are in peace, we address to them words of exhortation in the fear of God, and read the Scripture to them, with purity and in the concise and weighty words of the fear of God. We do everything as for their edification. And as to those who are married, we speak to them in the Lord in a manner suited to them. And if, moreover, the day decline and the eventide draw on, we select, in order to pass the night there, a woman who is aged and most exemplary of them all; and we speak to her to give us a place all to ourselves, where no woman enters, nor maiden. And this old woman herself will bring us a lamp, and whatever is requisite for us she will herself bring us. From love to the brethren, she will bring whatever is requisite for the service of stranger brethren. And she herself, when the time for sleep is come, will depart and go to her house of peace.

But if, moreover, we chance upon a place, and find there one believing woman only, and no other person be there but she only, we do not stop there, nor pray there, nor read the Scriptures there, but we flee as from before the face of a serpent, and as from before the face of sin. Not that we disdain the believing woman—far be it from us to be so minded towards our brethren in Christ!—but, because she is alone, we are afraid lest anyone should make insinuations against us in words of falsehood. For the hearts of men are firmly set on evil. And, that we may not give a pretext to those who desire to get a pretext against us and to speak evil of us, and that we may not be a stumbling-block to anyone, on this account we cut off the pretext of those who desire to get a pretext against us; on this account we must be "on our guard that we be to no one a stumbling-block, neither to Jews, nor to Gentiles, nor yet to the Church of God; and we must not seek that which is profitable to ourselves only, but that which is for the profit of many, so that they may be saved." For this does not profit us, that another stumble because of us. Let us, therefore, be studiously on our guard at all times, that we do not smite our brethren and give them to drink of a disquieting conscience through our being to them a stumbling-block. For "if for the sake of meat our brother be made sad, or shocked, or made weak, or caused to stumble, we are not walking in the love of God. For the sake of meat thou causest him to perish for whose sake Christ died." For, in "thus sinning against your brethren and wounding their sickly consciences, ye sin against Christ Himself. For, if for the sake of meat my brother is made to stumble," let us believers say, "Never will we eat flesh, that we may not make our brother to stumble." These things, moreover, does every one who truly loves God, who truly takes up his cross, and puts on Christ, and loves his neighbour; the man who watches over himself that he be not a stumbling-block to any one, that no one be caused to stumble because of him and die because he is constantly with maidens and lives in the same house with them—a thing which is not right—to the overthrow of those who see and hear. Evil conduct like this is fraught with stumbling and peril, and is akin to death. But blessed is that man who is circumspect and fearful in everything for the sake of purity!

If, moreover, it chance that we go to a place in which there are no Christians, and it be important for us to stay there a few days, let us be "wise as serpents, and harmless as doves;" and let us "not be as the foolish, but as the wise," in all the *self*-restraint of the fear of God, that God may be glorified in everything through our Lord Jesus Christ, through our chaste and holy behaviour. For, "whether we eat, or drink, or do anything else, let us do it as for the glory of God." Let "all those who see us acknowledge that we are a blessed seed," "sons of the living God," in everything—in all our words, in shamefastness, in purity, in humility, forasmuch as we do not copy the heathen in anything, nor are believers like other men, but in everything are estranged from the wicked. And we "do not cast that which is holy before dogs, nor pearls before swine;" but with all possible restraint, and with all discretion, and with all fear of God, and with earnestness of mind we praise God. For we do not minister where heathens are drinking and blaspheming in their feasts with words of impurity, because of their wickedness. Therefore we do not sing psalms to the heathen, nor do we read to them the Scriptures, that we may not be like common singers, either those who play on the lyre, or those who sing with voice, or like soothsayers, as many are, who follow these practices and do these things, that they may sate themselves with a paltry mouthful of bread, and who, for the sake of a sorry cup of wine, go about "singing the songs of the Lord in the strange land" of the heathen, and doing what is not right. Do not so, my brethren, let not these deeds be done among you; but put away those who choose thus to behave themselves with infamy and disgrace. It is not proper, my brethren, that these things should be so. But we beseech you, brethren in righteousness, that these things be so done with you as with us, as for a pattern of believers, and of those who shall believe. Let us be of the flock of Christ, in all righteousness, and in all holy and unblemished conduct, behaving ourselves with uprightness and sanctity, as is right for believers, and observing those things which are praiseworthy, and pure, and holy, and honorable, and noble; and do ye promote all those things which are profitable. For ye are "our joy, and our crown," and our hope, and our life, "if so be that ye stand in the Lord." So be it!

15

APOLOGISTS

15.1 The Apology of Athenagoras

The Greek word *apologia* means a speech for the defense in a court of law and was used for their open letters or tracts by second-century Christian writers, without any overtones of apology in the modern sense. Of the known apologies, the first six are in Greek (by Quadratus 120s c.e., Aristides 120s or 145, Justin 150, Athenagoras 177, Tatian 180, Theophilus 180—all approximate dates). They were relatively short works of explanation, justification, and attack, in various proportions. Latin apologists were Tertullian (197) and Minucius Felix (early 200s), writing at great length. The word "apologist" is not conventionally applied to writers of later apologies (Arnobius and Athanasius, for example, in the early 300s) but the arguments they use belong to the traditional range, developed over the decades and passed on. Most of them can be seen in germ even in early apologies like Athenagoras's.

Source: Athenagoras, *Legatio* 1–7, 10–15, 17–27, 30–37, trans. W. R. Schoedel (Oxford: Clarendon Press, 1972), amended.

To the emperors Marcus Aurelius Antoninus and Lucius Aurelius Commodus, conquerors of Armenia and Sarmatia, and, above all, philosophers.

1. The inhabitants of your empire, greatest of kings, follow many different customs and laws, and none of them is prevented by law or fear of punishment from cherishing his ancestral ways, however ridiculous they may be. The Trojan calls Hector a god and worships Helen, regarding her as Adrasteia [Nemesis]; the Lacedaemonian venerates Agamemnon as Zeus and Phylonoe the daughter of Tyndareus as Enodia [Hecate]; the Athenian sacrifices to Erechtheus as Poseidon; and the Athenians celebrate mysteries for Agraulus and Pandrosos who were considered impious for opening the chest. In a word the various races and peoples of mankind perform whatever sacrifices and mysteries they wish. The Egyptians regard even

cats, crocodiles, snakes, asps, and dogs as gods. All these both you and the laws permit, since you regard it as impious and irreligious to have no belief at all in a god and think it necessary for men to venerate as gods those whom they wish, that through fear of the divine they may refrain from evil. . . . For that reason individual men, admiring your gentle and mild natures, your peaceableness and humanity toward all, enjoy equality before the law; the cities have an equal share in honor according to their merit; and the whole empire enjoys a profound peace through your wisdom.

To us, however, who are called Christians, you have not given the same consideration, but allow us to be driven to and fro and persecuted, though we have done no wrong; in point of fact—as will be shown in what follows—we are the most pious and righteous of all men in matters that concern both the divine and your kingdom; for the crowd is hostile toward us only because of our name. For these reasons we have dared to set forth an account of our position—you will learn from it how unjustly and against all law and reason we suffer—and we ask you to show some concern also for us that there may be an end to our slaughter at the hands of lying informers. For the penalty our persecutors exact does not affect only our goods, nor does the disgrace they bring upon us affect only our civic standing, nor does the harm they cause us have to do with some equally trivial matter. These things we despise even though they seem matters of moment to the crowd. For we have been taught not to strike back at someone who beats us nor go to court with those who rob and plunder us. Not only that: we have even been taught to turn our head and offer the other side when men ill use us and to give our cloak should they snatch our tunic. No, when our property is gone, their plots against us affect our very body and soul. They spread a host of charges, of which there is not the slightest suggestion that we are guilty, but which are typical of those babblers and their kind.

2. Now if a man can convict us of any evil, great or small, we do not ask to be let off. On the contrary we consider it right that our punishment be severe and merciless. But if the charge stops short at our name—and to this day what is said about us amounts to only the low and untested rumor of the populace, and no Christian has yet been convicted of evil—then it is your task as mighty, humane, and learned kings to bring to an end by law the abuse we suffer, that just as all the world has enjoyed your benefactions both as individuals and as cities, we too may have reason to offer our solemn thanks to you that there has been an end to the laying of false information against us. For it does not become your reputation for justice that, whereas others found guilty of crimes are not

punished until convicted, in our case the mere name plays a larger role than legal tests. Our judges do not inquire whether the defendant is guilty of any crime; they simply heap abuse on our name as though that were a crime. But no name is considered good or bad in and of itself. Names appear praiseworthy or disgraceful only because of the good or bad deeds which are implied by them. All this you know very well; for you make philosophy and profound learning, as it were, the ground of your actions. That is why even those who are defendants before you do not lose heart though accused of the greatest crimes; and since they know that you will examine their conduct and not pay attention to meaningless labels or to false charges from the prosecution, they are equally disposed to grant the justice of a favorable or unfavorable decision.

We too, then, ask to enjoy the equity you show to all that we may not be hated or punished simply because we are Christians—for how could our name make us wicked?—but to be judged on the basis of our conduct, whatever it may be that men may wish to examine, and either to be let go when we show the groundlessness of the charges or to be punished if we are found guilty—not guilty merely because of our name (for no Christian is evil unless his profession is a pretence), but because of some crime. Such is what we observe in the case of defendants who pursue philosophy. None of them appears good or bad to the judge before trial because of his knowledge or skill. Only when he is shown to be guilty is he punished. He brings on himself no accusation because of his philosophy—for only the philosopher who breaks the law is evil; knowledge itself is not to blame—and when he rebuts the slanders against him, he is released. Let equity prevail also in our case. Let the conduct of the defendants be investigated. Let no mere name be subject to accusation.

As I begin the defense of our teaching, I must ask you, greatest emperors, to be fair as you listen and not be carried away and prejudiced by low and irrational rumor, but to direct your love of learning and truth also to the following account concerning ourselves. Thus you will not go wrong through ignorance, and we shall rid ourselves of the hostility against us by showing how unfounded are the accusations arising from the uncritical gossip of the crowd.

3. They bring three charges against us: atheism, Thyestean [cannibalistic] banquets, and Oedipean [incestuous] unions. If these are true, spare no class among us, prosecute our crimes, destroy us root and branch, including women and children—if indeed *any* human being could be found living like wild animals in that way! Even animals, however, do not eat members of their own kind; and they mate in accordance with the law of nature and at the one season appointed for the begetting of

offspring—not for any licentious purpose; and they also know by whom they are benefited. If then there be a man more savage than the beasts, what punishment does he not deserve to suffer for such enormities?

But if these charges are fabrications and empty slanders owing their existence to the fact that by a natural principle evil opposes virtue and that by divine law opposites war against each other, and if you yourselves are our witnesses that we are not guilty of any of these crimes since you merely command us not to confess (?), then it is only right that you examine our conduct, our teachings, and our zeal and obedience to you, your house, and the empire. By so doing, you will at length grant us a favor equal to that enjoyed by our persecutors. We shall surely overcome them, ready as we are to give up even our lives without flinching.

4. I shall now meet each charge separately. It is so obvious that we are not atheists that it seems ridiculous even to undertake the refutation of those who make the claim. It was right for the Athenians to charge Diagoras with atheism; for not only did he disclose Orphic doctrine, divulge the mysteries of Eleusis and those of the Cabiri, and chop up the wooden image of Heracles to cook his turnips, but he bluntly declared that there is no god at all. But surely it is not rational for them to apply the term atheism to us who distinguish God from matter and show that matter is one thing and God another and the difference between them immense; for the divine is uncreated and eternal, and can be contemplated only by thought and reason, whereas matter is created and perishable.

If we held opinions like those of Diagoras in spite of having such impressive signs conducive to piety in the order, the perfect harmony, the magnitude, the colors and the arrangement of the world, then we could not complain of having acquired a reputation for impiety and of having brought on ourselves this harassment. But since we teach that there is one God, the Maker of this universe, and that he is not created (since it is not Being that is created, but non-being) whereas all things were made by the Word that issues from him, it is irrational that either of these ills have befallen us. It is wrong that we are defamed and persecuted.

5. Poets and philosophers were not regarded as atheists for giving their attention to matters concerning God. Euripides, in expressing his perplexity concerning those whom common preconception ignorantly names gods, says:

> Zeus ought not, if he dwells in heaven,
> Reduce the same man to unhappy straits.

And in setting out his doctrine of that which may be understood of God's existence through rational insight, he says:

Do you see aloft the boundless ether,
Encircling the earth in its damp folds?
This esteem Zeus! This consider God!

He could not discern the substances thought to underlie the popular gods—substances of which the word god happened to be predicated ("for as to Zeus, I know not who Zeus is, except by hearsay"); nor could he grant that their *names* were predicated of underlying realities (for if the substances of things do not underlie them, is there anything more to them than their names?); but he discerned Another from his works, understanding the things that appear as providing a glimpse of things unseen. The one whose works they are and by whose spirit they are guided he took to be God. Sophocles also agrees with him when he says:

One in truth, yea, one is God,
Who formed heaven and the broad earth.

Thus concerning God's nature which fills heaven and earth with his beauty he teaches both where God must be and that God must be one. . . .

6.2 Plato and Aristotle—and note that it is not as one who intends to give an exact account of the doctrines of the philosophers that I run through what they say concerning God; for I know that you are as much superior to all men in an exact understanding of the whole range of learning as you exceed them in the wisdom and power of your rule, and that you can boast of having accomplished in every branch of learning what not even those who have specialized in one can lay claim to; but since it is impossible to show without mentioning names that we are not alone in insisting on the oneness of God, we have turned to the Opinions—so then, Plato says, "It is a hard task to find the Maker and Father of this universe, and having found him it is impossible to declare him to all." Here he understands the uncreated and eternal God to be one. If he acknowledges other gods such as sun, moon, and stars, he recognizes that they are created: "Gods, offspring of gods, whose Creator am I, as well as Father of those works which are indestructible except as I will; all that is bound can be undone." Now if Plato is no atheist when he understands the Creator of all things to be the one uncreated God, neither are we atheists when we acknowledge him by whose Word all things were created and upheld by his spirit and assert that he is God.

Aristotle and his school bring before us one God whom they liken to a composite living being and say that he consists of soul and body. They consider his body to be the ether, the planets, and the sphere of the fixed stars, all of which have a circular motion, and his soul to be the reason that controls the motion of the body—itself unmoved, yet cause of the body's motion.

The Stoics, although they multiply names for the divine being by means of titles corresponding to the permutations of matter through which they say the Spirit of God moves, in reality think of God as one. For if God is an artisan fire systematically proceeding to the production of the world, containing in itself all the generative principles by which everything takes place in accord with Destiny, and if his Spirit penetrates the whole world, then it follows from their teaching that God is one, receiving the name "Zeus" to correspond to the "seething" [*zeon*] elements of matter or "Hera" to correspond to the "air" [Greek *aer*] and being given all his names to correspond to every part of matter, which he pervades.

7. Seeing, then, that all admit, though reluctantly, when they get down to the first principles of everything, that the divine being is one, and since we insist that he who ordered our universe is God, why is it that *they* enjoy the license to speak and write what they want concerning the divine being, whereas a law has been imposed upon *us* who can establish with compelling proofs and arguments the correctness of what we think and believe—that God is one?

For poets and philosophers have gone at this and other matters by guesswork, each of them moved by his own soul through some affinity with the breath of God to seek, if possible, to find and understand the truth. But they were able to gain no more than a peripheral understanding; they could not find Being since they would not stoop to learn about God from God, but each relied upon himself. That is why they all came up with different doctrines concerning God, matter, the forms, and the world. We, however, have prophets as witnesses of what we think and believe. They have spoken out by a divinely inspired Spirit about God and the things of God. You too would admit, since you surpass others in wisdom and reverence for the truly divine, that it would be irrational to abandon belief in the Spirit from God which has moved the mouths of the prophets like musical instruments and to pay attention to human opinions. . . .

10. We have brought before you a God who is uncreated, eternal, invisible, impassible, incomprehensible, and infinite, who can be apprehended by mind and reason alone, who is encompassed by light, beauty, spirit, and indescribable power, and who created, adorned, and now rules the universe through the Word that issues from him. I have given sufficient evidence that we are not atheists on the basis of arguments presenting this god as one.

For we think also that there is a Son of God. Now let no one think that this talk of God having a Son is ridiculous. For we have not come to our views on either God the Father or his Son as do the poets, who create myths in which they present the gods as no better than men. On the contrary, the Son of God is the Word of the Father in Ideal Form and

Energizing Power; for in his likeness and through him all things came into existence, which presupposes that the Father and the Son are one. Now since the Son is in the Father and the Father in the Son by a powerful unity of spirit, the Son of God is the mind and reason of the Father.

If in your great wisdom you would like to know what "Son" means, I will tell you in a few brief words: it means that he is the first begotten of the father. The term is used, not because he came into existence (for God, who is eternal mind, had in himself his Word or Reason from the beginning, since he was eternally rational), but because he came forth to serve as Ideal Form and Energizing Power for everything material which is like an entity without qualities . . . and underlies things in a state characterized by the mixture of heavier and lighter elements.

The prophetic spirit also agrees with this account. "For the Lord," it says, "made me the beginning of his ways for his works." Further, this same Holy Spirit, which is active in those who speak prophetically, we regard as an effluence of God which flows forth from him and returns like a ray of the sun.

Who then would not be amazed if he heard of men called atheists who bring forward God the Father, God the Son, and the Holy Spirit and who proclaim both their power in their unity and their diversity in rank. Nor does our teaching concerning the godhead stop there, but we also say that there is a host of angels and ministers, whom God, the Maker and Artificer of the world, set in their places through the Word that issued from him and whom he commanded to be concerned with the elements, the heavens, and the world with all that is in it and the good order of all that is in it.

11. Do not be surprised that I go through our teaching in detail. I am making my points carefully to prevent you from being carried away by low and irrational opinion and to put you in a position to know the truth. For we can persuade you that you are not dealing with atheists precisely through the doctrines which we hold—doctrines not man-made but ordained and taught by God.

What then are the teachings on which we are brought up? "I say to you, love them who curse you, pray for them who persecute you, that you may be the sons of your Father in heaven who makes his sun rise upon the evil and the good, and sends rain on the just and the unjust" [Luke 6.27–28].

Since this teaching has made itself heard with a loud cry, allow me here to proceed with full liberty of speech as one who is making his defense before philosopher kings. For which of those who solve syllogisms and eliminate ambiguities and trace etymologies or who . . . homonyms and synonyms, predicates and prepositions, what the subject is and what the predicate . . . promise to make their followers happy with these and similar teachings—which of those, I say, are so pure in soul that they love rather than hate their enemies, bless (as most befits a man of moderation) rather than speak evil of those who are prompt with reproach for them, and pray for those who plot against their life? On the contrary, with ill will they constantly dig up just such abuse against one another and constantly seek to bring off some wickedness, for they have made the concoction of words their business rather than the doing of deeds.

In our ranks, however, you could find common men, artisans, and old women who, if they cannot establish by reasoned discourse the usefulness of their teaching, show by deed the usefulness of the exercise of their will. For they do not rehearse words but show forth good deeds; when struck they do not strike back; when robbed they do not prosecute; they give to those who ask; and they love their neighbors as themselves.

12. So then, if we did not think that God presided over the human race, would we remain so pure? Certainly not! But since we are convinced that we shall render an account of all our life here below to the God who made both us and the world, we choose the way of life that is moderate, that shows affection for men, and that is thoughtlessly despised. We do not think that we shall suffer so great an evil here below, even if they rob us of our lives, that it may be compared to what we shall gain beyond from the great Judge in return for a way of life that is gentle, affectionate, and kind. Plato said that Minos and Rhadamanthys would judge and punish evil men; we say that no one, not a Minos, or a Rhadamanthys, or the father of them both, will escape the judgement of God.

And yet are those to be credited with piety who think that the way to live is this, "Let us eat and drink, for tomorrow we die," and claim that death is a deep sleep and a forgetting ("sleep and death are twin brothers")? And are we at the same time considered to be irreligious despite the fact that to escape condemnation our behavior and our way of life are of so different a character? For we are men who consider life here below of very little worth. We are attended only by the knowledge of him who is truly God and the Word that issues from him—a knowledge as to what is the unity of the Son with the Father, what is the communion of the Father with the Son, what is the Spirit, what is the unity of these powers—the Spirit, the Son, and the Father—and their diversity when thus united. We know that the life we await is far better than words can tell if we are brought there pure from all blame. We show such affection for men that we love not only our friends; "for," it says, "if you love them who love you and lend to them who lend to you, what reward will you have?"

These points, then, represent a few small matters from among many important ones—few and small that we may not further burden you; for those who test the quality of honey and whey can tell if the whole is good by tasting one small sample.

13. Since the majority of those accusing us of atheism—though they have not even the foggiest notion of the nature of God, are ignorant of scientific or theological doctrine and have no acquaintance with them, and measure piety in terms of sacrifices—since they accuse us of not recognizing the same gods as do the cities, I ask you to take the following into account, my sovereigns, in dealing with both issues. First, concerning our refusal to sacrifice.

The Artificer and Father of this universe needs no blood, fat, or the fragrance of flowers and incense. He himself is the perfect fragrance and is in need of nothing from within or without. The best sacrifice for him is for us to know who stretched out the heavens and gave them their spherical form and established the earth as a center, who brought together water into seas and divided the light from the darkness, who adorned the sky with stars and caused the earth to make every seed spring up, who made animals and formed man. So then, when we regard the Artificer as a God who conserves and governs all things with the knowledge and skill by which he guides them and we raise up holy hands to him, what further need does he have of any hecatomb?

> And men in their petitions, when one sins and errs,
> Turn some of them [the gods] aside with sacrifices
> And pleasing votive gifts, with libation and with fat.

But what have I to do with whole burnt offerings which God does not need? And what have I to do with sacrificing, since what is required is to offer up our rational worship as an unbloody sacrifice?

14. What they have to say about our not coming forward and recognizing the same gods as the cities is very silly. Even those who accuse us of atheism for not acknowledging the same gods they know do not agree with each other about the gods: the Athenians set up Celeus and Metaneira as gods; the Lacedaemonians, Menelaus (to whom they sacrifice and celebrate festivals); the Trojans (who do not even want to hear the name of Menelaus) bring forward Hector; the Chians, Aristaeus (acknowledging him both as Zeus and Apollo); the Thasians, Theagenes (who even committed murder at the Olympian games); the Samians, Lysander for so much slaughter and destruction; the Cilicians, . . . ; the Sicilians, Philip the son of Butacides; the Amathusians, Onesilaus; the Carthaginians, Hamilcar. A day would not suffice for me to complete the catalogue.

Since they themselves are in disagreement about their own gods, why do they accuse us of not conforming? I cannot help thinking that what goes on among the Egyptians is ridiculous. For on the festivals they go to the temples and beat their breasts as though lamenting the dead, and yet they sacrifice to them as though to gods! And no wonder, considering the fact that they regard animals as gods, shave themselves when the creatures die, bury them in temples, and initiate public laments. If we are irreligious because our religiosity has nothing in common with theirs, all cities and all nations are irreligious; for all men do not recognize the same gods.

15. But suppose that they all did recognize the same ones. What then? Since the crowd, in its inability to distinguish what is God, what is matter, and what a gulf there is between them, reverently approaches material images, are we on their account also to draw near and worship statues—we who do distinguish and divide the uncreated from the created, being from non-being, the intelligible from the perceptible, and who give each of them its proper name?

To be sure, if matter and God are the same—two names for one thing—then we are irreligious if we do not regard stones and wood, gold and silver, as gods. But if there is a vast difference between them, as much as there is between the artisan and the materials provided for his craft, why are we accused? . . .

17. I ask you to examine them [pagan gods] briefly. For it is necessary in defending my cause to make precise observations both about their names, showing that they are very recent, and about their images, showing that they were made, so to speak, only yesterday or the day before. You yourselves know these things better than I, since you are deeply versed beyond all others in the ancients. I say then, that it was Orpheus, Homer, and Hesiod who gave genealogies and names to those they called gods. Herodotus also provides proof of this: "For I think that Hesiod and Homer preceded me by four hundred years, and not more. They are the ones who provided the Greeks with a genealogy of the gods, gave names to the gods, distributed to them their honors and crafts, and described their appearances."

Images were not in use before the discovery of molding, painting, and sculpture. Then came Saurius of Samos, Crato of Sicyon, Cleanthes of Corinth, and the Corinthian maid. Tracing out shadows was discovered by Saurius, who drew the outline of a horse standing in the sun. Painting was discovered by Crato, who colored in the outlines of a man and a woman on a whitened tablet. Relief modeling was discovered by the Corinthian maid; she fell in love with someone and traced the outline of his shadow on the wall as he slept; then her father, a potter, delighted with so precise a likeness, made a relief of the outline and filled it with clay; the relief is preserved to this very day in Corinth. After these there came Daedalus, Theodore, and Smilis, who went further and discovered sculpture and molding.

So short, then, is the time since the introduction of images and the making of statues that it is possible to name the craftsman of each god. Endoios, a disciple of Daedalus, made the statue of Artemis in Ephesus and the ancient olive statue of Athena (or rather of Athela; for she is Athela, the unsuckled, as those . . .) and the Seated Athena. The Pythian Apollo is the work of Theodore and Telecles. The Delian Apollo and the Artemis are the craftmanship of Tectaeus and Angelio. The Hera in Samos and in Argos are the works of Smilis. . . . The Aphrodite in Cnidus is another work of Praxiteles. The Asclepius in Epidaurus is the work of Phidias.

To put it in a word, not one of their images eludes identification as the work of a man. If, then, they are gods, why were they not so from the beginning? Why are they more recent than those who have made them? Why did they need human craftmanship for their existence? They are earth, stones, matter, and futile craftmanship.

18. Now some say that these are only images, but that there are gods for whose sake the images exist. They say that their processions to the images and their sacrifices are offered up to the gods and celebrated for them because there is no way other than this to approach them ("dangerous are gods when they appear visibly"). As evidence that this is so they refer to the activities associated with certain statues. With this in mind let us investigate the power of the divine names.

I shall request you, greatest of sovereigns, before beginning my examination, to excuse me if I bring forward my arguments polemically to establish their truth. Certainly I do not consider it my task to condemn images; but in dismissing the slanders against us I must provide the reason for the decision that we have made. May you find it possible to examine by your own efforts also the heavenly kingdom; for as all things have been subjected to you, a father and a son, who have received your kingdom from above ("for the king's life is in God's hand," as the prophetic spirit says), so all things are subordinated to the one God and the Word that issues from him whom we consider his inseparable son.

I ask you then to examine the following point before all else. The gods, so they say, were not in existence from the beginning, but each of them came into being as we do. And this is agreed by them all: Homer speaks of "Ocean, the origin of the gods, and Tethys their mother." Orpheus (who was the first to invent their names, to describe their births, and to recount the deeds of each, who is generally believed by them to treat of the gods with great accuracy, and who for the most part is followed even by Homer, especially in his treatment of the gods) affirms their ultimate origin from water—"Ocean, in whom is to be found the origin of all." For according to him water was the beginning of everything.

From water came slime. From both an animal was born—a serpent with the head of a lion attached, and between them the face of a god. Its name was Heracles and Chronos. This Heracles generated a huge egg which, when filled by the power of him who generated it, broke into two through friction. The upper part of it was fashioned into Heaven; the part which descended became Earth; a sort of two-bodied god came forth. Heaven in union with Earth begot female offspring—Clotho, Lachesis, and Atropos— and the male Hundred-hands—Cotys, Gyges, Briareus—and the Round-eyes—Brontes, Steropes, and Argos. Heaven bound and cast them into Tartarus when he learned that he would be deprived of his rule by his offspring. Consequently Earth in her anger brought forth the Titans:

> Our mistress the Earth brought forth children of Heaven
> To whom men also give the name of "Titans"
> Because they took vengeance [a form of the verb *tino*] on the
>   starry expanse of Heaven.

19. This is their version of the beginning of the generation of the gods and the universe. Take this then into consideration: each of the beings divinized by them, since it has a beginning, must also be perishable. For if they came into being from nothing, as those who theologize about them say, then they do not exist; for either they are something uncreated and so eternal; or they are created and so perishable.

On this point there is no disagreement between myself and the philosophers. "What is that which always is and does not come to be, or what is that which comes to be but never is?" Plato in his dialogues on the intelligible and perceptible teaches that that which always is, the intelligible, is uncreated, whereas that which is not, the perceptible, is created, having a beginning and an end.

For this same reason the Stoics say that there will be a cosmic conflagration and that all will be restored as the world begins again. According to them there are two causes, one active and efficacious insofar as it is Providence, the other passive and mutable insofar as it is matter; if it is impossible for the world which is subject to becoming to remain unaltered even though guided by Providence, how can these gods avoid dissolution, since they do not exist by nature but come into being? How can these gods be superior to matter when they derive their substance from water? But neither on their view can it be said that water is the beginning of all things. For what could arise from simple and uniform elements? Matter needs a craftsman and a craftsman needs matter. Or how could there be shapes without matter or a craftsman? Nor does it make sense to say that matter is more ancient than God, for the active cause necessarily precedes those things that come into being.

20. Now if the absurdity of their theology extended only to saying

that the gods came into being and have their substance from water, I would simply show that there is nothing created which is not also subject to dissolution and would pass on to the other charges. They go on, however, to give a description of the bodies of their gods. They say that Heracles is a coiled serpent-god and the others Hundred-handed. They say that the daughter of Zeus, whom he fathered by his mother Rhea, also called Demeter . . . had two eyes in the natural place and two more on her forehead and the face of an animal on the back of her neck and that she had horns. Consequently Rhea in a fright abandoned the monstrous child and did not offer her the breast. That is why she is called Athela, but commonly Persephone and Core [Maid]; though she is not the same as Athena, who is also named from the fact that she is a "maid."

They also go on to recount, accurately as they suppose, the deeds performed by the gods; that Cronus cut off the genitals of his father and threw him down from his chariot and that he slew his children by devouring his male offspring; that Zeus bound his father and cast him into Tartarus (just as Heaven had done with his sons) and fought with the Titans for sovereignty; that he pursued his mother Rhea when she resisted marriage with him; that when she became a serpent he likewise turned himself into a serpent, entangled her in the so-called knot of Heracles, and had intercourse with her (the rod of Hermes is a symbol of that kind of union); then that he had intercourse with his daughter Persephone, violating her also in the form of a serpent, and so having Dionysus by her.

Since this is their teaching, this much must at least be said: what nobility or value is there in such an account for us to believe that Cronus, Zeus, Core, and the rest are gods? And what man of discernment habituated to reflection would believe that a viper was the offspring of a god? Thus Orpheus:

> Phanes brought forth yet another fearful child
> From his sacred belly: the Viper, terrible to look upon.
> Hair indeed streaked from its head, and beautiful to see
> Was its face; but what remained below its neck
> Were the parts of a fearful serpent.

Or could he allow that this very Phanes, the first-born of the gods (for he was the one who emerged from the egg), had the body or form of a serpent or was devoured by Zeus so that Zeus could become infinite? For if the gods differ in no way from the vilest beasts (for it is clear that the divine must differ somewhat from earthly things and things derived from matter!), they are not gods. Why indeed do we reverently draw near to them who are born like dumb beasts and who themselves look like animals and are ugly in form?

21. Yet if all they said was that their gods were corporeal and had

blood, semen, and the passions of anger and lust, even then one would be bound to consider these doctrines laughable nonsense; for in God there is neither anger nor lust and desire nor yet semen for producing offspring.

Well then, let us suppose that they are corporeal yet superior to wrath and anger, so that Athena will not be seen "incensed with Zeus her father, as fierce anger seized her," and Hera will not be described as follows "Hera's heart could not contain her anger, but she cried out." And let them be superior to grief like this:

> Alas, I see pursued about the wall
> A man I cherish; and my heart grieves.

For my part I regard even men who yield to anger and grief as ignorant and foolish; but when the "Father of men and gods" bewails his son—

> Woe is me, when Fate decrees that by Patroclus, Menoetius' son
> Sarpedon, dearest of men to me, is now to be subdued—

and when for all his grief he cannot rescue him from danger—

> Sarpedon is son of Zeus, yet Zeus saves not his own child —

who would not condemn the foolishness of those who are ardent theists, or rather atheists, on the basis of such myths?

Let us suppose that they are corporeal, but let us not have Aphrodite's body wounded by Diomedes—

> Diomedes, proud son of Tydeus, has wounded me—

or her soul by Ares:

> Aphrodite, daughter of Zeus, always dishonours me
> Because I am lame; and she loves destructive Ares. . . .
> Fair flesh he tore asunder—

the mighty one in battle, ally of Zeus against the Titans, shows himself weaker than Diomedes!

> He raged as when Ares with his spear—

be silent, Homer, a god does not rage! Yet you tell me of a god who is bloodthirsty and a bane of men—

> Ares, Ares bane of men, bloodthirsty one—

and you tell a story of his adultery and bonds:

> They went to bed and slept together; but there fell about them
> Bonds cunningly contrived by the skilled Hephaestus,
> Not a limb could they move

Do they not reject this mass of impious nonsense concerning the gods? Heaven is castrated; Cronus is bound and cast down into Tartarus; the Titans revolt; the Styx dies in battle (already this shows that they regard them as mortal); they fall in love with each other; they fall in love with human beings—

> Aeneas, whom fair Aphrodite bore to Anchises,
> A goddess who slept with a mortal on the slopes of Mount Ida.

They do not fall in love. They experience no passion. For either they are gods and lust does not touch them. . . . Yet if a god assumes flesh by divine dispensation, is he forthwith a slave of lust?

> For never did love for goddess or woman
> Poured out in my breast so overcome my heart,
> Not when I loved the wife of Ixion,
> Nor when I loved Danae, fair daughter of Acrisius,
> Nor the daughter of far-famed Phoenix,
> Nor Semele, or Alcmene in Thebes
> Not the fair queen Demeter,
> Nor famed Leto, nor thyself.

He is created, he is perishable, with nothing of a god about him. They even serve men—

> O halls of Admetus, in which I, though a god
> Brought myself to praise menial fare—

and they tend cattle—

> I came to this land and herded cattle for a stranger
> And preserved this house.

Admetus then is superior to the god! Wise seer, you who foreknow what will befall others, you did not foresee the murder of your darling, but killed your friend with your own hand!

> I deemed Apollo's divine mouth to be unerring,
> Welling up with prophetic lore—

thus Aeschylus reproaches Apollo as a false seer—

> But he himself who sung the hymn, was present at the feast,
> And spoke these words, it is he who slew my son.

22. But perhaps all this is the deceit of poets, and there is a scientific explanation concerning the gods along lines such as this (as Empedocles says):

> Shining Zeus and life-giving Hera with Aidoneus
> And Nestis who with her tears fills the springs of mortals.

If then Zeus represents fire, Hera earth, Aidoneus air, and Nestis water, they are elements—fire, water, air—and none of them is a god, neither Zeus, nor Hera, nor Aidoneus. For they have their substance and origin from matter which has been given its diversity by God:

> Fire, water, earth, and the calm height of air,
> And with them all, Love.

Without Love the elements cannot be kept from being thrown into confusion by Strife. How then could anyone say that they are gods? Love is the ruling principle according to Empedocles, the composite entities are the ruled, and the ruling principle is their master. If then we attribute one and the same power to the ruled and the ruling, we shall inadvertently make perishable, unstable, and changeable matter equal in rank to the uncreated, eternal, and ever self-same God.

"Zeus" according to the Stoics is the element which "seethes," (*zei*), "Hera" the "air" (if the name is repeated in quick succession, both terms are actually sounded together) [in Greek the two words are distinguished only by the order of the letters], "Poseidon" what is "potable." Some give physical explanations of one kind, some of another. For some say that Zeus is air—dipolar, male-female. Others say that he is the season that turns time [*chronos*] and brings fine weather; consequently he alone escaped Cronus.

But in the case of the Stoics this can be said: "If you think that the supreme God is one, both uncreated and eternal, and you say that there are composite entities resulting from the mutation of matter and that the spirit of God pervading matter in its permutations receives now one name, now another, then material things will be God's body, and when the elements perish at the cosmic conflagration, such names must perish together with these things and the spirit of God alone remain." Who then could believe those to be gods whose bodies the permutation of matter destroy?

We have a reply to those who say that Cronus is time [*chronos*]; that Rhea is earth; that she conceived by Cronus and brought forth and is regarded, therefore, as mother of all; that he begat and consumed his offspring, and that the severing of his vital organs signifies the intercourse of the male with the female, since it severs semen and casts it into the womb and brings forth man with desire—that is, Aphrodite—within him; that the madness of Cronus is the change of season that brings destruction upon animate and inanimate things; that the bonds and Tartarus are time changing with the seasons and passing away. Our reply is this: if Cronus is time, he changes; if he is a season, he alters; if he is darkness or frost or moisture, none of these is abiding. The divine, however, is immortal, immovable, and unchangeable; so then neither Cronus nor any phantom of him in the mind is a god.

As to Zeus, if he, the offspring of Cronus, is air (the male aspect of which is Zeus, the female aspect Hera—and thus she is called both sister and wife), he is subject to change; if he is a season, he alters. But the divine neither changes nor decays.

Why should I burden you further with such accounts? You know better than I the various views of all who give physical explanations: you know what the writers have thought concerning nature or concerning Athena, who they say is thought pervading all things, or concerning Isis, who they say is the origin of the world from whom all sprang and through whom all exist, or concerning Osiris, who was slain by his brother Typhon and whose limbs Isis with her son Horus sought and found about . . . which she arranged in a tomb that to this day is called the Tomb of Osiris. They twist and turn themselves in every direction about material things and miss the God who is contemplated by reason. They divinize the elements and portions of them, sometimes giving one name to them, sometimes another: the sowing of grain is Osiris (hence they say that in the mysteries, when his limbs—that is, the fruits of the earth—are found, this acclamation is made to Isis: "we have found, we rejoice together"); at the same time the fruit of the vine is Dionysus, the vine itself Semele, and the flaming heat of the sun Zeus.

The fact is that those who divinize . . . the myths do anything but treat of God, since they do not realize that what they use to defend the gods confirms the arguments against them. What have Europa and the Bull or Leda and the Swan to do with earth and air so that the repulsive union of Zeus with these women would signify a union of earth and air?

They fail to see the greatness of God and are unable to rise up to it by reason (for they are not attuned to the heavenly realm). They have fixed themselves on material things and falling lower and lower divinize the movements of the elements. It is as if a man were to regard the very ship in which he sailed as performing the work of the pilot. Without a pilot it is nothing more than a ship even though it has been equipped with everything; just so, neither are the elements of any use, no matter how beautifully ordered, without the Providence of God. For the ship will not sail of itself, and the elements will not move without the Artificer.

23. Now you, who are wiser than all men, may reply: "Why is it, then, that some of the images actually effect things if the gods do not exist to whom we erect these statues? For it is not likely that inanimate and

motionless images would have such power of themselves if nothing were moving them." Not even we deny that in some places, cities, and nations certain things are brought about in the name of images; but although some have been benefited and others been harmed, we do not think that gods are responsible for what is brought about in either case; rather we have made a careful examination both as to the reason why you think that the images possess power and who they are who usurp the names of the images and bring these things about.

Now that I am about to show who they are who bring these things about by taking possession of the images and to show that they are not gods, I feel that I ought to make use of certain philosophers as my witnesses.

Thales, as those who know his doctrines well record, was the first to distinguish gods, demons, and heroes. He presents God as the mind of the world, but regards demons as psychic substances and heroes as souls separated from men—good heroes being good souls, evil heroes evil souls.

Even Plato himself, who suspended judgement in regard to all the rest, makes a division between, on the one hand, the uncreated God along with those produced by the uncreated One to beautify the heavens—the planets and fixed stars—and, on the other hand, the demons. Since he does not think it worth discussing these demons, he is satisfied to follow those who have already spoken of them:

"It is beyond our powers to tell of the rest of the demons or to know their origin, but we must put our trust in those who have told the story before, since they were the offspring of the gods (as they said)—gods who clearly know their own ancestors. We cannot, then, distrust the offspring of the gods even though they speak without pertinent and necessary proofs; but we must follow custom and believe them when they claim to be giving information about their family history. On their authority, then, we too are to hold and declare a like view of the origin of these gods: Ocean and Tethys were the offspring of Earth and Heaven, and from these came Phorcus, Cronus, Rhea, and all their company. From Cronus and Rhea came Zeus, Hera, and all the rest whom we know—all those called their brothers and sisters as well as others who are *their* offspring. . . ."

24. What need is there with you who are well versed in everything either to call to mind poets or to examine still other opinions? It is sufficient for me to say this: suppose that the poets and philosophers did not recognize that God was one and did not have critical opinions about the other gods, some regarding them as men who once lived, would it make sense to have us banished because we have a doctrine which distinguishes God and matter and their respective substances?

We say that there is God and his Son, his Word, and the Holy Spirit, united in power yet distinguished in rank as the Father, the Son and the

Spirit, since the Son is mind, reason [*logos*, word], and wisdom of the Father and the Spirit an effluence like light from fire. So also we have recognized that there are other powers which are concerned with matter and operate through it. One of them is opposed to God, not because there is a counterpart to God as Strife is a counterpart to Love in Empedocles or as Night is a counterpart to Day in the realm of nature (for if anything had stood opposed to God, it would surely have ceased to exist, its constitution dissolved by the power and might of God), but because the spirit which is concerned with matter is opposed to God's goodness. This goodness belongs to God as an attribute and is co-existent with him as color is with its corporeal substance; without it he does not exist. It is not as though it were a part of him but rather an accompanying quality necessarily associated with him, as united and allied with him as a yellowish-red is with fire and a deep blue with the sky. The spirit opposed to him was in fact created by God just as the rest of the angels were also created by him, and he was entrusted with the administration of matter and material things.

These angels were called into being by God to exercise providence over the things set in order by him, so that God would have universal and general providence over all things whereas the angels would be set over particular things. As in the case of men whose virtue and vice is a matter of choice (for you would neither honor the good nor punish the evil if virtue and vice were not in their hands) some take seriously what has been entrusted to them by you whereas others are found untrustworthy, so it is in the case of the angels. Some of them—they were, remember, created free by God—remained true to the task for which God made them and to which he had appointed them. Others violated both their own nature and their office. These include the prince over matter and material things and others who are stationed at the first firmament (do realize that we say nothing unsupported by evidence but that we are exponents of what the prophets uttered); the latter are the angels who fell to lusting after maidens and let themselves be conquered by the flesh, the former failed his reponsibility and operated wickedly in the administration of what had been entrusted to him.

Now from those who went after maidens were born the so-called giants. Do not be surprised that a partial account of the giants has been set forth also by poets. Worldly wisdom and prophetic wisdom differ from one another as truth differs from probability—the one is heavenly, the other earthly and in harmony with the prince of matter:

> We know how to tell many falsehoods which have the form
> of truth.

25. These angels, then, who fell from heaven, busy themselves about the air and the earth and are no longer able to rise to the realms above the heavens. The souls of the giants are the demons who wander about the world. Both angels and demons produce movements—demons movements which are akin to the natures they received, and angels movements which are akin to the lusts with which they were possessed. The prince of matter, as may be seen from what happens, directs and administers things in a manner opposed to God's goodness.

> Oft into my heart has come this thought:
> That either chance or demon rules men's lives.
> Against hope and against justice
> It casts some forth from homes
> Apart from God, and others it makes prosper.

If faring well or badly against hope and justice left Euripides speechless, to whom belongs the administration of earthly affairs which is of such a nature that a man could say:

> "How, then, when we see such things, are we to say
> There is a race of gods, or follow laws obediently?"

This is what made Aristotle also say that things below heaven are not guided by Providence, although the eternal providence of God rests equally on us all:

> "The earth by necessity, whether it wills or not,
> Makes the grass grow and thus fattens my flocks."

But the particular providence of God which is concerned with truth and not conjecture extends itself to those who are worthy whereas everything else is subject to providence by the law of reason as part of a total system.

But since the demonic impulses and activities of the hostile spirit bring these wild attacks—indeed we see them move men from within and without, one man one way and another man another, some individually and some as nations, one at a time and all together, because of our kinship with matter and our affinity with the divine—in light of this, some men, whose reputations are not small, have thought that our universe did not arise in an orderly fashion but is the random product of irrational chance. They do not recognize that none of the things of which the whole world is composed is disordered or neglected. Each of them is the product of reason, and that is why they do not go beyond their appointed order. Even man himself is a well-ordered creature to the extent that it depends on the One who made him: his nature in its origin has one common reason, his bodily form does not go beyond the law set for it, and the end of life remains common to all alike. But to the extent that it depends on the reason peculiar to each individual and the activity of the ruling prince and his attendant demons, one man is swept along one way, another man another way, even though all have the same rationality within.

26. It is these demons who drag men to the images. They engross themselves in the blood from the sacrifices and lick all around them. The gods that satisfy the crowd and give their names to the images, as you can learn from their history, were once men. The activity associated with each of them is your assurance that it is the demons who usurp their names. For some—I mean the devotees of Rhea [Cybele]—castrate themselves; others— I mean the devotees of Artemis—make incisions and gash their genitals. (And the Artemis among the Taurians slaughters strangers!) I shall not discuss those who mutilate themselves with knives and knuckle-bones and what form of demons they have. For it is not of God's doing to incite men to things contrary to nature.

> When the demon prepares evil for a man,
> He first perverts his mind.

But God, who is perfectly good, eternally does what is good.

Troy and Parium provide the best proof that it is others who operate through the images than those for whom they were erected: Troy has images of Neryllinus (a man of our own time); Parium has the images of Alexander and Proteus. Both the grave and the image of Alexander are still in the market-place. Almost all the images of Neryllinus serve simply as public monuments, since that is how a city is beautified. One of them, however, is thought to give oracles and heal the sick, and for this reason the Trojans sacrifice to the statue, overlay it with gold, and wreathe it. Then there is the statue of Alexander and that of Proteus. You know about Proteus—the one who threw himself into the fire at Olympia. His statue is also said to give oracles. To the statue of Alexander—"ill-starred Paris, in form most fair, mad for women"—public sacrifices are celebrated; it is treated as a god who hears man's prayers.

Well, then, are Neryllinus, Proteus, and Alexander the ones who are responsible for these phenomena associated with the statues, or is it the nature of the material used for them? The material, however, is bronze, and what can bronze do by itself when it is possible to change it into another shape as the Amasis referred to by Herodotus did with his foot-basin? [Amasis, king of Egypt, had the foot-basin made into a statue to reflect his own rise from humble station.] What more can Neryllinus, Proteus, and Alexander do for the sick? For what the image is said to accomplish now, it did while Neryllinus was alive and ill himself.

27. What is the solution? First, that the movements of the soul not

directed by reason but by fantasy in the realm of conjectures derive various images, now one, now another, from matter or simply mold them independently and give birth to them. A soul experiences this especially when it attaches itself to the spirit of matter and blends with it, when it does not look up to heavenly things, or, in general terms, when it becomes mere blood and flesh and is no longer pure spirit.

These movements of the soul not directed by reason but by fantasy give birth to illusory images, which bring with them a mad passion for idols. When the soul is weak and docile, ignorant and unacquainted with sound teachings, unable to contemplate the truth, unable to understand who the Father and Maker of all things is—when such a soul has impressed upon it false opinions concerning itself, the demons associated with matter, because they are greedy for the savor of fat and the blood of the sacrifices, and because their business is to delude men take hold of these deceitful movements in the soul of the many, and by invading their thoughts flood them with illusory images which seem to come from the idols and statues; and the demons harvest the fame of all the remarkable things which the soul, because of its immortal nature, brings about in a rational way of itself, whether it be foretelling the future or healing present ills. . . .

> 30. The Cretans are ever liars! For your tomb, O King,
> Have the Cretans contrived; and yet have you not died!

Although you believe, Callimachus, in the birth of Zeus, you do not believe in his tomb. Although you think that you will obscure the truth you proclaim him even to the ignorant as one who *has* died. Thus if you look upon his cave, you call to mind his birth from Rhea; but if you view his tomb, you cast a shadow over the one who has died. You do not know that the uncreated God is alone eternal. For either the popular myths about the gods recounted by poets are untrustworthy and the piety shown the gods useless (for they do not exist if the stories about them are false), or if these births, loves, murders, castrations, and thunderbolts are true, then they no longer exist, they have ceased to be, since from non-existence they came into being.

What reason is there to believe some stories and not to believe others, seeing that the poets have given such lofty accounts of them? For these men who caused the gods to be acknowledged by the lofty treatment of the stories about them would not have lied about their weaknesses and afflictions.

Proof has now been offered to show to the best of my ability, if not as it deserves, that we are not atheists when we recognize the Maker of the universe and the Word proceeding from him as God.

31. They go on to charge us, however, with godless banquets and sexual unions. They do so that they may believe their hatred reasonable, and because they think that by frightening people they can draw us away from the strictness of our way of life or make our rulers harsh and unyielding with their fantastic charges. They are wasting their time with men who know that from time immemorial, and not only in our own day, evil has habitually opposed virtue by some divine law or principle. That is why Pythagoras, too, with three hundred companions, was burned to death. Heraclitus and Democritus were driven out the one from the city of Ephesus, the other, accused of being mad, from the city of Abdera; and the Athenians condemned Socrates to death. But just as they were no worse in the scale of virtue because of the opinion of the crowd, neither does the indiscriminate slander of a few cast any shadow upon the uprightness of our life. For we have our good reputation with God. Still I shall also meet these complaints.

I am well aware that as far as you are concerned I have made my case by what I have already said. For you, whose wisdom is greater than that of all others, know that men whose life is regulated, so to speak, by God as their measure, so that each one of us may be blameless and faultless before him, have no intention of doing the least wrong. If we were persuaded that our life here below was the only one we would live, there would be reason to suspect us of wrong-doing in serving flesh and blood and yielding to the temptations of gain or lust. But since we are aware that God knows what we think and say both night and day, and that he who is totally light sees also what is in our hearts; and since we are persuaded that when we depart this present life we shall live another life better than that here, a heavenly one, not earthly, so that we may then abide with God and with his help remain changeless and impassible in soul as though we were not body, even if we have one, but heavenly spirit; and, alternatively, since we are convinced that, if we fall with the rest of men, we shall live another life worse than that here in realms of fire (for God did not create us like sheep or beasts of burden, and it would not be incidental if we were to be destroyed and disappear); since all this is so, it is not likely that we should want to do evil and deliver ourselves up to the great Judge to be punished.

32. It is not at all remarkable that they fabricate stories about us such as they tell of their own gods. They present the sufferings of their deities as mysteries; but if they are about to condemn promiscuous and licentious unions, then they ought to hate either Zeus, who begot children by his mother Rhea and his daughter Core and had his own sister to wife, or Orpheus, the creator of these stories, because he made Zeus even more irreligious and abominable than Thyestes. For it was in fulfillment of an

oracle that the latter had intercourse with his daughter, because he wanted to gain a kingdom and be avenged.

But we are so far from promiscuity that it is not even permissible for us to look with lust: for "he who looks at a woman to lust after, he," it says, "has already committed adultery in his heart." What doubt could there be of the chastity of such men? They are not permitted to look at anything other than that for which God has created the eyes, so that there may be a light for us. For them to look with pleasure is adultery since the eyes were created for other purposes; and they will be judged for something no more tangible than a thought!

For our teaching is not set forth with a view to human laws whose surveillance an evil man may well escape. At the beginning I assured you, my masters, that our doctrine is taught by God. We have a law, then . . . which prompts us to consider ourselves and our neighbors the measure for justice. For this reason we regard some, depending on their age, as our sons and daughters, others we consider our brothers and sisters, and to those advanced in years we give the honor due to fathers and mothers. But we are profoundly concerned that the bodies of those whom we consider brothers and sisters and who are known by all the other terms applied to kin remain inviolate and unsullied. Again, our teaching has it: "If anyone kisses twice because it was pleasurable, . . ." and it adds: "So then one must be scrupulous about the kiss, or more precisely, the reverential greeting," since it places us outside eternal life if our thoughts are the least bit stirred by it.

33. Since we hope for eternal life, we despise the things of this life, including even the pleasures of the soul. Thus each of us thinks of his wife, whom he married according to the laws that we have laid down, with a view to nothing more than procreation. For as the farmer casts seed into the ground and awaits the harvest without further planting, so also procreation is the limit that we set for the indulgence of our lust. You could find many among us, both men and women, growing old unmarried in the hope of being united more closely with God.

If to remain a virgin and abstain from sexual intercourse brings us closer to God, and if to allow ourselves nothing more tangible than a lustful thought leads us away from God, then, since we flee the thought, much more will we refuse to commit the deed. We are not concerned with the exercise of eloquence but with the performance and teaching of deeds—either to stay in the state in which a man was born or to remain satisfied with one marriage; for a second marriage is gilded adultery. For "whoever divorces his wife," it says, "and marries another, commits adultery." Neither does it allow a man to divorce a woman whose maidenhead he has taken, nor does it allow him to marry again. For he who detaches himself from his previous wife, even if she has died, is a covert adulterer. He thwarts the hand of God (because in the beginning God formed one man and one woman), and he destroys the communion of flesh with flesh in the unity characteristic of the intercourse of the sexes.

34. Since we are so oriented (indeed how can I even recount such abominations), there ring in our ears the words of the proverb, "The harlot presumes to teach her who is chaste!" For it is they who have made a business of harlotry and have established immoral houses of every base persuasion for the young. Nor have they neglected male prostitution. Men work their frightful deeds with men; they violate in every way those whose bodies are especially noble or comely; thus they dishonor even the beauty created by God (for there is no self-made beauty on earth; it comes from the hand and mind of God). They of all people, revile us for vices which they have on their own consciences and which they attribute to their own gods, boasting of them as noble deeds and worthy of the gods.

These adulterers and pederasts reproach men who abstain from intercourse or are satisfied with a single marriage, whereas they themselves live like fish. For they swallow up whoever comes their way, the stronger driving out the weaker. And this is what it really means to feed on human flesh: that when laws have been promulgated to further every form of justice, they violate these very ordinances so that the governors of the provinces which you have sent out cannot even handle all the lawsuits. Yet it is they who reproach us though we are not even permitted to draw back when struck nor to refuse to bless when ill-spoken of; for it is not enough to be just (justice is to return measure for measure); but it is required of us to be good and long-suffering.

35. What reasonable person, then, could say that we who are so oriented are murderers? It is impossible to devour human flesh without having previously killed someone! First then, they lie; second, if someone asks them whether they have seen what they report, none has the hardihood to say that they have. Further, we have slaves, some many, some few, and it is impossible to escape their observation. Yet none of them has ever told such monstrous lies about us.

Who can charge people with murder and cannibalism who are known not to allow themselves to be spectators at the slaying of a man even when he has been justly condemned? Who among you does not enthusiastically follow the gladiatorial contests or animal fights especially those which you yourselves sponsor? But since we regard seeing a man slain as the next thing to murdering him, we have renounced such spectacles. How, then, can we be capable of murder when we will not even look at such sights to avoid being polluted and defiled?

Again, what sense does it make to think of us as murderers when we say that women who practice abortion are murderers and will render account to God for abortion? The same man cannot regard that which is in the womb as a living being and for that reason an object of God's concern and then murder it when it has come into the light. Neither can the same man forbid exposing a child which has been born on the grounds that those who do so are murderers and then slay one that has been nourished. On the contrary, we remain the same and unchanging in every way at all times: we are servants of reason and not its masters.

36. What man who believes in a resurrection would offer himself as a tomb for bodies destined to arise? For it is impossible at one and the same time to believe that our bodies will arise and then eat them as though they will not arise, or to think that the earth will yield up its dead and then suppose that those whom a man has buried within himself will not reclaim their bodies. On the contrary, the likelihood is that those who would not shrink from any outrage are men who think that they will not render an account of their present life, whether bad or good, and that there is no resurrection, but who believe that the soul also perishes along with the body and is, so to speak, snuffed out. On the other hand there is no reason for those to commit the slightest wrong who believe that nothing will remain unexamined in the presence of God and that the body too will be punished which promotes the irrational impulses and lusts of the soul. . . .

37. Let our teaching concerning the resurrection be set aside for the present [it forms the subject of a second work by Athenagoras]; but do you, who by nature and learning are in every way good, moderate, humane, and worthy of your royal office, nod your royal heads in assent now that I have destroyed the accusations advanced and have shown that we are godly, mild, and chastened in soul. Who ought more justly to receive what they request than men like ourselves, who pray for your reign that the succession to the kingdom may proceed from father to son, as is most just, and that your reign grow and increase as all men become subject to you? This is also to our advantage that we may lead a quiet and peaceable life and at the same time may willingly do all that is commanded.

15.2   Two Passages from Lactantius's
Divine Institutes

At a much later date than that of the preceding apologetic work, Lactantius was called from Africa to Nicomedia by the emperor Diocletian to teach Latin declamation and literature (Lactantius was a professor of rhetoric); but in that eastern, Greek-speaking city, he found few pupils. Being converted to Christianity, just when is unclear, he gave himself up wholly to writing, and his *Divine Institutes* is one result, from the very period of the Great Persecutions (303–11 C.E.), and in their virtual capital. The following passage describes the persecutors in by-now-traditional Apologists' terms.

Source: Lactantius, *Divinae Institutiones* 5.20, trans. William Fletcher, *Ante-Nicene Christian Library,* vol. 21 (Edinburgh: T. & T. Clark, 1871), pp. 337–38.

They cause their own death by serving most abandoned demons, whom God has condemned to everlasting punishments; in the next place, because they do not permit God to be worshipped by others, but endeavour to turn men aside to deadly rites, and strive with the greatest diligence that no life may be without injury on earth, which looks to heaven with its position secured. What else shall I call them but miserable men, who obey the instigations of their own plunderers, whom they think to be gods?—of whom they neither know the condition, nor origin, nor names, nor nature; but, clinging to the persuasion of the people, they willingly err and favor their own folly. And if you should ask them the grounds of their persuasion, they can assign none, but have recourse to the judgement of their ancestors, saying that they were wise, that they approved them, and that they knew what was best; and thus they deprived themselves of all the power of perception: they bid adieu to reason, while they place confidence in the errors of others. Thus, involved in ignorance of all things, they neither know themselves nor their gods. And would to heaven that they had been willing to err by themselves, and to be unwise by themselves! But they hurry away others also to be companions to their evil as though they were about to derive comfort from the destruction of many. But this very ignorance causes them to be so cruel in persecuting the wise; and they pretend that they are promoting their welfare, that they wish to recall them to a good mind.

Do they then strive to effect this by conversation, or by giving some reason? By no means; but they endeavour to effect it by force and tortures. O wonderful and blind infatuation! It is thought that there is a bad mind in those who endeavour to preserve their faith, but a good one in executioners. Is there, then, a bad mind in those who, against every law of humanity, against every principle of justice, are tortured, or rather, in those who inflict on the bodies of the innocent such things as neither the most cruel robbers, nor the most enraged enemies, nor the most savage barbarians have ever practised? Do they deceive themselves to such an extent that they mutually transfer and change the names of good and evil? Why, therefore, do they not call day night—the sun darkness? Moreover, it is the same impudence to give to the good the name of evil, to the wise the name of foolish, to the just the name of impious. Besides this, if they have any confidence in philosophy or in eloquence, let them arm themselves, and refute these arguments of ours if they are able; let them meet us hand to hand, and examine every point. It is befitting that they should undertake the defence of their gods, lest if our affairs should increase (as they do increase daily), theirs should be deserted, together with their shrines and their vain mockeries; and since they can effect nothing by violence (for the religion of God is increased the more it is oppressed), let them rather act by the use of reason and exhortations.

Let their priests come forth into the midst, whether the inferior ones or the greatest; their flamens, augurs, and also sacrificing kings, and the priests and ministers of their superstitions. Let them call us together to an assembly; let them exhort us to undertake the worship of their gods; let them persuade us that there are many beings by whose deity and providence all things are governed; let them show how the origins and beginning of their sacred rites were handed down to mortals; let them explain what is their source and principle; let them set forth what reward there is in their worship, and what punishment awaits neglect; why they wish to be worshipped by men; what the piety of men contributes to them, if they are blessed; and let them confirm all these things not by their own assertion (for the authority of a mortal man is of no weight), but by some divine testimonies, as we do. There is no occasion for violence and injury, for religion cannot be imposed by force; that matter must be carried on by words rather than by blows, that the will may be affected. Let them unsheath the weapon of their intellect; if their system is true, let it be asserted. We are prepared to hear, if they teach; while they are silent, we certainly pay no credit to them, as we do not yield to them even in their rage. Let them imitate us in setting forth the system of the whole matter: for we do not entice, as they say; but we teach, we prove, we show. And thus no one is detained by us against his will, for he is unserviceable to God who is destitute of faith and devotedness; and yet no one departs from us, since the truth itself detains him. Let them teach in this manner, if they have any confidence in the truth; let them speak, let them give utterance; let them venture, I say, to discuss with us something of this nature; and then assuredly their error and folly will be ridiculed by the old women, whom they despise, and by our boys. For, since they are especially clever, they know from books the race of the gods, and their exploits, commands, and deaths, and tombs; they may also know that the rites themselves, in which they have been initiated, had their origins either in human actions, or in casualties, or in deaths. It is the part of incredible madness to imagine that they are gods, whom they cannot deny to have been mortal; or if they should be so shameless as to deny it, their own writings, and those of their own people, will refute them; in short, the very beginnings of the sacred rites will convict them. They may know, therefore, even from this very thing, how great a difference there is between truth and falsehood; for they themselves with all their eloquence are unable to persuade, whereas the unskilled and the uneducated are able, because the matter itself and the truth speaks.

Lactantius, a few pages earlier, had discussed the role of eloquence in the church's missionary efforts.

Source: Lactantius, *Divine Institutes* 5.1.9–10, *PL* 5.549–50, original translation.

Many people waver [in their Christian allegiance], those most of all who have some acquaintance with literature; for here the [pagan] philosophers, the orators, and the poets are a baneful influence through their ability so easily to ensnare the unguarded mind by the attractions of their speech and the soft modulations of their flowery verses. [But we should not therefore avoid all delights of style, ourselves.] Let the cup be lined with the honey of divine wisdom so that the bitter medicine may be drained by people unawares, and without distaste as the first enticing delight hides the sourness under a sugary surface; for this is the chief reason why, among the wiser people and the more educated and the leaders of our times, holy writings lack credibility. The prophets spoke too simply, in everyday unadorned fashion, as to the masses, and are therefore held in contempt by those who want to hear or read nothing which is not polished and learned. Nothing can gain a hold on their minds that does not caress the ear with a sweet sound. Whatever seems low is thought to be of the credulous, the ignorant, the vulgar. So much is this the case, that they judge nothing truth that is not a source of pleasure in the hearing, and nothing believable that does not produce delight; no one estimates a matter by its veracity, only by its decoration. Thus they do not believe divine things because they lack all pretence, nor even believe the expounders, because they too are quite untutored or at least have little education—for it is indeed very rare that they are really eloquent. The reason is evident: eloquence is in service to this world, it parades itself before the people and caters to pleasure of evil sort . . . [and he goes on to list as exceptions, in Latin, only Minucius Felix, Tertullian, and Cyprian among eloquent Christians].

16

HERMETISM AND
GNOSTICISM

Under the influence of Egyptian religion, Judaism, late Platonism, and Christianity (in various combinations), currents of mysticism and transcendentalism arose in late syncretistic religion. Two of these are Hermetism and Gnosticism.

16.1 Hermetism: A Selection from the Poimandres

Hermetism takes its name from the fact that its ultimate teacher is Thoth (Tat), the ibis- or baboon-headed scribe of the gods in Egyptian mythology whom the Greeks identified with Hermes, and to whom they also gave the name Trismegistos (Thrice-Greatest). A sample of the Hermetists' lore is given below, in which the indebtedness to the Hebrew *Genesis* are obvious, but also the differences.

Source: *Poimandres* 1.1–12, trans. Walter Scott, *Hermetica* 1 (Oxford: Clarendon Press, 1924) (frequently reprinted).

Once on a time, when I had begun to think about the things that are, and my thoughts had soared high aloft, while my bodily senses had been put under restraint by sleep—yet not such sleep as that of men weighed down by fullness of food or by bodily weariness—methought there came to me a being of vast and boundless magnitude, who called me by my name and said to me, "What do you wish to hear and see, and to learn and come to know by thought?" "Who are you?" I said. "I," said he, "am Poimandres, the Mind of the Sovereignty." "I would fain learn," said I, "the things that are, and understand their nature, and get knowledge of God. These," I said, "are the things of which I wish to hear." He answered, "I know what you wish, for indeed I am with you everywhere; keep in mind all that you desire to learn and I will teach you."

When he had thus spoken, forthwith all things changed in aspect before me, and were opened out in a moment. And I beheld a boundless view; all was changed into light, a mild and joyous light; and I marveled when I saw it. And in a little while there had come to be in one part a downward-tending darkness, terrible and grim. . . . And thereafter I saw the darkness changing into a watery substance, which was unspeakably tossed about, and gave forth smoke as from fire; and I heard it making an indescribable sound of lamentation; for there was sent forth from it an inarticulate cry. But from the Light there came forth a holy Word, which took its stand upon the watery substance; and methought this Word was the voice of the Light.

And Poimandres spoke for me to hear, and said to me, "Do you understand the meaning of what you have seen?" "Tell me its meaning," I said, "and I shall know." "That Light," he said, "is I, even Mind, the first God, who was before the watery substance which appeared out of the darkness; and the Word which came forth from the Light is son of God. Learn my meaning," said he, "by looking at what you yourself have in you, for in you too the word is son and the mind is father of the word. They are not separate one from the other; for life is the union of word and mind." Said I, "For this I thank you."

"Now fix your thought upon the Light," he said, "and learn to know it." And when he had thus spoken, he gazed long upon me, eye to eye, so that I trembled at his aspect. And when I raised my head again, I saw in my mind that the Light consisted of innumerable Powers, and had come to be an ordered world, but a world without bounds. This I perceived in thought, seeing it by reason of the word which Poimandres had spoken to me. And when I was amazed, he spoke again, and said to me, "You have seen in your mind the archetypal form, which is prior to the beginning of things, and is limitless." Thus spoke Poimandres to me.

"But tell me," said I, "whence did the elements of nature come into being?" He answered, "They issued from God's Purpose, which beheld that beauteous word and copied it. The watery substance, having received the Word, was fashioned into an ordered world, the elements being separated out from it; and from the elements came forth the brood of living creatures. Fire unmixed leapt from the watery substance, and rose up aloft; the fire was light and keen, and active. And therewith the air, too, being light, followed the fire, and mounted up till it reached the fire, parting from earth and water; so that it seemed that the air was suspended from the fire. And the fire was encompassed by a mighty power, and was held fast, and stood firm. But earth and water remained in their own place, mingled together so as not to be [distinguishable?]; but they were kept in motion by reason of the breath-like Word which moved upon the face of the water.

"And the first Mind—that Mind which is Life and Light—being bisexual, gave birth to another Mind, a Maker of things; and this second Mind made out of fire and air seven Administrators, who encompass with their orbits the world perceived by sense; and their administration is called Destiny.

"And forthwith the Word of God leapt from the downward-tending elements of nature to the pure body which had been made, and was united with Mind the Maker; for the Word was of one substance with that Mind, and the downward-tending elements of nature were left devoid of reason, so as to be mere matter.

"And Mind the Maker worked together with the Word, and encompassing the orbits of the Administrators, and whirling them around with a rushing movement, set circling the bodies he had made, and let them revolve, travelling from no fixed starting-point to no determined goal; for their revolution begins where it ends.

"And Nature, even as Mind the Maker willed, brought forth from the downward-tending elements, animals devoid of reason; for she no longer had with her the Word. The air brought forth birds, and the water, fishes— earth and water had by this time been separated from one another—and the earth brought forth four-footed creatures and creeping things, beasts wild and tame.

"But Mind the Father of all, he who is Life and Light, gave birth to Man, a Being like to Himself; for Man was very goodly to look on, bearing the likeness of his Father. With good reason then did God take delight in Man; for it was God's own form that God took delight in. And God delivered over to man all things that had been made."

16.2   Gnosticism: A Selection from the *Pistis Sophia*

Gnosticism is something of a catch-all term, referring to a variety of para-Christian religious movements which had in common their reliance on a secret *gnosis* (knowledge). We hear most about Gnostics from hostile Christian sources like Irenaeus and Epiphanius, for whom they represented a heresy to be combatted; but we are fortunate in having some original Gnostic documents preserved in Coptic. As a sample of this kind of thinking, we cite a cosmological account.

Source: *Pistis Sophia* (Belief-Wisdom) 3.126, trans. Violet MacDermot, *NHS* 9:635–36.

Maria [Magdalene] continued again, she said to Jesus: "My Lord, of what type is the outer darkness, or rather, how many places of punishment are there in it?"

Jesus however answered and said to Maria, "The outer darkness is a great dragon whose tail is in its mouth [cf. the common drawing in the Magical Papyri], and it is outside the whole world and it surrounds the whole world. And there is a great number of places of judgment within it, and it has twelve chambers of severe punishments, and an archon [ruler] is in every chamber and the faces of the archons are different from one another. The first archon moreover which is in the first chamber has a crocodile-face and his tail is in his mouth, and all freezing comes out of the mouth of the dragon, and all dust and all cold and all the various diseases; this one is called by his authentic name and his place: Enchthonin [cf. the power of nonsense words and names in the Magical Papyri]. And the archon which is in the second chamber, a cat-face is his authentic face; this one is called in their place: Charachar. And the archon which is in the third chamber, a dog-face is his authentic face; this one is called in their place: Archaroch. And the archon which is in the fourth chamber, a serpent-face is his authentic face; this one is called in their place: Archrochar. And the archon which is in the fifth chamber, a black bull-face is his authentic face; this one is called in their place: Marchur. And the archon which is in the sixth chamber, a mountain pig-face; this one is called in their place: Lamchamor. And the archon which is in the seventh chamber, a bear-face is his authentic face; this one is called by his authentic name in their place: Luchar. And the archon of the eighth chamber, a vulture-face is his authentic face; this one is called by his name in their place: Laraoch. And the archon which is in the ninth chamber, a basilisk-face is his authentic face; this one is called by his name in their place: Archeoch. And the tenth chamber: there is a great number of archons within it, each one having seven dragon heads with their authentic face. And the one over all is called by his name in their place: Zarmaroch. And the eleventh chamber: there is a great number of archons in that place, each of them having seven cat heads with their authentic face. And the great one over them is called in their place: Rochar. And the twelfth chamber: there is a very great number of archons in it, each of them having seven dog heads with their authentic face. And the great one over them is called in their place: Chremaor.

Now these archons of these twelve chambers are inside the dragon of the outer darkness. And each of them has a name according to the hour. And each of them changes his face according to the hour. And furthermore, to each of these twelve chambers, there is a door opening to the height, so that the dragon of the outer darkness has twelve chambers of darkness, and there is a door to every chamber opening to the height. And there is an angel of the height watching at each of these doors of the chambers, whom Jeu, the First Man, the Overseer of the Light, the Messenger of the First Ordinance, has placed to keep watch over the dragon, so that it does not rebel, together with all the archons of the chambers which are within it."

17

CONVERSION, PRE-CONSTANTINE

17.1 Conversions Wrought by St. Gregory the Wonderworker, as Recorded by Gregory of Nyssa

Conversions wrought by St. Gregory Thaumaturgus (the Wonderworker) are related by St. Gregory of Nyssa in a biography compiled from memories in the district preserved to his own day, a century later. The Wonderworker had been born in Pontus (that is, in north-central Turkey), at Neocaesarea, in about 213 C.E. Of a wealthy pagan family, he was sent away to Beirut for extended education. There he became converted to Christianity. Returning home in about 238, he soon left the city for the solitude of the wild countryside of the nearby hills. There he had a vision enjoining on him a more active role than he had wished or valued before. The miracles described below took place on his return from the wilderness or, only a little later, after the Christian community there had chosen him as their bishop, i.e., in the 240s.

Source: Gregory of Nyssa, *Life of St. Gregory Thaumaturgus, PG* 46.913Cff., original translation.

So, leaving the back-country, he turned his face toward the city [Neocaesarea] where he needed to raise a church to God. When (913D) he discovered that the whole region was under the spell of spirits' [*daimones,* pagan gods] deceits and that no temple to the true God had been prepared, while the city and its environs were filled with (pagan) holy altars, and chapels [*aphidrumata,* literally "branch-foundations," of an important cult elsewhere, including a copy of that cult's statue] and the population shared a common zeal in beautifying the precincts of the idols and shrines, and in seeing to it that men's idolatry might cling to them, fortified by processions, sacrifices and the defilements around altars, like a noble warrior engaged in combat with the chief of a company—and through him all the subordinates are defeated—, so this great man commenced from the very leadership of the spirits themselves. How did he do this?

While he was traversing the road from the back-country to the city, nightfall overtook him along with a violent drawn-out rainstorm. He found himself in a certain shrine with his companions. Now the shrine was one of the famous ones, in which the spirits being worshiped appeared openly to the temple-wardens, when a certain prophetic oracle was activated by them. (916A) Going up into the shrine with his companions, he intimidated the spirits on the instant by calling the name of Christ. He purified the air, polluted with the stench of sacrifices, by a gesture of the Cross, in his usual fashion (916B) and spent the whole night awake in prayers and psalm-singing, so transforming into a house of prayer a building befouled by the altar's filth and the chapels. Having passed his night in this fashion, he had his journey to pursue once again, at dawn. The temple-warden, however, at dawn went about his usual care of the spirits; and they say that the spirits appeared and spoke to him, saying the shrine was barred to them because of the man who had stayed there; and the temple-warden made use of certain purifications and sacrifices thereby to get the spirits to return and live in the temple, applying every means, but his zeal was unrewarded: the demons did not respond to his summons as had been their custom; and, roused by indignation (916C) and anger, the temple-warden then caught up with the great man, uttering the most terrible threats, saying he would bring charges before the magistrates and apply force against him and inform the emperor of the outrage and of his being a Christian, an enemy of the gods, who had dared to set foot inside the palace [i.e., the temple]; and his entrance had removed the force that worked within the shrines, and the spirits' oracular force was no longer present in those places as it had been. And when he [Gregory] put down the temple-warden's violent and boorish anger through his more elevated attitude, opposing the alliance of the true God to every threat and declaring that he so relied on the power of his champion that, by Jesus' authority, he could drive them away from wherever he wished or settle them in (916D) whatever place he wanted; and when he had promised to give proof of what he had just said, then the temple-warden was astonished and overwhelmed by the greatness of such authority and adjured him to demonstrate his power from these very deeds, by making the spirits return to the temple. When the great man heard this, he broke off a little bit of his book, inscribed in it a certain injunction to the spirits, and gave it to the man in charge of the temple; and the writing said verbatim, "Gregory to Satan: Enter." And they say that the temple-warden took the writing and put it on the altar and applied their accustomed (917A) fumes of sacrifice and foulnesses, and beheld again the things he earlier beheld, before the spirits were dislodged from the place of idols; and after these happenings he began to think that there must be some divine force with Gregory by which he appeared the superior of the spirits; and quickly catching up with him once more before he reached the city, he asked if he could learn the secret from him, and what that God was that held the whip hand over the nature of spirits. And when the great man briefly related the secret of piety, the man in charge of the temple reacted as might be expected of a person uninitiated in divine matters, by supposing it was beneath his conception of god to believe that the divinity had been persuaded to appear to man in the flesh; and, when the other replied, it was not by words that faith in this had prevailed but that belief arose from the miracles of the events themselves, (917B) the temple-warden still sought from him the sight of some marvel, so as thus to be brought around to agreement with the faith through what happened. Thereupon, it is said that the great man wrought the great miracle, the most incredible of all: for when the temple-warden asked that a stone of a good size right under their eyes, without a human hand but solely through the power of belief, by the command of Gregory, should be transferred to some other place, the great man hesitated not a moment, but immediately commanded the stone, as if it were alive, to move to that place that the temple-warden had indicated. When that happened, straightway he believed in the Word, giving up everything—clan, house, wife, children, friends, priesthood, (917C), hearth, possessions—considering it worth everything he had, to join the company of the great man and share his toils, and that divine way of life [*philosophia*] and teaching. . . . (920A) Henceforward, that great man, beginning from his triumph over the spirits, leading the temple-warden about with him like a trophy of victory over them, that awe might strike the population through report of him, advanced on the city with confidence and boldness of speech, not upon chariots and steeds and mules, not flaunting the multitude of his retinue, (920B) but rather having his miraculous deeds [*aretai*] as a guard about him. All the inhabitants in a mob poured out from the city as if at the news of some novel spectacle, all eager to see what sort of man Gregory was, who, though a man, by his command over the beings they considered gods, as if by a king's power, moved and led the spirits about by his command wherever he wished, and banished or recalled them, to all appearance, from wherever he wanted, just like slaves—a man who had that servant of his as if enslaved to some authority, now scornful of his previous status, having exchanged all his possessions for a new way of life with him. (920C) In this mood, everyone welcomed him on the outskirts of the city, and, when he was among them and everyone was looking at him earnestly, he moved past the men as if they had been lifeless matter, turning to none of those whom he encountered but walking steadily into the city; and so he aroused in them all the more astonishment, appearing to viewers even to surpass report. The fact that he was first entering the great city, though it had not been any custom of his, and was not overwhelmed by such a mass assembled on his account but walked as if in a desert with his eyes only for himself and his path, turning aside to nobody among those gathered about him, all this appeared to people to be something even beyond the miracle of the stone. For that reason—although, as was earlier said, there had been very few (920D) who had received the faith before his visitation—as virtually the entire city accepted his priesthood in honor, he entered thus, on all sides pressed by the crowd of those that accompanied him. From the moment he took up his *philosophia*, he freed himself from everything else at once, as if from a burden, so to speak, though he had none of the necessities of life—no field, no location, no house, but was himself everything to himself (rather his virtue and faith was his homeland and hearth and wealth). So he was in the city, but a lodging for him to rest in (921A) there was not— neither one belonging to the church nor privately owned. The crowd around was at a loss about how he would be lodged and from whom he might seek shelter. "Why," the teacher asked them, "are you at a loss about such things as where people should rest their bodies, as if you were beyond the shelter of God? Or do you think God is a small house, if in him we live and move and exist?" . . . (921B) While he was discussing these matters with his companions, one of the men notable through family and wealth came up, numbered among the leaders for all his power. His name was Musonius. When he saw the matter of such concern to so many, who were ready to take the man into their homes, he pushed ahead of them all and snatched the goodwill for himself: he invited the great man to stay with him and to honor his house by entering so that it might be more distinguished and of good repute in times to come, since time would transmit to others, later, the memory of (921C) such an honor. Since many others, however, turned up to beg the same favor, he thought it right to bestow it on him who asked first. The rest, he put off with words of kindness, and returned the honor they showed, and so was lodged with the man who got there first . . . . (922D) Since, however, only a few people had heard him earlier, so great a number added themselves to the gathering before the day ended and the sun set that the number of believers appeared like the assembly of the citizen body. The next day, once again the populace was on his doorstep, along with their wives and children and the aged and those on whom the spirits or some other misfortune had laid some bodily affliction. In their midst, that man measured out what was suitable to the needs of each person in the assemblage, (924A) through the power of the Spirit [*pneuma*, not *daimon*]—

preaching, jointly examining, admonishing, teaching and healing. For he won over the greatest number to his preaching because what they saw coincided with what they heard, and the tokens of divine power shone upon him through the divine power through both. His words confirmed what they heard, the miracles of healing astonishingly confirmed what they saw. The griever was comforted, youth made wise, the aged ministered to by appropriate words. Slaves were taught to be loyal to their masters; the powerful, to be kind to the lowly; the poor, that virtue alone is wealth and the winning of it is within everyone's reach; and the man fortunate in his riches was properly admonished that he should consider himself not the master but the steward of his possessions. To women he dispensed what was profitable to them; (924B) to children, what suited their age; to parents, what was proper. . . . (924D) At that time, then, all were astonished, both those in the city and round about, by the apostolic miracles. Everything he said and did they believed to be the work of divine power; nor did they rate any court more authoritative in disputes about earthly matters, but every judgment and every tangled situation was made straight through his counsel. The result was good government and peace for one and all, through his grace, and great abundance of good things, both privately and publicly. No evil disturbed mutual concord. It may not be out of place, perhaps, to make mention of one of his decisions, so (as the saying goes) that the whole cloth may appear just from the fringe. . . . (926B) There were two brothers, young in age, recently dividing their father's estate among themselves. Their dispute was over a lake, each claiming the whole of it and neither willing to accept the other (926C) as joint owner. The teacher became the judge of the case, and, arriving at the spot, he applied his own laws on their behavior, leading them to reconciliation and exhorting the youths to love, that they might set a higher value on concord than on profits; for peace abides forever among the living and the dead, whereas the enjoyment of profits is ephemeral, but entails an eternal judgment upon their wickedness. So he said what was suitable and repressed their ungovernable youth. (926D) His exhortation, however, availed nothing. Youth was on fire and burnt in their hearts and was swollen with hopes of gain. Each one got ready an army of his people, a bloodthirsty multitude of servants governed by wrath and youth. The day of conflict was set. But on the day before battle was to begin from both sides, the man of God, abiding on the banks of the lake, enduring the night through in sleeplessness, wrought a miracle like Moses' upon the waters. Not by a blow of his staff did he divide the deep in two; rather by prayer did he dry up the whole of it at once, (928A) and at dawn revealed the lake as dry land, parched and without moisture, having not even in its cavities any remnant of water, where before the prayer there had been a sea. And he thus giving judgment through God's power returned again to his home, while between the young men the decision that emerged from the events ended the strife. . . . (929A) Such were the sayings and doings in regard to the lake. But afterwards there was such another miracle of his pointed out and recalled. For a certain river flowed among them past that place, indicating by its name its rough, fierce nature: "Lykos," because it was destructive [like a wolf, *lykos*], so it is called by the people around. It is thus swollen because it comes down from the springs of Armenia where the countryside supplies an abundant stream from the overlying mountains. It is very eroded everywhere flowing beneath the foothills of the crags, especially when (929B) made savage by the winter gullies, since it gathers to itself the accumulation from the mountains. In the low part of the country through which it runs, however, at many points constricted by crags, it overflows its banks along its sides, setting awash with its stream all the ground above. Thus dangers were continually and unexpectedly afflicting the dwellers of those regions, at an untimely hour of the night when the river invaded the fields, or often by day. Not only were the crops or seeding of flocks destroyed by flooding, but the danger beset the inhabitants as well, unforeseeably shipwrecked, so to speak, in their very houses, by the overflow. (929C) Now, as the report of the wonders previously wrought by that great man spread over the whole province, the people resident along that part of the river—men, women, and children en masse—all arose and petitioned the great man, requesting him to find for them some release from their misfortunes, out of desperation. God, he said, could accomplish all things in him, such as are impossible to human plans or projects, and none of those things that present themselves to human planning and powers had been neglected by them, such as stones and dikes; and everything else that could be thought of against that sort of ill had been attended to; yet still they could not hold against the force of the evil. Since, then, he was greatly inspired with pity by them, they thought he should take a view himself of the situation so as to learn how it was that they were not able to move their dwellings and (929D) how death from the water threatened them every moment. When he found himself at the spot (for no hesitation held back his beneficent zeal), without asking for a cart, horses, or anything else needed for a crossing, but supported on a staff, he made the whole journey discoursing deeply with his road-companions about the ultimate hope. . . . (932B) Thus he spoke, and as if filled with the divine spirit from some holy inspiration, calling on Christ to come to him as ally in the task before him, he planted the staff which he bore in his hand in the broken section of the bank. Since the ground around was soaked and spongy, it easily sank in to the bottom, from the weight of the staff and from the hand that planted it.

Then, praying that it might be like a lock and barrier to the disorder of the waters, he went home, by the action showing that everything he did was accomplished through divine power. For straightway and after no long time, the staff, rooted in the bank, became a tree. The plant set bounds to the stream and is a spectacle (932C) and a story among the inhabitants to this day. Whenever the Lykos, swollen by winter rains and run-off, rises in its usual way and is borne along savagely, roaring fearfully in its course, then barely touching with its water around the trunk of the tree, once again swelling up it is confined to its center, as if afraid to approach the tree, and it sweeps past that spot with its wave bent. So great was the power of the great Gregory, or, rather, of God working wonders through him. . . . (953D) In this fashion he conducted the administration of the church, devoting his zeal, before he should quit this life, to seeing everybody converted from faith in idols to the saving faith. When he had foreknowledge of his own demise, he eagerly investigated the whole area around the city to learn if any persons remained outside the faith. When he discovered that those who remained in the old error numbered no more than seventeen, he declared, "This is a sad thing," raising his face to God, "that anything is lacking from the crew of the saved ones." But it was deserving of great thanks that he left behind him only as many idolaters to his successor in the church, as the Christians he himself received. And praying to those who already believed that there might be an increase to perfection, and a change among those without faith, he abandoned (956A) this human life, for God. . . . The conversion of the entire province from pagan folly to the recognition of the truth, let everyone behold with wonder (956B) who reads this, and let no one doubt, looking rather to the management whereby so great a change was wrought among those converted from lies to truth. For what happened in the first days of his ministration, something that my account passed by in its hurry to get to others of his miracles, I will now pick up and recount. There was a certain mass festival in the city conducted according to tradition in honor of one of the local spirits, and almost the whole province streamed in to it, all the countryside joining the city in the celebration. The theater filled up with visitors and the crowd that flowed in spread over all the seats, everyone eagerly looking down on the orchestra to see and hear the performance. The scene-area was filled with noise, and the magicians could not put on their show. The uproar not only prevented the crowd from enjoying the music but the magicians from having the opportunity to perform—whereupon the massed voice of the populace broke forth, calling upon the spirit honored by the festival and demanding that he make room for them all. When all of them were clamoring to each other, and the sound was raised aloft to the sky, it seemed as if the whole city spoke from one mouth, which bore the prayer to the spirit. The prayer, as one can hear verbatim, ran, "Zeus, make room for us!" When the great man heard the noise of those that called upon the spirit by name, and from whom they sought (956D) adequate space for the city, he said, through one of the persons standing around him, that more room would be given them than they had ever prayed for. This speech from him was borne out to them as a rather somber declaration; for a plague succeeded this mass holiday. Songs of lamentation were straightway mingled with the dances and turned the delights among them into grief and affliction: in the place of pipes and castanets, repeated dirges possessed the city. Once the disease struck, faster than any expectation it spread like wildfire feeding on households. And the temples were filled with people suffering from the disease who fled there in hopes of healing (957A). Springs, fountains, wells were filled with those on fire with thirst from the pestilential fever (whose fever the water could not quench and who both before and after drinking suffered alike, once the disease seized them). Many betook themselves like deserters to the cemeteries and the survivors no longer were enough to bury all the dead. An attack of the evil was not without forewarning for the people, but when a sort of phantasm appeared in a household about to be destroyed, then inevitably destruction would result. The cause of the disease was evident to everyone: the spirit invoked by them was evilly answering the prayers of the foolish, (957B) making a baneful space within the city by means of the sickness. So they became the supplicants of the great man and besought him to put a stop to the destruction wrought by this ill through the God he knew and preached, who, they agreed, was the one true God and ruled all things. For from that phantasm appearing before a household's destruction and producing an instant despair of life, there was for the endangered people only one means of salvation, through having the great Gregory in the house, and so through prayer to repel the disease that fell upon it. Quickly, through those people who had been the first to be saved in such a way, the report spread about to everyone else; and all seemed idle and in vain that had been valued previously by their foolishness—oracles, (957C) ablutions and hanging about idols. They all now looked to the great priest. Each of them claimed him for himself, to save his whole family. His reward for those he saved was the salvation of their souls. For by that sort of demonstration the holiness of the priest was made plain. There was no longer any delay in agreeing to the holy mystery among those who had, through deeds, been taught the power of the faith. In this manner did the disease prove more salutary than good health among those men, for, as weak as had been their thoughts in good health, so far as concerned the reception of the holy rites, to the same degree were they made stronger toward faith through bodily sickness. So their error about their idols was tested and discovered—they all were turned toward the name of Christ, some guided to the truth by the affliction of the disease (957D) while others opposed faith in Christ as a safeguard against the plague. There are other miracles of the great Gregory surviving in memory to this day, which we withhold from a disbelieving audience lest people be harmed supposing the truth a lie, through the sheer magnitude of the account; so we have not added these to what we have written. To Christ who performs such wonders through his servants be the fame, the glory and the supplication, now and forever, and for ages upon ages. Amen.

17.2 A Modern Comparison: The Conversion of Native Americans

For comparative purposes, the following glimpses of Native American responses to evangelizing are interesting. They are assembled from the first half of the nineteenth century.

Source: R. F. Berkhofer, *Salvation and the Savages* (Westport, Conn.: Greenwood Press, 1977), pp. 114f., 144f.

Not all halfbreeds converted, nor did all fullbloods remain loyal to the religion of their forefathers. The majority of conversions can no longer be explained, due to the lack of data from such modern devices as depth interviews and Rorschach and Thematic Apperception tests. Even the few detailed accounts that remain give only superficial reasons, such as old age and fear of death, or the fulfillment of a promise to embrace Christianity if a warrior escaped his enemy during battle. Rather than true reasons, these seem the culminating points of long psychological struggles. Probably not a few of the converts gathered about the mission to share the "loaves and fishes" more than the blood of Christ. Surely this seems to be the basis of Henry Spalding's early successes among the Nez Percés.

Frequently the customs of the old way provided gateways to the new. Due to the inferior status of women in the Sioux Tribe, women found it easier to convert than men. After six years of operation, one station in this tribe had forty members, of whom only two were men, who had joined within the last year. In this tribe the males engaged in the religious rites, and these activities as well as those in other areas were rigidly prescribed by custom, while the women took no part in the rites nor were their activities clear cut. Not only did this make conversion easier for a female, but her already modest dress was approved without change by the missionaries and her new religion simply meant from her husband's view a better kept house. On the other hand, a man had to cut off his hair, change his style of dress, and adopt new work patterns—in short, a whole new role.

In the battle against Satan, even so small a thing as medicine played a part. To prevent the Indians from attending the conjurers and medicine men of native tradition and religion, the missionaries sought to prove the superiority of white medicines and prove cures could be effected without "the idolatrous incantations of the devil over the sick." When traditional native "medicine" failed, the ill Indian called in the missionary and often promised to convert if the blackcoat's remedy was better than the old way. A rich Ottawa woman made such a bargain with Jotham Meeker, and a dull-witted Sioux man made the proposition to Stephen Riggs and thus became the first fullblooded Sioux male to join the church. A Potawatomi and an Ojibwa male also converted after recovery from severe illness. . . .

Illustrative of the second sequence was the most successful mission in this [Sioux] tribe. At the request of a halfbreed trader who wished his family educated, the American Board established a station at Laqui Parle in 1835 among the Wahpeton. Trader Renville helped the missionary to locate and in translation work. His wife was the first fullblooded Sioux to join the church, and most of the early church members and scholars in the mission school were his relatives. But even here as the Indians began to understand the implications of the religious and civil doctrines preached by the missionary and as the church slowly gained members, opposition arose. Whereas formerly the non-Christians had concealed their religious practices from the blackcoat, they made them as public as possible by 1840. Then in 1842 famine struck the Eastern Sioux, and the plight acted as a catalyst for violent opposition. The Indians believed the spirits had sent the drought as punishment for the departure from their forefathers' customs. While prior to this year the Sioux had occasionally killed mission cattle in revenge, they now began to slaughter three to ten a year. In 1845 the "soldiers" prevented the children from attending the school, and the Indians broke the school windows, stole vegetables, and damaged the mill. Opposition even halted the church's growth. In the years immediately preceding the drought, the church usually gained ten members annually; after the drought, only two Indians joined the church during the next four years. To make it even worse, the famine dispersed one-half of the older members, and of the remainder, one-half had been suspended by mid-1846.

After the drought, even Renville lost some of his influence. In the opinion of one missionary, only the trader's presence protected the station. So important did this man seem to the resident missionary, that Renville's death in 1846 caused him to leave in discouragement. When the Indians realized the missionary was not obliged to stay, they appreciated his replacement, Stephen R. Riggs, slightly more. The congregation increased by a few listeners, but opposition continued without abatement. Feasts were held simultaneously with Sunday services to attract men from the church. In 1848 an old chief wanted the "soldiers" to drive Riggs out, but the local band did not sustain him. Though the church had gained membership in recent years, still in 1850 the membership was only half of what it had been at the time of the famine.

18

THE PERSECUTIONS

18.1 Chronology of the Persecutions

Major acts of persecution of the Christians
and dates commonly suggested

C.E.

64	Rome (Nero, after the Great Fire)
ca. 90?	Rome (by order of Domitian?)
108	Rome (Ignatius)
111	Pontus, by Pliny the Younger
124–25	province of Asia (through Hadrian's letter to governor Minucius)
120s	Rome (bishop Telesphorus)
152–56	Rome (Ptolemaeus)
165?	Rome (Justin)
165–68	Smyrna (Polycarp)
160s	Athens, Rome, elsewhere? (Euseb., *Hist. eccl.* 4.23); also Laodicea? (Sagaris dies, Euseb., *Hist. eccl.* 4.26) and Pergamon (Papylas and Carpus)
177	Lyons and Vienne
178	Palestine? (Origen, *Contra Celsum* 8.69)
180	Africa (at Madaura and at Scilli near Carthage)
180s	Italy? (Hippolytus, *Elenchos* 9.2.11)
202–3	General Edict (Euseb., *Hist. eccl.* 6.1ff.): Africa, Egypt, Rome, & c
212–13	Africa (cf. Tertullian)
222	Rome (Bishop Callistus)
235?	Cappadocia (Origen, *Commentary on Matthew* 39ff.)
248	Alexandria (mob action, Euseb., *Hist. eccl.* 6.41.1)
249–50	General Edicts of Decius: Rome, Antioch, Jerusalem, Alexandria, Carthage, & c
257–58	General Edicts of Valerian: Africa, Egypt, Palestine, & c
270s?	Scattered martyrdoms; cf. W.H.C. Frend, *Martyrdom and Persecution in the Early Church* (Garden City, N.Y.: Anchor Books, 1967), p. 444

299–300 Diocletian from his capital Nicomedia clears Christians out of the army
303 Feb. 23–24: First Edict of the Great Persecutions posted, with supplement (aimed against buildings, books, civic rights—not persons)
Spring: Second Edict posted (for arrest of bishops)
Nov.?: Third Edict posted (bishops must sacrifice or be jailed)
304 Spring: Fourth Edict posted (all Christians must sacrifice)
305? The anti-Christian propaganda work, *The Deeds of Pilate*
May (until April 306): persecution in east lapses
May 1: Diocletian and Maximian abdicate (Diocletian †313)
306 April: Fifth Edict posted in Caesarea in Palestine (Christians must sacrifice on orders of Maximin Daia)
July 25, London: Constantius dies, Constantine succeeds him
Oct. 28: Maxentius claims rule in Rome
307 Severus dies; concord between Maxentius and Constantine (who marries Fausta, Maxentius's daughter)
308 Fall: "Congress of Carnuntum" for peace among emperors
Nov. 11: Licinius declared Augustus
309 July/Aug. to Nov.: Persecution in the East lapses
310 Maximian rises against Constantine and is destroyed
311 Constantia, sister of Constantine, betrothed to Licinius; secret treaty between Maxentius (Rome) and Maximin Daia
April 30: Galerius's Edict of Serdica for his east-central realm (ending persecutions there and in Maximin Daia's realm)
May 5: Galerius dies
Maximin Daia and Licinius sign Peace of Chalcedon
Maximin Daia begins to breach Edict of Serdica, after months of pro-pagan measures, propaganda, organization in Antioch
312 Oct. 28: After his vision, Constantine defeats Maxentius at the Battle of the Milvian Bridge
313 January: At Milan, Constantine and Licinius draft "Edict" of toleration, and Licinius marries Constantia
Feb.: Maximin Daia relaxes persecution (Euseb., *Hist. eccl.* 9.9A)
Feb./Mar.: Maximin Daia crosses Bosporus against Licinius
April 30: Maximin Daia defeated at Hadrianople
June 13: Licinius in Nicomedia issues Edict of Toleration
Sept.: Maximin Daia issues Edict of Toleration (Euseb., *Hist. eccl.* 9.10.7)
Oct.?: Maximin Daia dies

18.2 Persecutions of the Jews

Passages above have shown, among the non-Christian population of the empire, scorn or impatience or disagreement toward other people's religious beliefs, and stronger reactions still, in the setting of Alexander of Abonouteichos, against openly expressed atheism; but of *hostility* toward others' beliefs, there is no sign; so there were no persecutions. In the earlier Seleucid kingdom, toward Jews, it had been another matter: martyrs are familiar from the second century b.c.e. and the Old Testament. Among later illustrations relevant to the period on which this collection is focused, Jews' willingness to die for their religious beliefs may be seen in the following text. It was put into its final form around 200 c.e., and reports on a scene of the preceding century.

Source: S. Lieberman, *Annuaire de l'Institut de Philologie et d'Histoire Orientales et Slaves* 7 (1939/44), p. 418.

When Rabbi Haninah ben Teradyon was seized [while teaching the Law], sentence was passed on him to be burnt with his book [the Torah]. They informed him: "Sentence has been passed upon you to be burnt together with your book" . . . , they informed his wife: "Sentence has been passed upon your husband to be burnt with his book and on you to be executed" . . . , they informed his daughter: "Sentence has been passed on your father to be burnt, on your mother to be executed, on you to do work" [i.e., to be prostituted]. . . . Then one philosopher stood up before the proconsul and said: "My master, do not become proud [of the fact] that you burnt the scroll of the Law, for it has returned to the place whence it was issued, to its father's house." He said to him: "Tomorrow you will be punished like them." He retorted: "You have announced good tidings to me; tomorrow my share will be with them in the future world."

18.3   Contradictory Evidence for the Persecution under Septimius Severus: The *Historia Augusta* and Tertullian

Turning to the history of the persecution of Christians, we find much fuller and more familiar evidence, shot through, however, with puzzling questions. Some of them concern even the largest matters: the very reason for persecution—which, the more one studies it, turns into "reasons," plural, operating among different parts of society and at different levels of authority. It is likewise unclear just what was the extent of action taken by the state. Was there, for example, a "general edict" aimed by the emperors against Christians in the whole empire, in 202 c.e.? Besides the evidence of attested martyrdoms of that and the following years, there is testimony of the "Augustan Histories." In this collection of biographies of emperors compiled toward the end of the fourth century, along with a good deal of demonstrable fabrication, occurs this passage.

Source: *Life of Septimius Severus* 17, in *Scriptores Historiae Augustae,* trans. David Magie, LCL.

[In 202, Septimius promoted] his elder son and appointed him consul as a colleague to himself; and without further delay, while still in Syria, the two entered upon their consulship. After this, having first raised his soldiers' pay, he turned his steps toward Alexandria, and while on his way thither he conferred numerous rights upon the communities of Palestine. He forbade conversion to Judaism under heavy penalties and enacted a similar law in regard to the Christians. He then gave the Alexandrians the privilege of a local senate, for they were still without any public council.

On the other hand, there is Tertullian writing in 212 about the events he was familiar with in North Africa.

Source: Tertullian, *To Scapula* 4, trans. S. Thelwall, *Ante-Nicene Christian Library,* vol. 11 (Edinburgh: T. & T. Clark, 1869), pp. 49–50.

You see, then, how you [pagan authorities] trespass yourselves against your instructions to wring from the confessing a denial. It is, in fact, an acknowledgement of our innocence that you refuse to condemn us at once when we confess. In doing your utmost to extirpate us, if that is your object, it is innocence you assail. But how many rulers, men more resolute and more cruel than you are, have contrived to get quit of such causes altogether—as [the governor] Cincius Severus, who himself suggested the remedy [while hearing cases] at Thysdrus [in modern Tunisia], pointing out how the Christians should answer that they might secure an acquittal; as Vespronius Candidus, who dismissed from his court a Christian, on the ground that to satisfy his fellow citizens would break the peace of the community; as Asper, who in the case of a man who gave up his faith under slight infliction of torture, did not compel the offering of sacrifice, having owned before, among the lawyers and advisors at court, that he was annoyed at having to meddle with such a case. Pudens, too, at once dismissed a Christian who was brought before him, perceiving from the indictment that it was a case of vexatious accusation; tearing the document in pieces, he refused so much as to hear him without the presence of his accuser, as not being consistent with the imperial commands. All this might be officially brought under your notice, and by the very lawyers, who are themselves also under obligations to us, although in court they give their voice as it suits them. The clerk of one of them, who was liable to be thrown upon the ground by an evil spirit, was set free from his affliction; as was also the relative of another, and the little boy of a third. How many men of rank (to say nothing of common people) have been delivered from devils and healed of diseases! Even Severus himself, the father of Antoninus [Caracalla], was graciously mindful of the Christians; for he sought out the Christian Proculus, surnamed Torpacion, the business agent of Euhodias, and in gratitude for his having once cured him by anointing, he kept him in his palace till the day of his death. Antoninus, too, brought up as he was on Christian milk, was intimately acquainted with this man. Both women and men of the highest rank, whom Severus knew well to be Christians, were not merely permitted by him to remain uninjured; but he even bore distinguished testimony in their favor and gave them publicly back to us from the hands of a raging populace.

18.4 Origen on Persecution of Christians

Persecutions as they were experienced by Christians were both reported and interpreted by persons in pastoral positions. Origen, perhaps referring to events in Asia Minor in 235 C.E., provides an illustration of this in the course of his very long *Commentary on Matthew* (§39), known only in a Latin version.

Source: Origenes Werke 11, *Die Griechischen Christlichen Schriftsteller* 38, ed. Erich Klostermann (Leipzig: Hinrichs, 1933), original translation.

"Next (Matt. 24:9–10) they [the unbelievers] will deliver you over to sufferings, and will kill you; and you will be hated for my [Jesus'] name among all peoples . . ."—but if anyone should want to argue over the words "all the peoples," he will not find it clear enough that, among "all peoples" inhabiting the furthest parts of the earth, the people of Christ are indeed held in detestation; unless perhaps one might say that "all" was written instead of "many" for the purpose of emphasizing how many. . . . Those who are in the midst of calamities, arguing over their causes, always like to find something to talk about; so when such things do befall the world, it is a consequence—as if man were abandoning the cult of the gods—that they should say that wars and famines and plagues occur due to the great number of Christians. Pagans, and anyone wise in pagan wisdom, thus often have blamed famines on Christians and also referred the causes of pestilences to the Church of Christ. We, however, know that, in our own regions, there are earthquakes in some places, and some destruction has been wrought, with the result that persons impious and outside the faith declared Christians the cause of the earthquake; and on that account the churches have suffered persecutions and have been burnt down; and not only this, but the seemingly wise say things like that in public, that the worst earthquakes take place because of the Christians.

18.5 Clement of Alexandria on the Proper Response to Persecution

Proper response by Christians to persecution in Egypt was spelled out toward the turn of the third century by Clement of Alexandria.

Source: Clement, *Stromateis* 4.10.76f., trans. Beresford James Kidd, in *Documents Illustrative of the History of the Church* (London: SPCK,1920), 1:159.

When again [Jesus] says, "When they persecute you in this city, flee ye to the other," he does not advise flight as if persecution were an evil thing; nor does he enjoin them, by flight, to avoid death, as if in dread of it, but wishes us neither to be the authors nor abettors of any evil to any one, either to ourselves or the persecutor and murderer. For he, in a way, bids us to take care of ourselves. But he who disobeys is rash and foolhardy.

And if he who kills a man of God sins against God, he also who presents himself before the judgement-seat becomes guilty of his death. And such is also the case with him who does not avoid persecution, but out of daring presents himself for capture. Such a one, as far as in him lies, becomes an accomplice in the crime of the persecutor. And if he also uses provocation, he is wholly guilty, challenging the wild beast. And similarly, if he afford any cause for conflict or punishment, or retribution or enmity, he gives occasion for persecution. Wherefore, then, we are enjoined not to cling to anything that belongs to this life; but "to him that takes our cloak to give our coat," not only that we may continue destitute of inordinate affection, but that we may not by retaliating make our persecutors savage against ourselves, and stir them "up to blaspheme the Name."

18.6 Athanasius on Response to Persecution

Athanasius, successor to Peter, the last bishop of Alexandria mentioned by Eusebius, looking back from twenty years' vantage, recalls impressions about both prescribed and actual response to persecution.

Source: Athanasius, *Apology for His Flight* 22, trans. James Stevenson, in *A New Eusebius* (London: SPCK, 1957), p. 170.

Thus the saints, as I said before, were abundantly preserved in their flight by the providence of God, as physicians for the sake of them that had need. And to all men generally, even to us is this law given, that we should flee when we are persecuted and hide ourselves when we are sought after, and not rashly tempt the Lord, but should wait, as I said above, until the appointed time of death arrive or the Judge determine something concerning us, according as it shall seem to him to be good; that we should be ready that, when the time calls for us, or when we are taken, we may contend for the truth even unto death. This rule the blessed martyrs observed in their several persecutions. When persecuted, they fled; while concealing themselves, they showed fortitude; and when discovered, they submitted themselves to martyrdom.

18.7   Cyprian on Responses to Persecution

Cyprian, bishop of Carthage, later recalls the response of the city's Christians in 250 to the orders that initiated the persecution under the emperor Decius.

Source: Cyprian, *On Those Who Fell Away* (*De lapsis*) 8f., trans. James Stevenson, *A New Eusebius,* pp. 230f.

Alas! there are those from whom all this is fallen and passed out of memory. They did not even wait to be arrested before they went up [and offered sacrifice], or questioned before they made their denial [of their Christianity]. Many fell before the fight, many were laid low without meeting the enemy; they did not even give themselves the chance of seeming unwilling to sacrifice to the idols. They ran to the market-place of their own accord, they hasted to death of their own will; as if they had always wished it, as if embracing an opportunity which they had fervently desired. How many the magistrates put off at the time, as night was at hand! How many who even entreated that their undoing might not be delayed! How can any one make violence an excuse for his guilt, when the violence was rather on his own part and to his own destruction? When they came, thus willingly, to the Capitol [local center of Jupiter-worship], when they spontaneously submitted themselves to the commission of that dreadful deed, was there no tottering in the limbs, no blackness upon the face, no quaking of the stomach and collapse of the limbs? Did not the senses die, the tongue cleave, and speech fail? Could the servant of God stand there and speak and renounce Christ, he who before had renounced the Devil and the world? The altar where he went to perish, was it not his funeral pile? Ought he not to shudder at and flee from an altar of the Devil which he had seen in the smoke and redolence of its vile odor, as from the death and sepulchre of his existence? Why bring an offering with you, wretched man, why present a victim? You are yourself an offering at the altar, you are yourself come as a victim; you have slaughtered there your own salvation, your hope; your faith was burnt in those funeral flames.

Many, however, were unsatisfied with doing destruction upon themselves; men were urged to their ruin by mutual encouragements, and the fatal cup of death was offered from mouth to mouth. That nothing might be wanting to their load of guilt, even infants in their parents' arms, carried or led, were deprived, while yet tender, of what was granted them in their commencement of life. Will not these children in the day of judgement say, "We did not sin; it was not our will to hasten from the bread and cup of the Lord to an unhallowed pollution. We perish through the treachery of others, and our parents on earth have robbed us of our parentage in heaven: they forfeited for us the church as a mother, and God as a father, and thus, while young and unaware and ignorant of that monstrous act, we are included in a league of sin by others, and perish through their deceit."

18.8   Two Papyrus *Libelli* attesting to Christian Apostasy

Certificates on papyrus from Egypt (in Latin, *libelli*, mentioned in other texts) survive by the dozens from the persecution of Decius's reign. They date to 250, down to mid-July. Their format has little variety, as the following two examples indicate.

Source: John R. Knipfing, "The Date of the Acts of Phileas and Philonomus," *HTR* 16 (1923): 346–47, cited by J. Stevenson, *A New Eusebius*, p. 228.

First hand: To the commission chosen to superintend the sacrifices at the village of Alexander's Isle. From Aurelius Diogenes, son of Satabous, of the village of Alexander's Isle, aged 72 years, with a scar on the right eyebrow. I have always sacrificed to the gods, and now in your presence in accordance with the edict I have made sacrifice and poured a libation and partaken of the sacred victims. I request you to certify this below. Farewell. I, Aurelius Diogenes, have presented this petition.

Second hand: I, Aurelius Syrus, saw you and your son sacrificing.
Third hand: . . . onos
First hand: The year of the emperor Caesar Gaius Messius Quintus Trajanus Decius Pius Felix Augustus, Epeiph 2 [June 26, 250 c.e.]

To the commission chosen to superintend the sacrifices. From Aurelia Ammounos, daughter of Mystus, of the Moeris quarter, priestess of the god Petesouchos, the great, the mighty, the immortal, and priestess of the gods in the Moeris quarter. I have sacrificed to the gods all my life, and now again, in accordance with the decree and in your presence, I have made sacrifice and poured a libation and partaken of the sacred victims. I request you to certify this below.

18.9   Cyprian on Forgiveness for Apostasy

The emperor Valerian in 257 commanded that his subjects should indicate their reverence for "the religion of Rome" (the phrasing in the *Governor's Report* of Cyprian's martyrdom, echoed by accounts from other provinces). The next year he followed up with a further order in this form.

Source: Cyprian, *Letters* 80.1, trans. J. Stevenson, in *A New Eusebius*, p. 259.

Many various and uncertain rumors are going about, but the truth is as follows: Valerian had sent a rescript to the senate directing that bishops, presbyters and deacons should forthwith be punished; that senators and men of rank and Roman knights should lose their dignity and be deprived of their property, and if, when deprived of their possessions, they should still continue to be Christians, then they should lose their heads also; that matrons should be deprived of their property and banished; that whosoever of Caesar's household had either before confessed, or should now confess, should forfeit his property and be sent in chains as conscripts to Caesar's estates.

Cyprian, bishop of Carthage 248–58 C.E., lived through the Decian persecution of the mid-third century, and had at that time to deal with the pastoral problems raised by people's conduct under pressure. His letters contain advice on what distinctions were proper in regard to various degrees of failure and surrender, and what might be forgiven, and how. He refers often to the certificates, amounting sometimes to grants of forgiveness, sought from Christians who had not surrendered despite pains and penalties, and whose sanctity was thought to give them the power of remission of sins.

Source: Cyprian, *Letters* 13, 14, 18, 22, trans. Robert Ernest Wallis, *Ante-Nicene Christian Library* (Edinburgh: T. & T. Clark, 1868–69).

13. Cyprian to the presbyters and deacons, his brethren, greetings. I have read your letter, beloved brethren, wherein you wrote that your wholesome counsel was not wanting to our brethren, that, laying aside all rash haste, they should manifest a religious patience to God, so that when by his mercy we come together we may debate upon all kinds of things, according to the discipline of the church, especially since it is written, "Remember from whence thou hast fallen, and repent." Now he repents who, remembering the divine precept, with meekness and patience and obeying the priests of God, deserves well of the Lord by his obedience and his righteous works.

Since, however, you intimate that some are insistent in pressing quickly to be received into communion, and have desired in this matter that some rule should be given by me to you, I think I have written enough on this subject in the last letter that was sent to you: those persons who have received a certificate [*libellus*] from the martyrs [who did not hide or abandon their Christianity, but escaped death] and can be assisted by their help with the Lord in respect of their sins, if they begin to be pressed by some sickness or risk and when they have made confession, and have received from you the laying of hands on them in acknowledgement of their penitence—such persons should be given to the Lord with the peace promised to them by the martyrs. But others who, without having received any certificate from the martyrs, are arousing ill-will (and theirs is the condition not of a few, nor of one church, nor of one province, but of the whole world) must wait, relying on the protection of the Lord, for the public peace of the church itself. For this is suitable to the modesty and the discipline and the very life of all of us, that [with] the chief officers meeting together with the clergy in the presence also of the people who stand fast—to whom themselves, moreover, honor is to be shown for their faith and fear [of God]—we may be able to order all things with the religiousness of a common consultation. But how irreligious is it, and mischievous, even to those themselves who are eager, that while such as are exiles and driven from their country, and stripped of all their property, have not yet returned to the church, some of the lapsed should be hasty to anticipate even confessors themselves, and to enter the church before them! If they are so over-anxious, they have what they require in their own power, the times themselves offering them freely more than they ask. The struggle is still going forward, and the strife is daily celebrated. If they truly and with constancy repent of what they have done, and the fervor of the faith prevails [if they present now themselves as confessors], he who cannot be delayed may be crowned. I bid you, beloved brethren, ever heartily farewell; and have me in remembrance. Greet all the brotherhood in my name and tell them to be mindful of me. Farewell.

14. Cyprian to his brethren the presbyters and deacons assembled at Rome, greetings. Having ascertained, beloved brethren, that what I have done and am doing has been told to you in a somewhat garbled and untruthful manner, I have thought it necessary to write this letter to you, wherein I might give an account to you of my doings, my discipline, and my diligence; for, as the Lord's commands teach, immediately the first burst of the disturbance arose and the people with violent clamor repeatedly demanded me, I, taking into consideration not so much my own safety as the public peace of the brethren, withdrew for a while, lest, by my over-bold presence, the tumult which had begun might be still further provoked. Nevertheless, although absent in my body, I was not wanting either in spirit or in act or in my advice, so as to fail in any benefit that I could offer to my brethren by my counsel, according to the Lord's precepts, in anything that my poor abilities enabled me.

And what I did, these thirteen letters, sent forth at various times, declare to you, which I have transmitted to you; in which neither counsel to the clergy nor exhortations to the confessors nor rebuke, when it was necessary, to the exiles, nor my appeals and persuasions to the whole brotherhood, that they should entreat the mercy of God, were wanting, to the full extent that, according to the law of faith and the fear of God, with the Lord's help, my poor abilities could endeavor. But afterwards, when tortures came, my words reached both to our tortured brethren and to those who were as yet only imprisoned with a view to torture, to strengthen and console them. Moreover, when I found that those who had polluted their hands and mouths with sacrilegious contact, or had no less infected their consciences with wicked [forged] certificates [of sacrifice], were everywhere soliciting the martyrs and were also corrupting the confessors with importunate and excessive entreaties, so that, without any discrimination or examination of the individuals, thousands of certificates [of remission of sin] were given out daily, contrary to the law of the Gospel, I wrote letters in which I recalled by my advice, as much as possible, the martyrs and confessors to the Lord's commands. To the presbyters and deacons also was not wanting the vigor of the priesthood; so that some, too little mindful of discipline, and hasty with a rash precipitation, who had already begun to join in communion with the lapsed, were restrained by my interposition. Among the people, moreover, I have done what I could to quiet their minds and have instructed them to maintain ecclesiastical discipline.

18. Caldonius to Cyprian and his fellow presbyters abiding at Carthage, greetings. The necessity of the times induces us not hastily to grant peace. But it was well to write to you that they who, after having

sacrificed, were again tried, went into exile. And thus they seem to me to have atoned for their former crime, in that they now let go their possessions and homes and, repenting, follow Christ. Thus Felix, who assisted in the office of presbyter under Decimus and was very near to me in bonds (I knew that same Felix very thoroughly), and Victoria his wife, and Lucius, being faithful, were banished, and have left their possessions, which the treasury now has in keeping. Moreover, a woman, Bona by name, who was dragged by her husband to sacrifice and (with no conscience guilty of crime, but because those who held her hands, sacrificed) began to cry out against them, "I did not do it. It was you who did it!"— she also was banished. Since, therefore, all these were asking for peace, saying, "We have recovered the faith which we had lost, we have repented, and have publicly confessed Christ"—although it seems to me that they ought to receive peace—yet I have referred them to your judgement, that I might not appear to presume anything rashly. If, therefore, you should wish me to do anything by the common decision, write to me. Greet our brethren; our brethren greet you. I bid you, beloved brethren, ever heartily farewell.

22. Cyprian to the presbyters and deacons abiding at Rome, his brethren, greetings. After the letters that I wrote to you, beloved brethren, in which what I had done was explained, and some slight account was given of my discipline and diligence, there came another matter which, any more than the others, ought not to be concealed from you. For our brother Lucian, who himself is one of the confessors, earnest indeed in faith and robust in virtue but little grounded in the readings of the Lord's word, has attempted certain things, constituting himself for a time an authority for unskilled people, so that certificates written by his hand were given indiscriminately to many persons in the name of Paulus; whereas Mappalicus the martyr, cautious and modest, mindful of the law and discipline, wrote no letters contrary to the Gospel but only, moved with domestic affection for his mother who had fallen, commanded peace to be given to her. Saturninus, moreover, after his torture, still remaining in prison, sent out no letters of this kind. But Lucian, not only while Paulus was still in prison, gave out everywhere in his [Paulus'] name certificates written with his own hand, but even after his decease persisted in doing the same things under his name, saying that this had been commanded by Paulus, ignorant that he must obey the Lord rather than his fellow servant. In the name also of Aurelius, a young man who had undergone torture, many certificates were given out, written by the hand of the same Lucian, because Aurelius did not know how to write himself.

18.10 The Martyrdom of Cyprian, from the Official Records

The martyrdom of Cyprian, bishop of Carthage, took place in 258. It is known through his own writings, through a biography, and through a special separate account, the *Governor's Report.*

Source: Edward Charles Everard Owen, *Some Authentic Acts of the Early Martyrs* (Oxford: Clarendon Press, 1927), 95–96, altered; the longer doubtful parts are bracketed.

During the consulship of the emperors Valerian and Gallienus, Valerian being consul for the fourth and Gallienus for the third time, on August 30 at Carthage in his private room Paternus the proconsul said to Cyprian the bishop, "The most sacred emperors Valerian and Gallienus have thought fit to send me a letter in which they have commanded that those who do not observe the Roman religion must recognize the Roman rites. I have therefore made inquiries concerning yourself. What answer have you to give me?" Cyprian the bishop said, "I am a Christian and a bishop. I know no other God than the one true God who 'made heaven and earth, the sea, and all that in them is.' This God we Christians serve, to Him we pray day and night for ourselves and for all men, and for the safety of the emperors themselves." The proconsul Paternus said, "Is your will constant in this?" Cyprian the bishop answered, "A good will which knows God cannot be altered." The proconsul Paternus said, "Can you then in accordance with the orders of Valerian and Gallienus go into exile to the city of Curubis?" Cyprian the bishop said, "I will go." The proconsul Paternus said, "They have thought fit to write me not about bishops only but also about priests. I would know therefore from you who the priests are who reside in this city." Cyprian the bishop answered, "It is an excellent and beneficial provision of your laws that informers are forbidden. They cannot therefore be revealed and reported by me. They will be found in their own cities." The proconsul Paternus said, "I will seek them out here today." Cyprian the bishop said, "Since our discipline forbids anyone to offer himself unsought, and this is also at variance with your principles, they cannot offer themselves any more than I can report them; but if sought by you they will be found." The proconsul Paternus said, "They shall be found by me." And he added, "The emperors have also given instructions that in no place shall meetings be held nor shall anyone enter the cemeteries. If therefore any fail to observe these beneficial instructions, he shall suffer death." Cyprian the bishop answered, "Do as you are instructed." [Then the proconsul Paternus ordered the blessed Cyprian to be banished.

And as he stayed a long time in exile, the proconsul Aspasius Paternus was succeeded in the proconsulship by Galerius Maximus, who ordered the holy bishop Cyprian to be recalled and brought before him.] When Cyprian, the holy martyr chosen by God, had returned from the city Curubis, which had been assigned as his place of banishment by command of Aspasius then proconsul, by divine command he remained in his own gardens, whence he daily expected to be summoned, as had been shown. While he still lingered in that place, suddenly on September 13 in the consulship of Tuscus and Bassus there came to him two high officials, one an equerry of the staff of the proconsul Galerius Maximus and the other a member of the same staff, an equerry of the bodyguard. These lifted him into a carriage, placed him between them, and conveyed him to the house of Sextus, whither the proconsul Galerius Maximus had retired to recover his health. And so the same Galerius Maximus the proconsul ordered Cyprian to be remanded till the morrow. For the time being, blessed Cyprian withdrew under guard to the house of a high official, equerry on the same staff of the illustrious Galerius Maximus the proconsul, and remained with him at his house in the street which is called Saturn's between the temple of Venus and the temple of Public Welfare. There the whole congregation of the brethren gathered. When this came to holy Cyprian's knowledge, he gave orders that charge should be kept of the young women, for all had remained in the street before the door of the official's house.

On the morrow, being September 14, a great crowd gathered in the morning to the house of Sextus in accordance with the command of Galerius Maximus the proconsul. And so the same Galerius Maximus the proconsul ordered that Cyprian the bishop should be brought before him on the morrow where he sat in the Hall Sauciolum. When he had been brought before him, Galerius Maximus the proconsul said to Cyprian the bishop, "Are you Thascius Cyprian?" Cyprian the bishop answered, "I am." Galerius Maximus the proconsul said, ["Have you taken on yourself to be Pope of persons holding sacrilegious opinions?" Cyprian the bishop answered, "Yes." Galerius Maximus the proconsul said,] "The most sacred emperors have commanded you to perform the rite." Cyprian the bishop answered, "I refuse." Galerius Maximus the proconsul said, "Consider your own best interests." Cyprian the bishop answered, "Do as you are bid. In so clear a case there is no [need for] consultation." Galerius Maximus, having conferred with his advisors said, with difficulty and reluctance, "You have long lived in a sacrilegious mind and you have joined with yourself very many wicked men to your conspiracy, and you have set yourself up as the enemy of Roman gods and holy worship; nor have the pious and most sacred emperors Valerian and Gallienus, Augusti, and Valerian the most noble Caesar been able to recall you to membership in their rites. And therefore, since you have been convicted as an instigator and standard-bearer of wicked wrongdoing, you shall be an example to those whom you have made your associates by your crime. By your blood, good order shall be vindicated." And he read the verdict aloud from the record: It is our pleasure that Thascius Cyprian be executed by the sword. Cyprian the bishop said, "Thanks be to God."

After this sentence, the crowd of brethren cried, "Let us too be beheaded with him!" From this arose an uproar among the brethren and a great crowd followed him out. So the same Cyprian was led forth on to the land of Sextus behind the governor's palace, and there he took off his mantle and spread it where he would kneel, and prostrated himself on the ground. And then he took off his outer garment, giving it to the deacons, and stood in his linen and began the wait for the Guardsman. When the Guardsman had arrived, he told his followers to give the man 25 gold pieces. Many kerchiefs and towels were being placed before him by the brothers. Then Cyprian bound his eyes with his own hand but, when he couldn't fasten the ends of the kerchief, the priest Julian and the sub-deacon Julian did it for him. Thus Cyprian suffered his end, and his body was exposed for view nearby to satisfy the Gentiles' curiosity. At night, however, his body was removed and, accompanied by candles and tapers with prayer and rejoicing was brought to the cemetery of Macrobius Candidianus the procurator, which is on the Mappalian road near the fish-ponds. A few days later, moreover, Galerius Maximus the proconsul died. [The most blessed martyr Cyprian suffered on the 14th day of September under the emperors Valerian and Gallienus, in the reign of our Lord Jesus Christ, to whom belong honor and glory for ever and ever. Amen.]

18.11 Persecution of Manichaeism, from an Imperial Decree

Persecution of Manichaeism in the empire began with the following decree. Mani (216–276 C.E.), as the Apostle of Jesus active in Persia, had preached a Jesus who rescued the Kingdom of Light from a long struggle and complicated involvement with the Kingdom of Darkness. Mani had enjoyed Persian royal support until the accession of a new king, who had him executed. His universal church lived on—in China, from the seventh to the fourteenth century; in the eastern (modern) former Soviet Union from the eighth to the thirteenth; in Europe, with Augustine its most famous convert, until the fourteenth century. It was naturally seen as a Persian religion and therefore a hostile faith; hence, the character of its reception by the emperors in 296.

Source: *Mosaicarum et Romanarum legum collatio* 15.3.1, trans. Moses Hyamson (London: H. Frowde, 1913).

The emperors Diocletian and Maximian [and Constantius] and Maximian to Julian, proconsul of Africa: Well-beloved Julian, excessive leisure sometimes incites ill-conditioned people to transgress the limits of nature, and persuades them to introduce empty and scandalous kinds of superstitious doctrine, so that many others are lured on to acknowledge the authority of their erroneous notions.

But the immortal gods, in their providence, have thought fit to ordain that the principle of virtue and truth should, by the counsel and deliberations of many good, great and wise men, be approved and established in their integrity. These principles it is not right to oppose or resist, nor ought the ancient religion to be subjected to the censure of a new creed. It is indeed highly criminal to discuss doctrines once and for all settled and defined by our forefathers, and which have their recognized place and course in our system. Wherefore we are resolutely determined to punish the stubborn depravity of these worthless people.

As regards the Manichaeans, concerning whom you have reported to us, who, in opposition to the older creeds, set up new and unheard-of sects, purposing in their wickedness to cast out the doctrines vouchsafed to us by divine favor in olden times, we have heard that they have but recently advanced or sprung forth, like strange and monstrous portents, from their native homes among the Persians—a nation hostile to us—and have settled in this part of the world, where they are perpetrating many evil deeds, disturbing the tranquillity of the provinces and causing the gravest injuries to cities; and there is danger that, in process of time, they will endeavor, as is their usual practice, to infect the innocent, orderly and tranquil Roman people, as well as the whole of Our empire, with the damnable customs and perverse laws of the Persians as with the poison of a malignant serpent. And since all that your wisdom has set out in detail in your report of their religion shows that what our laws regard as their misdeeds are clearly the offspring of a fantastic and lying imagination, we have appointed for these people the condign pains and penalties which are their due.

We order that the founders and heads of these sects be subjected to severe punishment and, together with their abominable writings, be burnt in the flames. We direct that their followers, if they continue recalcitrant, shall suffer capital punishment, and their goods be forfeited to the imperial treasury.

And if those who have gone over to that hitherto unheard-of, scandalous and wholly infamous creed, or to that of the Persians, are persons who hold public office or are of any rank or standing, you will see to it that their estates are confiscated and the offenders sent to the Phaeno or Proconnesus mines.

And in order that this plague of iniquity shall be completely extirpated from this Our most happy age, let your zeal hasten to carry out our orders and commands. Given at Alexandria, March 31st.

18.12 The Martyrdom of Phileas, Bishop of Thmouis

> The martyrdom of the Alexandrine Christian Phileas in ca. 307 is known from both a Latin version and an earlier and more reliable Greek one, published only in 1964. The Greek represents an only slightly altered version of the actual court records, and can be compared with the court records that are translated in chapter 19, below. The two versions, however, must be taken together as a basis for translation, as the Greek is very incomplete. In the translation that follows, portions preserved only in the Latin are indicated in italics.

> **Source:** V. Martin, *Papyrus Bodmer* 20 (Geneva: Bibliotheca Bodmeriana, 1964), original translation.

The speech of Phileas, bishop of Thmouis and magistrate of Alexandria, in his own defense, when he was brought forward for the fifth time and subsequently put to death. At the time of his first speech, after much outrageous treatment from the governor and many outbursts [from the bystanders] and bone-breakings [the word normally refers to a rheumatic disease, but here seems to be used for a torture] at the hands of the legionaries, more than forty times, he was thrown [in jail] in Thmouis for two days. Afterwards, going about unshod and manacled . . . he came to Alexandria and was thrown into prison . . . maltreated and given beatings, he was not deflected; and in the same fashion on the third and fourth appearances, after much maltreatment and beating, Phileas heard [the charges]: You have killed many men through not sacrificing. Pierius saved many by following orders.

Summoned for the fifth time, along with twenty of his clergy, Phileas heard the governor [say]: Can you now finally speak sensibly?

Phileas said: I have done so right along, and I exercise myself in sensibility.

The governor said: Sacrifice to the gods.

Phileas said: I don't sacrifice.

Culcianus said: *Why?*

Phileas replied: Because the sacred and divine scriptures say, "Whoever sacrifices to the gods, and not to God alone, will be uprooted."

Culcianus said: Sacrifice to the Lord alone.

Phileas said: I will not make a burnt offering, for God does not desire such sacrifice. For the sacred and divine scriptures say, "What use to me are the multitude of your sacrifices? The Lord says, 'I am full. Holocausts of rams and fat of lambs and blood of he-goats I do not want.' Nor offer flour."

But one of the lawyers said: Are you being judged about flour, or fighting for your soul?

Culcianus said: Come on, sacrifice.

Phileas replied: I do not sacrifice. I haven't learned how.

Culcianus said: Didn't Paul sacrifice?

Phileas replied: No. Far from it.

Culcianus said: Didn't Moses sacrifice?

Phileas replied: The precept was for the Jews alone to offer sacrifice only in Jerusalem *to God alone* and the Jews break the law now in doing so anywhere else.

Culcianus said: What manner of sacrifice does God require?

Phileas said: A pure heart, unsullied soul, reasoned ideas, which lead to piety and just deeds. . . . There only will the soul receive rewards.

Culcianus said: Do we take care, then, of the soul?

Phileas said: Yes, both the soul and the body.

Culcianus said: Why?

Phileas said: I told you, so that you will receive there the reward for what it [the soul] did well for God.

Culcianus said: Just the soul, or the body too?

Phileas said: The soul and the body.

Culcianus said: This body?

Phileas said: Yes.

Culcianus said: This very flesh rises?

And amazed, he repeated: This very flesh rises?

Phileas said: The flesh itself rises, and that of those in sin being judged receives its punishment, but that which has justice receives salvation and eternal life [conjectural restoration].

Culcianus said: Spare yourself and all your people. Sacrifice.

Phileas said: I am sparing myself and all the people I'm responsible for, in not sacrificing.

Culcianus said: Didn't Paul deny [Jesus]?

Phileas said: Far from it!

Culcianus said: Who was it denied [Jesus]?

Phileas said: I will not say!

Culcianus said: I challenge you on your oath, it was Paul,

Phileas said: Far from it! The apostle of my Lord never denied [Jesus].

Culcianus said: I swore. Now you swear too.

Phileas said: It is not permitted to us to swear. For the holy divine scripture declares, "Let your Yes be Yes and your No, No."

Culcianus said: Have you never sworn?

Phileas said: If I did, I erred.

Culcianus said: Err now.

Phileas said: There are differences in error.

Culcianus said: Was Jesus God?

Phileas said: Yes.

Culcianus said: How was it then that he did not say of himself that he was God?

Phileas said: Because he had no need of such a declaration. He did God's business through actual working powers.

Culcianus said: What did he do?

Phileas said: He cleansed lepers, made the blind to see and the deaf to hear, the lame to walk and the dumb to speak; he healed the withered and commanded demons to depart from bodies; he healed the paralyzed; he restored the dead to life and performed many other signs and wonders.

Culcianus said: And if he was God, how was he crucified?

Phileas said: He knew that at the hands of the unjust he would be scourged and he was beaten and slapped and wore a crown of thorns and suffered death . . . furnishing a pattern of our salvation in this too. And wittingly he gave himself to [the cross] for our sakes, and thereby has. . . . *Likewise the holy writings predicted this, those writings which the Jews think they hold, but do not. So let whoever wants come, and he will see if these things are not so.*

Culcianus said: Was Paul God?

Phileas replied: No. He was the first to announce justice to men. Spirits and divine powers from God were in him, and he did good deeds through divine power and spirit.

Culcianus said: Wasn't he just an ordinary person, and spoke in Syriac?

Phileas said: He was a Jew, the first of the heralds, and spoke Greek as the best of the Greeks.

Culcianus said: Was he not just an ordinary man? Perhaps you mean he is to be ranked with Plato?

Phileas said: Not just Plato, but he was wiser than all philosophers. For he persuaded the wise, and, if you wish, I will tell you his words.

Culcianus said: Sacrifice.

Phileas said: I do not sacrifice. Perish the idea!

Culcianus said: The conscience exists?

Phileas said: Yes.

And he said again: The conscience exists?

Phileas said: As I said, it does exist.

Culcianus said: In regard to your sons and wife, why don't you follow your . . . conscience?

Phileas said: Because conscience towards God is greater, and precedes everything else. For the holy scripture says, "You shall love the Lord your God who made you."

Culcianus said: What God?

Phileas, raising his hands to heaven, [said]: The God that made the [heaven] and the earth and the sun and everything in them, invisible, immovable, unchanging, inconceivable, to whom all creation is servant and obedient and subject.

The lawyers stopped Phileas, who was speaking at length, and said to him: Why do you resist the governor?

Phileas replied: I am answering his question.

Culcianus said: Sacrifice now.

Phileas replied: I do not sacrifice. I spare my soul. Because not only Christians spare their souls, but also pagans. Take the example of Socrates. When he was being led to death, with his wife and sons standing by, he did not turn back, but took the hemlock eagerly.

Culcianus said: Remember the honor I showed you. I could have maltreated you in your city, but wishing to honor you, I did not.

Phileas replied: I thank you. Do me the following favor.

Culcianus said: What do you want?

Phileas replied: Use your full force. Carry out your orders.

Culcianus said: Do you want to die this way without a reason?

[Phileas] said: That is not irrational. I am rather taking good care of myself.

Culcianus said: I'm doing your brother a favor, and you can pay me back for it.

Phileas said: I ask as a final kindness that you apply your rigor and do as you've been commanded.

Culcianus said: If you were one of the yokels who give themselves up out of desperation, I wouldn't spare you. But since you have so much wealth that you could feed and take care not only of yourself but of the whole city, spare yourself for that reason, and sacrifice.

Phileas said: I do not sacrifice.

The lawyers standing around said: He did sacrifice in closed session.

Phileas said: If I did or if I didn't, let the governor say.

And, since he would not alter or budge, the lawyers and all the court, together with the fiscal officer, wanted the governor to give him [time for] reflection.

Culcianus said: Do you want me to give you a chance to think it over?

Phileas said: I have thought it over, often, and that's what I choose.

At that, the lawyers and the court, along with the fiscal officer, wanted to persuade the blessed Phileas to obey the commands. As he would not budge, however, they went at him, exhorting him to think it over. Peace to all the saints!

18.13 Maximinus Daia Encourages Persecution: The Epigraphical Record from Arycanda

An inscription consisting of a Greek petition and a Latin response, from Arycanda in southern Turkey, records the proposal made to the emperors in 312 (actually, only to Maximin Daia, ruling in the east), on behalf of the two provinces there, and the imperial response. The fragmentary Latin text is restored on the basis of Eusebius's report of a similar response given the people of Tyre.

Source: CIL 3.12132, original translation; see Euseb. *Hist. eccl.* 9.4.1., for background.

To the Caesar-Augusti Galerius Valerius Maximinus and [. . .] Valerius Licinianus Licinius, saviors of every province and nation of mankind: a request and supplication of the Lycian and Pamphylian provinces: Your kinsmen the gods have rendered kindnesses to everyone who concerns himself with their cult on behalf of the eternal well-being of your all-conquering majesties. We have thus thought it right to apply to your eternal monarchy to request that the Christians, long raging mad and to this day maintaining their mania unchanged, should at last be stopped and not trespass against the cult due to the gods, with any sinister novelty of worship; and this may be achieved if, by your divine and eternal decree, it will be established among all that the power of the atheists to pursue their detestable devotions is forbidden and barred, while all men show their zeal, on behalf of your eternal and incorruptible emperorship, in the worship of your kinsmen the gods. For this, it is obvious, is of the greatest benefit to all your subjects.

[Reply, the opening lost:] We leave it to your own piety to ask however great a boon you may wish, in recognition of this your devout proposal; and you may be sure it is as good as done and given; for you will obtain it without any delay. And that will both testify, to every age, our piety toward the immortal gods, and declare what truly merited rewards from our Mercifulness you have obtained for your children and their posterity.

18.14 A Former Victim of Persecution Becomes a Bishop, from an Inscription of Laodicea Combusta

An inscription from near Laodicea Combusta (central Turkey) of ca. 340, in memorial for a man known in other texts, who was forced out of a career by Maximin's decree of 307 and was persecuted in 311.

Source: William M. Calder, *Journal of Roman Studies* 10, (1920): 42–59 = *MAMA* I:1928, no. 170; original translation.

M. Julius Eugenius son of Cyrillus Celer of Kouessos of the [Laodicean] senate, having served [as an officer] in the bureau of the governor of Pisidia, and having married Flavia Julia Flaviana daughter of Gaius Nestorianus, a man of [Roman] senatorial rank; and having served with distinction; and when a command had meanwhile gone forth in the time of Maximinus that Christians should offer sacrifice and not quit the service, having endured very many tortures under Diogenes the governor of Pisidia, and having contrived to quit the service, maintaining the faith of the Christians; and having spent a short time in the city of the Laodiceans and having been made bishop by the will of Almighty God; and having administered the episcopate for twenty-five full years with great distinction; and having rebuilt from its foundations the entire church . . . [follows, more on the church he rebuilt and on his provisions for his own tomb].

19

THE GREAT PERSECUTIONS IN
NORTH AFRICA

After the period of St. Paul's letters, for many centuries, surviving
evidence allows a direct glimpse inside only three churches, all in
North Africa, all seen in the early 300s: Carthage, Cirta (which honored
its benefactor by taking his name, Constantine), and Aptungi (Abthugni).
This evidence is of the best quality, tested in court before witnesses of
both sides. From it can be derived a sense of the tone of conversation,
serious but confidential in letters among the local leaders, ungrammat-
ical among their followers; also a sense of relations between high and
low; of facilities for church use; practices regarding charity and episco-
pal elections; and the response to persecutions. All of this, however,
must be picked out of a much larger and confusing record, meant not
for history students, but for litigants in a split, an envenomed wound,
in the African Christian community: the schism called Donatism. In
order to find one's way through the following selections, the origins of
the split must be recalled, in mutual accusations of having surrendered
church vessels and scripture to the officials of the Great Persecutions,
beginning in 303 C.E. Christians who were "betrayers" (*traditores*) were
seen thereafter as unfit to serve in office; therefore their acts, such as
ordaining a bishop or serving communion, were invalid.

In such a case, to determine who was a legitimate bishop and what
was a legitimate church, the litigants tried to prove each other *traditores*. The two sides were the Caecilianists and the Donatists, so-named
after bishops appointed early in the developments that split the
Carthaginian church. Appeals by the two sides to Constantine, soon
after his conversion, led to many special hearings, for which many
documents were prepared and many witnesses heard. Discussion of all
this material in modern times has been voluminous. Enough to cite the
influential work of W.H.C. Frend (*The Donatist Church*, rev. ed.
[Oxford: Clarendon Press, 1985]) and the very full work of Jean-Louis
Maier on whose edition and French translation the following English
translation is based. Documents read into the court record are indicated
in italics.

19.1 The Acquittal of Felix, Bishop of Aptungi

First, the *Acta purgationis Felicis episcopi Autumnitani.* In this document, Felix, Bishop of Aptungi of the Caecilianist side, is acquitted of
charges of being a *traditor,* and it is shown that the Donatists had
trumped up these charges against him by falsifying letters. The preserved text starts awkwardly, not with part of the record of the main
trial, but with an account of a previous hearing being read into the
record. Here as farther into the dossier, we give such supporting
documents, as opposed to living testimony at the trial, in italics.

Source: Jean-Louis Maier, *Le Dossier du Donatisme* 1, *Texte und Unter-
suchungen zur Geschichte der altchristlichen Literatur* 134 (Berlin:
Akademie-Verlag, 1987), pp. 174–87, original translation.

1. *In the municipality of Abthugni, the duumvir [co-mayor] Gallienus said, "Since you are present, Caecilianus [a former magistrate, not to
be confused with his namesake, the anti-Donatist bishop of Carthage], listen
to the letter of my lord Aelius Paulinus,* vir spectabilis, *vice-prefect. This is
what he deigned to order according to the letter sent to us: it obliges you to
explain yourself, and I will write down what archivist you had at the time
of your magistracy. But since the archivist of that time is deceased, you will
have to bring with you all the records of your magistracy according to the
letter of the same, my master, and you must leave for the colony, Carthage,
with your writings. The curator, in whose presence we compel you, is
present. What do you have to reply?"*

*Caecilianus said, "Recently you brought me a letter from Aelius
Paulinus,* vir spectabilis, *vice-prefect; I immediately sent someone to the
scribe Miccius; he came to bring me the records drawn up at that time, and
he is still looking for more; and since it is no short time since I was
duumvir—it is eleven years—, as soon as he finds them, I will obey so great
an order."*

*Gallienus the duumvir said, "It is in your interest to obey the com-
mand; you see, it is a sacred [i.e., imperial] command."*

Caecilianus said, "I am devoted to so great an order."

2. *Likewise, when a little later the scribe Miccius arrived, Fuscius the
duumvir added, "You also heard, Miccius, that you must go with Caecilianus to the office of the vice-prefect,* vir spectabilis, *and that you are to take
with you an account of that time. What do you say to that?"*

*Miccius replied, "When the year of the magistracy was over, he took
all his records home. . . ."* [*There is a considerable lacuna here, at the end
of which we find ourselves in the record of the main trial.*]

3. ". . . I am looking to see whether a page of them can be found."

And, while he was looking, Quintus Sisenna the duumvir said, "What the office knows, he told us."

Apronianus said, "If he took all the records of his magistracy, where could one find acts issued then or drawn up at so important a time?"

And when he said this, Aelianus the proconsul said, "Both my interrogation and the responses of individual persons are contained in the acts."

Agesilaus said, "There are also other letters necessary for this affair. It behooves us that they be read."

Aelianus said, "Read them with Caecilianus present so that he can tell whether he dictated them."

Agesilaus recited:

4. *When Volusianus and Annianus were consuls [314 c.e.], on the nineteenth of August, at law before Aurelius Didymus Speretius, priest of Jupiter Optimus Maximus, duumvir of the splendid colony of Carthage, Maximus said:*

"I speak in the name of the elders of the Christian people of the Catholic name [i.e., the Donatists]. It is before the greatest emperors that the case must be heard against Caecilianus [the bishop] and Felix, who try with all force to usurp the leadership of that law. The documentation of his [Felix's] crimes is being gathered against them. Because when the persecution was announced against the Christians, that is, that they sacrifice and hand over whatever scriptures they had to be burned, Felix who was then bishop at Abthugni gave permission that scriptures be handed over by Galatius, so that they could be consumed by fire. And the magistrate at that time was Alfius Caecilianus, whom you may see present. And since his office at that time made him responsible for everyone's sacrificing according to the proconsul's orders, and if anyone had scriptures, his producing them according to the sacred [imperial] law, I request, inasmuch as he is present and you see that he is an old man and cannot go to the sacred [imperial] court, that he make a sworn declaration whether, according to the agreement which he made on record, he gave a letter and whether what is in the letter is true, so that these people's actions and faith can be detected in the sacred [imperial] court."

In Caecilianus's presence, Speretius the duumvir said, "Do you hear what has been entered in to the record?"

Alfius Caecilianus said, "I had gone to Zama with Saturninus to buy some linen, and when we got back, the Christians themselves sent to me in the praetorium, to say, 'Did the sacred [imperial] order reach you?' I said, 'No, but I already have seen copies; both at Zama and at Furnos I saw basilicas being destroyed and scriptures burned. Therefore produce any scriptures you have, so that you may obey the sacred [imperial] command.'

Then they sent to the house of bishop Felix to get scriptures from there so that they could be burned according to the sacred [imperial] order. And thus Galatius, together with us, reached the place where they were in the habit of holding their prayers. From there we removed the bishop's chair and letters of greeting, and everything was burned according to the sacred [imperial] order. And when we sent public agents to the house of the same Felix, they reported that he was absent. For when at a later time Ingentius came, the scribe of Augentius with whom I shared the aedileship, I dictated to this same colleague a letter which I had sent to this same bishop Felix."

Maximus said, "It is present. Let this letter be shown him so he can identify it."

He answered, "That's the one."

Maximus said, "Since he recognizes his letter, I read it and ask that it be entered in to the record in its entirety."

And he recited:

5. "Caecilianus to his kinsman Felix, greetings! When Ingentius met Augentius, my colleague and his friend, and asked whether, in the year I was duumvir, any writings of your law had been burned according to the sacred [imperial] law . . . Galatius, one of the followers of your law, had publicly brought forth letters of greeting from the basilica. I wish, dearest kinsman, that you may enjoy good health for many years. By the sign that you sent me from the praetorium . . . unless you and I and the person the praetorium belongs to, and you said, 'Take the key and the books you find in the bishop's chair and the codices on the stone, take them. But see to it that the agents don't take the oil and the grain.' And I said, 'Don't you know that where sacred scriptures are found the house itself is torn down?' And you said, 'What then shall we do?' And I told you all, 'Let someone move them to the cemeteries where you all make your prayers and leave them there. And I will come with the agents and take them.' And we came there and took everything as we had agreed and burned it according to the sacred [imperial] order."

Maximus said, "Since the contents of this letter, which he himself acknowledged that he sent, have been read into the record, we ask that what he said be entered into your records."

Speretius the duumvir said, "What you all said is written down."

6. Agesilaus said, "As far as, 'I wish, dearest kinsman, that you may enjoy good health,' he recognized the present letter, but the remaining part that he now read he says is false."

Caecilianus said, "Lord, I dictated up to the point where it says, 'I wish, dearest kinsman, that you may enjoy good health.'"

7. Apronianus said, "Always false like this by terror, by trickery, by irreligious mentality are the actions of those who don't want to agree with

the catholic church! For since Paulinus is representing the prefects here, some private person who would get a messenger's pittance was suborned to go to the faithful of catholic unity to mislead and terrorize them. This way of doing things has thus been discovered: For a lying story was made up against the most religious bishop Felix so that he would seem to have handed over and burned scriptures. For Ingentius, since whatever he did would injure the sanctity and the religious spirit of Caecilianus, was suborned to come with a letter pretending to be that of Felix the bishop to Caecilianus the duumvir and pretend to him that he was sent by Felix. He should say the very words in which this is made up."

Aelianus the proconsul said, "Tell us."

Apronianus said: "He said, 'Tell my friend Caecilianus that I received eleven precious divine codices and that it is now convenient for me to return them. Say that in the year of your magistracy you burned them, so that I cannot give them back.' Wherefore Ingentius must be asked to what extent these things were devised or fabricated and to what extent he wanted to take the magistrate into a lie to vilify Felix's character. He should say by whom he was sent, and furthermore if that machination against Felix's conscience . . . whereby he might belittle him through Caecilianus's shamefulness and vice. There is someone who has been sent as a delegate by the other side throughout Mauritania and Numidia."

8. And in the presence of Ingentius, Aelianus the proconsul said, "On whose orders did you undertake to do those things with which you are charged?"

Ingentius said, "How so?"

Aelianus the proconsul said, "Since you are pretending that you don't understand what you are being asked, I will say more openly: Who sent you to the magistrate Caecilianus?"

Ingentius said, "Nobody sent me."

Aelianus the proconsul said, "So how did you come to the magistrate Caecilianus?"

Ingentius said, "When we got there and the case of Maurus, bishop of Utica, who had bought his bishopric back, was being discussed, Felix, bishop of Abthugni, came up to the city to preach and said, 'Let no one have communion with him, because he has committed a falsehood.' And I said in opposition, 'Neither with him nor with you, since you are a betrayer.' I was upset because of my host, Maurus, because I had taken communion with him abroad, because I had avoided the persecution. Then I went to the hometown of Felix himself. I took with me the elders to see whether he was really a betrayer or not."

Apronianus said, "It wasn't like that. He went to Caecilianus. Ask Caecilianus about it."

Aelianus the proconsul said to Caecilianus, "How did Ingentius come to you?"

Caecilianus answered, "He came to my house. I was having lunch with the workers. He came there, stood in the door, and said, 'Where is Caecilianus?' I answered, 'Here.' I said to him, 'What's up? Everything OK?' 'Everything,' he said. I answered him, 'If you don't mind having lunch, come have some.' He said to me, 'I'll come back here.' He came there by himself. He started to tell me, 'Look, I'm concerned about inquiring whether any scriptures were burned the year you were duumvir.' I said to him, 'You're bothering me, you don't have any business here, get the hell gone.' And I pushed him away. And he came there again with my colleague with whom I was aedile. My colleague said, 'Felix our bishop sent this man so that you could write a letter for him that he received precious codices and didn't want to give them back. You should write to him that they were burned the year you were duumvir.' And I said, 'This is your Christian fidelity!?'"

Ingentius said, "Lord, Augentius should also come. I am honorable, and my honor may perish and we have his clique."

Aelianus the proconsul said to Ingentius, "You will be refuted by other evidence."

Aelianus the proconsul said to the attendants, "Prepare him [for torture]."

And when he was prepared, Aelianus the proconsul said, "Let him be hung up."

And when he was hung up, Aelianus the proconsul said to Caecilianus, "How did Ingentius come to you?"

He answered, "He said, 'Our Felix sent me here so that you could write to him that there is a one wretch, somebody or other, [who says] that having with him very precious codices he doesn't want to give them back. So write a letter that they are burned, so that he won't have to return them.' And I said, 'Is this the fidelity of a Christian?' And I started to upbraid him, and my colleague said, 'Write to our friend Felix.' And so I dictated the letter which you see, up to the point that I dictated it."

9. Aelianus the proconsul said, "Hear without fear the recitation of your letter; indicate how far you dictated it."

Agesilaus recited, ". . . *I wish, dearest kinsman, that you may enjoy good health many years.*"

Aelianus the proconsul said to Caecilianus, "Did you dictate this far?"

He answered, "This far. The rest is false."

Agesilaus recited, *"By this sign that you sent me from the praetorium . . . unless you and I and the person the praetorium belongs to and you said, 'Take the key and the books you find in the bishop's chair and the codices on the stone, take them. But see to it that the agents do not take the oil and the grain.' And I said, 'Don't you know that where sacred scriptures are found, the house itself is torn down?' And you said, 'What then shall we do?' And I told you all, 'Let someone move them to the cemeteries where you all make your prayers, and leave them there. And I will come with the agents and take them.' And we came there and took everything as we had agreed and burned it according to the sacred [imperial] order."*

Maximus said, "Since the contents of this letter, which he acknowledged that he sent, have been read into the record, we ask that what he said be entered into your records."

Speretius the duumvir said, "What you all said is written down."

Caecilianus replied, "From that point on it is false, after my letter ends, after I said, 'Be in good health, dearest kinsman.'"

Aelianus the proconsul said, "Who do you say added to the letter?"

Caecilianus said, "Ingentius."

Aelianus the proconsul said, "Your statement is entered in the record."

10. Aelianus the proconsul said to Ingentius, "You will be tortured so you won't lie."

Ingentius said, "I was wrong. I added to this letter because I was upset on account of Maurus, my host."

Aelianus the proconsul said, "Constantine the greatest, always Augustus, and Licinius, the Caesars, so deign to show their good-will to the Christians in that they do not want discipline corrupted, but rather wish that religion be observed and cultivated. Do not therefore flatter yourself that when you tell me you are a worshiper of God you therefore cannot be tortured. You will be tortured so you won't lie, something [i.e., lying] which seems foreign to Christians. Therefore speak simply, so you won't be tortured."

Ingentius said, "I already confessed without torture."

Apronianus said, "Deign to ask of him by what authority, by what trickery, by what insanity he has traveled throughout all parts of Mauretania and Numidia, for what reason he stirred up dissension for the Catholic church."

Aelianus the proconsul said, "Were you in Numidia?"

He answered, "No, Lord. Let someone try to prove it!"

Aelianus the proconsul said, "Nor in Mauretania?"

He answered, "I was there on business."

Apronianus said, "And in this he lies, Lord; for one can't get to Mauretania except via Numidia, insofar as he says that he was in Mauretania and not in Numidia."

Aelianus the proconsul said to Ingentius, "Of what station are you?"

Ingentius answered, "I am a decurion [town councillor] of Ziqua."

Aelianus the proconsul said to the attendants, "Let him down."

After he was let down, Aelianus the proconsul said to Caecilianus, "Did you say falsely what you said?"

Caecilianus answered, "No, Lord. He who wrote the letter, order him to come. He is a friend of this guy. He will say how far I dictated the letter."

Aelianus the proconsul said, "Who is this whom you want to come?"

Caecilianus said, "Augentius, with whom I was aedile. I can't prove except by Augentius himself who wrote the letter; how far I dictated, he can tell."

Aelianus the proconsul said, "It is certain that the letter was falsified?"

Caecilianus answered, "It is certain, Lord. On my blood, I do not lie."

Aelianus the proconsul said, "Since you were duumvir in your hometown, it is necessary to trust your words."

Apronianus said, "It is not new for them to do this. Also they added to the records what they wanted. It's their usual trick."

11. Aelianus the proconsul said, "From the statement of Caecilianus, who says that the records were falsified and a lot added to the letter, it is clear with what plan Ingentius did these things, and therefore let him be sent to jail. He is needed for a closer interrogation. But it is clear that Felix, the religious bishop, is free of the charge of burning divine documents, since no one could prove anything against him, to the effect that he betrayed or burned the most religious scriptures. The interrogation of everyone written hereabove has demonstrated that no divine scripture was found or destroyed or burned. It is contained in the record that Felix, the religious bishop, was not present at those times, nor did he compromise his conscience, nor order anything of the sort done."

Agesilaus said, "Concerning those who came to instruct your Power, what does your Power order?"

Aelianus the proconsul said, "Let them return home."

19.2 The Trial Held before Zenophilus

Next, the *Gesta apud Zenophilum*. The background is that there has been a rift between Silvanus, Donatist bishop of Cirta, and the deacon Nundinarius, who was even stoned at Silvanus's instigation. Nundinarius, who knows all about Silvanus's collaboration with the persecutors, subsequent irregular installation as bishop, and other misdeeds, has decided to drag the whole dirty business out in court. Purpurius of Limata is another Donatist bishop whose record is hardly clear of malfeasance. It appears that Nundinarius appealed to him first about Silvanus's behavior, as well as to Fortis (whose position on Donatism seems to be unclear), and to others, before bringing the matter into court. All bishops seem equally secretive.

Source: Ibid., pp. 214–39, original translation.

When Constantine the greatest Augustus and the younger Constantine, most noble Caesar, were consuls, on the Ides of December [13 Dec., 320] . . . with Sextus of Thamugadi, Victor the schoolteacher being brought in and put on the stand, in the presence also of the deacon Nundinarius, Zenophilus, *vir clarissimus consularis* [i.e., a nobleman who had served as consul; hereafter v.c.c.] said, "What is your name?"

He answered, "Victor."

Zenophilus v.c.c. said, "What is your profession?"

Victor said, "I am a teacher of Roman literature, a Latin grammarian."

Zenophilus v.c.c. said, "What is your rank?"

Victor said, "My father was a decurion of Constantine [Cirta], my grandfather a soldier: he served with the emperor, for our blood is of Moorish origin."

Zenophilus v.c.c. said, "Mindful of your faith and your honesty, state simply what the cause was of the dissension among the Christians."

Victor said, "I don't know the origin of the quarrel; I am just one of the Christian people. But when I was at Carthage, when bishop Secundus [of Tigisi, a Donatist] finally came there, they were said to have found bishop Caecilianus improperly appointed by some people or other, and they installed someone else in his place. So the quarrel started at Carthage and I clearly cannot know the origin of the quarrel, since our city always has had only one church. And if there was a quarrel, we don't know anything about it."

2. Zenophilus v.c.c. said, "Are you in contact with Silvanus?"

Victor answered, "Yes."

Zenophilus v.c.c. said: "Why then to the neglect of someone whose innocence has been proved by trial? [i.e., Caecilianus]" And he added, "And it is stated that you know something else very certain, that Silvanus is a betrayer. Make a statement about that."

Victor said, "I don't know that."

Zenophilus v.c.c. said to deacon Nundinarius, "Victor says that he doesn't know that Silvanus is a betrayer."

Nundinarius said, "He does so, because he handed codices over."

Victor answered, "I had fled this storm, and if I lie, may I perish! When we suffered the onslaught of sudden persecution, we fled to the mountain of Bellona. I was living with the deacon Mars and the priest Victor. When all the codices were demanded of the same Mars, he denied that he had them. Then Victor gave the names of all the readers. They came to my house when I was absent. The magistrates went upstairs and took my codices. When I came back, I found the codices gone."

Nundinarius the deacon said, "But you replied on the record that you gave over codices. Why are these things that can be demonstrated being denied?"

Zenophilus v.c.c. said to Victor, "State [matters] simply so that you won't be interrogated more strictly."

Nundinarius the deacon said, "Let the records be read."

Zenophilus v.c.c. said, "Let them be read."

And Nundinarius gave them over and the clerk read aloud:

3. *When Diocletian was consul for the eighth time, Maximian for the seventh, on the nineteenth of May [303], from the acts of Munatius Felix, perpetual flamen and curator of the colony of Cirta: When people came to the house in which the Christians congregated, Felix, perpetual flamen and curator of the state [rei publicae], said to bishop Paulus, "Bring forth the scriptures of the law and whatever else you all have here, as has been ordered, so that you can obey the command."*

Paulus the bishop said, "The readers have the scriptures. But we are giving you what we have here."

Felix, perpetual flamen and curator of the state, said to bishop Paulus, "Show us the readers or send for them."

Bishop Paulus said, "You know them all."

Felix, perpetual flamen and curator of the state, said, "We don't know them."

Bishop Paulus said, "The public agents know them, that is, Edusius and Junius the clerks."

Felix, perpetual flamen and curator of the state, said, "Leaving aside the matter of the readers, whom the public agents will make known, you all give what you have."

When bishop Paulus sat down, as did Montanus and Victor Deusatelius and Memorius, the priests, the deacons Mars and Helius standing nearby, the sub-deacons Marcuclius, Catulinus, Silvanus [the future bishop], and Carosus, the grave-diggers Januarius, Meraclus, Fructuosus, Miggin, Saturninus, Victor son of Samsuricus, and others bringing things out, Victor son of Aufidus keeping a list, as follows: Two golden chalices, likewise six silver chalices, six silver ewers, a small silver basin, seven silver lamps, two candle-holders, seven short bronze lamp-stands with their lamps, likewise eleven bronze lamps with their chains, eighty-two women's tunics, thirty-eight veils, sixteen men's tunics, thirteen pairs of men's shoes, forty-seven pairs of women's shoes, nineteen rustic capes(?). [There is no main verb in the preceding sentence.]

Felix, perpetual flamen and curator of the state, said to the grave-diggers [error for sub-deacons] Marcuclius, Silvanus, and Carosus, "Bring what you have."

Silvanus and Carosus said, "We have emptied out whatever was here."

Felix, perpetual flamen and curator, said to Marcuclius, Silvanus, and Carosus, "Your answer is written in the record."

4. Then after empty wardrobes were found in the libraries, there Silvanus brought out a small silver case and a silver lamp that he said he had found behind a trunk. Victor son of Aufidus said to Silvanus, "You were a dead man if you hadn't found them!"

Felix, perpetual flamen and curator of the state, said to Silvanus, "Look more diligently if anything remains here."

Silvanus said, "Nothing remains here. We have emptied everything out."

And when the dining hall was opened, there were found six storage jars and six trunks. Felix, perpetual flamen and curator of the state, said, "Bring out the scriptures that you have, so that we can obey the commands of the emperors and the orders."

Catulinus produced one extremely big codex. Felix, perpetual flamen and curator of the state, said to Marcuclius and Silvanus, "Why did you all give just one codex? Bring out the scriptures that you have."

Catulinus and Marcuclius said, "We don't have any more because we're sub-deacons. But the readers have the codices."

Felix, perpetual flamen and curator of the state, said to Marcuclius and Catulinus, "Point out the readers."

Marcuclius and Catulinus said, "We don't know where they live."

Felix, perpetual flamen and curator of the state, said to Catulinus and Marcuclius, "If you all don't know where they live, tell us their names."

Catulinus and Marcuclius said, "We aren't traitors. Here we are. Order us killed."

Felix, perpetual flamen and curator of the state, said, "Let them be arrested."

5. And when they arrived at the house of Eugenius, Felix, perpetual flamen and curator of the state, said to Eugenius, "Bring out the scriptures which you have, in order to obey the command."

And he brought out four codices. Felix, perpetual flamen and curator of the state, said to Silvanus and Carosus, "Point out the other readers."

Silvanus and Carosus said, "The bishop already said that Edusius and Junius, the clerks, know them all. They can show you to their houses."

Edusius and Junius the clerks said, "We will show them, Lord."

And when they came to the house of Felix the tailor, he brought out five codices. And when they came to the house of Projectus, he brought out five large and two small codices. And when they came to the house of the grammarian, Felix, perpetual flamen and curator of the state, said to Victor the grammarian, "Bring out the scriptures which you have, so as to obey the command."

Victor the grammarian offered two codices and four notebooks. Felix, perpetual flamen and curator of the state, said to Victor, "Bring out the scriptures. You have more."

Victor the grammarian said, "If I had had more, I would have given them."

And when they came to the house of Euticius of Caesarea, Felix, perpetual flamen and curator of the state, said to Euticius, "Bring out the scriptures which you have, so as to obey the command."

Euticius said, "I don't have any."

Felix, perpetual flamen and curator of the state, said to Euticius, "Your statement is on the record."

And when they came to the house of Coddeo, his wife brought out six codices. Felix, perpetual flamen and curator of the state, said, "Look to see if you all have any more, and bring them out."

The woman replied, "I don't have any more."

Felix, perpetual flamen and curator of the state, said to Bos the public slave, "Go in and look if she has any more."

The public slave said, "I looked and didn't find any."

Felix, perpetual flamen and curator of the state, said to Victorinus, Silvanus, and Carosus, "If anything too little has been done, the danger is yours."

6. After this had been read, Zenophilus v.c.c. said to Victor, "Confess simply."

Victor answered, "I wasn't present."

Nundinarius the deacon said, "We are reading the letters of the bishops, made by Fortis."

And a copy of the memorandum given to the bishops by the deacon Nundinarius is read:

Christ and his angels are witness that those with whom you [bishops] are in communion, that is Silvanus of Cirta, is a betrayer and a thief of the property of the poor, since all you bishops, priests, deacons, and elders know about the four hundred folles [a monetary unit] *of Lucilla, clarissima femina* [i.e., of Roman senatorial rank], *on account of which you conspired to make Majorinus bishop—that was the beginning of the split. For Victor the fuller [clothes-cleaner] also, in your presence and that of the people, gave twenty folles to become priest, which Christ and his angels know.*

7. And there was read a copy of a letter:

Purpurius the bishop to Silvanus, his fellow bishop, greetings in the Lord! Our son the deacon Nundinarius came to me and asked me, most holy one, to send this request from me to you, that there might be peace, if possible, between you and him. And I want that to be the case, so that nobody will know what goes on between us; if you so desire in writing, I will go there by myself for the matter in hand and settle the dispute between you all. By his own hand, he [Nundinarius] gave me a memorandum on the matter, by reason of which he would have been stoned on your order. It is not just for a father to punish his son contrary to the truth; and I know that what is written in the memorandum given me is true. Seek a remedy, so that this wickedness can be extinguished before a flame arises which cannot subsequently be put out without the blood of the faithful. Gather with the clerics the elders of the people, men of the church, and let them inquire diligently what the dissensions are, so that what happens may happen according to the precepts of faith. You will not stray either to the right or to the left. And do not willingly bend your ear to evil counsellors who do not wish peace. You all are destroying us.

And in another hand, *Farewell.*

8. Likewise a copy of a letter:

Purpurius the bishop to the clergy and the elders of Cirta, eternal greetings in the Lord! Moses cried to the entire assembly of the children of Israel and told them what the Lord ordered done. And nothing was done without the advice of the elders. Then you too, dearest ones, whom I know to have all heavenly and spiritual wisdom, inquire with all your strength what the dissension is and lead it to a peaceful solution. For Nundinarius the deacon says that nothing escapes you about the origin of this dissension between him and our dearest Silvanus. For he gave me a memorandum in which everything is written down. For he said you also knew everything. I know that it is not for [general] hearing. Seek a good remedy, so that this matter may be extinguished without danger to your souls, lest suddenly when you have accepted a person (?) you be haled into court. Make a just decision between the parties according to your seriousness and justice. Take care not to stray either to the left or the right. The matter at hand concerns God, who scrutinizes the thoughts of individuals. Take pains that no one may know what this conspiracy is. What is in the memorandum concerns you. It is not good; for the Lord said, "You will be condemned out of your own mouth, and out of your own mouth you will be justified."

9. Likewise another one was recited:

Fortis to his dearest brother Silvanus, eternal greetings in the Lord! Our son the deacon Nundinarius came to me and recounted what had gone on between you and him, as if by the intervention of the evil one who wants to divert the souls of the just from the way of truth. When I heard this, my wits failed, that such dissension comes between you. That a priest of God would come to this! . . . let what is not to our advantage take place.

Now therefore ask him that, as is possible, the peace of our Lord Savior Christ be with him, lest we come before the public and be condemned by the pagans. For it is written, "Take care, while you bite and blame each other, that you be not consumed by each other." Therefore I ask the Lord that this scandal be lifted from our midst, so that the matter of God can be celebrated with thanksgiving, the Lord saying, "My peace I give you, my peace I leave with you." What peace can there be where there are dissensions and rivalries? For when I was [verb missing] by the soldiers . . . separated and I came with him amid such violence, I commended my soul to God and I pardoned you, because God sees men's minds and hearts, and because I was led by you to them. But God freed us and we serve him with you. Thus, as we were pardoned, you two become reconciled in peace, so that in Christ's name we may celebrate peace with joy. Let no one know!

10. [Another letter was read:]

Fortis to his brothers and sons, the clergy and the elders, eternal greetings in the Lord! My son, your deacon Nundinarius, came to me and reported about what was done against you. Certainly you should have arranged matters so that things would not get to the point of insanity that people would be stoned for the truth. This both you and we know, as you reported to us. And it is written, "Is there no wise man among you, who can judge among brothers? But brother is judged with brother, but before the infidels"—as will happen with you in court if you are not careful. Have we gone so far as to give such an example to the pagans, so that those who believed in God through us may themselves curse us when we come before the public? Therefore lest it get to this point, you who are spiritual see to it that no one knows, so that we may celebrate Easter in peace. And encourage them to be reconciled in peace and let there be no dissension, so that, when it becomes public, you too may not start to be in danger. If this happens, you will have only yourselves to blame. And you will give as much as you can, Possessor, Dontius, individual priests Valerius and Victor, since you know everything that has been done; make an effort that peace be with you.

11. And another was read:

Sabinus to his brother Silvanus, eternal greetings in the Lord! Your son Nundinarius came to us, not just to me, but also to our brother Fortis, reporting a serious complaint. I am astounded at your Seriousness that you acted so with your son, whom you nourished and ordained. For if a building is founded on earth, is not something heavenly added because it is built by the hand of a priest? But you should not be amazed when the scripture says, "I will destroy the wisdom of the wise, and the prudence of the prudent will I reprove," and again says, "Men enjoyed darkness more than light," as you are doing. Let it be sufficient for you to know everything. On this matter, our brother Fortis also wrote to you. Now I would ask your

Charity, most well-intentioned brother, that you carry out the saying of the prophet Isaiah, "Remove evil from your souls, and come, let us discuss, says the Lord," and again, "Reject evil from your midst." Thus you do too: subject and turn aside the trouble-making of those who did not want there to be peace between you and your son. But let your son Nundinarius celebrate Easter in peace with you, lest this matter, which is known to all of us, become public. I would ask you, most well-intentioned brother, to hear the petition of my Humility. Let no one know!

12. Likewise another was read:

Sabinus to his brother Fortis, eternal greetings in the Lord! I am in a particularly good position to know what your charity is towards all your colleagues. Nonetheless, according to the will of God who said, "I love certain people more than my soul," I am certain that you honored Silvanus. Wherefore I did not hesitate to send you this letter, because I had your letter to him sent on account of Nundinarius' name. Whoever acts quickly, God's affair is always advanced thereby. Do not make an excuse: for the business presses us in these days and disturbs us without respite until the most solemn day of Easter, so that through you a most rich peace may be made and we be found worthy co-inheritors of Christ, who said, "My peace I give you, my peace I leave with you." And again I ask you to do this.

And in another hand, *I hope that you are well in the Lord and mindful of us. Farewell. But I ask you, let no one know!*

13. When these letters had been read, Zenophilus v.c.c. said, "Both by the records and by the letters that have been read it is clear that Silvanus is a betrayer."

And he said to Victor: "Confess simply whether you know that he handed anything over."

Victor said, "He handed things over, but not in my presence."

Zenophilus said, "What was Silvanus's function at that time among the clergy?"

Victor said, "The persecution started when Paul was bishop and Silvanus was sub-deacon."

Nundinarius the deacon responded, "He means, when he came there to be made bishop, the people responded, 'Let someone else be made bishop; hear us, God.'"

Zenophilus v.c.c. said to Victor, "Did the people say, 'Silvanus is a betrayer'?"

Victor said, "I myself fought against his becoming bishop."

Zenophilus v.c.c. said to Victor, "So you knew he was a betrayer?"

Victor replied, "He was a betrayer."

Nundinarius the deacon said, "You elders were shouting, 'Hear, God, we want our fellow-citizen. He [Silvanus] is a betrayer.'"

Zenophilus v.c.c. said to Victor, "So did you shout with the people that Silvanus was a betrayer and should not become bishop?"

Victor said: "Both I and the people shouted. We wanted our fellow-citizen, a man of integrity."

Zenophilus v.c.c. said, "For what reason did you think he did not deserve it?"

Victor said, "We were demanding a man of integrity and a fellow-citizen. For I knew we would get to this, the emperor's court, when things are entrusted to people like these."

14. Then when the grave-diggers Victor son of Samsuricus and Saturninus were brought in and put on the stand, Zenophilus v.c.c. said, "What is your name?"

He answered, "Saturninus."

Zenophilus v.c.c. said, "What is your profession?"

Saturninus replied, "Grave-digger."

Zenophilus v.c.c. said, "Do you know that Silvanus is a betrayer?"

Saturninus said, "I know that he handed over a silver lamp."

Zenophilus v.c.c. said, "What else?"

Saturninus replied, "I don't know anything else, except that he got it from behind a trunk."

And when Saturninus was removed, Zenophilus v.c.c. said to the man who remained, "You, what is your name?"

He answered, "Victor son of Samsuricus."

Zenophilus v.c.c. said, "What is your profession?"

Victor said, "I am an artisan."

Zenophilus v.c.c. said, "Who handed over the silver table [*sic!*]?"

Victor said, "I didn't see; I say what I know."

Zenophilus v.c.c. said to Victor, "Granted that it is already evident from the responses of those previously interrogated, still you declare that Silvanus is a betrayer."

Victor said, "The second time he was asked how he let it go that we be led to Carthage [the previous several words are of unclear meaning], I heard from the mouth of the bishop himself, 'A silver lamp and a small silver case were given to me and I handed them over.'"

Zenophilus v.c.c. said, "From whom did you hear it?"

Victor said, "From Silvanus the bishop."

Zenophilus v.c.c. said to Victor, "You heard it from himself?"

Victor said, "I heard from him that he handed them over with his own hands."

Zenophilus v.c.c. said, "Where did you hear it?"

Victor said, "In the basilica."

Zenophilus v.c.c. said, "At Constantine?"

Victor said, "There he started to address the people, saying, 'On what account do they say that I am a betrayer? Because of a lamp and a case!'"

15. Zenophilus v.c.c. said to Nundinarius, "What else do you think should be asked of these people?"

Nundinarius said, "About the treasury's barrels, who took them."

Zenophilus v.c.c. said to Nundinarius, "What barrels?"

Nundinarius said, "They were in the Sarapis-temple, and bishop Purpurius took them. The acetum [vinegar or cheap wine] that was in them, bishop Silvanus, the priest Dontius, and Lucianus took it."

Zenophilus v.c.c. said, "Do those present know that it was done?"

Nundinarius said, "They know."

The deacon Saturninus said, "Our ancestors used to say that they were stolen."

Zenophilus v.c.c. said, "By whom are they said to have been stolen?"

Saturninus said, "By bishop Purpurius, and the acetum by Silvanus and the priests Dontius and Superius and the deacon Lucianus."

Nundinarius said, "Did Victor give twenty folles and get to be a priest that way?"

Saturninus said, "Yes."

And when he said that, Zenophilus v.c.c. said to Saturninus, "So he gave a bribe of twenty folles to Silvanus to become a priest?"

Saturninus said, "Yes."

Zenophilus v.c.c. said to Saturninus, "Was it put in front of Silvanus?"

Saturninus said, "In front of the bishops' seat."

Zenophilus v.c.c. said to Nundinarius, "By whom was the money taken?"

Nundinarius said, "The bishops themselves divided it among themselves."

16. Zenophilus v.c.c. said to Nundinarius, "Do you want Donatus called?"

Nundinarius said, "Let him come [and testify] about what the people shouted two days after the peace, 'Hear, God; we want our fellow-citizen.'"

Zenophilus v.c.c. said to Nundinarius, "Is it certain that the people shouted that?"

He answered, "Yes."

Zenophilus v.c.c. said to Saturninus, "Did they shout that Silvanus was a betrayer?"

Saturninus said, "Yes."

Nundinarius said, "When he was made bishop, we had no relations with him, because he was said to be a betrayer."

Saturninus said, "What he says is true."

Nundinarius said, "I saw that Mutus the gladiator was carrying him on his shoulders."

Zenophilus v.c.c. said to Saturninus, "Did it happen that way?"

Saturninus said, "Yes."

Zenophilus said, "Is everything Nundinarius says true about Silvanus being made bishop by the gladiators?"

Saturninus said, "It's true."

Nundinarius said, "The prostitutes were there!"

Zenophilus v.c.c. said to Saturninus, "The gladiators carried him?"

Saturninus said, "They and the mob carried him, for the citizens were shut up in the cemetery."

Nundinarius the deacon said, "Were the people of God there?"

Saturninus said, "They were shut up in the larger house [i.e., chapel]."

Zenophilus v.c.c. said, "Is it certain that everything Nundinarius says is true?"

Saturninus said, "It's true."

Zenophilus v.c.c. said to Victor, "What do you say?"

Victor said, "It's true, Lord."

17. Nundinarius said, "Bishop Purpurius took a hundred folles."

Zenophilus v.c.c. said to Nundinarius, "About those hundred folles, what people do you think should be questioned?"

Nundinarius said, "Let Lucianus the deacon be called, because he knows everything."

Zenophilus v.c.c. said, "Let Lucianus be called."

Nundinarius said, "They knew that four hundred folles were taken, but that the bishops divided them up, they don't know."

Zenophilus v.c.c. said to Saturninus and Victor, "Do you know that money was received from Lucilla?"

Saturninus and Victor said, "We do."

Zenophilus v.c.c. said, "The poor didn't receive it?"

They said, "Nobody received anything."

Zenophilus v.c.c. said to Saturninus and Victor, "Wasn't anything taken from the Sarapis-temple?"

Saturninus and Victor said, "Purpurius took the barrels, and bishop Silvanus and the priests Dontius and Superius and the deacon Lucianus took the acetum."

Zenophilus v.c.c. said, "From the response of Victor the grammarian and Victor son of Samsuricus and Saturninus it is clear that everything alleged by Nundinarius is true. Let them be removed and go out."

18. Zenophilus v.c.c. said, "What other people do you think should be questioned?"

Nundinarius said, "Castus the deacon, so that he can say if Silvanus is not a betrayer. He ordained him."

And when the deacon Castus was brought in and put on the stand, Zenophilus v.c.c. said, "What is your name?"

He replied, "Castus."

Zenophilus v.c.c. said to Castus, "What is your profession?"

Castus said, "I don't have one."

Zenophilus v.c.c. said to Castus, "Even though Nundinarius' charges have been confirmed by Victor the grammarian, as well as by Victor son of Samsuricus, and by Saturninus, still you too state whether Silvanus is a betrayer."

Castus replied, "They said that he found a lamp behind the chest."

Zenophilus v.c.c. said to Castus, "Likewise make a statement about the barrels taken from the Sarapis-temple and the acetum."

Castus replied, "Bishop Purpurius took the barrels."

Zenophilus v.c.c. said, "Who took the acetum?"

Castus replied that bishop Silvanus and the priests Dontius and Superius had taken the acetum.

Zenophilus v.c.c. said to Castus, "State how many folles Victor gave to be made priest."

Castus said, "My lord, he offered a bag and how much was in it, I don't know."

Zenophilus v.c.c. said to Castus, "To whom was the bag given?"

Castus said, "Silvanus took it in the larger chapel."

Zenophilus v.c.c. said, "The money was not divided among the people?"

Castus said, "It wasn't given and I didn't see anything."

Zenophilus v.c.c. said to Castus, "About the folles that Lucilla gave, the common people didn't get anything?"

Castus said, "I didn't see anybody get any."

Zenophilus v.c.c. said to Castus, "Where did the money end up?"

Castus said, "I don't know."

Nundinarius said, "Did you hear or see that the people were told, 'Lucilla is giving you too some of her fortune'?"

Castus said, "I didn't see anybody get any."

Zenophilus v.c.c. said, "Castus's statement is clear that he doesn't know that the folles which Lucilla gave were divided among the people. So let him be removed."

19. Likewise when Crescentianus the sub-deacon was brought in and put on the stand, Zenophilus v.c.c. said, "What is your name?"

He replied, "Crescentianus."

Zenophilus v.c.c. said to Crescentianus, "State simply like the others whether you knew Silvanus to be a betrayer."

Crescentianus said, "Our predecessors who were clerics reported the details."

Zenophilus v.c.c. said, "What did they report?"

Crescentianus said, "They reported that he was a betrayer."

Zenophilus v.c.c. said to Crescentianus, "They called him a betrayer?" And he added, "Who said that?"

Crescentianus said, "Those who had relations with him among the people said that once he had been a betrayer."

Zenophilus v.c.c. said, "They said that about Silvanus?"

Crescentianus said, "Yes."

Zenophilus v.c.c. said to Crescentianus, "When he was made bishop, were you there?"

Crescentianus said, "I was present and shut up with the people in the larger chapel."

Nundinarius the deacon said, "Country people and gladiators made him bishop!"

Zenophilus v.c.c. said to Crescentianus, "Did Mutus the gladiator really pick him up?"

He said, "Obviously."

20. Zenophilus v.c.c. said to Crescentianus, "Do you know that the barrels were taken from the Sarapis-temple?"

Crescentianus said, "A lot of people used to say that bishop Purpurius himself took the barrels and the acetum that ended up with our venerable Silvanus; the sons of Aelion used to say that."

Zenophilus v.c.c. said to Crescentianus, "What did you hear?"

Crescentianus said, "That the acetum was taken by the venerable Silvanus and Dontius and Superius the priests, and Lucianus the deacon."

Zenophilus v.c.c. said to Crescentianus, "And of the four hundred folles that Lucilla donated, did the people receive anything?"

Crescentianus said, "Nobody got anything from that; I don't even know who spent them."

Nundinarius said, "Did the little old ladies ever get anything from it?"

Crescentianus said, "Nothing."

Zenophilus v.c.c. said, "Certainly whenever anything of the sort is donated, all members of the congregation get their share publicly?"

Crescentianus said, "I didn't hear or see that he gave any of the money."

Zenophilus v.c.c. said to Crescentianus, "So none of the four hundred folles were given to the people?"

Crescentianus said, "Nothing; otherwise some small part would have ended up with us."

Zenophilus v.c.c. said, "So by whom was the money taken?"

Crescentianus said, "I don't know; nobody got anything."

Nundinarius said, "How many folles did Victor give to be made priest?"

Crescentianus said, "I saw some baskets brought with money in them."

Zenophilus v.c.c. said to Crescentianus, "To whom were the baskets given?"

Crescentianus said, "To bishop Silvanus."

Zenophilus v.c.c. said, "They were given to Silvanus?"

He replied, "Yes."

Zenophilus said, "Was nothing given to the people?"

He answered, "Nothing. It is necessary that we too receive something if there is a distribution, as usually happens."

Zenophilus v.c.c. said to Nundinarius, "What else do you think should be asked of Crescentianus?"

Nundinarius said, "That's it."

Zenophilus v.c.c. said, "Since Crescentianus made a simple statement about everything, let him be removed."

21. Likewise when the sub-deacon Januarius was brought in and put on the stand, Zenophilus v.c.c. said, "What is your name?"

He replied, . . .

20

CONSTANTINE

20.1 Constantine's Vision in Lactantius's and Eusebius's Accounts

The accident or miracle of Constantine's conversion, which was, for various reasons, a most unlikely thing to happen, brought Christianity abruptly to the very top of the Roman world. The event is reported in quite different terms, the cause of some incorrigible uncertainties about it. Lactantius is the earliest source (317 C.E.), here quoted in part.

Source: Lactantius, *De mortibus persecutorum* 44.1-11, trans. William Fletcher, *Ante-Nicene Christian Authors* (Edinburgh: T. & T. Clark, 1871), amended.

The civil war between Constantine and Maxentius had now broken out, and though Maxentius remained within Rome because the soothsayers had foretold that he would die if he went outside, yet he conducted the military operations with able generals. In size of forces he had the advantage, having not only received his father's army by desertion from Severus but also his own which he had recently raised out of Mauretanians and Gaetuli [of Numidia]. They fought and at the beginning Maxentius' troops were winning, until Constantine, with redoubled courage, and resolved on death or victory, led his whole force to the vicinity of the city and encamped them opposite the Milvian Bridge. The anniversary of Maxentius' accession day was near, that is October 28th, and the five-year celebrations were ending. Constantine was directed in a dream to have the heavenly sign of God inscribed on the shields of his men and thus to proceed into battle. He did as he had been commanded, and marked on their shields the letter Chi (*X*) of Christ, turned over at the top, with a letter I crossing through it. Armed with this sign, the soldiers took up their weapons. The enemy advanced but without their emperor, and crossed the bridge. The armies met and fought with the utmost strenuousness, and neither side thought of flight. In the meantime, sedition arose in the city and Maxentius was reviled as having abandoned the safety of the state. While he was staging the Circensian Games on his anniversary, the people suddenly cried out in unison, "Constantine cannot be overcome." Dismayed by this, Maxentius burst from the gathering and, calling together some senators, ordered the Sibylline books to be consulted. In them it was found that "On the same day an enemy of the Romans will perish." Induced by this oracle to hope for victory, he went out and took up battle. The bridge in his rear was broken down. At this sight the fighting grew fiercer, and the hand of God prevailed. The forces of Maxentius turned to flight. He himself fled toward the bridge, which had been broken down. The multitude pressing on him in their flight, he was driven into the Tiber. When at length this grievous war was over, Constantine was hailed emperor with great rejoicing by the senate and people of Rome. He now came to know the treachery of Maximin Daia: for he found letters written to Maxentius and statues and busts [of Maxentius and Maximin] set up together. The senate, in acknowledgement of Constantine's bravery, bestowed on him the title Greatest . . .

> In addition to a very brief account of the above scene, without mention of Constantine's vision or Maxentius's recourse to the Sibylline books (*Hist. eccl.* 9.9.2ff.), Eusebius after Constantine's death reported more fully on the same events.
>
> **Source:** Eusebius, *Vita Constantini* 1.26f., anonymous translation, *Nicene and Post-Nicene Fathers of the Christian Church,* Ser. 2, 1 (1890, New York; reprint, Grand Rapids: Wm. B. Eerdmans, 1961), adapted.

[When Constantine saw] the imperial city of the Roman empire bowed down by the weight of a tyrannous oppression, at first he had left the task of liberation to those who governed the other divisions of the empire, as being senior to himself, but when none of these proved able to afford relief, and those who had attempted it had experienced a disastrous termination of their enterprise, he said that life was without enjoyment to him so long as he saw the imperial city thus afflicted, and prepared himself for the overthrow of the tyranny. Being convinced, however, that he needed some more powerful aid than his military forces could provide, on account of the wicked, magical enchantments which were so diligently practised by the tyrant [Maxentius], he sought divine assistance, deeming the possession of arms and a numerous soldiery of secondary importance, but believing the cooperating power of deity invincible and not to be shaken. He considered, therefore, on what god he might rely for protection and assistance. While engaged in this inquiry, the thought occurred to him that his predecessors had been deceived by hopes lodged in the gods, except for one (his father Constantius), who alone had honored the one supreme God during his whole life [and] had found him to be the savior and protector of his empire and the giver of every good thing. . . . Accordingly he called on him with earnest prayer and supplications that he would reveal to him who he was, and stretch forth his right hand to help him in his present difficulties. And while he was thus praying with fervent entreaty, a most marvelous sign appeared to him from heaven, the account of which it might have been hard to believe had it been related by any other person. But since the victorious emperor himself long afterwards declared it to the writer of this history, when he was honored with his acquaintance and society, and confirmed his statement by an oath, who could hesitate to credit the story, especially since the testimony of after-time has established its truth? He said that about noon, when the day was already beginning to decline, he saw with his own eyes the trophy of a cross of light in the heavens, above the sun, and bearing this inscription: Conquer by this. At this sight he himself was struck with amazement, and his whole army also, which followed him on this expedition, and wit-nessed the miracle. He said, moreover, that he doubted within himself what the import of this apparition could be; and while he continued to ponder and reason on its meaning, night suddenly came on, when in his sleep the Christ of God appeared to him with the same sign which he had seen in the heavens, and commanded him to make a likeness of that sign which he had seen in the heavens, and to use it as a safeguard in all engagements with his enemies.

At dawn of day he arose and communicated the marvel to his friends; and then, calling together the workers in gold and precious stones, he sat in the midst of them and described to them the figure of the sign he had seen, bidding them represent it in gold and precious stones. And this representation I myself have had an opportunity of seeing. Now it was made in the following manner. A long spear, overlaid with gold, formed the figure of the cross by means of a transverse bar laid over it. On top of the whole was fixed a wreath of gold and precious stones; and within this, the symbol of the Savior's name, two letters indicating the name of Christ by means of its initial characters. . . . Being struck with amazement at the extraordinary vision, and resolving to worship no other God save him who had appeared to him, he sent for those who were acquainted with the mysteries of his doctrines, and inquired who that God was, and what was intended by the sign in the vision he had seen. They affirmed that he was God, the only begotten son of the one and only God. . . . Assuming therefore the supreme God as his patron . . . and setting the victorious trophy, the salutary symbol, in front of his soldiers and bodyguard, he marched [against Maxentius into Italy, and thereafter toward Rome; from which God drew Maxentius far out beyond the gates to his defeat. Thereafter, entering the capital,] by loud proclamation and monumental inscriptions he made known to all men the salutary symbol, setting up this great trophy of victory over his enemies in the midst of the imperial city, and expressly causing it to be engraved in indelible characters, that the salutary symbol was the safeguard of the Roman government and of the entire empire. Accordingly, he immediately ordered a lofty spear in the figure of a cross placed beneath the hand of a statue representing himself, in the most frequented part of Rome, and the following inscription to be engraved on it in the Latin language: "By virtue of this salutary sign which is the true test of valor, I have preserved and liberated your city from the yoke of tyranny. I have also set at liberty the Roman senate and people, and restored them to their ancient distinction and splendor" . . .

20.2   A Letter from Constantine regarding the Building of Churches

Besides various laws (see below, from the *Codes*) favoring the church, Constantine issued directives recorded by the church historians. Eusebius quotes many, including those in his biography of the emperor, one of which is offered here. This letter, given also by Socrates, *Hist. eccl.* 1.9, Theodoret, *Hist. eccl.* 1.15.1–2, Gelasius, *Hist. eccl.* 3.3.1–4, and Nicephorus, *Hist. eccl.* 8.27, was sent to other bishops besides Eusebius, bishop of Caesarea. By it the prelates are empowered to ask from the praetorian prefect and the provincial governors, who had received instructions to co-operate with the bishops, whatever aid might be needed in the project of repairing and building Christian churches. Such projects were made more easily practicable by Constantine's final victory over Licinius, his brother-in-law and colleague, whose persecution of Christians in the east perhaps came from the suspicion that they desired Constantine to enjoy alone the sovereignty—which indeed he did from this year, 324 C.E.

Source: Eusebius, *Vita Constantini* 2.46, trans. P. R. Coleman-Norton, in *Roman State and Christian Church* (London: SPCK, 1966), 1:103f.

Victor Constantine, Greatest, Augustus, to Eusebius: Because until the present time the unholy will and tyranny have persecuted the savior God's servants, I have believed and carefully have convinced myself, best beloved brothers, that the edifices of all the churches either by neglect have been ruined or through fear of the imposed injustice have become less than their proper worth. But now, since freedom has been recovered and that dragon has been chased from the administration of public affairs by the providence of the highest God and by our effort, I believe both that the divine power has been made manifest to all and that those who through either fear or unbelief have fallen into some errors, when they have learned to know the true being, will come into the true and right course of life.

Therefore, with respect to either whatever churches you yourself preside over or whatever other bishops and priests or deacons you know are presiding in the several places, do you suggest that they should be concerned about the buildings of the churches: either to restore or to enlarge those in existence or, whenever need demands, to construct new ones. Both you yourself and the rest through you also shall ask the necessary things from both the provincial governors and the prefectural office. For to these it has been commanded to assist to the utmost with all zeal your Sanctity's words.

God guard you, beloved brother.

21

JULIAN

21.1 Some Letters of Julian the Apostate

The emperor Julian, called "the Apostate" for his conversion from his childhood beliefs, in the latter half of his reign (362–63) and in the eastern provinces actively encouraged and attempted to restructure and vitalize traditional cults by various measures. These are mentioned in other writers but can be seen best in some of his own letters and directives.

Source: Julian, *Letters* 18–20, 22, 36, trans. Wilmer Cave Wright, LCL.

To an Official: (. . .) Is it not right to pay to human beings this respect that we feel for things made of wood? For let us suppose that a man who has obtained the office of priest is perhaps unworthy of it. Ought we not to show forbearance until we have actually decided that he is wicked, and only then by excluding him from his official functions show that it was the overhasty bestowal of the title "priest" that was subject to punishment by obloquy and chastisement and fine? If you do not know this you are not likely to have any proper sense at all of what is fitting. What experience can you have of the rights of men in general if you do not know the difference between a priest and a layman? And what sort of self-control can you have when you maltreated one at whose approach you ought to have risen from your seat? For this is the most disgraceful thing of all, and for it in the eyes of gods and men alike you are peculiarly to blame. Perhaps the bishops and elders of the Galilaeans sit with you, though not in public because of me, yet secretly and in the house; and the priest has actually been beaten by your order, for otherwise your high-priest would not, by Zeus, have come to make this appeal. But since what happened in Homer seems to you merely mythical, listen to the oracular words of the Lord of Didymus [more correctly, Didyma], that you may see clearly that, even as in bygone days he nobly exhorted the Hellenes in very deed, so too in later times he admonished the intemperate in these words: "Whosoever with reckless mind works wickedness against the priests of the deathless gods and plots against their honors with plans that fear not the gods, never shall he travel life's path to the end, seeing that he has sinned against the blessed gods whose honor and holy service those priests have in charge." Thus, then, the god declares that those who even deprive priests of their honors are detested by the gods, not to mention those who beat and insult them! But a man who strikes a priest has committed sacrilege. Wherefore, since by the laws of our fathers I am supreme pontiff, and moreover have but now received the function of prophecy from the god of Didymus, I forbid you for three revolutions of the moon to meddle in anything that concerns a priest. But if during this period you appear to be worthy, and the high-priest of the city so writes to me, I will thereupon take counsel with the gods whether you may be received by us once more. This is the penalty that I award for your rash conduct. As for curses from the gods, men of old used to utter them and write them, but I do not think that this was well done; for there is no evidence at all that the gods themselves devised those curses. And besides, we ought to be the ministers of prayers, not curses. Therefore I believe, and join my prayers to yours, that after earnest supplication to the gods you may obtain pardon for your errors.

To a Priest: I should never have favored Pegasius unhesitatingly if I had not had clear proofs that even in former days, when he had the title of bishop of the Galilaeans, he was wise enough to revere and honor the gods. This I do not report to you on hearsay from men whose words are always adapted to their personal dislikes and friendships, for much current gossip of this sort about him has reached me, and the gods know that I once thought I ought to detest him above all other depraved persons. But when I was summoned to his headquarters by Constantius of blessed memory I was traveling by this route, and after rising at early dawn I came from Troas to Ilios about the middle of the morning. Pegasius came to meet me, as I wished to explore the city—this was my excuse for visiting the temples—and he as my guide showed me all the sights. So now let me tell you what he did and said, and from it one may guess that he was not lacking in right sentiments towards the gods.

Hector has a hero's shrine there and his bronze statue stands in a tiny little temple. Opposite this they have set up a figure of the great Achilles in the unroofed court. If you have seen the spot you will certainly recognize my description of it. You can learn from the guides the story that accounts for the fact that great Achilles was set up opposite to him and takes up the whole of the unroofed court. Now I found that the altars were still alight, I might almost say still blazing, and that the statue of Hector had been anointed till it shone. So I looked at Pegasius and said, "What does this mean? Do the people of Ilios offer sacrifices?" This was to test him cautiously to find out his own views. He replied: "Is it not natural that they should worship a brave man who was their own citizen, just as we worship the martyrs?" Now the analogy was far from sound; but his point of view and intentions were those of a man of culture, if you consider the times in which we then lived. Observe what followed. "Let us go," said he, "to the shrine of Athene of Ilios." Thereupon with the greatest eagerness he led me there and opened the temple, and as though he were producing evidence he showed me all the statues in perfect preservation, nor did he behave at all as those impious usually do, I mean when they make the sign on their impious foreheads, nor did he hiss to himself as they do. For these two things are the quintessence of their theology, to hiss at demons and make the sign of the cross on their foreheads.

These are the two things that I promised to tell you. But a third occurs to me which I think I must not fail to mention. This same Pegasius went with me to the temple of Achilles as well and showed me the tomb in good repair; yet I had been informed that this also had been pulled to pieces by him. But he approached it with great reverence; I saw this with my own eyes. And I have heard from those who are now his enemies that he also used to offer prayers to Helios and worship him in secret. Would you not have accepted me as a witness even if I had been merely a private citizen? Of each man's attitude toward the gods who could be more trustworthy witnesses than the gods themselves? Should I have appointed Pegasius a priest if I had any evidence of impiety towards the gods on his part? And if in those past days, whether because he was ambitious for power or, as he has often asserted to me, he clad himself in those rags in order to save the temples of the gods, and only pretended to be irreligious so far as the name of the thing went—indeed it is clear that he never injured any temple anywhere except for what amounted to a few stones, and that was a blind, that he might be able to save the rest—well then, we are taking this into account, and are we not ashamed to behave to him as Aphobius did, and as the Galilaeans all pray to see him treated? If you care at all for my wishes you will honor not him only but any others who are converted, in order that they may the more readily heed me when I summon them to good works, and those others may have less cause to rejoice. But if we drive away those who come to us of their own free will, no one will be ready to heed when we summon.

To the high-priest Theodorus: I have written you a more familiar sort of letter than to the others because you, I believe, have more friendly feelings than others towards me. For it means much that we had the same guide, and I am sure you remember him. A long time ago, when I was still living in the west, I learned that he had the highest regard for you, and for that reason I counted you my friend, and yet because of their excessive caution, I have usually thought these words well said—"For I never met or saw him . . ."—and well said is "Before we love we must know, and before we can know we must test by experience." But it seems that after all a certain other saying has most weight with me, namely, "The Master [Plato] has spoken." That is why I thought even then that I ought to count you among my friends, and now I entrust to you a task that is dear to my heart, while to all men everywhere it is of the greatest benefit. And if, as I have the right to expect, you administer the office well, be assured that you will rejoice me greatly now and give me still greater good hope for the future life. For I certainly am not one of those who believe that the soul perishes before the body or along with it, nor do I believe any human being but only the gods; since it is likely that they alone have the most perfect knowledge of these matters, if indeed we ought to use the word "likely" of what is inevitably true; since it is fitting for men to conjecture about such matters, but the gods must have complete knowledge.

What then is this office which I say I now entrust to you? It is the government of all the temples in [the province] Asia, with power to appoint the priests in every city and to assign to each what is fitting. Now the qualities that befit one in this high office are, in the first place, fairness, and next, goodness and benevolence towards those who deserve to be treated thus. For any priest who behaves unjustly to his fellow men and impiously towards the gods, or is overbearing to all, must either be admonished with plain speaking or chastised with great severity. As for the regulations which I must make more complete for the guidance of priests in general, you as well as the others will soon learn them from me, but meanwhile I wish to make a few suggestions to you. You have good reason to obey me in such matters. Indeed in such a case I very seldom act offhand, as all the gods know, and no one could be more circumspect; and I avoid innovations in all things, so to speak, but more peculiarly in what concerns the gods. For I hold that we ought to observe the laws that we have inherited from our forefathers, since it is evident that the gods gave them to us. For they would not be as perfect as they are if they had been derived from mere men. Now since it has come to pass that they have been neglected and corrupted, and wealth and luxury have become supreme, I think that I ought to consider them carefully as though from their cradle. Therefore, when I saw that there is among us great indifference about the gods and that all reverence for the heavenly powers has been driven out by impure and vulgar luxury, I have always secretly lamented this state of things. For I saw that those whose minds were turned to the doctrines of the Jewish religion are so ardent in their belief that they would choose to die for it, and to endure utter want and starvation rather than taste pork or any animal that has been strangled or had the life squeezed out of it; whereas we are in such a state of apathy about religious matters that we have forgotten the customs of our forefathers, and therefore we actually do not know whether any such rule has ever been prescribed. But these Jews are in part god-fearing, seeing that they revere a god who is truly most powerful, and most good, and governs this world of sense, and, as I well know, is worshipped by us also under other names. They act as is right and seemly, in my opinion, if they do not transgress the laws; but in this one thing they err, in that, while reserving their deepest devotion for their own god, they do not conciliate the other gods also; but the other gods they think have been allotted to us Gentiles only, to such a pitch of folly have they been brought by their barbarous conceit. But those who belong to the impious sect of the Galilaeans, as if some disease (. . .)

To Arsacius, High-priest of Galatia: The Hellenic religion does not yet prosper as I desire, and it is the fault of those who profess it; for the worship of the gods is on a splendid and magnificent scale, surpassing every prayer and every hope. May Adrasteia pardon my words, for indeed no one, a little while ago, would have ventured even to pray for a change of such a sort or so complete within so short a time. Why then do we think that this is enough, why do we not observe that it is their benevolence to strangers, their care for the graves of the dead and the pretended holiness of their lives that have done most to increase atheism? I believe that we ought really and truly to practise every one of these virtues. And it is not enough for you alone to practise them, but so must all the priests in Galatia, without exception. Either shame or persuade them into righteousness or else remove them from their priestly office, if they do not, together with their wives, children and servants, attend the worship of the gods, but allow their servants, or sons, or wives to show impiety towards the gods and honor atheism more than piety. In the second place, admonish them that no priest may enter a theater or drink in a tavern or control any craft or trade that is base and not respectable. Honor those who obey you, but those who disobey, expel from office. In every city establish frequent hostels in order that strangers may profit by our benevolence; I do not mean for our own people only, but for others who are in need of money. I have but now made a plan by which you may be well provided for this; for I have given directions that 30,000 modii of grain shall be assigned every year for the whole of Galatia and 60,000 pints of wine. I order that one fifth of this must be used for the poor who serve the priests, and the remainder be distributed by us to strangers and beggars. For it is disgraceful that, when no Jew ever has to beg and the impious Galilaeans support not only their own poor but ours as well, all men should see how our people lack aid from us. Teach those of the Hellenic faith to contribute public service of this sort, and the Hellenic villages to offer their first fruits to the gods; and accustom those who love the Hellenic religion to these good works by teaching them that this was our practice of old. At any rate Homer makes Eumaeus say, "Stranger, it is not lawful for me, not even though a baser man than you should come, to dishonor a stranger. For from Zeus come all strangers and beggars. And a gift, though small, is precious." Then let us not, by allowing others to outdo us in good works, disgrace by such remissness, or rather utterly abandon, the reverence due to the gods. If I hear that you are carrying out these orders I shall be filled with joy.

As for the government officials, do not interview them often at their home, but write to them frequently. And when they enter the city no priest must go to meet them, but only meet them within the vestibule when they visit the temples of the gods. Let no soldier march before them into the temple, but any who will may follow them; for the moment that one of them passes over the threshold of the sacred precinct he becomes a private citizen. For you yourself, as you are aware, have authority over what is within, since this is the bidding of the divine ordinance. Those who obey it are in very truth god-fearing, while those who oppose it with arrogance are vainglorious and empty-headed.

I am ready to assist Pessinus if her people succeed in winning the favor of the Mother of the gods [whose famous shrine was in that city]. But if they neglect her, they are not only not free from blame but, not to speak harshly, let them beware of reaping my enmity also. "For it is not lawful for me to cherish or to pity men who are the enemies of the immortal gods." Therefore persuade them, if they claim my patronage, that the whole community must become suppliants of the Mother of the gods.

Rescript on Christian Teachers: I hold that a proper education results, not in laboriously acquired symmetry of phrases and language, but in a healthy condition of the mind, I mean a mind that has understanding and true opinions about things good and evil, honorable and base. Therefore, when a man thinks one thing and teaches his pupils another, in my opinion he fails to educate exactly in proportion as he fails to be an honest man. And if the divergence between a man's convictions and his utterances is merely in trivial matters, that can be tolerated somehow, though it is wrong. But if in matters of the greatest importance a man has certain opinions and teaches the contrary, what is that but the conduct of hucksters, and not honest but thoroughly dissolute men, in that they praise most highly the things that they believe to be most worthless, thus cheating and enticing by their praises those to whom they desire to transfer their worthless wares. Now all who profess to teach anything whatever ought to be men of upright character, and ought not to harbor in their souls opinions irreconcilable with what they publicly confess; and above all I believe it is necessary that those who associate with the young and teach them rhetoric should be of that upright character; for they expound the writings of the ancients, whether they be rhetoricians or grammarians, and still more if they are sophists. For these claim to teach, in addition to other things not only the use of words, but morals also, and they assert that political philosophy is their peculiar field. Let us leave aside, for the moment, the question whether this is true or not. But while I applaud them for aspiring to such high pretensions, I should applaud them still more if they did not utter falsehoods and convict themselves of thinking one thing and teaching their pupils another. What! Was it not the gods who revealed all their learning to Homer, Hesiod, Demosthenes, Herodotus, Thucydides, Isocrates and Lysias? Did not these men think that they were consecrated, some to Hermes, others to the Muses? I think it is absurd that men who expound the works of these writers should dishonor the gods whom they [the writers] used to honor. Yet, though I think this absurd, I do not say that they ought to change their opinions and then instruct the young. But I give them this choice: either not to teach what they do not think is admirable or, if they wish to teach, let them first really persuade their pupils that neither Homer nor Hesiod nor any of these writers whom they expound and have declared to be guilty of impiety, folly, and error in regard to the gods, is such as they declare. For since they make a livelihood and receive pay from the works of those writers, they thereby confess that they are most shamefully greedy of gain, and that, for the sake of a few drachmas, they would put up with anything. It is true that, until now, there were many excuses for not attending the temples, and the terror that threatened on all sides absolved men for concealing the truest beliefs about the gods. But since the gods have granted us liberty, it seems to me absurd that men should teach what they do not believe to be sound. But if they believe that those whose interpreters they are and for whom they sit, so to speak, in the seat of the prophets, were wise men, let them be the first to emulate their piety towards the gods. If, however, they think that those writers were in error with respect to the most honored gods, then let them betake themselves to the churches of the Galilaeans to expound Matthew and Luke, since you Galilaeans are obeying them when you ordain that men shall refrain from temple-worship. For my part, I wish that your ears and your tongues might be "born anew," as you would say, as regards these things in which may I ever have part, and all who think and act as is pleasing to me.

For religious and secular teachers let there be a general ordinance to this effect: Any youth who wishes to attend the schools is not excluded; nor indeed would it be reasonable to shut out from the best way boys who are still too ignorant to know which way to turn, and to overawe them into being led against their will to the beliefs of their ancestors. Though indeed it might be proper to cure these, even against their will, as one cures the insane, except that we concede indulgence to all for this sort of disease. For we ought, I think, to teach, but not to punish, the demented.

21.2   Late Pagan Theology: Sallustius's *On the Gods and Ordered Creation*

A Neoplatonist essay entitled *By Sallustius, On the Gods and Ordered Creation* is usually but not firmly ascribed to Julian's friend and supporter Sallustius, the praetorian prefect of the Gallic provinces (361–63) and consul (363). It presents in a convenient form a sort of summary, as it were, a teacher's handbook, of "Hellenic" theology, drawn from entirely traditional, mostly Neoplatonic, ideas.

Source: Sallustius, 1–4, 9, 14–16, 21, trans. Gilbert Murray, *Four Stages of Greek Religion* (New York: Columbia University Press, 1912).

1. Those who wish to hear about the gods should have been well guided from childhood, and not habituated to foolish beliefs. They should also be in disposition good and sensible, that they may properly attend to teaching. They ought also to know the "common conceptions." Common conceptions are those to which all men agree as soon as they are asked: for instance, that all god is good, free from passion, free from change. For whatever suffers change does so for the worse or the better: if for the worse, it is made bad, if for the better, it must have been bad at first.

2. Let the disciple be thus. Let the teachings be of the following sort. The essences of the gods never came into existence (for that which always is never comes into existence; and that exists for ever which possesses primary force and by nature suffers nothing): neither do they consist of bodies; for even in bodies the powers are incorporeal. Neither are they contained by space; for that is the property of bodies. Neither are they separate from the First Cause nor from one another, just as thoughts are not separate from mind nor acts of knowledge from the soul.

3. We may well inquire, then, why the ancients forsook these

doctrines and made use of myths. There is this first benefit from myths, that we have to search and do not have our minds idle. That the myths are divine can be seen from those who have used them. Myths have been used by inspired poets, by the best of philosophers, by those who established the mysteries, and by the gods themselves in oracles. But why the myths are divine it is the duty of philosophy to inquire. Since all existing things rejoice in that which is like them and reject that which is unlike, the stories about the gods ought to be like the gods, so that they may both be worthy of the divine essence and make the gods well disposed to those who speak of them: which could only be done by means of myths.

Now the myths represent the gods themselves and the goodness of the gods—subject always to the distinction of the speakable and the unspeakable, the revealed and the unrevealed, that which is clear and that which is hidden: since, just as the gods have made the goods of sense common to all, but those of the intellect only to the wise, so the myths state the existence of the gods to all, but who and what they are only to those who can understand.

They also represent the activities of the gods. For one may call the world a myth, in which bodies and things are visible but souls and minds hidden. Besides, to wish to teach the whole truth about the gods to all produces contempt in the foolish, because they cannot understand, and lack of zeal in the good; whereas to conceal the truth by myths prevents the contempt of the foolish and compels the good to practise philosophy.

But why have they put in the myths stories of adultery, robbery, father-binding, and all the other absurdity? Is not that perhaps a thing worthy of admiration, done so that by means of the visible absurdity the soul may immediately feel that the words are veils and believe the truth to be a mystery? 4. Of myths, some are theological, some physical, some psychic, and again some material, and some mixed from these last two. The theological are those myths which use no bodily form but contemplate the very essence of the gods: e.g., Kronos, swallowing his children. Since god is intellectual and all intellect returns into itself, this myth expresses in allegory the essence of god. Myths may be regarded physically when they express the activities of the gods in the world: e.g., people before now have regarded Kronos as Time, and, calling the divisions of time his sons, they say that the sons are swallowed by the father. The psychic way is to regard the activities of the soul itself: the soul's acts are thoughts; though they pass on to other objects, nevertheless they remain inside their begetters. The material and last is that which the Egyptians have mostly used, owing to their ignorance, believing material objects actually to be gods and so calling them: e.g., they call the earth Isis, moisture Osiris, heat Typhon, or again, water Kronos, the fruits of the earth Adonis, and wine Dionysus. To say that these objects are sacred to the gods, like various herbs and stones and animals, is possible to sensible men, but to say that they *are* gods is the notion of a madman—except perhaps in the sense in which both the orb of the sun and the ray which comes from the orb are colloquially called "the sun."

The mixed kind of myth may be seen in many instances. For example, they say that in a banquet of the gods Discord threw down a golden apple; the goddesses contended for it, and were sent by Zeus to Paris to be judged; Paris saw Aphrodite to be beautiful and gave her the apple. Here the banquet signifies the hyper-cosmic powers of the gods; that is why they are all together; the golden apple is the world which, being formed out of opposites, is naturally said to be "thrown by Discord." The different gods bestow different gifts upon the world and are thus said to "contend for the apple." And the soul which lives according to sense— for that is what Paris is—not seeing the other powers in the world but only beauty, declares that the apple belongs to Aphrodite. Theological myths suit philosophers, physical and psychic suit poets, the mixed suit religious initiations, since every initiation aims at uniting us with the world and the gods.

To take another myth, they say that the Mother of the gods seeing Attis lying by the river Gallus fell in love with him, took him, crowned him with her cap of stars, and thereafter kept him with her. He fell in love with a nymph and left the Mother to lie with her. For this the Mother of the gods made Attis go mad and cut off his genital organs and leave them with the nymph, and then return and dwell with her. Now the Mother of the gods is the principle that generates life; that is why she is called Mother. Attis is the creator of all things which are born and die; that is why he is said to have been found by the river Gallus; for Gallus signifies the galaxy or Milky Way, and the point at which body subject to passion begins. Now as the primary gods make perfect the secondary, the Mother loves Attis and gives him celestial powers. That is what the cap means. Attis loves a nymph: the nymphs preside over generation, since all that is generated is fluid. But since the process of generation must be stopped somewhere, and not allowed to generate something worse than the worst, the creator who makes these things casts away his generative powers into the creation and is joined to the gods again. Now these things never happened, but always are. And mind sees all things at once, but reason (or "speech") expresses some first and others after. Thus, as the myth is in accord with the cosmos, we for that reason keep a festival imitating the cosmos, for how could we attain higher order?

9. This is enough to show the providence of the gods. For whence comes the ordering of the world if there is no ordering power? And

whence comes the fact that all things are for a purpose—e.g., irrational soul, that there may be sensation, and rational, that the earth may be set in order? But one can deduce the same result from the evidences of providence in nature, e.g., the eyes have been made transparent with a view to seeing, the nostrils are above the mouth to distinguish bad-smelling foods, the front teeth are sharp to cut food while the back teeth grind it. And we find every part of every object arranged on a similar principle. It is impossible that there should be so much providence in the last details, and none in the first principles. And too, the arts of prophecy and of healing, which are part of the cosmos, come of the good providence of the gods. All this care for the world, we must believe, is taken by the gods without any act of will or labor. As bodies which possess some power produce their effects by merely existing—e.g., the sun gives light and heat by merely existing—so, and far more so, the providence of the gods acts without effort to itself and for the good of the objects of its forethought. This solves the problems of the Epicureans, who argue that what is divine neither has trouble itself nor gives trouble to others.

Therefore, to believe [in astrology] that human beings, especially their material constitution, are ordered not only by celestial beings but by celestial bodies, is a reasonable and true belief. Reason shows that health and sickness, good fortune and bad fortune, arise according to our deserts from that source. But to attribute men's acts of injustice and lust to fate is to make ourselves good and the gods bad—unless by chance a man meant by such a statement that, in general, all things are for the good of the world and for those who are in a natural state, but that bad education or weakness of nature changes the goods of fate for the worse. Just so, it happens that the sun, which is good for all, may be injurious to persons with ophthalmia or fever. Else why do the Massagetae eat their fathers, the Hebrews practise circumcision, and the Persians preserve rules of rank? Why do astrologers, while calling Saturn and Mars "malignant," proceed to make them good, attributing to them philosophy and royalty, generalships and treasures? And if they are going to talk of triangles and squares, it is absurd that gods should change their natures according to their position in space, while human virtue remains the same everywhere. Also the fact that the stars predict high or low rank for the father of the person whose horoscope is taken, teaches that they do not always make things happen but sometimes only indicate things. For how could things which preceded the birth depend upon the birth?

14. If anyone thinks the doctrine of the unchangeability of the gods is reasonable and true, and then wonders how it is that they rejoice in the good and reject the bad, and are angry with sinners and become propitious when appeased, the answer is as follows: god does not rejoice—for

that which rejoices also grieves; nor is he angered—for to be angered is a passion; nor is he appeased by gifts—if he were, he would be conquered by pleasure. It is impious to suppose that the divine is affected for good or ill by human things. The gods are always good and always do good and never harm, being always in the same state and like themselves. The truth simply is that, when we are good, we are joined to the gods by our likeness to them, and when bad, we are separated from them by our unlikeness; and when we live according to virtue we cling to the gods, and when we become evil we make the gods our enemies—not because they are angered against us but because our sins prevent the light of the gods from shining upon us, and put us in communion with spirits of punishment. And if by prayers and sacrifices we find forgiveness of sins, we do not appease or change the gods, but by what we do and by our turning towards the divine, we heal our own badness and so enjoy again the goodness of the gods. To say that god turns away from the evil is like saying that the sun hides himself from the blind.

15. This solves the question about sacrifices and other rites per-formed to the gods. The divine itself is without needs, and the worship is paid for our own benefit. The providence of the gods reaches everywhere and needs only some congruity for its reception. All congruity comes about by representation and likeness; for which reason, the temples are made in representation of heaven; the altar, of earth; the images, of life (which is why they are made like living things); the prayers, of the element of thought; the mystic letters, of the unspeakable celestial forces; the herbs and stones, of matter; and the sacrificial animals, of the irrational life in us. From all these things the gods gain nothing; what gain could there be to god? It is we who gain some communion with them.

16. I think it well to add some remarks about sacrifices. In the first place, since we have received everything from the gods, and it is right to pay the giver some tithe of his gifts, we pay such a tithe of possessions in votive offerings—of bodies, in gifts of [hair and] adornment, and of life, in sacrifices. Then, secondly, prayers without sacrifices are only words, and with sacrifices they are live words; the word gives meaning to the life, while the life animates the word. Thirdly, the happiness of every object is its own perfection; and perfection for each is communion with its own cause. For this reason we pray for communion with the gods. Since therefore the first life is the life of the gods, but human life is also life of a kind, and human life wishes for communion with divine life, a mean term is needed. For things very far apart cannot have communion without a mean term, and the mean term must be like the things joined; therefore the mean term between life and life must be life. That is why men sacrifice animals; only the rich do so now, but in old days everybody did, and that

not indiscriminately but giving the suitable offerings to each god together with a great deal of other worship. Enough of this subject.

21. Souls that have lived in virtue are in general happy, and when separated from the irrational part of their nature, and made clean from all matter, have communion with the gods and join them in the governing of the whole world. Yet even if none of this happiness fell to their lot, virtue itself, and the joy and glory of virtue, and the life that is subject to no grief and no master, are enough to make happy those who have set themselves to live according to virtue and have achieved it.

21.3   An Epigraphic Record of a Late Pagan Sacrifice

To illustrate from nonliterary sources the impact of Julian's religious teachings, an inscription may serve best: one carved on an altar from Rome (near St. Peter's) of around the mid-fourth century. In cryptic and arcane phrases such as are common in oracular utterances or sacred texts, this one *may* refer to the renewal of sacrifices to Attis (the Mighty One) by Julian after intermission under a series of Christian rulers.

Source: *SEG* 2.518, trans. Herbert J. Rose, *Journal of Hellenic Studies* (1925): 82.

I present in this offering the works, thought, action, excellence of life, and all the goodness of wise Ga (. . .) lios; for he dedicated and brought once more unto the Mighty One that rose again the Bull and Ram [in sacrifice—the so-called *taurobolium* and *criobolium*] that is the symbol of fair hap. Yea, he scattered the darkness that had endured eight and twenty barren years, and made the light of salvation to shine again.

22

CONVERSION, POST-CONSTANTINE

22.1 Requirements for Church Membership, from Theodore of Mopsuestia and the *Didascalia Apostolorum*

The pace of Christianization in the empire quickened at a great rate in the wake of a Roman emperor's own conversion and his very active advocacy and patronage of the church thereafter; but it is rarely possible to see in detail just how, and through exactly what words and thoughts, these results followed. Certain external features along the path to conversion in this period are, however, indicated by the text given below. Here, Theodore, eventually bishop of Mopsuestia (in southern Turkey) over the years 392–428 C.E., describes certain forms required for reception into the church. They center in baptism. Theodore is talking about practices in Antioch, where he had been a priest, after studying under Libanius and some years as a lawyer. The date of the composition is not long before he became bishop, i.e., 380s. The modern translator summarizes the ceremony of the sacrament first.

Source: Alphonse Mingana, *Commentary of Theodore* (1933), pp. xiiif., 39f., 42f.

[The catechumen comes to church attended by his godfather, and his name is written down in the church books by the Registrar of baptisms. The godfather answers the questions put to the catechumen by the Registrar of Baptisms and becomes his surety for his past life, his preparedness and his competence to receive the sacrament of baptism. Then the exorcists come and "ask in a loud and prolonged voice that our Enemy should be punished and by a verdict from the Judge (God) be ordered to retire and stand far." During all this time the catechumen remains silent and stands barefooted on sackcloth; his outer garments are taken off from him while his head is bent and his arms are outstretched. Then he goes to the priest before whom he genuflects and recites the Creed and the Lord's

Prayer and the words of abjuration which are: "I abjure Satan and all his angels and all his works and all his service and all his deception and all his worldly glamor; and I engage myself and believe and am baptized in the name of the Father and of the Son and of the Holy Spirit." Then the priest "clad in a robe of clean and radiant linen" signs him on the forehead with the holy chrism and says, "So-and-So is signed in the name of the Father and of the Son and of the Holy Spirit."]

[Mingana, pp. 39f. and 42f.] . . . After saying: "I abjure Satan" you add, "and his angels." You call angels of Satan all those who serve his will for the purpose of deceiving people and causing them to fall. We must believe to be servants of Satan all those who occupy themselves with the outside wisdom and bring the error of paganism into the world. Clearly are angels of Satan all the poets who maintained idolatry by their vain stories and strengthened the error of heathenism by their wisdom. Angels of Satan are those men who under the name of philosophy established devastating doctrines among pagans, and corrupted them to such an extent that they do not acquiesce in the words of the true religion. Angels of Satan are also the heads of heresies, those who after the coming of Christ our Lord devised in an ungodly way, and introduced into the world, doctrines contrary to the true faith.

. . . Are service of Satan: the purifications, the washings, the knots, the hangings of yeast, the observances of the body, the flutterings or the voices of birds and any similar thing. It is service of Satan that one should indulge in the observances of Judaism. Service of Satan is also that service which is found among the heretics under the name of religion, because although it has some resemblance to an ecclesiastical service, yet it is devoid of the gift of the grace of the Holy Spirit, and is performed in impiety.

. . . After this you say, "And all his worldly glamor." They called his glamor, the theater, the circus, the racecourse, the contests of athletes, the profane songs, the water-organs and the dances, which the Devil introduced into this world under the pretext of amusement, and through which he leads the souls of men to perdition.

The above procedures may be compared with those in the *Didascalia Apostolorum,* the *Teachings of the Apostles,* compiled in the earlier third century by another Syrian bishop for use in his church.

Source: *Didascalia et Constitutiones Apostolorum,* ed. Franciscus X. Funk (Paderborn: Schoeningh, 1895), 1:126f., original translation.

. . . As likewise the heathen, when they desire to repent [*meta-noein*] and to turn from their erroneous ways, we accept them in the congregation to hear the word, but we do not share communion with them until they are initiated through being sealed (i.e., baptized).

22.2 Sozomen on the Conversion of Alaphion

One of those unusual glimpses referred to above, where the actual moment of conversion is described in a post-Constantinian setting, appears in the following. Conversion is wrought by the ascetic Hilarion at a date around 350 (since in 353 he had already gone to Egypt), as later recalled by Sozomen.

Source: Sozomen, *Hist. eccl.* 5.15, anonymous translation, *Nicene and Post-Nicene Fathers of the Christian Church*, Ser. 2, 2 (New York, 1890; reprint, Grand Rapids: Wm. B. Eerdmans, 1957), p. 337.

My grandfather was of pagan parentage, and, with his own family and that of Alaphion, had been the first to embrace Christianity in Bethelia, a prosperous town near Gaza, in which there are temples highly reverenced by the people of the country on account of their antiquity and structural excellence. The most celebrated of these temples is the Pantheon built on an artificial eminence commanding a view of the whole town. The conjecture is that the place received its name from the temple, that the original name given to this temple was in the Syriac language, and that this name was afterwards rendered into Greek and expressed by a word which signifies that the temple is the residence of the gods. It is said that the above-mentioned families were converted through the instrumentality of the monk Hilarion. Alaphion, it appears, was possessed by a devil, and neither the pagans nor the Jews could, by any incantations and enchantments, deliver him from this affliction; but Hilarion, by simply calling on the name of Christ, expelled the demon, and Alaphion with his whole family immediately embraced Christianity.

22.3 Jerome on Conversions Wrought by Hilarion

Here Jerome adds another scene from the biography of a holy man which he composed. The location is the area south of Gaza, the time 380s C.E.

Source: Jerome, *Life of Hilarion* 25, *PL* 23.42, 380s C.E., original translation.

Journeying with an enormous troop of his monks into the desert of Cades to see one of his disciples, [Hilarion] arrived at Elusa on the very day, by chance, when a general ceremony had drawn the population of the entire town to the Venus-temple. They paid worship to her because of Lucifer, to whose cult the Saracens [i.e., the local Arabs] are quite devoted. But the town itself is generally backward because of its location. When it was learned that Saint Hilarion was passing by, he who had healed so many Saracens that were possessed by some demon, the people came out to meet him in crowds, with their wives and children, bowing their heads and calling on him, "Barech!"—that is, in Syriac, "Bless us!" He received them kindly and modestly, begging them to worship God rather than stones. With abundant tears he looked up to the sky and promised them, if they would believe in Christ, that he would often come to them. Marvelous is God's grace!—for they would not allow him to leave before he laid down the ground plan of a church to be built, and before their priest, who wore a crown as a badge of office, had been marked with the cross.

22.4   Rufinus on Conversion in Egypt

The church historian Rufinus describes events of 373 c.e., or a little later which concern people he was familiar with, and at a time when he himself was in the same region: in Egypt, near Nitria. He writes, however, about twenty years after the events (the story is repeated in Socrates, *Hist. eccl.* 4.24).

Source: Rufinus, *Hist. eccl.* 2.4, *PL* 21.512Cf., original translation.

[The Arian heretic Lucius] gave instructions that the very [monastic] fathers, though exiled from their flock, should be secretly arrested and deported to a certain island of Egypt, a swampy one where he had found there to be no Christians. Thereby they should live without any relief or any of their usual employments. The old men therefore were taken at night with only [!] two slaves to the island; and there the local inhabitants tended a certain temple with great veneration. Just at the time the barge bearing the old men touched the shore of that place, on a sudden the maiden daughter of that temple's priest was possessed by a spirit, giving vent to monstrous howls and shouts to the very heavens, and she began to career about among the people, making many gyrations and shrieking, and she began vibrating this way and that her foaming mouth. And when the people ran together to see such a great wonder, most of all because it was the daughter of the priest whom they held in such honor, and followed her about as she was torn along through the breezes, they came on the barge of the old men. There she flung herself at their feet and, prostrate, began to cry out, "Why come you here, servants of the Highest God, to tumble us out of our ancient sleepy dwellings? Here, driven from everywhere else, we lay hidden. But how at all [?] could we conceal ourselves from you? We retire to our ancient seats. Take now your people and your lands!" While she was speaking in this fashion, the deceitful spirit, rebuked by them, was put to flight. The girl, being now sane, lay with her parents at the feet of those apostles of our time; and they, preaching the faith of our Lord Jesus Christ to them, from such beginnings brought them quickly around to so great a change of heart that, on the spot, that very day, they tore down with their own hands that most ancient temple, held in the highest veneration, and straightway erected a church. They needed no long time for reflection, those people among whom not words but a wonderful power [*virtus*] produced belief in the events.

22.5 Libanius on the Futility of Forced Conversions by Christians

The pagan professor of rhetoric in Antioch, Libanius, in 386 C.E. had the courage needed to protest, to a devout and savagely impulsive emperor, against some of the processes of Christianizing that the orator was aware of in his own region. He suffered no ill consequences, but provoked no help from the emperor, by whom, a few years later, the forces of the state were more sharply brought to bear against the unconverted (still a majority of the population). See the laws quoted a little below.

Source: Libanius, *Oration* 30 [*Pro templis*], 26–29, trans. A. F. Norman, LCL, altered.

But they [zealous Christians who took it upon themselves to destroy pagan shrines] alone of all were judges of the charges they brought, and, having judged, themselves played the part of executioner. To what end? For the worshippers of the gods thenceforth to be barred from their own rites and be converted to theirs [the Christians']? But this is utter nonsense. Who doesn't know that, as a result of their very sufferings, people have come to admire more than ever their previous condition, just as in physical desire the lover has only to be barred from the act and he does it all the more and becomes more ardent towards the object of his affections. If such conversions of mind could be effected simply by the destruction of the temples, they would have been long ago destroyed by your [Theodosius's] decree, for you would long since have been glad to see this conversion. But you knew that you could not, and so you never laid a finger on these shrines. These people [the zealous Christians], even if they looked forward to such result, ought to have advanced toward it in step with you, and should have let the emperor share in their ambition. It would have been better, surely, to succeed in their objective by staying on the right side of the law rather than by abusing it.

And if they tell you that some other people have been converted by such measures and now share their religious beliefs, do not overlook the fact that they speak of conversions apparent, not real. Their converts have not really been changed—they only say they have. This does not mean that they have exchanged one faith for another—only that this crew [the zealous Christians] have had the wool pulled over their eyes. They go to their ceremonies, join their crowds, go everywhere where these do, but when they adopt an attitude of prayer they either invoke no god at all or else they invoke the gods. It is no proper invocation from such a place, but it is an invocation for all that. In plays, the actor who takes the part of a tyrant is not a tyrant, but just the same as he was before putting on the mask; so here, everyone keeps himself unchanged, but he lets them think he has been changed. Now what advantage have they won when adherence to their doctrine is a matter of words and the reality is absent? Persuasion is required in such matters, not constraint. If a person fails in persuasion, fails and employs constraint, nothing has been accomplished, though he thinks it has. It is said that in their very own rules it does not appear, but that persuasion meets with approval and compulsion is deplored. Then why these frantic attacks on the temples, if you cannot persuade and must needs resort to force? In this way you would obviously be breaking your own rules.

22.6   Provisions in the *Theodosian Code* against Pagan Survivals

The compilation of laws announced by emperors from Constantine on, published as one *Theodosian Code* by Theodosius II in 438, contains over 2,500 laws, of which some dozens have to do with pagans and paganism.

Source: *The Theodosian Code and Novels, and the Sirmondian Constitutions*, trans. C. Pharr (Princeton: Princeton University Press, 1952).

16.10.2 (341 c.e.). Emperor Constantius Augustus to Madalianus, Vice Pretorian Prefect: Superstition shall cease, the madness of sacrifices shall be abolished. For if any man in violation of the law of the sainted emperor our father [Constantine], and in violation of this command of Our Clemency, should dare to perform sacrifices, he shall suffer the infliction of a suitable punishment and the effect of an immediate sentence.

16.10.3 (342, 346 C.E.). The same Augustuses [Constantius and Constans] to Catullinus, Prefect of the City: Although all superstitions must be completely eradicated, nevertheless, it is Our will that the buildings of the temples situated outside the walls [of Rome] shall remain untouched and uninjured. For since certain plays or spectacles of the circus or contests derive their origin from some of these temples, such structures shall not be torn down, since from them is provided the regular performance of long established amusements for the Roman people.

16.10.4 (346, 354, 356 C.E., or [Piganiol, *Empire chrétien* 288, n.3] 352 C.E.). The same Augustuses [Constantius and Constans] to Taurus, Pretorian Prefect: It is Our pleasure that the temples shall be immediately closed in all places and in all cities, and access to them forbidden, so as to deny to all abandoned men the opportunity to commit sin. It is also Our will that all men shall abstain from sacrifices. But if perchance any man should perpetrate any such criminality, he shall be struck down with the avenging sword. We also decree that the property of a man thus executed shall be vindicated to the fisc [confiscated]. The governors of the provinces shall be similarly punished if they should neglect to avenge such crimes.

16.10.11 (391 C.E.). The same Augustuses [Theodosius, Gratian, and Valentinian II] to Evagrius, Augustal Prefect [governor of Egypt] and Romanus, Count of Egypt: No person shall be granted the right to peform sacrifices; no person shall go around the temples; no person shall revere the shrines. All persons shall recognize that they are excluded from profane entrance into temples by the opposition of Our law, so that if any person should attempt to do anything with reference to the gods or the sacred rites, contrary to Our prohibition, he shall learn that he will not be exempted from punishment by any special grant of imperial favor. If any judge [governor] also, during the time of his administration, should rely on the privilege of his power, and as a sacrilegious violator of the law, should enter polluted places, he shall be forced to pay into Our treasury fifteen pounds of gold, and his office staff a like sum, unless they opposed him with their combined strength.

16.10.14 (396 C.E.). The same Augustuses [Honorius and Arcadius] to Caesarius, Pretorian Prefect: If any privileges have been granted by ancient law to civil priests, ministers, prefects, or hierophants of the sacred mysteries, whether known by these names or called by any other, such privileges shall be completely abolished. Such persons shall not congratulate themselves that they are protected by any privilege, since their profession is known to be condemned by law.

16.10.15 (399 c.e.). The same Augustuses [Arcadius and Honorius] to Macrobius, Vicar of Spain, and Proclianus, Vicar of the Five Provinces [in Gaul?]: Just as We forbid sacrifices, so it is Our will that the ornaments of public works shall be preserved. If any person should attempt to destroy such works, he shall not have the right to flatter himself as relying on any authority, if perchance he should produce any rescript or any law as his defense. Such documents shall be torn from his hands and referred to Our Wisdom.

22.7   Theodoretus on Anti-Pagan Miracles

In the Syrian city of Apamea in about 391 c.e., the bishop engaged in physical campaigns against paganism, as Theodoret explains. It is worth noticing that we come here full circle to an account of Christian miracles such as we touched on in our very first selection, from Epiphanius.

Source: Theodoret, *Hist. eccl.* 5.21, *PG* 82.1244–45, original translation.

John, bishop of Apamea, whom I have already mentioned, had died, and the divine Marcellus, fervent in spirit, according to the apostolic law, had been appointed in his stead. Now there had arrived in Apamea the prefect of the East with two tribunes and their troops. Fear of the troops kept the people quiet. He [the prefect] attempted to destroy the huge and richly adorned shrine of Jupiter, but finding the building was firm and solid he understood that it was beyond the power of man to break up its closely compacted stones; for they were huge and well and truly laid, and moreover clamped fast with iron and lead. When the divine Marcellus saw the prefect's timidity, he sent him on to the rest of the towns while he himself prayed to God to aid him in the work of destruction. Next morning there came uninvited to the bishop a man who was no builder, or mason, or artificer of any kind, but only a laborer who carried stones and timber on his shoulders. "Give me," said he, "two workmen's pay and I promise you I will easily destroy the temple." The holy bishop promised to do as he was asked, and the following was the fellow's contrivance. Round the four sides of the temple went a portico united to it and on which its upper story rested. The columns were of great bulk, commensurate with the temple, each being sixteen cubits in circumference. The quality of the stone was exceptionally hard, offering great resistance to the masons' tools. In each of these the man dug through its entire diameter, propping up the superstructure with olive timber before he went on to another. After he had hollowed out three of the columns, he set fire to the timbers. But a black demon appeared and would not suffer the wood to be consumed, as it naturally would be, by the fire, and stayed the force of the flame. After the attempt had been made several times and the plan was proved ineffectual, news of the failure was brought to the pastor, who was taking his afternoon siesta. Marcellus forthwith hurried to the church, ordered water to be brought in a vessel, and placed the water under the divine altar. Then, bending his head to the ground, he besought the loving Lord in no way to give in to the usurping power of the demon but to lay bare its weakness and exhibit His own strength, lest unbelievers should henceforth find excuse for greater wrong. With these and other like words he made the sign of the cross over the water and ordered Equitius, one of his deacons who was armed with faith and enthusiasm, to take the water, run fast, and sprinkle it in faith, and then apply the flame. His orders were obeyed, and the demon, unable to endure the approach of the water, fled. Then the fire, affected by its foe the water as though it had been oil, caught the wood and consumed it in an instant. When their support had vanished, the columns themselves fell down and dragged twelve others with them. The side of the temple which was connected with the columns was dragged down by violence of their fall and carried away with them. The crash, which was tremendous, was heard throughout the town, and all ran to see the sight. No sooner did the multitude hear of the flight of the hostile demon than they broke into a hymn of praise to the God of all.

22.8 A Council of African Bishops Requests Aid against the Pagans

At one of their provincial gatherings at Carthage (in June of 401 C.E.) the bishops of Africa agreed to the following.

Source: Exerpts from the Register of the Church of Carthage, in C. Meunier, *Concilia Africae a.345–a.525*, CCSL 149 (1974): 196f., original translation.

§58. There remain still other requirements to be sought from the most pious emperors: that they should command the remaining idols throughout all Africa to be utterly extirpated, for in a number of coastal areas and in various rural estates the wickedness of such error flourishes, and that they should direct both the idols themselves to be destroyed and their temples which have been set up in rural parts or remote sites, without identification.

§60. This too is to be requested, that, inasmuch as religious social gatherings occur in many places contrary to decrees, brought together by pagan error, so that now Christians are under pressure from pagans to join in such celebrations (and hence, under Christian emperors, another Persecution seems to be carried on in secret), the emperors should order them prohibited and banned from cities and estates, by imposing a penalty, particularly since they [the pagans] show no compunction about celebrating them on the birthdays of the most blessed martyrs in some cities, and in the sacred spots themselves. On those days, indeed—shameful to declare!—the dancing of the most wicked folk goes on in town squares and open spaces, and the respect due to the marital state and the modesty of countless women assembled in piety for the most sacred day is assaulted by lascivious insults, while access to holy worship itself is almost barred.

§61. Furthermore, this too is to be requested: that theatrical shows and those of the games be removed from the Lord's day and the other most celebrated Christian days, especially because on the Eighth Day of holy Easter the people gather more at the Circus than at church. The day of their worship will have to be moved—if indeed they do foregather—nor should any Christian be obliged to attend such shows, especially because, in putting them on, contrary to God's commands as they are, no pressure of persecution should be applied by anyone, but rather (as ought to be the case) a man should stand on his free will, divinely granted him. And in particular, concern is to be shown most for the danger to members of the public work associations who are forced, against God's instructions and in great fear, to gather at the shows.

22.9   Socrates on Conversion
of the Barbarians

The church historian Socrates records events of the 430s in Germany.

Source: Socrates, *Hist. eccl.* 7.30, anonymous translation, *Nicene and Post-Nicene Fathers of the Christian Church,* Ser. 2, 2, (New York, 1890; reprint, Grand Rapids: Wm. B. Eerdmans, 1957), p. 170.

There is a barbarous nation dwelling beyond the Rhine under the name Burgundians. They lead a peaceful life, for, being almost all artisans, they support themselves by the exercise of their trades. The Huns, by making continual irruptions on this people, devastated their country and often destroyed great numbers of them. In this perplexity, therefore, the Burgundians resolved to have recourse not to any human being but to commit themselves to the protection of some god; and, having seriously considered that the god of the Romans mightily defended those that feared him, they all with one consent embraced the faith of Christ. Going therefore to one of the cities of Gaul, they requested the bishop to grant them Christian baptism—who, ordering them to fast seven days, and having meanwhile instructed them in the elementary principles of the faith, on the eighth day baptized and dismissed them. Accordingly becoming confident thenceforth, they marched against the invaders; nor were they disappointed in their hope. For the king of the Huns, Uptar by name, having died in the night from the effects of surfeit, the Burgundians attacked that people then without a commander-in-chief and, although they were very few in numbers and their opponents very many, obtained a complete victory; for the Burgundians were altogether but three thousand men and destroyed no less than ten thousand of the enemy. From that period this nation became zealously attached to the Christian religion.

ACKNOWLEDGMENTS

The editors gratefully acknowledge permission to reprint the following excerpts which previously appeared in other publications. Selections from the Loeb Classical Library are reprinted by permission of its publishers and the Loeb Classical Library.

Chapter 1. Magic, Dreams, Astrology, "Superstition"

1.2 From *The Greek Magical Papyri in Translation*, vol. 1, ed. Hans Dieter Betz (Chicago: The University of Chicago Press, 1986).

1.4 From *Oneirocritica*, trans. Robert J. White (Park Ridge, N.J.: Noyes Press, 1975). Reprinted by permission of Original Books, Torrance, California.

1.5 From Manilus, *Astronomica*, trans. G. P. Goold (Cambridge, Mass.: Harvard University Press, 1977).

1.6 From Firmicus Maternus, *Mathesis*, trans. Jean R. Bram (Park Ridge, N.J.: Noyes Press, 1975).

1.7 From Cicero, *De Divinatione*, trans. William A. Falconer (Cambridge, Mass.: Harvard University Press, 1923).

1.8 From Pliny, *Natural History*, trans. W.H.S. Jones, Loeb Classical Library, vol. 8 (Cambridge, Mass.: Harvard University Press, 1963).

1.9 From Pliny the Younger, *Letters*, trans. Betty Radice, Loeb Classical Library, vol. 1 (Cambridge, Mass.: Harvard University Press, 1969).

1.10 From Apuleius, *Metamorphoses*, trans. Jack Lindsay (Bloomington: Indiana University Press, 1962). Reprinted by permission of the publisher and the Murray Pollinger Literary Agency.

Chapter 2. Healing Shrines and Temple Management

2.1 From Strabo, *Geography*, trans. Horace L. Jones, Loeb Classical Library, vols. 5 and 8 (Cambridge, Mass.: Harvard University Press, 1928 and 1932).

2.2 From Diogenes Laertius, *Lives of the Philisophers*, trans. R. D. Hicks,

Loeb Classical Library, vol. 2 (Cambridge, Mass.: Harvard University Press, 1925).

2.3/ From *Corpus Inscriptionum Latinarum* (Leiden: Inter Documenta-
2.4 tion Co., n.d.).

2.5 From *Select Papyri*, trans. A. S. Hunt and C. C. Edgar, Loeb Classical Library, vol. 2 (Cambridge, Mass.: Harvard University Press, 1934).

Chapter 3. Cult Scenes

3.1 From Pliny, *Letters*, trans. Betty Radice, Loeb Classical Library, vol. 2 (Cambridge, Mass.: Harvard University Press, 1969).

3.4 From Pausanias, *Guide to Greece, Vol. 1: Central Greece*, trans. Peter Levi (Penguin Classics, 1971), copyright © 1971 by Peter Levi.

3.6 From Lucian, *On the Dance*, trans. A. M. Harmon, Loeb Classical Library, vol. 5 (Cambridge, Mass.: Harvard University Press, 1936).

3.7 From *The Oxyrynchus Papyri*, vol. 7, trans. Arthur S. Hunt (London: The Egypt Exploration Society, n.d.).

Chapter 4. Hymns

4.1 From *The Oxyrynchus Papyri*, vol. 11, trans. Bernard P. Grenfell and Arthur S. Hunt (London: The Egypt Exploration Society, n.d.).

4.4 From *Collectanea Alexandrina* by John U. Powell (Oxford: Oxford University Press, 1925).

4.5 From *Orphic Hymns*, trans. Apostolos A. Athanassakis (Missoula, Mont.: Scholars Press, 1977).

4.8 From *Select Papyri*, ed. Denys L. Page, Loeb Classical Library, vol. 3 (Cambridge, Mass.: Harvard University Press, 1963).

4.9 From Menander Rhetor, trans. D. A. Russell and N. G. Wilson (Oxford: Oxford University Press, 1981).

4.10 From *On the World* in *Harvard Theological Review*, vol. 56, copyright © 1963 by the President and Fellows of Harvard College.

Chapter 5. Cult Groups

5.3 From *Readings in the History of the Ancient World*, trans. William C. McDermott and Wallace E. Caldwell (New York: Rinehart and Co., 1958), copyright © 1951, 1979 by William C. McDermott and Wallace E. Caldwell. Reprinted by permission of Holt, Rinehart and Winston, Inc.

5.4 From *Classical Quarterly* (Oxford: Oxford University Press, 1932).

5.5 From *Arethusa Monographs*, vol. I (Buffalo: SUNY Buffalo, 1969).

Chapter 6. Imperial Cult

6.2 From *Corpus Inscriptionum Latinarum* (Leiden: Inter Documentation Co., n.d.).

6.4   From Tertullian, *Apology*, trans. T. R. Glover (Cambridge, Mass.: Harvard University Press, 1931).

Chapter 7. Religious Attitudes

7.1   From Seneca, *Letters from a Stoic*, trans. Robin Campbell (Penguin Classics, 1969), copyright © 1969 by Robin Alexander Campbell.

7.5   From Seneca, *Moral Letters*, trans. Richard L. Gummere, Loeb Classical Library, vol. 2 (Cambridge, Mass.: Harvard University Press, 1920).

7.6   From Augustine, *City of God*, trans. William M. Green, Loeb Classical Library, vol. 2 (Cambridge, Mass.: Harvard University Press, 1963).

7.7   From *Didascalia Apostolorum*, vol. 13, trans. R. Hugh Connolly (Oxford: Clarendon Press, 1929).

7.9   From *The Oxyrynchus Papyri*, vol. 42, trans. P. J. Parsons (London: The Egypt Exploration Society, n.d.).

Chapter 8. Marcus Aurelius

8.1   From Marcus Aurelius, *Meditations*, trans. A.S.L. Farquharson (Oxford: Clarendon Press, 1944).

Chapter 9. Theology

9.1   From Plutarch, *Isis and Osiris*, trans. Frank Cole Babbitt, Loeb Classical Library, vol. 5 (Cambridge, Mass.: Harvard University Press, n.d.).

Chapter 11. Holy Men and Women

11.1   From Philostratus, *Vita Apollonii*, trans. F. C. Conybeare, Loeb Classical Library, vol. 2 (Cambridge, Mass.: Harvard University Press, n.d.).

Chapter 12. Missionizing (Non-Christian)

12.3   From Philo, *On the Virtues* and *The Special Laws*, trans. F. H. Colson, Loeb Classical Library, vol. 8 (Cambridge, Mass.: Harvard University Press, 1939).

Chapter 13. Perceptions of Judaism

13.2   From *Select Papyri*, trans. A. S. Hunt and E. C. Edgar, Loeb Classical Library, vol. 2 (Cambridge, Mass.: Harvard University Press, 1934).

13.3   From Josephus, *Jewish War*, trans. H. St. J. Thackeray, Loeb Classical Library, vol. 2 (Cambridge, Mass.: Harvard University Press, 1927).

13.6   From *R. Abbahu of Caesarea*, trans. Lee I. Levine, in *Christianity, Judaism and Other Greco-Roman Cults: Studies for Morton Smith at Sixty*, ed. J. Neusner, part 4 (Leiden: E. J. Brill, 1975).

Chapter 14. Perceptions of Christianity

14.3 From Marcus Aurelius, *Meditations*, trans. A.S.L. Farquharson (Oxford: Clarendon Press, 1944).

14.4 From *Galen on Jews and Christians*, trans. Richard Walzer (Oxford: Oxford University Press, 1949).

Chapter 15. Apologists

15.1 From Athenagoras, *Legatio*, trans. W. R. Schoedel (Oxford: Clarendon Press, 1972).

Chapter 16. Hermetism and Gnosticism

16.1 From *Poimandres*, trans. Walter Scott in *Hermetica*, vol. I (Oxford: Clarendon Press, 1924).

16.2 From *Pistis Sophia*, trans. Violet MacDermot in *Nag Hammadi Studies*, vol. 9 (Leiden: E. J. Brill, 1978).

Chapter 17. Conversion, Pre-Constantine

17.2 From *Salvation and the Savages* by R. F. Berkhofer (Lexington: University Press of Kentucky, 1965).

Chapter 18. The Persecutions

18.3 From *Life of Septimius Severus* in the *Scriptores Historiae Augustiae*, trans. David Magie, Loeb Classical Library, vol. 2 (Cambridge, Mass.: Harvard University Press, 1922).

18.5 From Clement, *Stromateis*, trans. Beresford James Kidd in *Documents Illustrative of the History of the Church*, vol. I (London: SPCK, 1920).

18.6 From Eusebius, *Apology for His Flight*, trans. James Stevenson in *A New Eusebius* (London: SPCK, 1957).

18.7 From Cyprian, *On Those Who Fell Away*, trans. James Stevenson in *A New Eusebius* (London: SPCK, 1957).

18.8 From *Harvard Theological Review*, vol. 16, copyright © 1923 by the President and Fellows of Harvard College.

18.9 From Cyprian, *Letters*, trans. James Stevenson in *A New Eusebius* (London: SPCK, 1957).

18.10 From *Some Authentic Acts of the Early Martyrs* by Edward Charles Everard Owen (Oxford: Clarendon Press, 1927).

18.12 From *Papyrus Bodmer*, vol. 20 (Cology-Geneve: Bibliotheca Bodmeriana, 1964).

18.13 From *Corpus Inscriptionum Latinarum* (Leiden: Inter Documentation Co., n.d.).

Chapter 20. Constantine

20.2 From Eusebius, *Vita Constantini*, trans. P. R. Coleman-Norton in *Roman State and Christian Church*, vol. I (London: SPCK, 1966).

Chapter 21. Julian

21.1 From Julian, *Letters*, trans. Wilmer Cave Wright, Loeb Classical Library, vol. 3 (Cambridge, Mass.: Harvard University Press, 1923).

Chapter 22. Conversion, Post-Constantine

22.5 From Libanius, *Oration*, trans. A. F. Norman, Loeb Classical Library, vol. 2 (Cambridge, Mass.: Harvard University Press, 1977).

22.6 From *The Theodosian Code and Novels, and the Sirmondian Constitutions*, trans. C. Pharr, copyright © 1952, 1980 Princeton University Press.

INDEX OF
NAMES AND TOPICS

295